A Ship's Tale

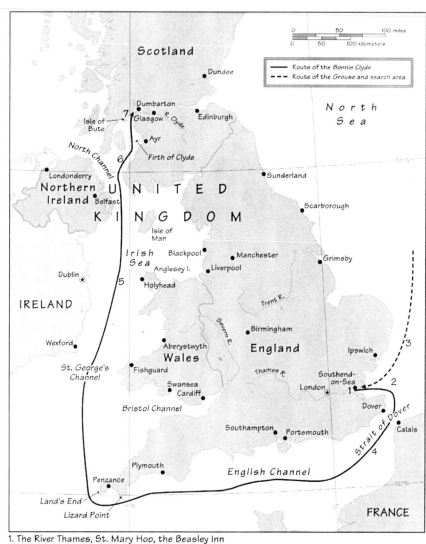

1. The River Thames, St. Mary Hoo, the Beasley Inn
2. Scuttling Point, the *Bonnie Clyde* pirated away
3. Route of the training ship, route of the *Grouse*, first search area
4. Submarine contact
5. Ferryboat sights the *Bonnie Clyde*
6. Accidental brief grounding of the *Bonnie Clyde*
7. Overtaken, beginning of the River Clyde

A Ship's Tale

A NOVEL

by

N. Jay Young

C&M Online Media, Inc.
Raleigh

Published by
C & M Online Media, Inc.
Raleigh NC
www.cmonline.com

ISBN: (print) 978-1-932482-03-4
ISBN: (ebook) 978-1-932482-12-6

Cover graphic: adapted from a photograph supplied with permission by the National Maritime Museum, Greenwich, LONDON SE10 9NF.

Back cover photo credit: Ann Callicrate.

Design by Once Removed

*This is dedicated to every old salt
and deep-water dreamer*

Contents

Preface

In post-World War II England, countless thousands of returning soldiers and sailors wanted a turnaround in the political status quo. Members of the British armed forces were considerably better educated than they had been in the First World War. The soldiers returning from the Second World War were no longer in awe of their leaders, and had extremely mixed loyalties. There was the resentment of unemployment, and men returning from the military were demanding a greater share in the nation's post-war restructuring. They didn't trust a conservative government to tackle the enormous social, economic, and political problems that the conservative government had done very little to solve. They demanded that changes be made.

As a consequence, Winston Churchill, who led Britain to victory during the World War II, found himself a member of the opposition when the election of 1945 returned the Labour Party to power with a huge majority. Under the Parliament of the new government, some of the greatest changes in Britain's history began. This meant nothing less than a reconstruction of the entire nation.

The management of the economy, which proved successful in wartime, was now a major undertaking in peacetime. Stringent financial measures, imposed to meet the enormous war debt, caused undue hardship that was made worse by one of the worst winters on record. Monstrous gales and floods wiped out farms and destroyed agricultural products. A fuel shortage severely curtailed exports, and food was still severely rationed. Even bread and potatoes were rationed, although both had been exempt during the war. This shortage forced the government to sell horses for food in place of beef.

The fact that there was a black market cannot be denied. Beer and whisky were luxuries that were quite sought after and often times were easily obtainable through the right connections. Ration coupons were issued for just about everything, but not nearly enough clothing coupons were issued to buy much, not even a pair of shoes.

Stallholders in shops would often strike a bargain by selling or trading extra coupons. Why were transactions carried out like this? Because appearances had to be maintained that things were being done in the proper way.

Every Briton—man, woman, and child—was issued a ration card and a National Registration card. The ration cards, sometimes worth more than money, were presented to shopkeepers who cut the appropriate number of coupons for the rationed item at the time of purchase.

The Ministry of Food determined the number of coupons cut. Sometimes more or less were taken depending on the supply of any particular commodity. Fruits and most vegetables were not fresh unless they were privately grown. Items of food rationed included meat, bacon, milk, and milk powder. Petrol and oil were reserved for essential services. The ordinary person had no or little access to petrol, and not many had cars.

I doubt that anyone could give you an accurate account of the amount allowed for each item; it was little enough. For one person there was one or two eggs a week and two ounces of butter. The wrapper of a pound pat of butter was printed in two-ounce segments, so that it was easy to cut the allotted portion.

Heavy workers got the larger amounts of food stores. Miners also received other privileges. And so that was the pattern of things. What one did not eat, others did, and there was swapping among friends and neighbours.

Rationing did not starve people and the balanced diet benefited the whole population's gaining in health. For a time the beer was brewed a bit weaker, except in Scotland. Clothing and footwear were made to a wartime standard, bearing a special brand mark.

Use of the ham radio was forbidden during the war because of fears of spying and espionage. After the war its use flourished.

The Beasley Inn had connections to the black market and access to food that wasn't easily obtained during rationing. This gave the inn a small, but loyal clientele. Subsequently, everyone kept quiet about deliveries that appeared with some regularity. Customers were content to enjoy access to these items and seldom asked how the Beasley Inn was able to stay well supplied throughout the rationing and shortages.

Mr. Beasley, who died during the Great War, had been aware that in order to bring people into such a small village as Allhallows, the inn was required to have things one couldn't find elsewhere. He had been trading and selling to farmers and bootleggers for many years. For sailors the Beasleys had cared little and never knew that they were part of one of the biggest black market supply lines coming into the UK by ship. When Mrs. Beasley took over running the inn, she merely filled out her requests and submitted them to the people doing her deliveries, never asking or caring about their origin.

Harris had known about these things for years and was connected with a great supplier of items unknown to most. Bowman also knew of these things, but never was personally involved. When Harris and Bowman were reunited on the *Bonnie Clyde*, their connections started coming in very handy.

During the war everything that could float was used for the war effort, but after World War II most such vessels were no longer necessary and were cleared from the waterways of commerce by selling them off, cutting them up for scrap, or scuttling them at sea.

And so it was.

NJY

Chapter 1
KENT, ENGLAND, OCTOBER 1946

The weathered masts were reaching into a driftwood sky that morning when I first saw the derelict ships, old square-riggers from a bygone era. Chained to makeshift moorings, they tugged like giant seahorses, but with nearly all the life gone out of them. Tattered rigging, loose fittings, and green unpolished bright work enough to make a sailor cry. They were the monarchs of sail in their day, but their day had long passed. Their once-proud masts now served as perches for the occasional passing gull among the twisted trees along the south shore of the River Thames. No more would they await the arriving tug for the tow upriver, with their holds full and lads eager to walk the shore again. They were used up and turned out like whores in the wind.

Gone were the days of the great clipper and packet ships, once a common sight here. They had fallen victim to progress. The steam engine had made them obsolete, and upriver, bridges of a newer more efficient time now restricted the passage of tall ships forever. Oh, but they made a magnificent picture when under full sail with a stiff wind at their backs! No wonder that hundreds of writers and millions of spectators have expressed the opinion that this was among the most splendid sights ever to be witnessed. Alas, even the greatest of spectacles fade from favour with the passage of time.

The three ships lay moored together along the Kent side of the Thames Estuary, not far from the great river's mouth, across the mud banks and sand that were tied together by a field of tussocky grass. Looking upriver I could see a number of support ships from the war painted grey and identified only by white numbers and letters rusting in the rains. Farthest from shore wallowed the remains of a once-proud four-masted barque, now a rusted hulk long since demasted. Rivets and steel plates had been peeled back to reveal the main hatchway in an attempt to use her as a coal barge, the ultimate humiliation for any sailing ship. She lay awash in the mud as if serving as a breakwater for the other two, and that she did quite well.

The ship closest in was a three-masted barque with a steel hull. She looked more sound than the wooden three-master in the middle, which had some of her yardarms either missing or in disrepair. The shoreward vessel had a gangway down to the nearby bank, so it appeared that one could use it to board all three. I took care walking across the wood and metal planking that made a path across the marshes and had a closer look. The name was still discernible on her bow: *Bonnie Clyde*.

As I wandered along the shore, I thought of all they had been. Aboard these ships seamen once lived in quarters that today would be considered intolerable; their diet dreadful, their work hard and extremely dangerous. Voyages often took months to reach destinations, and it was not uncommon for a man to spend several years travelling different trade routes before returning home with little money to show for his efforts. Voyages were always dependent upon the hope of favourable weather. Sailing had long been regarded as one of the most hazardous ways to travel, for ship disasters were commonplace. Vessels sometimes disappeared without a trace or clue as to their fate.

The busy Thames was every bit as challenging as the English Channel, for collisions and obstacles were a constant hazard to all craft navigating these waters. So it had been for centuries, but seafaring men were still drawn to sign on and ship out before the mast. Now the masts were gone, except for these.

I spent time walking along the bank looking each ship over, remembering when a friend arranged passage for me aboard such a vessel, and what a fine adventure it had been! I stood a long while at the bottom of the gangway waiting for some sign of life, but saw no one about. With absence of ceremony, I climbed the ageing wooden planks to the deck.

As I came aboard, there was no officer of the watch to speak with, so I was left to wander her deck alone. I thought of the past few years that had brought me from the war in Europe to this peaceful spot. It was a year after World War II and there were not enough jobs for sailors, or anyone else for that matter. Times were hard for those of us returning home as well as those who fought the war on their own doorsteps.

I looked about with a sigh at the twisted cable and untidy ropes. It was sad to see her in such a state. Her wooden deck was in remarkably good condition, as were the steel masts and standing rigging, with every yardarm accounted for. In fact, there was new rope around the main yardarm, showing that work had recently been done. Surely everyone here knew and cared little that these ships were nothing short of wrecks awaiting some grim fate. Damned shame, I thought. Damned waste of a good ship here!

Walking up through the fo'c's'le, I passed two new mechanical brace and halyard winches designed to ease the backbreaking task of hoisting and turning the enormous yards. With their use, much of the arduous work at the capstan could be avoided. Walking the capstan round is backbreaking work, as anyone knows who's done it.

The winches seemed out of place here, a little too modern for an old ship. They didn't look as though they were completely installed either. The main yard had been lowered, and rested on the port and starboard rails, lashed with new chain and good running rigging all around. I ducked under the huge yard and headed towards the stern. Of the two starboard lifeboats I passed, one had rotted out and collapsed on its chocks, the wood warped and split. The others were equally dismal, and were not even capable of retaining rainwater. I sighed. What a mess!

It was a crisp afternoon on the water. Turning my collar up and reaching for my pipe and lighter, I put one foot up against the old boat chock and struck the lighter. With a hand cupped around to deflect the wind, I was enjoying my third puff when the old timber under my foot suddenly gave way to my weight, sending me to the deck with a resounding crash. An indignant wharf rat scurried off down the deck to hide elsewhere, and a gull, equally offended, took wing. I was glad that the lifeboat didn't fall as well.

I collected myself and began to rise. I was startled as a booted figure, clad in a heavy sweater and with piercing blue eyes, appeared out of nowhere. With an embarrassed smile, the hello had just left my lips as he burst out in a hard Scottish burr, "What the bloody hell d'ye think ye're doin' here?"

"Well," I replied, "I was just passing, and—"

"Ye've been sent by those government officials, have ye?"

"What? Which officials?" I said, bewildered.

He pursed up his leather-like face and raised the brim of his cap an inch. "Those who want tae take her tae her grave," he answered darkly.

"Take who?" I gasped. I didn't know if he was just trying to scare me or was some old crank gone mad. Still, he was a bit frightening.

"This 'ere ship, lad. Are you telling me ye know nothing of it?" he demanded.

"Look, I'm...that is, I just returned from the war and..."

"In the war? Army, eh?" he scoffed.

"No, Navy."

"Well! We have a sailor here, do we?" he said, looking me over with a keen eye.

"I was a ship's officer in the Royal Navy aboard the—"

"I don't bloody care about the Royal Navy!" he snapped. "This ship had nae a gun on her, but by gaw for two years we sailed through the U-boats carrying ammo and shells whilst the Jerries thought our hold was filled with guano."

"Guano?" I asked.

"Aye, bird shit!" he grimaced, taking his pipe from a pocket.

We laughed at having thus established ourselves as fellow seamen; then went and sat down on the main hatchway to relight our pipes and chat. Looking at this old man, a deep water square-rigger sailor, I could hardly wait to hear his story.

As I struggled with my lighter, the old man reached into his pocket and brought out a box of Swan Vestas to light his own pipe first, before passing the box to me without comment. The flaring match revealed every wrinkle in his face and hands, evidence of his many years of gruelling shipboard toil. He looked over at me, out of the corner of his eye, as I grew more self-conscious. I felt less like a naval officer, and more like some callow cabin boy.

The old man cleared his throat ceremoniously. "Now then," he began, "I've been at sea fifty-two years, man and boy. I was a master on other rigs thirty-some years and then five years master aboard this one. My taking charge of her now, is what any captain would call his last command. I hate tae waste a good ship because of government fools, who sit in small rooms and make big decisions. Three years ago they took her oot o' service and left her here to rust with the last of them. She's been a fine ship. Now it's either cut them up or scuttle them. If the government officials get their way, they'll take them out for target practise. And still another tap-dancing political twit thinks she'd make a fine pub if they put her up dry!"

"You mean permanent dry dock?" I asked.

"Aye," he said sadly.

"Well, I suppose that's better than the other two options."

"That's no bloody option at all!" he cried. "This ship belongs on the water and nae here getting weather beaten by the North Sea gales. Well, it's a mercy that at least the auld barque on the seaward side still makes a fair breakwater. Never wished any ship harm, except them German ones. She was slammin' into baith o' these, so we sank her to the mud, and a good job too."

"You sank her?" I exclaimed.

"You ask a lot o' questions, young man. For all I know you're in with some o' those government officials."

"I've got no reason to lie to you sir. I told you, I just returned —"

"Aye, aye, from the war. I heard ye. Can't be too careful. Anyway, I expect ye're too young."

"Too young! Too young for what?" I said, bristling.

"To be one of those government officials," he growled. "Are ye nae listening, lad?"

"Yes, well, I just wasn't sure what you meant," I said. I hadn't the slightest idea what he was on about and was about to tell him to put a sock in it.

He gave me a quizzical look. "What did ye think I meant, eh? Here, just what is your name, laddie?"

"Flynn," I said, putting out my hand.

"Right," he answered. "And Bowman's mine." He wiped his hand on his trousers and extended it to me. His grip was as firm and rough as his words. "Now answer me, Flynn. What was it you thought I meant? Eh, lad?"

"I thought you meant I was too young to understand the way you feel, and it isn't so. When I was fifteen, I sailed with the maritime service on the *Jackson*, a four-masted barque, training for entry into the Merchant Navy. I put in some good years, and just when I was ready to qualify, along came Hitler. I finished up as a lieutenant aboard a destroyer in the North Atlantic, escorting convoys. Wretched duty, that was."

The old man's mouth opened as if to speak, and then clamped down on his pipe. He sat quietly reflecting behind clouds of smoke. I hoped he had developed a bit of respect for me for the training I'd received, along with the dangers I'd faced. To this he said nothing.

I could hear only the sounds of the water and the creaking of the ship. The old man sat with eyes fixed, gazing within and beyond. The late afternoon sun was fading, and a fog was forming out beyond Sheerness. Still he took scant notice, and sat without a word. I could hardly continue sitting near without trying to make some conversation, so I pondered exactly what to say. I stood up and stretched, looking at the masts towering above us.

"Kind of romantic, the era of sail," I said, then stopped, realising how trite that sounded.

The old man jumped up as if he'd been stung by a bee. "Romantic!" he cried. "Romantic? Aloft, hauling in wet canvas sail in a damned cold ocean gale, hands so frozen they can hardly grip, with only the wind at yer back holding ye against the yardarms, hoping ye can make it down the ratlines without taking a fall to the pitching deck below? Ye hae a damn strange idea of romance, Flynn. Little wonder ye're not married."

"I didn't know it showed," I said in surprise.

"It does," he answered.

"And you?"

He knocked the ash from his pipe and refilled it before speaking. "Thirty-two years we were," he said at last in a low voice. "Lost her in the bombing. Stayed in London where we thought it safe. And at first Hitler only sent his packages over to the military targets. Nineteen-forty…October, it was. Direct hit on our house and me down river. I could hear the planes coming in from the deck of this very ship and the sirens wailing like lost souls…Aye well, at least after that we had no more need to worry over one another when I was at sea. 'Missing,' they said." He cleared his throat. "She was a fine lass, my Meg."

"I'm sorry, Mr. Bowman," I said quietly.

I recalled when last I said goodbye to my best girl. I remember her in a nurse's uniform and cape. We both looked quite dapper in our new uniforms as we stood on a corner of a street with rows of flats, one with a large red cross.

"I'll be right here when you return," she said.

I recall looking at the name of the street on the sign. After the war, I stood alone on the same street corner surrounded by buildings re-duced to rubble with the same sign bent and rusted—it was raining. A tattered awning slapped in the wind. Suddenly a flap of torn canvas made the same sound on the *Bonnie Clyde*, and Bowman's words brought me to conscious thought.

"No matter." He turned and walked aft up the ladder to the bridge deck so I followed him up to the helm. He then sat with one hand on the large double wheel, which I saw had a foot brake to help control or slow the turning of the helm in rough seas. "Put in many an hour at this helm. It seemed only fitting that I should be caring for the auld *Bonnie* once she was retired." He patted the wheel in a comforting manner.

"What do you do now?" I asked.

"Answer stupid questions," he said, turning away. After a moment he looked back at me almost apologetically. "I'm a pensioner of the company now. Enough to keep me in food and almost enough to keep the rain off me head."

"You live aboard?" I asked.

"Aye, till they drag me off," he said, looking grim.

I wasn't too sure who they were, the old shipping company or the government officials, but I said, "They wouldn't do that, would they?

Surely they wouldn't bother you. After all, you've taken care of things around here."

"They don't want us around, Flynn. Taking care of things isn't what they want either. And bother us? Why ye'd think they'd naught better to do."

"Mr. Bowman," I began, "at the risk of asking another stupid question, who exactly are us?"

"Meself and some others who feel the same about this ship. Sailors, deep water men all."

"So then, that was who helped you sink the old coal barque. That's spot on, just grand," I said, thinking I was being complimentary.

"You keep that under yer hat, young man," he cautioned.

"Not to worry sir. I work at the inn down the end of the lane from here, so if I can help you…"

"And what makes ye think help is needed? Besides, have ye naught better to spend your time at?" he snapped.

"Well, if you think being at the beck and call of a fussy bitty hen of a landlady is a better way to pass the time, then you must be mad."

"Mad I'm not," he snorted, "a bit daft I may be." A thought lit his eye. "Would that inn be the old Beasley place?"

I nodded. The path I'd followed down to the water led right back to the Beasley Inn. No one could miss it in passing, for it stood just off the roadway.

"I know it well," he laughed.

I returned to our original subject, "At the risk of sounding daft myself, this ship doesn't look as if she's a total loss. The standing rigging looks to be taut and sound. Now, if enough good line could be found…the main running rigging could easily be replaced. Ah, and I couldn't help noticing those winches, they could certainly handle the yards if properly rigged."

I kept on, pointing out this and that as I went, and spouting on about everything that I came across. "This deck," I continued, "surely all it needs is a bit of caulk and holystone…" I stopped suddenly, realising that my mouth was running away at a clip. I turned to meet Bowman's condescending stare. There was an uncomfortable silence.

"Well, first we'd need some sweepers fore and aft," he suggested.

"Right," I agreed.

With one quick motion, he snatched a broom from its resting place and shoved its handle into my hand. I blinked. He almost grinned, but his beard made it hard to tell. "Wouldn't ye agree that we've no need of officers on this ship as yet? Now manpower—of that we have need." I stared at him, surprised at the sudden steely ring of command in his voice.

"I suppose so," I responded. I had worked hard to become an officer, and sweeping was for ordinary seaman. Thankfully Bowman didn't pursue this line.

"Getting a bit cauld this day, eh lad? Care for a wee dram?" he asked.

I was surprised "Oh no! I couldn't deprive you of..." but he waved me off impatiently.

"There's always a drop of the right stuff for lads like you. Come along now."

I followed him over to the hatch, where a shove at the cover revealed the ladder to the deck below. As we climbed down, my eyes became accustomed to the darkness, and many things began to make even less sense to me. Below decks, the wood on the bulkhead and ladder were every bit perfect. A brass lamp shone above a table I could see down another ladder below. So much for this being a wreck, I thought!

Through another bulkhead and down a small passage aft was the captain's cabin. The old man walked right in, so I followed suit. This room probably looked as good as it did the day she was launched, save for some upholstery. The aft ports gave a grand view of the Thames waterway and the light reflected the water on the overhead.

"Blimey, you do live here!" I exclaimed, wide-eyed.

"Thought I told ye that," he said.

"Yes, but this is wonderful! And the captain's cabin, no less."

"She's got a captain. She's got me, and I her captain remain." There was real pride of place in his voice. Even to be captain of a derelict was no cause for shame!

He reached inside the cabinet and placed an unlabelled green glass bottle and two heavy mugs on the chart table. With a steady hand, he poured two equal portions, handing one to me. "Air do slainte," he toasted.

"That's grand. Sure to warm the blood," I concurred. "Cheers," I added, lifting the mug to my lips. Another surprise: this was good malt whisky! We sat sipping and savouring the amber liquid as if it were gold itself.

"So then, Captain Bowman. Isn't that how I should address you?"

"I've been called worse," he assured me.

"Yes sir," I said under my breath. I looked about the cabin, "I must say sir, this ship isn't what she seems from above. Topside is a bloody wreck from a distance, yet close up she's not so bad. The wood is fine, the seams appear tight, and then there's down below here. Tell me, is her hull sound?"

He glanced up from his drink and sat back in the chair with a crafty look. Freed from his scarf and turned-up collar, his grey whiskers looked much like a lion's mane and thick dark eyebrows bristled over his eyes. He made quite a picture.

"Quite sound. Been easier to work below," he remarked. "No one to see."

"To see what?" I enquired.

"What ye noticed a'ready, lad. With a few weeks of bustin' arse topside, we could get her out with half or better sail."

"Out? Sail?" I cried. "This? Aboard this ship?"

"Aye, this very ship," he said.

"But her rigging is a mess! Those lines couldn't hold half their load. No one knows if the upper topsails or topgallant yards would stand the strain. Good lord, it would take a pretty penny to put it right!"

He laughed. "So you know a bit about sailing these ships, do ye? Ha! Now you sound just like those government officials. Well it don't take but strong backs and quick minds."

"That doesn't quite pay the piper." I said, and then wondered if that was a wise expression to use with a Scotsman.

"Bugger the bloody piper! Look here, young man." Taking up the bottle, he replenished our mugs and tucked the bottle into the pocket of his watch coat. Reaching under the table, he pulled out two large Navy torches and handed me one. "Come along now," he said, and it did sound like an order.

Down a darkened passage we went, shining our lights as if in a coal mine. We went from his cabin down another ladder to the 'tween deck, and moved forward until we came to another bulkhead amidships. The air was damp and musty, and the overhead so low in places, even ducking would lose my cap.

The old man stopped outside one of the hatches, "Know where this goes?" he asked.

"To the main cargo hold?" I guessed.

"Aye, that it does." Turning his light first on me, then onto my cup, he produced the bottle from his coat and refilled our cups. "Come now lad, drink up."

I leaned half sitting against the inside hatch with my mug, and had one more nip. If I tried to match him sip for sip, I'd be plastered in no time. I was already feeling a bit loose in the joints. Bowman's face was in shadow but I could see he was serious.

"I'm going to show ye something, Flynn, and ye must never speak of it to anyone. I ask ye now for yer word." He gravely put out his palm and I shook his hand and promised. Sounded quite the mystery to me, but I quietly listened on.

"Aye," he said, "ye're right about the rigging, but if it were replaced before we're ready, it might give us away."

"I don't follow," I said. "You'd be hard pressed to come up with half of what you'd need."

He made no answer to this, but simply reached over and threw open the dogs that secured the hatch. Because I was leaning against it, I fell through the opening like baggage, tumbling over a dozen or so objects before reaching the bottom, and finding myself once again in the unenviable position of being flat on my arse looking up at Bowman.

"Take care now, lad! Now up wi' ye," he said impatiently.

Angry and incensed, I stood up to confront him, but when I picked up my torch, what I saw took all the words from my lips. Filling the hold were hawsers and lines of every size, both hemp and wire. There were all types of line, modern winding tackle, and shrouds with ranks of manila, and nylon ropes hanging and piled neatly in coils. As I moved my light around, I thought this was a bo'sun's gold mine. I sat down on a barrel next to a makeshift table covered with marlinespikes, serving mallets, sail-maker's palms, and an assortment of tools for sail making and rigging work. I looked at Bowman.

Even in the sharp shadows cast by the torches, the grin on the old man's face was plain to see. Here was a cargo hold filled with enough line to re-rig the entire ship—and then some.

"Captain Bowman," I began, "Where on earth did you get...I mean where did all this come from?"

"Not yet lad. Maybe all things being right, ye'll know enough in time. Come along now," he chuckled, and turned to go out.

I pulled on my cap and backed out of the hold. As I turned to follow him, I forgot about the low overhead and caught myself a hearty smack. It felt as though I'd nearly knocked my head off, but luckily it was only my cap. I snatched it up hastily, hoping the old man had not seen me, and hurried along the dark passage after him. Walking along the 'tween deck, I shone my torch into the old cabins and divided rooms, still looking in remarkably good condition. When we came back to the chart table, Bowman set the bottle on the table and fell into a chair.

"Well Flynn, do ye think I'm a crazy old fool?"

"I never thought you a fool, Captain Bowman. I don't know what to think. If you could re-rig this ship, what then? Surely she's property of the Crown. It would be much like an act of piracy to make off with her."

"Piracy? When something is thrown away and ye save it, is it theft?" he asked indignantly.

"Well no, but this isn't quite the same."

"No one said a word about stealing. Relocation is what we're talking about. Liberating her, ye might say. Taking her back to Scotland where she was built. There she'll be looked after."

"How do you know that?" I asked.

"We've people there and they have a real dock to give her a home port. 'Tis the only way, lad. We've tried everything and talked to everyone." His expression hardened. "A nod is as good as a wink to a blind man. They don't give a damn up in London," he said bitterly pounding the table with a gnarled fist. Giving a long sigh, he took up the bottle and added to our mugs.

We sat back in silence, listening to the waves. The last of the sun was streaming through the round porthole, casting an amber hued spotlight beam over the chart table. The ship's clock on the bulkhead sounded its bell, and I reached for my pocket watch to check the hour. Just then, the distant sound of voices and footsteps of men coming aboard could be heard. I looked to Bowman for some reaction, but he showed no surprise. He got up slowly and drew out his pocket watch. Mumbling something under his breath, he took three more mugs from the shelf and placed them on the table. The voices grew louder, the compartment hatch opened, and down came three figures of a distinctly salty character, all well bundled against the wind.

Two made directly for the bottle, greeting Bowman with jokes and chaffing, while the third ploughed his way towards the warmth of the cabin's pot-bellied stove near my end of the table. He was swathed in a long macintosh and his face was muffled by yards of scarf. As he set to unwinding himself, a blunt old face emerged. The watery grey eyes suddenly grew large as they lit upon me, and quickly narrowed with suspicion. I started to put on my best smile, but it didn't get far. His lips quivered, then twitched open.

"And what would it be you're doin' here?" he asked in a heavy Irish brogue. The room was instantly silent, as all eyes were cast on me. I didn't feel like defending my presence to this lot, but I had to say something.

"That's the second time today someone's asked me that." I said, motioning to Bowman, who now remembered to introduce me.

"This is Flynn, lads. Royal Navy. But in spite o' that, he's worked on proper ships and could be of real use to us."

"Oh," stuttered the scarved one, "and how is it you'll be doin' that?"

"I'm not sure really," I admitted, "but I've a strong back and some real sailing experience…"

"Ah, experience!" he said sarcastically. "Perhaps I'll learn something."

"Yes," I agreed with equal sarcasm, "perhaps you will." I turned away, leaving him muttering soundlessly.

"That's our Ned…Edward, if ye will," said Bowman. "Bloody good navigator. Not much on first impressions, just what you'd expect from an old mick." I looked to Edward for some sort of reaction, but his face was quite expressionless.

Bowman turned to the next man, "This is Boris. He's a Russian. Not good with English, but a damned fine rigger. None like him."

Boris pulled off his woollen cap and gave me a nod, dark eyes glinting.

I held out my hand, "Flynn's the name."

Though not an especially large man, Boris seemed impressively fit. He had a likeable earnestness about him. A smile gleamed through his moustache as he took my hand in a wiry grip. Ironically, as I would learn, Boris had left Russia years earlier, and had come to London to get a better life. Then the war came and life got worse. Here we were, impoverished and war-torn in England, but it was really the sea he regarded as his home now.

"Boris," he grinned. He pointed to the bottle on the chart table. "Is good, yes?"

"Excellent," I agreed.

My thoughts turned to the rigging. "I must say, you have a daunting task ahead of you."

"Thank you very good, Na Zdorovye!" Boris said, taking a long drink.

Bowman cleared his throat. "Told ye, not much on English."

"But big in heart," added Boris modestly, with an expansive gesture.

I lifted my cup. What a strange lot. I began to wonder if my tentative offer to help was wise. I decided to reserve judgment for the time being.

Edward fixed a sharp look on me, "Young man," he began then paused for a swallow of Scotch. His lips took on a quivering.

"If your work is as good as your words, well eh, a strong back is welcome. There's much to be done, and no time to do it all."

I was about to say something in return but the last of the three, a huge burly great bear of a man, now leaned towards Bowman and spoke in a quiet voice, "You'll want to know, no one followed. As soon as it's dark, we'll unload."

"Good show," nodded Bowman. He jerked a thumb in my direction, "This chap calls himself Flynn."

"Yes, I heard." The giant hove near and loomed over me.

"Harris," he said, extending a massive hand that all but swallowed up my own. I had to wonder if I'd get it back whole.

The expression on the face above me, with its sandy jaw-lined beard, was reassuringly mild. The beard was repeated in a fringe of hair around the back of his head, which left the top bare and shining pink. The overall effect was that of a vast benevolence, yet one had the overwhelming impression that in any fray this was someone you'd want to see in your own corner.

Finally he released my hand, which I cautiously flexed. "Excuse me a moment," he said, and made his way to a large armchair. He lowered himself with a grateful sigh, and with a piteous groan from the chair, poured himself a measure of whisky.

Giving me an appraising glance, he then looked towards Bowman. "How much does he know?" he asked.

"Enough," grunted Bowman.

Harris turned back to me, "Well Flynn, as Edward said, we've much to do and it means the world to us. I hope you'll not give us up, but bust your arse along with the rest of us, else I'll kick it into proper shape for you." And he gave a gentle, kindly smile that made the hairs stand up on the back of my neck. "Cheers," he added, lifting his mug.

"I'll do my very best, Harris," I gulped. Good God, I did seem to be committing myself, and, intriguing as it all sounded, I hadn't even known Bowman more than a few hours. "Never a good idea to always do your best. People will then always expect it of you," Harris joked.

The company looked about at one another and took this in without further comment, then pulled up their chairs closer to the pot-bellied stove. Harris leaned forward, opened the door, and stirred the coals with the poker. Taking up the tongs, he extracted a large bit of coal from a nearby box and tossed it in, then fell back into his chair and began his report.

"The spare wireless parts were hard to find, but I've enough to put the radio right with the exception of a proper handset. I've got two pumps and several tins of petrol to keep them going a few days. Good new hoses and lots of rigging parts. Boris, go through and see what's of use and what's rubbish."

"Aha, yes," said Boris, pulling on his watch cap.

Harris waved a hand, "Not yet, wait until dark. Oh, and deep-six anything with ship's markings if we can't paint over them." Boris nodded that he understood.

Whilst we waited for darkness, Harris and Bowman sat and told tales of their innumerable adventures during their many years at sea, some of it as shipmates. Between them, they had lived an odyssey that spanned many years and could probably fill a score of volumes if written down. Edward and Boris howled with laughter and volunteered little stories of their own as the evening wore on.

The place was cheery now, and we were starting to get to know one another. I could see that Edward, except when giving forth his low choked laugh, was a taciturn and reserved man. When he began to speak, his lips took on a nervous quiver, as if the words were stirring within, waiting to fall out. Boris was more easygoing and casually accepted most of life's tasks as not too much trouble. He'd been a rigger most of his life and was more at home aloft than on deck. That Russian accent of his was thicker than a London fog, but I suspected that he knew or understood more English than Bowman gave him credit for.

About seven o'clock, Harris got up and looked out of the porthole. "Well, Flynn, let's put that strong back of yours to some use. You help Boris unload. Bowman and I need to chat a moment. You too, Edward."

"Right," I replied. Rising, I laid hold of my coat and followed Boris up to the main deck. The instant the hatch opened we were greeted by a blast of frigid night air.

I hustled shivering into my coat, while Boris turned his face into the breeze as though it were a balmy summer's evening.

"Good night, not too cold," observed Boris.

"I expect it is, if you live in Siberia," I said.

He gave me an amused look. "No my friend, Siberia very, very cold."

I shuddered, "I'll take your word for it, Boris."

As we reached the gangway, I could make out an old ex-Royal Navy lorry parked on the bank. With the grace of a cat, Boris shot down the creaking old planks of the gangway, not even bothering to use the rope handrails. As I started after him I felt the ship roll a bit with the tide, and grasped the ropes whilst my knees struggled to keep my two feet under them. Finally reaching the bank, I looked over at Boris. "You make it look so easy!"

"Is only hard up top there," he said, pointing aloft to the towering masts. "You slip here, you only splash. You slip there, you splat."

"Right, well I shall try not to splat," but I wasn't feeling at all reassured as I looked up into the darkness.

Reaching into the back of the lorry, Boris threw back the tarpaulin. There were buckets of paint, great tins of petrol, and boxes of damned near everything one could wish for. It was staggering.

"Where did all this come from?" I asked in amazement.

Boris looked through the mass of goods, and lifted out a hauling block marked *HMS Princeton*. "From this," he said, indicating the letters on it.

"Good Lord man, don't tell me we're reduced to theft," I said in alarm.

"Hardly," came a voice behind me. I turned to see Harris making his way towards us. "The *Princeton* is in the scrap yard. Damned pig of a ship. She'll be broken up soon and needing none of this."

Then it came to me. Harris was more than a mere deckhand, and might be the inside connection to the scrap yards of the Royal Navy, whence he could easily smuggle things out bit by bit unnoticed. After a moment I worked up the courage to ask him about the possible connection. Even as I spoke, I thought I might have overstepped so I made my question short. He could always laugh it off, but I was rewarded with a ready reply.

"Aye that's true, every word," he said carefully. Then he looked me in the eyes and gave me that kindly smile again. "And a word to no one," he added sweetly.

I suppressed a shiver. "Well, I have to say it's brilliant. Up to now I was thinking that the ship couldn't ever be saved, but with that main cargo hold, you might carry it off."

Harris smiled, "Not a thing done slapdash."

"I had no idea that you were so well organised," I added lamely. "So much in fact, you must be the one who *organises* the endless supply of whisky in green unmarked bottles."

"No, that was sent up by Betty, a long-time friend of Bowman's wife, Meg. She runs a distillery on the Isle of Islay and gave a gift of a keg some time ago."

Harris once more bent his disquieting smile upon me, but mercifully at this point took his smile and clambered up into the back of the lorry with Boris. Each threw out a sack to me. I caught one while the other well-nigh caught me. I gathered them both awkwardly into my arms and began to trudge back towards the gangway. The fog that I had earlier seen gathering was now rolling in thicker by the minute.

"I feel like a grave robber in a Sherlock Holmes mystery," I called back to Harris.

"Sherlock Holmes robs graves?" asked Boris.

Harris looked up with an amused glint in his eye. "Yes indeed, simply doted on it," he remarked blandly. "Everyone knows that grave-robbing and the violin were the great Sherlock's favourite pastimes, mate."

Boris turned and gazed at him narrowly. Harris rolled his eyes skyward, "Oh never mind," he said absently, "let's have at it now."

It took a long hour to unload that bloody lorry. It seemed as though a bit of every ship scrapped must have been in there. Bowman, Edward, and Harris sorted things for storage locked together in a constant fray over what was or wasn't useful. Boris stood by silently, perhaps unable to determine what exactly they were on about. I envied him his poor English; then again he seemed to have an unflappable nature.

When the last bit of gear was safely stowed on board, we all filed back below deck. Between the pot-bellied stove and the heat of our labours, the cabin seemed positively tropical, a welcome change from the crisp night and the thickening fog.

"I must be getting soft," I groaned as I pulled off my coat, and fell into a chair. I was ready for a nice cup of tea, but Bowman was busily pouring another round of whisky, so I held out my hand for a mug of the restorative.

"It's a shame the sail locker doesn't shape up to the cargo hold," Bowman said.

"Why?" I asked, "How much sail is there?"

"Not much that's useful. Too much mildew and rot. Ha! I know what ye're thinking. All that rigging won't move a wind ship with nothing to catch the wind. Aye, but we're hoping to get lucky."

"Lucky?" I asked. I turned to Harris, who sat back with his eyes closed smoking a pipe comfortably held in the corner of his mouth.

"Good canvas is hard to come by, and what we do find is too small," Harris sighed. "Why, you'd have to stitch so much together, it'd probably split in a dozen places in the first hard blow. It's simply not for the doing."

"How would you sew it if you had it?" I asked. "Doing it by hand would take forever."

Harris settled back even further and blew out a smoke ring. "No need for that. We've friends in the garment trade, Jewish folk I helped get out of Europe when things got bad. Really nice people and they have quite a fleet of sewing machines, including some heavy-duty industrial ones. They're watching out for a volume of canvas. We already contacted some retired sail-makers to help with the sewing on the bolt ropes, making the cringles, and all those other finishes, without which the sails would be useless. I think I'll pop by there tomorrow and see if there's anything in the wind, so to speak. Care to come along Flynn?"

My aching muscles reproached me. "Well, I work all day, you know. I'm not sure that I could tackle another load so soon."

Harris laughed, "Small chance we'll fetch a cargo tomorrow."

I thought for a moment, "I'll give it a go, but it has to be at tea-time."

"Not to worry," said Harris airily. "No place is far away when I'm driving."

"I've just remembered, I've some work to finish up at the inn," I said. Reaching for my pocket watch, I winced as I saw that it was after two o'clock in the morning. It was late...or early, depending how you looked at it. "I really must be going. I've enjoyed this evening, despite the work, and I look forward to seeing you again soon. Captain Bowman, Boris, Edward, and you, Harris—good night, everyone."

As I bundled up against the night, I was wondering just what the devil I had blundered into, and what I had let myself in for. Soon I would have to be making other plans, and this sounded a good deal more exciting than working at the inn. We shook hands all around, and I quickly climbed the ladder into the night.

Chapter 2
THE BEASLEY INN

Next morning the shrill voice of Mrs. Beasley, landlady of the Beasley Inn, woke me. As she was directly beneath the window of my attic room, I couldn't pretend to ignore her presence.

"Oh, Mr. Flynn, please come straightaway. Purdy has a poor little bird!"

I rolled out of bed and pulled on my shirt, then went to the old casement and peered out. Below, my esteemed landlady and employer, her round figure swathed in an overcoat and a most astonishing nightdress, flitted heavily about the garden, arms flailing helplessly and grizzled hair flying. "Mr. Flyn-n-n," she wailed.

I had to wonder why people who own cats seem surprised whenever their pets capture a prize. These conquests, of course, customarily finish up with the termination of the luckless victim, following a lively round of recreational torture. Poor bird indeed. Miserable cat!

Purdy! Overweight, overindulged, and into trouble several times daily. Damned thing. Until I pruned back a branch that was too close to my little room, I never dared leave my window open for air, since Purdy made it his job to creep in whilst I was asleep or away. Once inside, he would not only give the bedclothes a liberal spraying, but was also thoughtful enough to leave a similar, more solid gift in my shoe. Once he ate a bird—or part of it—on my pillow. Of course, Mrs. Beasley refused to believe that her darling could be guilty of such villainy and in fact now regarded me with a degree of suspicion for having suggested it. I thought wistfully, what a handsome fur neckpiece one could fashion from a large cat pelt.

"Mr. Flynn, Martin, Katherine!" Mrs. Beasley cried. "You bad puss! Drop it! Drop it, I say!" I knew that neither the barman, Martin nor Katherine, the combined pastry cook and waitress, would pay any attention to her. It was *my* job. What a fearsome spectacle, to see this formidable lady acting the helpless female.

I heaved a martyr's sigh as I pulled on my trousers and shoes. I descended stairs and stepped into the sunshine, blinking with a slight bit of hangover from the night before. I was new to this area and had been here almost a week. Aside from Mrs. Beasley's alarms and her abrasive personality, it was quiet and restful. It was just a temporary job, but I was pleased with my position as gardener and groundsman for the property. The main pub building boasted a few guestrooms with combination pub and dining room in addition to three small one-bedroom cottages in the surrounding gardens. Mrs. Beasley was proud of her culinary prowess but she was not opposed to taking some credit for the skill of the pastry cook as well. A placard at the door of the pub read: Serving Luncheon, Tea, High Tea And Late Suppers By Arrangement. Another card advised: Bed And Breakfast Seasonally. By all accounts, the place was quite lively in the summer.

As I crossed the lawn, I encountered the thoroughly dishevelled Mrs. Beasley standing near her parlour door holding Purdy, a bulky ginger tom. "You nasty thing! How could you?" she was saying, as if the cat understood or cared in the least. He simply yawned as some stray bits of down floated gently off his mouth in the morning breeze. She turned and spied me. I averted my eyes from the undesired sight of her filmy nightdress, which may have looked more at home on Lana Turner or Hedy Lamarr.

"Oh Mr. Flynn, isn't it dreadful?" and she pointed to a scattering of feathers spread over the lawn.

"Yes. I'll see to it," I said, and fled off to the shed for a rake.

Nothing meant more to Mrs. Beasley than her cat and her birds, though tragedy was the frequent and inevitable result of combining the two interests. The suet and crumbs she lavished on her little feathered friends would have been more sustaining if they'd been placed where a cat couldn't reach them.

Bells rang out from the old stone church, for it was Sunday. I planned to get a bit of work done on this quieter day. It was not until later in the day that I saw Mrs. Beasley neatly dressed in tweed, with her salt-and-pepper locks perfectly coifed. It was quite a contrast to the wood nymph of the morning.

"Oh, there you are Mr. Flynn. Out till all hours last night?" she enquired.

"I suppose so," I began. "I took the footpath at the bottom of the garden to have a look at those old moored-up ships." Her expression grew stiffer. Now what? Talking to her was like having to answer to my mum when I was younger. "It's a grand sight," I added.

She looked down her nose at me and adjusted her glasses. "It will be far nicer when those wretched things are gone, and the people off them. Why, they're like shanties on the tide and home to a pack of tramps on the dole."

"Oh?" I said in surprise.

"Indeed, yes," she nodded. She lowered her voice to speak confidentially, eyes widening in dread, "And there is one worse than the lot, a horrid person called Bowman."

I laughed. "I think I may have met the man," I said as I clipped away at the hedge.

She became annoyed at this, "He's forever after the children."

"Children?" I asked.

"Yes, from what's left of the orphanage up there." She pointed to where the gently sloping downs climbed higher to the east above the water. I could make out part of a grey stone building. "The boys are drawn to those old wrecks and he's forever filling their heads with stories, even letting them climb the masts as if they weren't bad enough off loitering about such a filthy place. Oh! What a world!" She threw up her arms, and giving a tragic sigh, stalked back to the inn.

By the location of the orphanage, I guessed it afforded a tantalising view of the vessels and waterway below. It came as no surprise that children were drawn there. I remember many times when I was young how my elders disapproved of me "hanging about that unsavoury element," but to no avail. Nor did I find it surprising that Mrs. Beasley should find Bowman less than enchanting, remembering my own first encounter with him.

As I worked through the afternoon, I thought of last night and the courage and devotion each man brought to that grand old shanty on the tide. I had to laugh at the way Mrs. Beasley regarded it all, but I resolved to be very careful of what I said in her presence.

Promptly at four, a battered old Morris came bumping along the road and rolled to a stop with a jerk a few feet away. There was a loud hoot of the horn. Having never seen it before, I didn't look round until there was another hoot. It was Harris, and the little car was all but bursting at the seams with him. "Hello!" I called out.

Harris looked from the driver's window. "Get in before the old bat comes round again," he said, trying to whisper.

I glanced back at the inn amused. "I take it you mean Mrs. Beasley?"

"Aye, her Royal Hind-Arse," he growled, keeping his voice low. "She's into everyone's back garden, has a kettle on the whole of mankind with a paddle that reaches clear to the bottom of the pot. You'd best watch yourself around her."

He shook his head in disgust, and then creased his face up into the sinister leer of a cinema underworld chief. "Look 'ere mate, if that old tabby peaches on our mob, she won't live to see *us* do porridge," he grated.

I chuckled, "Point taken," I said. "She'll hear nothing from me. I just need a moment to clean myself up."

"No time for that. In the car, in the car!" He insisted.

As I squeezed in beside him, Harris's knees seemed to be bent up under his chin. I pitied his discomfort until we got under way. I found I had to slump down and shrink against my door to allow room for his elbow whilst he changed gears. The car rattled, shook, and clanked in an ominous manner. Once we left the inn behind, he raised his cap and slowly pulled it off. Now he was getting down to business. I found his driving skilful, but very fast. I held on like a white-knuckle flyer as he took the bends and weaved in and out of cars, carts, pedestrians, and bicycles.

I was surprised by the sight of others' equally startled faces flashing by outside my window.

"Is it really necessary to drive this fast?" I gasped.

"Oh, absolutely," he replied cheerfully, giving the throttle an extra boost. The car shuddered, as did I.

Harris told me he had served over twenty years on various ships, and had known Bowman since he was a boy, even serving with him and under him on occasion and was perhaps the only living person to get away with calling him Uncle Billy. Harris currently worked for the Royal Navy as a storeman in the Chatham Dockyard. It was not just fate that brought him and Bowman together this time; it was now the items in the scrap yards from many ships no longer useable.

I wondered what "Uncle Billy" thought of Harris's driving as I clung on for dear life, watching trees, houses, and villages rush by at a perilous speed. After a time I remembered to breathe. I had to remind myself that it was only the county of Kent, and not my life, which was passing before my eyes.

"Are we almost there?" I asked as we ran through Gravesend. "Surely it can't be much farther."

"Almost there m'boy," said Harris, his eyes fixed on the road.

Half reassured I watched the countryside as we passed, and suffered silently through another stretch of the journey. Behind the clouds, daylight would soon be failing. I became aware that we had moved into a built-up area and the traffic was increasing.

"Harris! I do need to be back soon. Where exactly are we going?"

He glanced at me from the corner of his eye. "Well, it's sort of East End-ish."

I digested this morosely. "You rotten cheat!" I exclaimed. "You knew I'd never come along if I'd known we were going all the way to London. Haven't you heard that petrol is still being rationed?"

"Don't worry over that, it's special Navy reserve fuel. It's a nice outing for you, laddie," he said. "Don't tell me you prefer the company of La Belle Beasley?"

This deserved no answer from me and I kept some colourful language to myself as we swung down Shooters Hill. Passing Greenwich and New Cross onto the Old Kent Road, we turned right and rattled over Tower Bridge. The traffic seemed to part miraculously at our approach; when it didn't, Harris cursed and chafed. I think he would have driven *over* the vehicles if he could. As we came into Whitechapel, looking at the bomb devastation was rather humbling. Whole stretches were flattened from the Blitz and by the latest super weapons. My own worries seemed very trivial by comparison. The East End had been hard hit, with the Luftwaffe being especially attentive to dockland warehouses, treating them to its full menu of destruction. The Germans used high explosives, incendiaries, and landmines in 1940, and then "doodlebugs" and V1 and V2 rockets in 1944. Of poor old Limehouse, the setting for many a tale of dark suspense, little remained. The Port of London had never shut down during the war, and river traffic had been periodically interrupted for mine sweeps.

We rumbled along for a time, before turning into a street having ruins to the left and the occasional intact structure to the right. Harris suddenly swerved, the engine whining, as he changed into bottom gear and ran into the kerb. *That* was how he stopped his car when there was no uphill available. "Here we are," he said.

After bouncing for the past two hours, I sat numbly in the silence. I felt that some comment was warranted, but reproaches were pointless. "Wherever did you come by this car?" I asked.

"'Tis all mine," he said. "I traded some magic beans for it," then grunted as he pried himself out from behind the wheel.

I opened my door and all but fell out. I stretched my limbs painfully, wondering if my spine was now permanently deformed.

"What about that lorry you had last night?" I asked.

He looked at me blankly, "Why?"

"Well," I said, "I thought we were coming to pick up sails. This car won't carry much."

"As I said last night, I doubt we'll be so lucky as to have much to carry," he said, "but we'll soon see." He turned and crossed the battered cobbles of the street. I hurried along behind him, his pace nearly twice my own. He halted before one of the few undamaged buildings, an ancient-looking brick warehouse, and stood surveying its blackened façade.

"I don't suppose that Whitechapel is anyone's idea of heaven, but compared to what der Fuhrer had in mind for them..." He shook his head, led the way up the steps to the loading platform, and went to the warehouse door. Removing his glove, he knocked on the door with a heavy hand. The door opened a crack and an eye peered out at us.

"Don't break it in!" protested a foreign-sounding male voice. "My God, you sound just like the Gestapo."

"Sorry," Harris replied.

"Never mind. I should know by now it could only be you," said a slender middle-aged man as he opened the door. He had dark curly hair and a thick beard. In his eyes I could see the shadow of grief, which was all too familiar these days. He wore his tailor's apron with an air of dauntless professionalism. The scissors at his belt and tape measure about his neck he wore as though they were the insignia of office.

As we entered, I looked about with interest. There were massive cutting tables heaped with bolts of cloth. Next to them a line of sewing machines, including some large heavy-duty ones, able to sew all sorts of materials. The whole place was a well-organised and successful workshop. Harris's refugees had done very well for themselves, and they had him to thank for making it possible.

The tailor was looking at me with curiosity, but Harris was already asking for news. "We've seen nothing," he said to Harris. "There are many small lots of material as heavy as you need, not nearly enough. It would take too long to sew it together, and I couldn't guarantee the results in a strong wind. We have to find some very big rolls, long pieces large enough to sew for sails. Oh, but how rude I am!" He turned to me and held out his hand, "Brian," he smiled.

"Flynn," I replied, giving him a warm handshake.

"Harris got us out of France you know, only two steps ahead of the German army. Never was there such a great heart! I know he put his life at hazard for us many times over. My family and I will always be happy to help him, and any friend of his. We can sew almost anything, but we must have the material. Not even the black market people have enough of the canvas you need." Brian threw up his hands in resignation.

Harris tried not to show his disappointment. "Well my friend, please keep your ears open," he said, "We'll have to be getting straight back as it's already late and we have a good drive ahead of us."

"Won't you stay for dinner?" Brian asked. "You never seem to have time for social visits these days."

"No, I'm sorry," Harris answered, "but thanks anyway. Could we have a couple of these?" he said eyeing a bowl of apples. "We missed our tea." He pulled out two, tossing one to me.

"Come along, Flynn." He made a quick exit, forcing me to scurry after him.

"Nice meeting you Brian," I said waving goodbye. "Thanks for the apples."

"Stay well, my friends," he called, and closed the door.

We were making for the car when suddenly Harris turned aside. He climbed over the bench at a nearby bus stop and slid down onto the seat, looking glum. The gaslight from a twisted street lamp emerging from a pile of rubble cast a wan light over us.

"That wasn't the news I'd hoped for," Harris said. "I don't think that much canvas exists in all of London." He gave a great sigh. We sat in silence for a time. To put the proper finish to our dismal mood, it now began to drizzle in the grey twilight. Harris gave no sign that he was even aware of this dampness.

Looking up the street, a red double-deck London bus had appeared and was making its way in our direction. Arriving at our stop, it drew up to let off two children. The conductor stepped off briefly, and walked to the front to have a quick word with the driver. As he got back on board and pulled on the bell cord, I happened to glance up at the advertising on the side of the bus. There were pictures of lions, tigers, and elephants, with blaring letters trumpeting CHIPPERTON'S CIRCUS, UNDER THE BIG TOP. A large circus tent occupied the background. All at once my mouth grew dry and I gulped.

"I say, Harris?"

"Yes?" he rumbled, chewing on his apple.

"When was the last time you saw the circus?"

"Circus?" he said, giving me an unfavourable look. "Have you gone round the bend Flynn? Who cares about that rubbish when there are more important matters at hand?"

"No, no," I said with a smile. "I have a friend I think you should meet."

"I've no time to run around a bloody circus," he protested.

"You'll have nothing *but* time for what I've in mind." I cajoled.

"Oh? And why do you think so?" he gazed at me with suspiciously.

"You'll just have to trust me on this one," I said.

"Beats pissin' to windward. That's what this day has come to," he muttered as he pitched his apple core.

The bus advertisement had also mentioned the place: Gravesend. It was not so far from the ships. I got Harris to agree to pick me up the next day. It was too late to go now, as my circus friend Robert would be busy with the evening performance.

We crossed the street, crammed ourselves into the car, and set off for Kent. With a roar of the mighty Morris engine, Harris resumed terrorizing the populace at large. I wondered what sort of reception I'd get back at the inn after my flagrant truancy. Fortunately, Mrs. Beasley had gone to the village of St. Mary Hoo on a long visit and never noticed my absence. Relieved at surviving the excursion and not facing an inquisition, I found myself some cold dinner from the kitchen and then crept into bed by ten o'clock. I had a feeling that I'd need all the sleep I could manage in the days to come.

Chapter 3
THE CIRCUS

Next day, Harris and I stood on Windmill Hill at Gravesend overlooking the circus. It was a crisp October day with enough wind to set the bunting and flags fluttering in the sun, but we only had eyes for the tents. There was the big top itself, a huge circle with its twin poles climbing up at least sixty feet. There were three other tents, where animal cages were kept, and several caravans dotted around the site.

"I thought you weren't keen on being reduced to theft?" Harris chuckled.

"Well, yes, but I thought where there's some canvas, there might be more. I have a friend who works here, so I'm hoping that we can find out."

"No harm in a bit of a look-see, eh?" Harris said with a smile. With that, we started down the hill. He looked over the tents gloatingly, as though they were already in the cutting room. As we were walking, one of the circus staff passed carrying a monkey that reached over and pulled off Harris's cap. Some passersby laughed, but Harris was not amused. He snatched it back, and put it back on his head. He drew himself up, the picture of wounded dignity, and cast a chilly eye upon the little creature. "Cheeky bugger, ought to be put in a pie," he growled. The monkey made a rude noise as it was borne off. Harris's eyes bulged out.

"Steady on," I laughed.

We'd been walking for a while taking in the festivities when I decided to ask a gateman for my friend. He directed us to one of the animal tents. There we found him cleaning out a lion's cage.

"Attention on deck!" I called out. Robert looked up and then dropped everything he held into a clattering heap.

"Flynn!" he cried. "You're a sight for sore eyes! How the devil are you? I haven't seen you in months. I thought you'd moved on without leaving word."

Robert and I were old friends and served two years as shipmates. Being demobbed from the Navy, or as some say "mustered out," we were doing what we could, and times were hard. There were no more convoys to escort and not much work available.

"No, I'm still around, Robert," I said, giving his hand a good pumping. "Oh, and this is my friend Harris."

"Hello," Robert said, "welcome to show business," and he reached out for his first Harris handshake. Robert's face may have turned a bit purple, but he bore this unexpected initiation in the spirit it was intended. He held his released hand out before him as a dog would an injured paw. "Here, sit down," he said, indicating some bales of straw with the other hand.

"How have you been?" I asked.

"Bare-arsed and bleeding from every pore," said Robert. "And you?"

"Much the same mate. Just going at it day by day," I responded. "I wasn't sure I'd still find you working here."

"Not much else for the doing. I was aspiring to become a rich drunk by now, but I'm afraid I've only achieved the latter." He laughed ruefully; then he gave me an enquiring look.

"Well, let's have it. You didn't come here to see a lion hula-dance in the sideshow." Robert was always one for getting to the point.

"Right you are," I answered. "We are looking for a large amount of canvas. Where does all this come from?"

"Is *that* all? Well then, how much of a supply? I've got enough to make suits for an elephant or two," and he waved a hand at the nearest tent.

Harris spoke, "I was thinking of a bit more, say perhaps 3500 square yards."

Robert's mouth opened to speak, and then he burst into laughter. "You're not serious? Starting up a circus of your own, are you?"

"No, just interested in the canvas." Harris replied.

"You could rig sail on a lot of small craft with all that," he said.

"Or a large one," added Harris. He stood up, his immense frame casting the only shade around. He pulled off his cap with one hand and with the other mopped his head with a handkerchief. "Let's take a walk round," he said in a low voice.

We strolled off away from the crowd. "Now how would one go about finding that much canvas, Robert?" Harris asked.

"Join the circus?" Robert said with a shrug.

"Why, it would never have crossed my mind without you asking," Harris returned with faint sarcasm.

Robert waved a hand at the large tents. "All this will be taken down and packed away a week from now, and I'll soon be looking for work again." He turned to me. "What the devil would you be wanting sail canvas for anyway?"

"Care for a drop?" Harris suggested, producing a flask from his coat.

"Not here," said Robert nervously. "I'd get sacked if someone saw me. What's all this about sail canvas? Doing a bit of seamanship these days, Flynn?"

"It's a long story, but if you come for a drink tonight, perhaps we can shed more light on the matter," said Harris.

Robert frowned, "Right. Where and what time?"

"Eight o'clock," Harris began. "From Gravesend take the country lane that goes east out across the marshes signposted to Lower Higham, then follow it onto High Halstow and head south past St. Mary Hoo to Allhallows. Allhallows is a tiny village with a few houses and an old Norman Church on a slight hill overlooking the estuary, literally in the middle of nowhere. There is a cosy little pub with the nicest barman and the nastiest landlady—"

"Oh my God," Robert exclaimed, rolling his eyes, "you don't mean the Beasley place?"

"Then you've met Mrs. Beasley?" I asked. "I just started working there."

"That old bat! She's gone completely doolally tap. We should have dropped her on the Germans. The bloody war would have been over years earlier," he laughed. "A couple of months back, she ordered me out of the pub because there was a fight. Mind you, I wasn't even *in* the fight—I just happened to be the last one in the place when she arrived. 'Out!' she said, 'you young hooligan! You ruffian, just look at my floor! I'll have the authorities on you!' Well, her beastly floor had nothing to do with me, and I was a bit annoyed. When I left, I slammed the door a bit too hard, and it came completely off its hinges. The blasted door chased me down the steps. She raised bloody hell and told me to 'never set foot in here again, you young jackanapes!'" He chuckled, "I wonder if she'd recognise me again."

"She's a bit of a strange one. She's also quite touchy and rude. After all, she's been a widow since the Great War," I said.

"Oh, and this war wasn't great enough?" Robert replied sarcastically.

"Ha!" Harris burst in, "Poor blighter. Her old man probably committed suicide after the Armistice when he realised he was being sent home to her." We all laughed.

Robert said, "See you at eight o'clock."

It was time for us to get back. Fortunately, the circus grounds were less than twenty miles from Allhallows, and the return trip to the inn was not long, especially in a flying Morris. I had taken a very generous break for lunch, and hoped it wouldn't arouse any suspicions. I had Harris leave me down the road from the inn just to be sure that Mrs. Beasley wouldn't see his car. I then got back to my work, thinking about everything that had transpired. It was good to see Robert again, for it had been several months since our last visit. I was now curious what would come of our meeting at the inn. The last twenty-four hours had held more intrigue than I'd been accustomed to. Although there was an element of intrigue, I had to admit all this made me extremely nervous.

Chapter 4
AN EVENING AT THE INN

The fog was billowing up like great clouds of smoke in the chilly air as I went to the pub side of the inn. It was one place we were not likely to run into Mrs. Beasley. Even though the pub bore her name, the licensee was actually a seasoned tapster by the name of Martin who was a pleasant character and well liked by his customers. In the evening Mrs. Beasley liked to stay safely in her parlour sipping sherry.

I paused at the shed long enough to throw in the rake and clippers I'd been using in the garden. I was too tired to walk in and hang them up. I'd find them tomorrow right enough.

As I got to the entrance, Harris's car came bumping along the road and parked on the other side. A young lad ran over to meet it, and after a few words disappeared into the fog. Bowman and Edward had just arrived and we all met up at the door of the pub. Bowman straightaway asked, "Do ye think yer friend will help us?"

"If he can, I'm sure he will. He's been there only a few months, so it may...wait a moment. Let's get inside and talk. I, for one, need a drink," I said shivering. Everyone nodded and we pushed open the pub door. "Who was that boy?" I asked Harris.

"Just a kid," said Harris. "You'll soon meet him."

Going in, my first impression was that it seemed no less foggy inside than out, so thick was the tobacco smoke. It was a damned sight warmer at least. This was the local and boasted a good view of the water. Men were sipping and storytelling as a game of darts was in progress. Luck was on our side, for the table nearest the fireplace was just coming free. We quickly took our seats by the welcome glow of the flames. I saw Boris at the bar with the collar of his wool coat still turned up and his knit cap pulled down. Harris hailed him, "Ahoy there, Boris!" The Russian smiled and came over, pulling off his watch cap. He sat down and whispered something of interest to Harris. I strained to hear, but it was lost in the noise of the pub.

"Right then," I said, "looks like we're all here except Robert. I'm sure he'll be along any time now."

Bowman gestured to our group, "No introductions for this part of the crew."

"You mean there are more?" I asked.

"Questions, questions," said Bowman. "Everything in its own good time."

A dart game was being played by a couple of drunken lads. The more they drank, the wilder the contest and their aim became. The murky air buzzed with flitting darts. Suddenly, Harris snapped at the air with one hand as though catching a fly. Then he brought his hand down and opened it on the table. There, plucked in mid-flight, was a stray dart. I couldn't believe my eyes.

"Christ, Edward!" Harris boomed. "This quite nearly flew up your nose." Everyone laughed. Edward's lips moved, but without words.

Harris rose and stood looming, "Now then boys, game's over." It seemed for a moment as if all talk in the pub stopped. "Let me have the other darts," he said, walking over to the two drunks. He spoke to them in a soft but steady voice. "I think you've had too many pints to be throwing these about."

"Oh, do you now?" began one of the two, as his friend tried to dissuade him from offering any further challenge. The first fellow truculently shrugged off the other's restraining hands and stood his ground. Harris extended one hand towards him, holding the dart in his fist point up, thumb against its shaft. As the fellow reached for it, Harris pushed his thumb forward, and with one flick, broke it neatly in two and placed it in the drunk's hand. From the look on the poor lad's face, one could see that he was not entertaining the notion of any further discussion. Harris returned to the table with a pleased look on his face.

"Why didn't ye just crush the damn thing to a powder?" grumbled Bowman.

"Ah, but then you would have said I was showing off," Harris smiled.

The laughter and chat picked up again when Robert came through the door. "Good evening everyone. I trust I haven't kept you waiting."

"No," I said, "This is only my first round." I held up my glass in illustration.

"Thanks for coming down," Harris began. "This is Bowman and Edward. We've ordered a pint for you, and that's Boris getting our drinks there."

We all looked up just in time to see the barmaid slap Boris. He came back to the table with our drinks, grinning. "She likes me, yes?"

"Oh, that much was quite obvious to all," Edward said laughing.

"What brought on the violence?" asked Harris, trying to hide his amusement.

Boris looked blank, "Language misunderstanding I think so, but she still smile."

"Oh, ever the ladies' man, aren't ye?" coughed Bowman, "but ye haven't reached Harris's deviant level of behaviour around the ladies, praise be."

Harris pretended to look elsewhere, but gave a nasty cackle.

I stood up and took Robert's arm. "Excuse me, but may I chat with you a moment?" I asked, tugging at his arm.

"But it's warm here by the fire," he objected. "'Tis colder than a whore's heart this night. It's the blasted fog. Besides, this is the best show in town, eh?"

"You would know," I said, abandoning my plan for a private word.

It was obvious to me that Robert was a possible recruit to the project, now that his job was coming to an end. First we needed to settle the matter of the canvas.

"Did you find out anything more about canvas?" I asked.

Robert took a good long drink before answering. "I've asked around for canvas everywhere," he said, "but there's not a spare foot in all London, let alone 3500 square feet. I talked to a few old shipmates who work in the Chatham Dockyard and London Docks. There's not a bit of canvas. Even if there was, scrap yard security is pretty tight. It seems a good deal of stuff goes missing."

Harris's eyes grew big as he cleared his throat noisily, taking a long drink. In fact, he found that he'd quickly drained his glass and waved to the barmaid to order another.

"But what I'd like to know," Robert continued, "is what the devil do you need all that canvas for? And what's all this bit about sailing, anyway?"

"Hush lad, lower your voice," Bowman interposed. "All things in due course."

Suddenly from outside there arose the agonised yelp of a dog. A few heads turned, but in the main room the heart-rending sound was ignored by the pub-goers as it disappeared into the distance. One man rose and went out.

"What in God's name was that?" Robert exclaimed.

Harris raised a placating hand. "Don't let it alarm you. It's just the landlady's tomcat. Himself likes to lie in wait by the steps and attack dogs. Curse the little bastard."

Harris leaned back in his chair. "Now, this afternoon you mentioned that they were taking the circus down for the winter soon."

"Yes, this is the last week of work for me," said Robert. "Then I don't know what I'll be doing."

Harris thought for a moment. "What happens to everything after that?" He asked blandly.

"When the circus comes to town, all of the equipment is carried by rail in six goods wagons. They're packed with everything needed to put the circus together: animals, games, tents, and enough rubbish to invade France all over again. Those tents are a pain in the arse! So damn many parts, and every one of them is heavy. We lay out the canvas, put up the poles, rig everything so the horses can pull it all up, and get some of the local kids to work for free passes. In a few days, we're going to warehouse everything except the animals. They go back to the zoos."

"Warehouse?" Harris asked, as he set the two front legs of his chair down and leaned forward to listen closer.

"Right," said Robert. "We can't leave it all in the goods wagons— they have to be returned to the railway company after the season. Trouble is, the kids are frantic to help put the tents up when we first get in, but they vanish when it comes time to taking it all down."

Robert eyed us thoughtfully. "Say, would you gents like a day's work?"

Harris turned to the table, and took piece of a paper and a pencil out of his coat. "How many people do you need?"

"There's no such thing as enough people when you're packing a bloody circus," said Robert.

"There will be this time," grinned Harris, "I'm quite sure I can get you plenty of willing lads."

"How?" laughed Robert. "At gunpoint?"

"No," said Harris. "I know someone who runs an orphanage. They just barely get by, and I'm sure the boys'll be worth their wages. I'll be needing twenty or so free passes for them right away. They won't be of much use come closing day."

Robert was interested, "Tell the headmaster to come and see us."

"I will," Harris smiled. "We've plenty of lads. Will twenty be enough?"

"With some of the present company along," said Robert, eyeing the massive Harris, "we should have the job well in hand. We've a whole bloody trainload to move."

He drained his glass and shoved it towards Harris, who signalled the barmaid with a raised finger. As soon as we got a refill, Robert looked at Harris, "Now then, I've been doing all the talking about the circus. Who's going to tell me what's going on?" We looked at one another, wondering who would speak up. Bowman was the leader, but so far Harris was doing all the talking.

"Right," said Harris. "Let's take a walk." The others nodded in approval. "I've a little something for the road," Harris said. He pulled open his coat, showing a flask peeking from an inner pocket.

Robert and I put on our coats in expectation of the cold and damp awaiting us outside.

"Hold this table at all costs," Harris said over his shoulder as we left and, with the laughter behind, we hustled through the door. "Let's take the car, it'll be faster."

I stopped in my tracks, remembering his driving. I called over to Robert, "Oh, God! Now we're in for it, old friend." Harris looked over his shoulder and shook his head sadly at my lack of faith.

We crammed into the Morris. This time I was in the rear seat as we bumped and clattered down the road towards the ship. Robert dodged Harris's elbow just as I had to. While it was not far on foot, we were glad to ride. The wipers strained to keep the windscreen clear in the dense damp. We slowed to a stop, and Robert wound down his window. His eyes grew wide at the sight of the old masts rising up dimly in the fog. We opened the doors and stepped out.

"I'll be damned!" he exclaimed. "You've outdone yourself this time, Flynn. Does the Royal Navy know you've hidden these ships in plain sight?" He shook his head in disbelief. "Blimey, as soon as you trimmed the sails they'd know, and in short order. You'll never outrun a Lighter, let alone a Motor Torpedo Boat. Those MTBs are fast and are still used by the Costal Patrol."

"What makes you think we hadn't considered that already?" said Harris.

Robert folded his arms. "Very well then, what's the plan?"

"The plan is all right here," Harris said, pointing to his great dome of a head. "We desperately need sail canvas. You tell us when those tents come down, and we'll send you more help than you ever dreamed of. This is our only chance. I'll tell you as much as you need to know." He repeated to Robert what I knew of the *Bonnie Clyde*, and why he and Bowman had the only chance of making this rescue happen successfully. He brought out the flask and passed it round.

Robert stood giving the *Bonnie* a good looking-over. "Sound is she?"

"Sound!" Harris replied.

Robert was still puzzled. "I don't understand how you're going to sail this off without notice. You'll have all the luck of a waxed cat running through Hell chased by an asbestos dog."

Harris stood pulling on his pipe for a while, blowing smoke into the fog. "There will be some onlookers, even some of those government officials, but no one will figure it out till it's too late to do anything to stop us."

With this last statement, Harris suddenly became deadly serious, and his soft voice exuded even more than its usual degree of veiled potential mayhem to any who dared cross him.

"What I am proposing to you now is something that you either take or leave. If you leave it, you'd best be aware of the consequences if you repeat the story to *anyone*. On the other hand," he laughed, "if you take it, then we'll have another badly needed friend."

All this was very solemn, and I knew that the rescue of the *Bonnie* had become something of a sacred duty. I became acutely aware of the situation now created for Robert. This had gone from looking for canvas to something I had not anticipated. Now I was concerned that I'd landed Robert in an awkward position, one from which he could not easily retreat. I had to say something.

After a moment I cleared my throat, "I do hope you'll agree with what we have planned Robert, because I simply cannot bear to think what these unfeeling civil servants have in store for the *Bonnie*. We can do nothing to save the other ship, the one without a name. Bowman calls her the *Auld Lass*. She's too far gone already, and the "coal barge" died long ago. But by God we can save this one. I'm not asking you to sign aboard. We just need the canvas, even if that's all you can help with."

Harris went on without further ado, "What we propose is that the tents from the circus never reach their storage place. That is, we will *requisition* them for the best of reasons. I don't think the owners of the circus would happily agree to this, so we must act as thieves for the moment. Time is of the essence. Already the men in suits have scheduled the *Auld Lass* for scuttling, and the *Bonnie* is soon to follow."

There was silence for quite a while as we went aboard and walked her deck. Harris took Robert below to show him around. Still there was silence. I could tell Robert was weighing the pros and cons. I knew the expression he wore very well.

He looked at me, then Harris, and began to laugh. "Perhaps I've gone daft, but I'm in! I believe there's a pint with my name on it back at the pub. I have quite a few questions though, quite a few, but they can wait."

Harris seized Robert's hand in a strong silent shake of gratitude. Once it was released, Robert looked over his hand, pretending to assess the damage. Harris then handed his flask around as we took another look about the ship. We made small talk of the work ahead, and short work of the flask. At last we piled into the car and rumbled back up the road.

"I don't see how you're going to sail her out of here free and clear," Robert said. Harris smiled, "As I said, I've no intention of doing so."

"You don't?" I said baffled.

"You don't know either, Flynn?" Robert asked in shock and surprise.

"Uh…well, all things in good time," I said sheepishly.

We clambered from the car and bolted for the inn door to find all as we'd left it. I made a point of going for a drink, but I needn't have bothered. The lovely bar maid met me with a glass of my favourite beer. Seeing her close up like this, I understood my attraction. Her hair flashed with glints of chestnut and auburn, all in a lovely halo for such a sweet face. I couldn't understand why I had not noticed all this about her before. I realised that I was staring and turned away in embarrassment as she continued on her rounds. Bowman noticed my interest.

"If I were you, I'd keep my rod in my britches and my tongue in my mouth," he said.

"You'd do no such thing," I said firmly. "Besides, if you did do so you'd piss yourself while starving." Bowman gave me an evil look as Harris laughed.

"Hold your hand out, naughty boy!" sang Robert.

"Come on, come on," Harris clucked, "let's keep to the business at hand. Now then, this is Monday and most of us have got work to do, so let's get together on Thursday and decide how to handle the circus and anything else that's not been decided."

"And why not sooner?" asked Robert. "I don't have that much on the go by day."

Harris raised a finger. "We all have our little missions to accomplish in the next few days. Plus we should be going about our usual business, so no one will take notice of what's about to happen."

Boris lifted his head off the table, "Something is going to happen?" he asked blearily.

"No, not now," Bowman sighed. "We'd best be off. Come on Boris, get up."

We all got ready to brave the cold again and headed for the door. I found that I had to pass the barmaid and paused to lose myself in her blue eyes once more. "Good night love," I said, tipping my cap. "See you around if Mrs. Beasley doesn't kill me first."

She smiled a glowing smile and I felt myself go soft inside. In the next instant Harris had brusquely pulled me out the door.

"And just what are you on about?" I barked, sourly.

"Didn't want you making a fool of yourself," he laughed.

"I wasn't doing so badly!" I said in protest.

"Quit while you're behind, Flynn," Robert laughed.

"Come on boys, I'll give you a ride," Harris said, leading the way towards his car.

"Courage lads!" I called after them thinking of Harris's driving. I turned to the stairs that led to my waiting pillow, all the while remembering that warm smile and those haunting blue eyes.

Chapter 5
THE ORPHANAGE

The sun was just peeping through the trees on the hill, but I was already on the job. I was locked in a life-and-death struggle with a hateful vine whose roots were sprawling everywhere. I had already spent most of a rainy Wednesday sweating over the wretched thing. Here it was Thursday, and I was still slaving away at it. I looked up and saw Mrs. Beasley approaching from the kitchen garden with a large spray of rosemary in her hand.

"Good morning, Mr. Flynn," she said stiffly. By her floury apron I guessed that she was at her baking, and when she was at her baking she was even testier than usual.

"Good morning, Mrs. Beasley," I panted from atop a mountain of torn-up growth. "However did this come to be so overgrown?"

"Well, we've been at war," she said pettishly.

"So I heard," I responded dryly, "in fact, it was in all the papers."

She gazed at me for a moment, her expression blank. "Yes of course," she said, with evident annoyance, and then fixed me with an accusing eye. "As you well know, there's been no one to keep up this place as it once was, since my young gardener ran off and joined the RAF. I promised that his position would still be here for him after the war. But really! Years on duty and another year in hospital. He *says* he expects to be fit enough to return in the spring. You young men!" she sighed, as though it were *our fault*.

"And there's the pond over there." She pointed to the well-tended haunt of a chattering flock of assorted waterfowl.

"Yes, that's a fine little pond," I said, making an effort to be agreeable. "I've cleaned it out and cut back the weeds and trimmed the edges."

She scowled, "Well, it was never intended that there should be a pond there you know. What a single German bomb accomplished in one night would have taken five men weeks of work. But there it was in the morning, a monstrous great hole in the place where my nice larch trees had stood. The poor things simply vanished. The rains kept it full, and then the ducks and geese came. That was some consolation at least. I do have the odd egg or two from them. After the bomb, I had to replace nearly every pane of glass on the inn. And the roof! Slates every-where!"

Again I had the impression that she felt it was somehow all our doing. She turned to go, then paused, "I do hope you'll be finished with this vine soon. I can't think why you're taking so long over it. Thank heavens I'm not paying you by the hour! Oh, yes, I nearly forgot, I've put together a few things for the orphans. When you have a moment, perhaps you can drive them up."

From where I stood, I had a clear view of the orphanage on the rise to the west. Pulling a thorn from my finger I said, "Perhaps it's time I took a break. I could run your donations up to the headmaster straight-away." This vine was beginning to take its toll on my patience, not to mention my epidermis, so I welcomed the opportunity to escape it for a little while. And escape *her* too!

Most of the time Mrs. Beasley was one of earth's most irritating people, and could drive anyone mad. But she must have had a grain of kindness, for she regularly donated food and clothing to make life a bit easier for the boys who lived at the orphanage. I had never been there before and had heard only little about it.

I cleaned myself up a bit, and then slid into the seat of the land-lady's decrepit Austin. Driving the road up to the old building provided a great view. The rolling hill sloped gently downward until it flattened into the marshy banks of the Thames estuary. As I wound along, I looked back where the Beasley Inn stood among its few trees, with the water behind it. To the east, past the Isle of Grain, was the naval base of Sheerness on the Isle of Sheppey, lost in the haze. To my eye, the broad waters and the land merged into a murky distance. I knew that not far beyond lay the foot of the North Sea, hard by the Straits of Dover. I stopped the car for a few minutes and enjoyed the sight of the river's traffic. There was a little Tyneside collier coming in with her hold full of sea-coal, and an outbound merchantman with the Channel Pilot escort she had picked up at Tilbury. Here the estuary was four miles wide at high water, but I could make out nothing of Southend or its mile long pier, which I knew lay across on the Essex side.

There was precious little working sail on the river these days, so it was a thrill to see one of the old Thames barges come into view upriver. With russet sails, it looked much as Thames barges had for centuries. Below and eastward, I could see the ships with no proper pier or land-ing. They stretched out what masts and yards they had between them, tasting the sea wind that once made them skim proudly over the waves.

The sight of them caught at my heart. By God, I thought, soon *one* of them will have her keel in deep water again! Somehow.

I came to myself and remembered my errand. I gave a salute to the old hulks, climbed back into the car, and continued on my way to the orphanage. Pulling up by the building, I could see it had once been a stately and elegant mansion. As I climbed out of the car, a man walked over to meet me. He looked for all the world like some sort of vampire with his thin form and pasty colour. His formal black suit, sombre but costly looking, only served to reinforce that Dracula impression.

"I am Mr. O'Connell, the headmaster here," he said in a haughty tone, without offering his hand.

"Flynn's the name. I work for Mrs. Beasley. She's sent along some things."

The skull-like features softened almost imperceptibly. "Ah, the dear lady," he responded in the same lofty manner, glancing into the car with genteel interest. "Boys!" he cried, "Please assist Mr. Flynn in carrying these goods inside."

Two thin young men in threadbare blazers came pelting down the steps. The headmaster bent a malevolent look upon them. "Boys, please, have you no manners? Are we animals here? Are we savages?"

They looked to be about thirteen, but I later learned both were fifteen.

The boys, with a murmuring of "No, Headmaster, sorry, Headmaster," duly composed themselves into a semblance of respectful orderliness and stood at attention. They waited there uncomfortably as O'Connell continued to glare. After a few moments O'Connell seemed satisfied with his authority, and directed them to carry on. Springing into action, they unloaded the car, doing their best to appear well behaved as they peered eagerly into the boxes and bags. They exchanged excited glances as the unmistakable fragrance of Mrs. Beasley's baking wafted from a cloth-shrouded basket.

"Never you mind what is there," snapped the headmaster, "just take it to the dining hall."

"Yes, Headmaster, sorry, Headmaster," the boys chanted mechanically, as they laboured up the old stone steps after him. I followed on, carrying the rest while O'Connell stalked ahead empty-handed, plainly above such a menial task.

We made our way through a still-splendid marble and stone entry, surmounted by a great bronze plaque of a rather later vintage which read: The Jacob Newington Starke Benevolent Home for the Care and Instruction of Unfortunate Boys. Well, there was no mistaking that these boys were unfortunate, having to endure life under the heel of a dried-up old tyrant such as O'Connell. I later learned that they referred to the Home, with fitting irreverence, as Jake Starkers. Once inside the entry, I looked about curiously. Ahead, much of the solid Georgian structure stood intact, but to my right there had been appalling destruction. I stopped in my tracks. Picking my way through a ruined doorway, I surveyed the remains of the bombed-out wing. It was all too familiar a sight: a jumble of broken stones lay heaped within what survived of the walls. The vanished roof, a skeleton of charred beams was all open to the elements. This was no blessing in disguise like Mrs. Beasley's surprise duck pond. I wondered if any boys had been caught in the explosion.

"Mr. Flynn! Mr. Flynn!" the headmaster protested fussily from without, "We do not go in there."

"Oh? Are you afraid I might damage something?"

His thin nostrils flared, "I shan't dignify that with an answer, young man. Just get out of there. Out this instant, I say!"

Arrogant sod! I had one or two such schoolmasters, the sort I would like to meet with a fresh cowpat in my hand—preferably produced by the largest bovine ever to walk a field. I mastered my resentment and withdrew from the forbidden area with good grace. As I passed the old man, I half expected to feel a cane fall on the backs of my legs. I didn't argue with him, as I reasoned the boys would pay for his subsequent bad temper. I privately reserved the right to settle with him in my own time.

I followed him through the main doorway, up a flight of stairs and into a large, nearly empty room in which our footsteps echoed dismally on the stone floor. This bleak cavern served as the dining hall. There were no rugs, and the only furniture was a long wooden table lined with benches, on which Mrs. Beasley's donations were heaped. I added my own burden to the lot. The two boys stood warming their hands at the hearth, in which glowed a sorry bit of coal that did nothing to take the chill off this immense space. Over the mantel hung a large Victorian-style painting I presumed to be the likeness of the benevolent Mr. Starke. The painting glowered dourly upon the room. Clearly, the present headmaster was carrying on in the spirit of this founding father. These were but the sorry remains of the original orphanage, but I doubted conditions were as bleak as what I saw now. The boys appeared ill clad and ill fed and the gaunt O'Connell was obviously not fattening on provisions denied his young charges. One did have to wonder, however, how he managed to afford such an expensive new suit amidst all this privation.

I began to feel that I had wandered into a Dickens novel and looked about half-expecting to see a great copper of gruel all a-bubble. This had to be the most cheerless place I'd ever visited. The one-time beauty and comfort of this hall had faded due to more than just the war. Pure neglect was everywhere. To one side of the hearth lay a fishing net filled with coal. I guessed at once it had been brought up from the old coal barge by some of the men there. At least *they* cared enough to send along a bit of warmth.

The eyes of the two young men darted from me to the donations and back again with the liveliest curiosity. O'Connell regarded them sourly; he then clapped his hands brusquely. "Boys!" he barked, "back to your History. You wouldn't want to fall behind, now would you?"

The boys marched out hastily, with a murmured "No, Headmaster," seemingly an automatic response. I wondered what the penalty was for falling behind. Flogging?

O'Connell turned his attention to me. "Thank you, Mr. Flynn," he said in a dismissive tone, "Now I must return to the managing of this establishment. Do convey my thanks to Mrs. Beasley, and tell her that I will call on her in the near future."

"Yes, I must be off. I wouldn't want to keep you from your duties," I returned levelly. "I know how devoted you are to the welfare of these unfortunate boys. I'll show myself out." As I turned to leave, I fancied that I could feel steam leaving my ears. One more minute of him, and I don't know what I might have done. I had visions of swabbing the floor with this pale skinny twit. Grief!

I went down the great stairs into the morning, only to be startled by the sound of a bo'sun's pipe. Looking back, I noticed a courtyard beyond the high stone wall alongside the building. Again I heard the familiar shrill sound.

As I headed towards the gate, O'Connell came hurrying along behind me. "Mr. Flynn! Oh, Mr. Flynn!" he called out, but I pretended not to hear. I stopped at the gate, which stood slightly ajar, and looked in. A mast had been erected as a flagpole, complete with yardarms and rigging. Standing with the boys were Harris and Boris. Puzzled, I pulled at the gate just as O'Connell came up and seized hold of my arm. I was so surprised that I did not react immediately.

"Mr. Flynn!" he said sharply, "I thanked you for delivering Mrs. Beasley's goods, and I'll now thank you not to interfere with my boys at their studies. Your presence is no longer required."

I shook him off with considerable force, protesting that I knew these men and had heard about their work with the boys.

O'Connell scoffed, "That does not surprise me in the least, nevertheless it is absolutely none of your affair. These two teach a class in seamanship every week, though it will never be of use in the modern world. I consider it no more than history instruction. Those crude, vulgar sailormen cause quite enough disruption on their own without the further intrusion of common and ill-mannered strangers."

I moved closer and he, seeing the look in my eyes, stepped back involuntarily as my blood began to boil. "Mr. O'Connell," I said as evenly as I could manage, "it is my best guess that those crude vulgar sailormen have done a good deal more to better the lot of *your* boys than you could possibly understand. And I am also sure those crude, vulgar sailormen have helped keep a bit of the cold out of this place. I'm willing to wager that much of the coal you use comes from the wrecked coal barge down there," and I pointed to the masts of the old ships, just visible at the bottom of the hill.

"Nonetheless, I must ask you to leave," he said. This was pronounced with such a starchy presumption of authority that words are not adequate to describe just how utterly obnoxious it sounded. I had had enough of this nasty little man. I began to feel impulses of a distinctly common and ill-mannered nature coming over me.

"Headmaster O'Connell," I said firmly, "have you ever had your nose broken?" I clenched my fist in anticipation. Just then, the heavy wooden gate was thrown open with such force that I was robbed of my opportunity. The black-suited figure was swept neatly away behind the great panel, which slammed back against the wall. Out walked Harris.

"Flynn!" he said in surprise, "what brings you up here?" There came a thud, and then a crash from behind the gate. Before I could answer, the door was pushed back and a distinctly damaged headmaster struggled into view, holding his nose.

"For pity's sake man, you shouldn't stand behind that gate!" cried Harris. Then he looked back at me with a twinkle. "Well, I see you've met Headmaster Mr. O'Connell."

"Quite," I answered. I looked on happily and much gratified as that thoroughly distasteful personage tottered wordlessly towards the stairs, still gingerly cradling his nose.

"Come along," Harris whispered, "let's have a chat." He put his huge hand on my shoulder and directed me towards a path round the outside of the courtyard wall. "Sorry there, O'Connell," he called back,

"I'd put some ice on that." He turned back to me. "Or pack it in horse dung," he added softly.

I began to laugh. "Hush now," he cautioned, "I know he's bloody irritating and he's a right mardy-arse, but we need him for a bit."

"Good heavens," I said in dismay, "don't tell me he's with us!"

"Oh no!" he laughed. "That chap's about as useful as tits on a worm. You see we've been training these lads in the art of seamanship."

A light dawned. "So they can act as a crew?" I exclaimed.

"Quite right," he replied. "The only ones at home in the rigging are Boris and myself. Boris is an expert, the best I've seen. But we need nimble lads who can go aloft to set and reef the sails, and walk the capstans to brace the yards. This lot is lean, but they're tough, and stronger than they look. We've been supplying them with as much extra food as we can find."

"Up in the rigging is a hard proving ground. Are you sure they're capable, and understand the dangers?" I asked.

"We've been training them for six months, here and down at the ship," Harris replied. "We rigged up one mast on the *Bonnie* with new sheets and stays, with the best canvas we could find on the other ships. I'm sure they'll do, even in a gale. I managed to find some oilskins and the lads have spent a good deal of time up there in the wind and rain." Harris paused for a long while thinking, and then continued. "You might think it hard on them, but they've been the most enthusiastic apprentices I've ever had. And that's not surprising, really, when you think of the kind of life they have with that cold stone dungeon for a home." He cast a hard look back at the old hall. "Look how thin and ragged they are! We do our best to smuggle in extra supplies. Mrs. Beasley sends what she can, but it's not nearly enough. She has no idea what the place is like nowadays. It seems bloody odd that she hasn't been up here for nearly twenty years. She thinks it's full of frolicking cherubs instead of deprived hungry teenagers. They surely get no proper schooling either. What could they learn from O'Connell? Calls himself headmaster! He's only headmaster by default."

"Should he be reported to the authorities? It's simply monstrous. The Dark Ages are over!"

Harris shook his head. "It's a legacy from the war and they'll catch up with him eventually. Meanwhile, we have plans of our own."

"But surely someone needs to know that the funds have been improperly used. He's only keeping those boys so he can suck their blood." I said.

Harris looked as if showing his disdain mirthlessly. "You know, he drives a Bentley while these boys don't even have bicycles. They don't seem to get their share, poor kids. Bloody hoighty-toighty two-faced bastard! You know, he and Beasley are cut from the same cloth. I've never met two more thoroughly disagreeable people."

"Perhaps we should introduce them for courtship," I suggested in jest.

He gave me a sly sidelong look. "Oh, they've met," he said knowingly.

"You're joking!" I exclaimed. Appalling images paraded before my mind's eye. I thought back to Sunday morning's cat chase. That glamorous nightie now showed in quite a different light!

He grinned at my horrified expression. "Oh yes, they're quite the back door item. Most of us aren't taken in by their façade of propriety. I would be sick if I knew everything they get up to. Why, it's been going on for years."

I shuddered and tried to turn my thoughts to other matters as we stopped, overlooking the sea. The wind was mild as the afternoon sun shone on the downlands that were taking on their sparse autumn colours. "Will the boys have a better home waiting for them, just as the ship has?" I asked.

Harris nodded. "They damn sure will," he smiled. "Jolly nice to see you really care, Flynn." He eyed me approvingly. "Uncle Billy was always a good judge of a man."

"Uncle Billy…Bowman?"

"One and the same," he laughed, "but don't you ever call him that. He'd ream you a new bumhole with a marlinespike."

"As you were saying the other day, you've known him a long time, eh?" I asked.

"Since I was fifteen. Too damn long. Can't quit him now. He's one of a kind, he is. I believe he could sail a matchstick up a gutter in a flood. We're lucky to have him," he sighed. "Well now, to return to the lower orders: do try to get on with that O'Connell twit. I know it's going to be hard, and God knows it too. At least when he and Beasley get together, we know they won't be watching *us*. This is one good reason we meet in the evening. It's good to keep Bowman away from Beasley—else hell itself will come to life."

"I'm just glad I wasn't standing behind that gate," I said with a grimace. "You had no way of knowing anyone was there."

"Oh, I saw you," he smiled, "and I've a keen set of ears as well."

"You dog!" I said, laughing.

Harris grinned complacently. "Come on, you'd best be getting back."

As I walked away, I gazed down on the distant Beasley domain and up at O'Connell's with a sense of amusement. Lord, how could I keep a straight face around either one of that pair now?

Chapter 6
INTERRUPTIONS AND SURPRISES

Mrs. Beasley's car was in a terrible state of disrepair, but fortunately I was up the hill and could roll it to start the engine. I hurtled down the road, trying to get back to the inn before my employer began to wonder what kept me. Most of the morning fog had burned off, and I could see trees displaying the first signs of autumn. It was a luxury to be free to enjoy the beauty of leaves turning red and golden. For six years I had come to regard the seasons as times to change camouflage and stations. Autumn had signalled only the approach of further hardships brought on by winter.

So many years of war, so many friends left behind. But this year, there was the prospect of a better winter to come, and that thought gave me a pleasant new sense of well-being, which quickly evaporated when I tried to apply the brakes. It was borne in upon me that Mrs. Beasley's car was a greater liability than that belonging to Harris. It was hard to imagine how they could keep these disintegrating machines going up and down the hills without serious mishap. One was compelled to assist the failing brakes by dragging a foot out the open door, a dangerous and nerve-racking operation at best, and only feasible at a very low speed—if one could achieve it.

As I reached the bottom of the hill, a Yank came tearing along the roadway towards me in a shiny new red Sunbeam, forcing me to swerve onto the verge to avoid him. I was fairly certain it was a Yank because only they had the money and the connections to get their hands on things like new Sunbeams. I entertained a series of uncharitable thoughts regarding the motoring habits of Yanks. After all, they nearly always forgot which side of the road to drive on. One could excuse right-hand driving on the Continent, it would be expected of the French and Italians! But Americans claimed to speak English, so they should jolly well learn to *drive* English too!

When I arrived back at the inn it was time for lunch. The barmaid, now waitress, gave me a heart-stopping smile and waved me to a table. As I sat waiting for my bit of fish and chips, I glanced out the window and spied the red Sunbeam that had figured so prominently in my brush with disaster minutes before. At a window table overlooking the car park sat a cocky-looking young man.

I stalked over to his table and pointed out of the window. "I take it you drive that red thing," I said, my anger growing.

"Yeah, sure do," he replied in the nasal tones of the New World.

"I was the other driver you nearly ran off the road back there," I grated. "This is England, and here we drive on the left-hand side of the roadway."

"Sorry about that, old boy," he said, lifting his glass. "Sometimes I forget. Can I stand you to a pint by way of apology?"

"No," I exploded. "You Yanks seem to think that money buys everything." I then returned to my table and sat down feeling happier for having said my piece. This feeling was quickly dispelled when the barmaid, *my* barmaid, *my* Venus of the taps brought him a pint and began to chat with him. By then I was thoroughly embittered. If he started pulling nylon stockings and chocolate bars out of his pockets, I'd ram them down his throat.

I had to get hold of myself. There were only three things I could bring to mind that were wrong about having Yanks here after the war: they were overpaid, they were oversexed, and they were still over here! I drained my glass, taking the last piece of fish along rolled up in a napkin and went out, slamming the door shut behind me. Not realising just how angry I'd been, I nearly forced the door off its hinges. It was just my luck; I now came face to face on the steps with Mrs. Beasley. I immediately thought of Robert's story, Headmaster O'Connell, and the negligee, and all but gagged.

"Mr. Flynn!" the landlady cried in tones of horrified reproof. "Please! Never, *ever* slam that door! It has been mended time and again all because you beastly brutal men must drink! Oh, why did I ever tie myself down to a low public house?"

"I'm sorry," I apologised sulkily, "it's been a long day, and not yet over."

"Yes, well you needn't take it out on the door," she said, wagging her finger.

I doffed my cap and placed it solemnly over my heart. "I'll be more careful in the future." Just then, the door opened behind us and I turned. There stood the lovely barmaid looking at us. The golden light from the windows in the room beyond made a halo about her hair and I felt rude and uncouth in comparison. I awkwardly adjusted my cap again and beat a hasty retreat in the face of this celestial vision, and hurried down the path to take up my duties in the garden.

I climbed back up to the Ornamental Rock where I had been struggling with the vine earlier in the day. Suddenly, something stirred in the shrubbery.

"Mr. Flynn! Mr. Flynn!" whispered a youthful voice.

"Yes, who's there?" I asked.

A tousled, red-headed boy from the orphanage emerged from the foliage. "Mr. Flynn, please hurry down to the ship." "Mr. Bowman and Mr. Harris need to see you at once. You'll come, won't you?" I nodded. After a last entreating look, the smudged young face winked out of view. I looked about and saw that Mrs. Beasley had withdrawn, so I put down my tools and hiked slowly down. Once the inn was lost to sight, I took off at a brisk pace, trotting along the footpath down to the water.

As I came in sight of the old vessels, I saw an official-looking black car parked along the road, and men moving about on board the ship. Climbing the gangway, I could see two alien figures uniformed in black coats and striped trousers, with regulation bowlers and umbrellas. Official Number One was hotly maintaining to Bowman that the middle ship tied up along our starboard side, the one he called *Auld Lass*, was going to be taken out and disposed of, and he was giving final notice to all concerned. He was shaking his perfectly furled umbrella in a neatly gloved fist for emphasis. Harris sat on a hatch cover, apparently dozing, with his back against the mainmast. Undoubtedly, these were the government officials of whom Bowman had spoken so fondly.

As they walked along the deck, nearly side-by-side, I could see Bowman was becoming increasingly agitated. This quickly deteriorated into a heated argument. When Bowman got angry, the veins in his neck and head stood out, making one fear an aneurysm. His face was an alarming beet-red. Official Number Two now decided to join in, and informed Bowman that they were nothing more than a gang of derelicts camping on these old wrecks. The old ships were going to be towed out, and everyone must make arrangements to vacate the premises, to wit, the said wrecks, and vacate them forthwith.

I took a seat on the hatchway next to Harris. He appeared to be asleep, with his head resting against the mast. His cap was pulled down over his eyes, no doubt listening very alertly to the whole of this rattling going on about him.

Harris's presence had been noted by one of the officials. Official Number Two, in his smart Savile Row attire and spotless bowler, marched over and kicked Harris's foot. "Did you hear me?" he barked, "I am talking to *you* as well."

Harris slowly raised the cap from over his eyes. "You're talking to *me*?" he said with ominous sweetness. I could feel an uneasiness mounting and feared the worst for anyone going up against Harris.

"Yes, I am addressing you," replied Official Number Two.

Harris rose and quickly seized him by his lapels, lifting his feet off the deck. He set him on the rail of the ship, leaned him backwards and roared, "Don't you *ever* lay hand or foot on me again! Do *you* understand?" Harris then shook him as a terrier would a rat.

Once he'd caught his breath, Official Number Two urgently protested. "Let me go! Unhand me this instant!" He waved his umbrella, making futile swipes at Harris.

Official Number One, incredulous at what was happening, now asserted himself. "I say!" he squeaked from a safe distance, "let him go! I say there!"

Harris shrugged his shoulders and let him go. Since the fellow was perched on the rail leaning back over the water, he hadn't far to go to end up in the river, and that he did straightaway. There was a resounding splash and spluttering as the floundering bureaucrat tried to move with his feet stuck firmly in the Thames mud.

Official Number One scrambled down the gangway with cries of dismay and danced about ineffectually on the shore. Bowman rushed over to the side to see what had happened.

"Harris!" he cried, "yer damned temper!"

"There's the pot calling the kettle black," smiled Harris. "Uncle Billy, you've been raving at these people yourself for the best part of an hour."

"Why did ye have to put him over side?" Bowman asked.

Harris smiled innocently. "But you heard them…they both ordered me to let him go." Bowman's face got even redder. "Since *when* have ye ever obeyed each and every order?"

"Well," Harris said softly, smacking his hands together, "some people are just born to command."

Official Number Two had dropped his umbrella before going overboard. Harris now reached down and picked it up from the deck. Unsnapping it, he shook out the neat furling and opened it. Holding the point daintily between thumb and forefinger, he leaned over and lowered the crook end of the umbrella to the man flailing about in the water below. "Here, here! Get hold of this." The wretched fellow grasped the handle, then vanished under the black dome of his brolly as the point escaped Harris's grip. "Ooh, it slipped," said Harris. "It's always useful to keep an umbrella on hand in case of need. You never know when you're going to get wet," he added. Idling back over to the hatchway, he sat down, tilted his cap back over his eyes, and resumed feigning his nap.

Official Number Two still foundered about with the ruin of his unhelpful umbrella and managed to snap up his bowler, as it was about to float away. He clambered soggily up the bank and stood soaking wet beside the car with Official Number One, less a shoe lost to the Thames mud. Neither seemed disposed to return to the ship. Both men began to hurl threats back at those still aboard. Not to be outdone, Bowman was shouting and kicking things about, still furious at having been told to pack up and leave.

Just then, the cheerful strains of a Russian song were heard, and Boris strolled into view on the road, with a sack over his shoulder. He halted, confused by the goings-on. Before him were two government officials, one wet and one dry, both shouting while a stream of Bowman's meaty curses were issued from the deck of the old barque.

The wet Official was straining to close the wreck of his umbrella just as Boris was passing. Boris cast an eye skyward.

"You are much wet, but I think today no rain," he remarked affably.

That was too much for Official Number Two. He made one last vain attempt at restoring order to the chaos of ribs and silk that had one been his pride and joy; he then flung the mess into the water. Snatching Official Number One's umbrella, he set upon Boris with an incoherent cry of rage.

One could see that he knew something about fencing, but slash or thrust as he would, the agile Russian easily kept clear of the menacing bumbershoot. There was no telling how long this game might continue had not Official Number One reclaimed his umbrella, and secured it out of harm's way in the boot of the car. Official Number Two stood panting with rage and frustration. Boris uttered a few inaudible words to him—then walked up the gangway.

"Mudak!" yelled Boris, shaking his head.

Finally, the government officials got into their car and headed back up the road in a cloud of smoke and dust. Bowman shook his fist after them.

Harris raised his cap from over his eyes. "Well now," he sighed, "we shall have to get our plans ready very quickly, because I'm certain they're going to make good on theirs." He sat up, yawned, and stretched. "There's little rest to be had now. Flynn, let's go for a walk."

Bowman stared at him in outrage. "Ye hurl government officials into the river, and then ye two decide ye're going to be taking a jolly little stroll off down the lane? Ye big fool. Try not to keep us from getting any deeper into the big muddy."

Leaving Bowman muttering darkly to himself, Harris and I walked up the lane back to the inn. I explained that I had left my work undone and was afraid Mrs. Beasley would notice my absence.

Harris digested this. "Well, we'll just walk a little faster and talk as we go," he said. "I think it's about time we made proper arrangements with O'Connell to get the boys up to the circus. We're going to need their help soon, and they can use their free passes for a holiday. Beforehand, a number of things must be properly organised." We reached the spot where I had been working earlier, when Mrs. Beasley returned from her daily pilgrimage to the pond where she fed the waterfowl and gathered what eggs she could.

She looked up the hill and saw me talking to Harris. I saw her stiffen. She beckoned me to come down. I asked Harris to wait and quickly presented myself before her. She was staring at Harris as though she feared he would suddenly produce a machine gun and open fire.

"That's one of the men from the boats," she said in a whisper. "Heaven knows what mischief he's about. Don't let him waste your time. We've nothing to say to them."

"Oh, very well Mrs. Beasley, as you wish. Actually, he was giving me a few tips on using fertiliser in the shrubbery. You wouldn't think it to look at him, but the man is a marvel in the garden." Her expression was decidedly doubtful.

"H'mph," she responded, and with a last glance at Harris, she turned and went back to the inn, presumably to her cooking.

With only four more days before the circus closed, Harris planned to visit the orphanage and have some words with the boys and Headmaster O'Connell. It suddenly dawned on me; the orphanage was where I had last seen Harris before being summoned away. How the devil did he get to the ship so quickly on that meandering road?

He smiled at my bafflement. "One of the lads likes to keep watch with my old spyglass, and he alerted me when he saw the black government car heading along the shore. By the way," he added, apparently apropos to nothing, "coming down from the orphanage there's a daisy of a shortcut for someone on foot.

He then advised me to be careful driving Beasley's car up to the orphanage. It would only be a matter of time before its brakes were extinct. The trick, he said, was to only drive it *uphill.*

"Oh, that's a great comfort," I said, with my enthusiasm thoroughly dampened.

He gave me a hearty slap on the back. "That's the spirit! Well, I'll be calling for you later," and off he went.

I sighed and returned to my unending assault upon the vine with roots in Hell, though this time I thought to first make a quick raid on the shed and get myself a pair of heavy gloves. Thus armoured, I could consider myself a bit more equal to the struggle. I returned to my assault upon the vine.

That night, I was awakened by the sound of someone tossing pebbles at my window. Still half asleep, I couldn't account for this and did my best to ignore it. After a time, I gave over holding the covers over my head, and went shivering to the window. I opened it just in time for a pebble to come crashing through one of the small glass panes. Fetching my torch, I soon spied Harris, looking up from the shrubbery below.

Oh damn, I thought, there goes another night's sleep out the window. I listened to see if the noise had roused Dame Beasley, but all was still. I pulled on my clothing, gazing sorrowfully at my warm bed. I went down the stairs as silently as was possible, then stole outside. I looked to be sure no one else was about and found Harris lurking amongst the oleanders.

"You've broken one of my little windows with your gravel pitching," I whispered. "And to what do I owe this visit?"

He put a warning finger to his lips and led me down the road. He said he spoke with Robert and arranged for the lads to take down the tents in four days. We had already discussed this at length earlier and his latest tidings could have easily waited till morning.

"Don't you ever sleep?" I asked, feeling very put-upon.

"No, I've been pacing and thinking," he said.

"Then go think somewhere else and don't fling stones while you're about it. Some of the world is trying to sleep, in case that had escaped your notice."

"It doesn't leave us a lot of time," Harris continued as if I hadn't spoken. "Taking down the tents will be a good day's work, and then cutting and sewing them for sails may be a problem because of the time involved. I'm not certain how long that's going to take, but I'll get some idea tomorrow when I go back up to London and see Brian."

"Very well, splendid—but why must you drag me out of bed to tell me this?"

"Because I want to keep you up to date on what's going on. When things start happening, they're going to happen fast." This still didn't seem like a reasonable explanation for my lost sleep. I told him that it made me unhappy to see him becoming an insomniac, and if he woke me again, I would cure him of it with a large heavy object.

Harris simply ignored this threat and we stood off in the darkness as he talked a bit more. He shared his plan for how the rigging would be set. The powers that be planned to leave the sunken outermost vessel, the old coal barge, permanently where she lay in the mud. There was something that had to be rehearsed, but on this point he was mercifully brief. I was nearly falling asleep by then. The *Auld Lass*, long since looted for parts, would be taken first. He estimated that it would be another three weeks before "they" could get about doing anything with the *Bonnie Clyde*. One could almost hear the little wheels whirring busily inside his head as he spoke.

"Harris," I said.

"Yes?" His fanatic eyes glinted.

"Go and get some sleep, so this weary figure before you can too," I yawned.

I started walking back to the inn, but before long I fancied I could detect stealthy footsteps behind me. I had momentarily thought that I heard them when Harris and I were walking along before, but between trying to stay awake and taking in all he said, I had dismissed it as imagination. Then I heard the unmistakable snap of a twig. I pretended not to have noticed the sound, and walked on until I was level with a tall bunch of marsh grass standing at the edge of the road, and I quickly sidestepped behind it. As my follower came by, I jumped out, tripped, and fell, knocking the other over as well. There was a muffled scream, and we finished up in a heap at the side of the road.

I took the torch from my pocket and flashed it on the face of the sinister figure, only to find myself looking into the startled blue eyes of the beautiful barmaid.

I was so embarrassed at having thus assaulted her that I hardly knew what to do or say. I hastily released her and we brushed ourselves off. We sat looking awkwardly at one another.

"What on earth are you doing here at this hour?" I demanded; then I winced at my ungallant words.

"I might be asking the same of you," she sniffed, tugging a leaf from her hair. "You've been keeping such interesting company of late, I was curious what you were up to."

"Why are you following me? Spying for Mrs. Beasley?"

She rolled her eyes. "Mrs. Beasley?" she laughed. "Oh, really! I may be her barmaid and cook, but she doesn't own my soul. I'm longing for the day this job will all be a memory long forgotten."

"Why then?" I said, adding, "please?"

"Ever since you came here, Mr. Flynn, I've been doing my best to make your acquaintance, or even to engage in polite conversation with you. You know, I only started here a week before you. But you've made it difficult, especially when you've been storming in and out of places, and always in the company of certain men who are not regarded very highly by the landlady." She blinked and shaded her eyes, "Now could you get that light out of my eyes, please?"

"I'm sorry." I said humbly, switching off the torch. I offered her my hand and pulled her to her feet. "I *am* sorry about knocking you over. I didn't know who was following me or for what reason. The least I can do is walk you back to the inn."

Now that the ice was broken, although a bit roughly, she told me a little about herself. Being Mrs. Beasley's slave was hardly what she fancied as a career, but it allowed her to put aside the odd penny against the day to make a proper start elsewhere.

Suddenly she stopped and I carried on a pace or two and stopped. I turned to look back at her. "Is there something wrong?" I asked.

"Here," she said in a suspicious tone, stepping up to me. "You don't even know my name, do you?" she asked in that soothing Irish lilt of hers. I could see her smile in the dark.

"Katherine. I know because I'm always hearing Mrs. Beasley calling after you," I admitted. I wondered why I hadn't noticed till this moment what an enchanting name that was, or was I just so captivated that any name attached to her would have seemed the essence of grace?

"Well, Katherine, we'd best get back to the inn before someone thinks we're carrying on together," I laughed.

She laughed as well. "Oh, I wouldn't fret myself over that. I saw Mrs. Beasley slinking off with Mr. O'Connell about an hour ago. Mind you, she always tries to get back before dawn."

I laughed at the picture this conjured up. I didn't realise so many others knew about their sordid little affair. It was amusing to find that Harris was not the only one who was privy to the dark secret of Mrs. Beasley's great romance. I related to her my encounter with O'Connell earlier that day and how Harris had come near breaking his nose with the gate, thus depriving me of the pleasure of performing the operation myself. She giggled delightedly.

We went round the inn to Katherine's cottage door. As she paused in the doorway, I plucked up my courage. "I say, Katherine?"

She turned. "Yes?"

"Would you care to have tea with me tomorrow?"

Her face lit in a warm smile. "Yes, Mr. Flynn, I'd like that very much."

"That's great," I exclaimed in relief. "Well, then, good night."

"Good night," she said softly, as the door closed between us. Moments later I was full of euphoria as I struggled up the stairs to my bedroom. I crawled into bed and stayed awake till dawn, not so much because of Harris and his disturbance, but because of nearly being drowned in those blue eyes, and the prospect of having tea with their owner later in the day.

Chapter 7
THE GOOSE, THE CAT, AND HIGH TEA

I woke the next morning to the sounds of waterfowl screaming. I suppose they wake up before the rest of the world and demand that everyone else follow suit. The shore of Mrs. Beasley's pond was less than forty feet from my window. Like it or not, I had a proper box seat to fully appreciate all the activity.

The sun had hardly made its appearance, but I knew it was high time I addressed the day. I spent a restless night assailed by thoughts of the ship, Harris, and above all, Katherine. I put on my gardening clothes and hunted about, wondering what I had done with my boots the night before. I have this pernicious habit of brutally kicking them off across the room at night, and they take their revenge by going to earth and cunningly hiding themselves in the most improbable places. The left boot I surprised in the open, but it took ten solid minutes of searching to track the right to its cover in the bin by the desk. Well, score one for me.

I went downstairs to take my breakfast in the kitchen with the rest of Mrs. Beasley's help. To my disappointment, Katherine was not in attendance. She probably didn't care to linger when Mrs. Beasley had no duties for her. I joined Martin, the licensed barman, and we chatted pleasantly over our food. I noticed that he always read *The Times*, not the usual paper for a man running the bar, and I asked him how this came about.

"Oh, you could blame it on my misspent youth," Martin said. "It was the paper my father read, so I've got used to its style. Also, I get it cheap because I'm still registered as a student with them," he laughed. "I had a friend working at the paper who arranged it some years ago, and although he's now at the *Daily Mail*, somehow the sub stays the same. Personally I couldn't abide the thing, especially with its front page nothing but small ads, but then I usually got my news from the radio at six o'clock each evening.

Our breakfast was suddenly interrupted by a commotion at the pond. Amidst a rising babel of honking, quacking, splashing, and flapping, there came the sharp tortured scream of a cat. Martin and I exchanged glances. The noise got closer, passed through the garden, and rounded the corner by Mrs. Beasley's parlour. Then came a chilling shriek. We knew those dulcet tones only too well, but didn't know what the kerfuffle was about. A moment later Mrs. Beasley burst into view, running full tilt, and sped through the garden with her precious Purdy close behind. What an odd sight. "Miserable beast!" I muttered, then gasped in delight.

In hot pursuit of the cat was a large goose, about the size of a mastiff and to my eyes much more formidable. Perhaps Purdy had ventured too close to the pond while trying to pick off lesser waterfowl. Whatever the reason, the sight was one destined to live in the memory.

I was cheering for the goose. There was flapping and hissing as the enraged bird chased the desperate cat. Relentlessly, with neck outstretched and parallel to the ground, the goose kept close to Purdy's heels. Flee where he would, the goose ran after. Martin and I moved from one window to another to follow the action.

"Now *there* is a goose with a mission," Martin sputtered. The two of us stood with hands and noses pressed against the glass like boys looking in at a toyshop window.

Purdy darted with surprising speed for a cat of his bulk, running flat out with the goose behind every inch of the way. At last he decided that discretion was the better part of surrender and shot up the nearest tree, a powerful bill snapping scant inches from his tail. Every hair on the cat stood on end. He clung to the topmost branch and hissed furiously, while the goose matched him hiss for hiss below. All of this had taken very few seconds in reality and we had hardly time to react when the landlady burst in, nearly hysterical, imploring us to "save poor little puss!"

Breathless and weeping with rage, Mrs. Beasley glared wildly from one to the other of us.

"If you catch that goose, I'll pluck it alive, I will, and roast the horrid thing over a slow fire!" She was alarmingly savage, her ample bosom heaving with primitive bloodlust. She composed herself and said in a more civilised tone, "Of course, if you fetch Purdy instead, I'd be ever so pleased." She seated herself at the table, and with a shaky hand poured out a cup of tea. I looked at Martin and he at me. There was nothing for it but to go and try to remedy the situation.

"Shall we go after Purdy or have a go at the goose?" I asked.

"To the hunt," said Martin.

I fetched along a few slices of toast by way of provision, and we went out. We stood for a moment surveying the field. The goose still fizzed about under the tree with undiminished zeal while Purdy still fizzed above. One would think that given time they'd simply run out of fizz and go their separate ways. This seemed a hopeful thought, but a glance back at the inn revealed Mrs. Beasley now posted at the window, urging us on to battle with vigorous gestures. Clearly, as Minions of the Amazon Queen we must now perform as warriors born.

"Well, goose or cat, which do you think would be easier?" I sighed, nibbling at my toast.

"It's not so much a question of being *easier*, as of being the lesser ordeal," said Martin. If we try to get the cat, we have to dodge the goose. Either way, we've got to deal with that bird." He rubbed his eyes. "Damn it, I hate mornings."

I heard later this particular goose had acquired quite a reputation as a tireless pursuer of intruders who wandered too near the pond. No watchdog could rival it for vigilance and sheer viciousness.

"I don't much fancy going up the tree and getting myself scratched to bits by Purdy. As much as I love roast goose, I suppose that our safest course would be to chase the blasted bird back to the pond from whence it came," I began.

Martin eyed the creature, "And how do you propose doing that?"

"There are ways," I said airily. I walked round to the tool shed and came back with two brooms. I handed one to Martin. "Now, you stay constantly on its left and I'll be constantly on its right, and we'll just move it along back to the pond." With my toast securely clenched in my teeth, I hefted my broom, feeling quite the valorous knight. The elegant simplicity of this plan made me confident of success. I remember thinking it far easier than herding cattle, admittedly an occupation with which I was quite unfamiliar.

At *first* things seemed to go very smoothly. But this definitely *was* in fact a goose with a mission, and an opponent to be reckoned with. After falsely encouraging us with a moment's surprise at our unfamiliar weaponry, to our shock, it bent to the attack in earnest. With a mad snapping, horrible to behold, it did its best to tear off every tuft from the brooms and was plainly looking for any opening to get at us. The wind of its flapping wings buffeted us, and my confidence seemed but a flimsy delusion now. I cursed my folly at not having brought rakes or spades instead. Martin's broom had taken the brunt of the attack.

"My God," he gasped, "you don't suppose it's carnivorous, do you?"

"Mmph," I replied through my toast, still held between my teeth, and then had a sudden inspiration. While the goose was busy with Martin, I impaled some of the mangled toast onto my bristles. I thrust the toast into the gaping bill of the monster, where it was immediately torn to bits. I thought my ploy had failed, but then fancied I could see a wait—what-was-that?—light come into his eyes.

"Stand off," I cried to Martin, and we quickly stepped back.

The great bird feinted at us, but was clearly preoccupied in finding the bits of that nice food that had fallen to the ground. It hastily gobbled them up, darting glances at us all the while. At the same time we were carefully backing away. I broke up and strewed the remaining remnants of the toast. When every bit of toast was eaten and it had picked through the grass for stray crumbs, it seemed a much more peaceable goose and no longer interested in us.

I daresay it had quite forgotten Purdy, who was now quietly observing developments from his perch above. The goose turned its head to favour us with a last long look, shook its feathers, and then took itself off unhurriedly towards the pond.

When we returned indoors, perspiring but laden with glory, Mrs. Beasley, visibly pleased, thanked us for the rescue of dear little puss and fetched our breakfasts back out from the oven. We thanked her in turn and set to eating. She was still standing by in what I dared to hope was a sort of solicitous kindly-old-mum posture.

That notion was soon dispelled as she began grilling me over every minute detail of the garden work I had done. Martin and I did our best to make short work of our food, while my inquisitress picked over each point.

I felt the need to change the topic. "I say," I began, "about the pond and that goose. I'm sure some of those larger rocks could be set a bit closer to the water's edge, and that would slow him down should he think to attack Purdy again."

"I should hope that Purdy has learnt his lesson about going near the goose," she said. "Just look at poor little puss up there in the tree."

Martin and I looked first at one another and then out the window again. It was easy to see Purdy sitting comfortably in a crotch of the highest branch, languidly grooming himself. He seemed in no imminent peril, and surely would come down of his own accord in due course. All he lacked was attention, and every now and then he looked about and gave an enquiring meow.

Mrs. Beasley wrung her hands. "You simply *must* get him down from there," she agonised. "Be very gentle with him, Purdy is a sensitive creature. I don't think you properly understand cats, Mr. Flynn."

Martin looked at me expressionlessly and then rose from the table. "I've some straightening yet to do before we open the pub." He began to drift almost imperceptibly in the direction of the inner door.

I snagged him by the back of the collar. "If you so much as *try* to leave, I'll throw you to the goose!" I threatened. "Now, we are going to get the cat down!"

"We're going to get the cat down," he echoed woodenly. Then he shrugged unenthusiastically, and we both trudged to the door with all the alacrity of condemned men on their way to the gibbet.

Once we were outside, clear of the kitchen and its ears, I looked him earnestly in the eye. "Now, Martin, we're going to get the bloody cat down because we'll never hear the end of it if we *don't*, even though the bloody cat is quite capable of getting himself down!"

"Just how do we do that?" he asked.

"Well, I could give you a leg up and you could just climb to the top of the tree, grab hold of him, and carry him down again. Of course, you'd be flayed alive in the process."

Martin scoffed unappreciatively at my levity. "I have a better idea," and picked up a handful of good-sized stones.

"Here, none of that!" I said, "Mrs. Beasley would probably have you behind bars if she suspected you even *thought* of such a thing."

"I know, but a man can dream!" He sighed, dropping the stones. "Very well then, have you got any better ideas?"

I looked idly about at the garden. I noticed a garden hose neatly coiled nearby. Inspiration coiled likewise, then struck.

I showed a smug face to Martin. "I have a plan. Such a lovely plan! One which takes us no closer to the tree than we are now."

"Is there a gun in it?" said Martin.

"Don't be crude," I admonished. I went and turned on the water, adjusting the nozzle of the hose to its most powerful spray. I directed it at the herbaceous border, admiring the sparkling effect of the droplets in the sun.

"I need you to keep close watch out for Mrs. Beasley. This won't take long, but she mustn't see."

No sooner had I spoken than we heard the door behind us. Turning, I hastily turned off the nozzle, and hid it behind me as our dread sovereign lady herself appeared.

"Have you thought of a way to get him down yet?" Mrs. Beasley asked anxiously.

"Nearly there, Mrs. Beasley. We're working on it right now," I said. "We must go carefully. After all, these things must be done delicately."

"I'm relieved that you understand," she said, turning to go back inside. "Oh dear, I can't think what's keeping the milkman! I suppose I shall have to go out front and watch for the worthless wretch myself. I do so want a bit of cream to help comfort poor Purdy when he's safely down."

Once she had gone, I clasped my hands together and cooed, "Poor Purdy!" Martin laughed. I wasted no more time and brought round the hose, making sure my position afforded me a good clear shot at the cat. Purdy looked down at me, and I up at him. I thought of those nights I had come in to find a damp, cat-sprayed bed. "Well, my little man," I murmured, "a spray for a spray. Turnabout is fair play!"

I twisted the nozzle on, aimed carefully, and gave that ginger devil a proper dousing. He tried several times to avoid the water by leaping from branch to branch, but the merciless stream always sought him out. In a scrambling bound, he was down the tree and halfway across the lawn. I turned to Martin triumphantly and he gave me a pat on the back. There came the clinking of bottles. Quick as a flash I hid the hose out of view, and was looking quite innocent as Mrs. Beasley came round the building with the long-awaited milk and cream.

Suddenly she exclaimed in surprise, "Purdy is out of the tree. Thank heavens!"

"Oh yes," I said smoothly, "It didn't take very long."

She looked about eagerly. "Well, where has he got to?"

"I haven't the least idea. Did you see which way he went, Martin?"

Martin shook his head, and then cleared his throat. "Well, I'd best go and set up. Must open on time!" And he took himself off.

Mrs. Beasley poked about the garden for a time, calling, "Oo-ooh, Purdykins, lovely cream! Puss puss puss! Come to mumsy, Purdypoo!" Finding no sign of him, she turned to go back inside. The Orange Peril was crouched under the roses, sodden, rumpled, and in mortal dread of his new nemesis, the Hose. Mumsy would just have to wait.

"He'll be back soon," she said. "He knows the sound of milk bottles." She made the bottles give off an enticing clatter and went back into the kitchen. Unlimited fresh milk was a distant luxury to many thousands in these lean days, but Purdykins must never want.

I shut the water off and coiled up the hose. Brushing off my hands, I felt the satisfaction of a job well done. An instant later, I was startled to hear a voice behind me.

"If I were you, I'd have cut down the bloody tree," boomed Harris.

"Shush! Mrs. Beasley is nearby," I cautioned.

"I know exactly where she is," said Harris. "I've been watching this business for the last five minutes. Your method of separating cat from tree was very effective."

"Thank you," I replied. "Yours seems a trifle extreme. Why are you here this early? Don't you ever sleep?" I asked again.

He fixed me with a serious look, "Flynn, they seem to be wasting little time over the hauling-off of the *Auld Lass*. It could happen as early as tomorrow. If she doesn't go out then, they won't get to it till Monday, which is also the day the circus comes down. I wanted to alert you, so we can arrange to be aboard the tug that's taking her. It's all part of the scheme."

"Really?" I said, puzzled.

"Trust me," he answered. Those were loaded words.

"I don't understand how this fits into the plan."

"Soon enough," he said reassuringly.

"Damn you, Harris! Now you're starting to sound like Bowman. 'All things in good time.' Go chase a goose!" I stalked away with my arms flailing, like a mad goose myself. At least tonight I might get some answers to my questions as our group of conspirators was meeting again. I surely had questions enough, not the least of which was: where and how would all this finish up?

The day dragged on interminably while I worked in the garden, waiting for teatime. I was determined to complete my work as quickly as possible and get paid. My employment would last just a few days longer. It would have been wiser to extend my free room and board by proceeding at a more leisurely pace, but I had fallen behind lately, and I did want to get paid. Plus, I didn't care to prolong any ties to this place save those of Katherine.

Teatime was only minutes off, and I knew that my appearance must not much resemble anything presentable at table. A violent growling started up under my belt at the thought of *table* and the edibles associated with it. I had worked straight on through lunchtime, and my stomach was reproaching me bitterly for my neglect.

I had a quick wash at the tap, then with a window for a mirror, I combed back my hair and straightened my shirt. I shook out my jacket and draped it casually over my arm. I was ready! I trotted up the steps of the pub restaurant and, taking a deep breath, pushed open the door.

Martin hailed me from the bar. "Hello, Flynn! Have you anymore cats you want stewed?" I waved him off in mock disgust and looked about. I couldn't see Katherine anywhere, so I sat by the bar.

"Have you come for your tea, lad?" Martin asked. "We have some nice rock cakes."

"I'd say it's tea plus lunch, and I'm absolutely famished." A delicious aroma suddenly struck me. "Here, what's that lot?" I pointed to a fragrant platter, steaming seductively on the back counter.

"Ah," he said, "a new crop of nice pork pies. They've just come out of the kitchen. And no Spam this time, really." He brought them over and set the plate on the bar.

My stomach squealed with delight, anticipating those plump little pies. "Bless you, kind sir," I gushed, laying hold of one. I was about to take a bite, when a voice said softly, "Mr. Flynn, would you pass me one as well?"

I turned round and there stood Katherine, looking very fetching in a sweater and wool skirt, holding a tray and looking at me expectantly. Waves of relief swept over me. I had begun to fear that I was too late or that she forgot the time. This was silly of course, since she was working today. The tray was quickly laden with plates and pies. Joining these was some of Mrs. Beasley's pickles, along with a bit of cheese, Scotch eggs, celery, boiled potatoes from the garden, and a clutch of rock cakes. A pint and a half-a-pint kept them company. To me, it looked fit for the King. Katherine seemed amused.

"So it's high tea then?" she smiled. "Well, I'm game, but you'll spoil my girlish figure yet."

We bore the feast to a table overlooking the pond. For the next few minutes only my eyes spoke to her, while I stuffed my mouth with culinary delights. Katherine watched me with interest, nibbling at a pie. Once the edge was off my hunger, I recounted the morning's exploits to her. She laughed and related some Purdy tales of her own. She occasionally slipped off to wait on customers, but, fortunately, it was a bit slow. I wanted to know everything about her.

"So tell me," I asked, "How did you come to be here, and where are you from?"

Her laughter ceased. Into her eyes crept such a haunted look of sadness that I bitterly regretted having asked.

Her story was much like many others nowadays, the war having torn so many families and friends apart. Her words came slowly. She'd emigrated from Dublin with her parents before the war and they'd lived in Islington, not far from some of the London railway terminuses. She had been through the Blitz and battled incendiaries at her home and at her neighbours' houses with her family many a night. Two years ago, while she was away, a V2 came down on the house next door, destroying both houses and sweeping away several others along with her parents inside. She had two brothers, but they'd gone missing in action in Europe. This long after the war, she had no hope of ever seeing them again.

"I've a married cousin in the north," she continued, "had I wanted to live with them. I could have lived with friends in London, but I didn't care to be anywhere near the place. Too much had changed. I know I can make another life for myself, but it's strange being on my own. If it weren't for this job, I'd have nothing at all. Well, one doesn't dwell on such things. We're all too busy surviving. At least I've managed to keep clear of the less savoury career opportunities."

I thought of all the others struggling to put their worlds back together. We had our finest hour, and a by-God bloody long hour it had been. I thought of Bowman and his wife and the widespread shambles left behind by the half dozen years of death and destruction.

The war had come too late to touch my family where we'd lived in Basingstoke. My parents had died of diphtheria when I was ten, and I went to live with my uncle near Portsmouth. My father had instilled in me a love of green growing things, of working the soil. Later, it was Uncle George who had stirred up my passion for the seafaring life. He emigrated to New Zealand in thirty-eight and we'd fallen out of touch with one another. I went back to Basingstoke to have a look at my family's former house, but all had been pulled down to make way for a street of flats. Even the fondly remembered little shop where I had once bought copies of *Comic Cuts* and my favourite sweet, farthing turnovers, which sometimes had a lucky silver thrupenny piece inside, though I never got one, was long gone. I had well and truly joined the ranks of displaced persons. As I told all this to Katherine, and how chance had brought me to the Beasley Inn, I realised how good it felt to be able to talk to someone about it.

She smiled in that reassuring way of hers. "Chance is sometimes part of a master plan, you know," she said.

If so, I thought, let it be a *good* master plan: one with her in it!

We lingered an hour and a half over our high tea. I mentioned that tomorrow was my day off, and asked if I might come and annoy her during her breaks. She coloured, and replied that it would be lovely. I was beaming from every pore in my face and didn't care who saw it!

I made my way outside into the early dusk. As I passed Mrs. Beasley's door, I was surprised to find Headmaster O'Connell standing there with his bandaged nose, looking, if possible, more sour than usual. In his bony hand was the rake I'd been using earlier. It seemed unaccountable. He had evidently just left the flat, so I wondered at his less-than-blissful expression.

Feeling self-assured, I couldn't resist a bit of cheek. "Well, Mr. O'Connell," I said affably, "are you after my job, or do you just fancy a little wholesome exercise?"

He eyed me balefully. "You left that rake lying about," he hissed. "I could not avoid stepping on it and was brutally struck on the head by it." He pulled off his homburg, which bore a perceptible dent. "Look at this!" There was the slightest red mark on his temple, for my money just where he should have been hit with a much larger object…such as a steam engine.

"Terribly sorry, how careless of me," I said, suppressing an impulse to laugh outright. I fixed an innocent gaze on him. "How nice that you've given the boys a holiday from school to see the circus. And how kind of you to favour us with a visit."

He glanced surreptitiously at the landlady's door, and a blush briefly struggled to bloom on that colourless face. He flung down the rake, and without further discussion, got into his car and drove up the road. As I picked up my rake, I could hear his car backfiring on its way up the hill. It reminded me of the sounds of combat. It would be too much to hope that he'd be picked off by a sniper or that his car might hit just the least little land mine. Well, a man could dream! I went back to my room for a short rest before tonight's meeting.

Dreaming was my happy occupation well after dark later on, this time peacefully in my bed, when I was again woken by stones rattling against the window. Of course it was Harris come to fetch me for to-night's meeting, which I had conveniently managed to forget. I had really been working hard all day and so had gone to bed early. Sighing, I dressed and slipped downstairs to where he waited outside in a drizzle.

"Look lively, Flynn," he said, "let's go into the pub for a drink."

"Harris, I've slaved all the day long, and now you've torn me from my well-earned rest. Are you quite sure that I'm really needed?" I protested.

Harris gave no sign of having heard me. With a deep sigh, I stomped along behind him. As we entered, I could see that Bowman was already installed at the fireside next to Edward. There was no sign of Robert or Boris. With Katherine's aid we were soon nursing a pint along with the others. Once everyone was settled, Harris launched into his latest report.

According to his sources, there was no definite word yet as to when our ship would be moved. We got a reprieve on the impending removal of the *Auld Lass*. She was now due to be taken off on Wednesday. Bowman nodded in approval, and even the taciturn Edward guardedly displayed pleasure at this development. Now we had more time in which to prepare, and Monday's "canvas operation" would be well out of the way before the first tug went to work.

Harris went on, "Flynn, I hope you're planning to join us at the circus on Monday, when the tents come down. We'll need all available hands."

I told him I didn't think Mrs. Beasley would appreciate my running off for an entire day. My work here was still not finished, and I didn't care to provoke her with further unexplained absences.

He smiled. "Ah, but it needn't be unexplained. You see, if you were simply to make a direct appeal—tell her you'd like to help chaperon the dear little orphans on their outing. One can't have too much supervision when boys go to the circus, after all, even if it's only to work there."

I knew it was futile to resist. "Well," I began reluctantly, "I suppose I could ask to take Monday off instead of Saturday. Perhaps I could even finish up by Monday, but you know, once I have no more work to do here, Mrs. Beasley will start charging me room and board if I'm to stay."

"Not to worry," Harris said, draining his glass. "Nothing we can't attend to." He rose. "But now I've much to do. I'll call for you at six o'clock Monday morning on the way to the circus. Don't be late." He made his way towards the door.

Bowman and Edward followed him out. They had said little during our meeting, and I got the impression they wished to talk more out of my hearing. I daresay it was obvious to them that I wasn't ready to quit the pub. I wanted another word with a certain barmaid. I sat for a time staring into the fire, my pipe unlit, and then forced myself to my feet and managed to catch Katherine's eye. Without going into specifics, I explained that something had come up and I'd be working tomorrow.

"Very well then, you'll just have to annoy me during meals," she said, looking faintly curious at the change of plans, which obviously had some connection with my departed visitors.

"Starting with breakfast?" I asked, feeling shy.

She nodded, and I went off into the dark drizzle floating in a warm glow. I went to my room and hung up my clothes a second time, then fell into bed completely exhausted. I was unable to quiet my thoughts as I watched the spider-webs on my window, wondering what it would all come to.

The next two days were all I'd hoped. Lingering over breakfast with Katherine was so agreeable that I decided to take elevenses in the pub in order to extend my time to be with her. What with these self-indulgences, plus luncheon, tea, and dinner, I was simply not spending much time outdoors, thus letting good dry working weather go to waste. At least on Sunday she had her half-day, and could keep me company as I picked at my tasks.

I arranged the change of schedule with Mrs. Beasley, who was surprisingly cooperative, once I invoked the sacred name of the Orphanage. She did know that on Sunday the boys were going to Gravesend to make use of their free admission on the closing day of the circus, otherwise the tickets couldn't be used till spring. Apparently not quite *all* her maternal instincts were lavished on that obnoxious cat of hers. Still, she couldn't forbear grumbling over how long I was taking over everything, and that her young gardener etc., etc....I had to wonder if he really intended returning at all, having escaped her this long. But I couldn't overly concern myself with her complaints. For the moment I was concentrating on enjoying the weekend to the fullest!

Chapter 8
CLOSING DOWN THE CIRCUS

Monday morning I rose in the chilly dark *before* the birds. I descended the stairs, wishing that I could have another glorious breakfast in the company of Katherine. But, alas, such was not to be. I helped myself to tea, bread, and a bit of cold meat, then went off to meet Harris. As I came round the front of the inn, Mrs. Beasley looked out from her door, her head bristling with rag-tied curls.

"Mr. Flynn," she called, "would you care to take my car? We're doing very well with our petrol rations, and you know I don't like to drive it myself. And perhaps, if you happened to be going into Gravesend there are some shops, and I could give you a list..."

I tipped my cap. "Thank you, Mrs. Beasley. You're very kind, but I've arranged to ride with some of the other helpers."

"Very well then, I won't detain you."

Thankfully, she withdrew and closed her door.

I suddenly remembered that my driver would be Harris. What a choice: driving Mrs. Beasley's car, which guaranteed me the life expectancy of a kamikaze pilot, or riding with Harris, which was an exercise in passive terror.

Hastening away from the inn, I found the Scourge of the Carriageways waiting in his car down the road. I approached with a feeling of doom. After saying good morning, I opened the door.

"May I have a blindfold?" I asked.

"I get the distinct impression that you don't like my driving," Harris said, in an injured tone.

"Oh, I like it well enough—from a distance." I said. I flicked my lighter, and by its flame, I looked in at the tiny space intended to receive my person. I cleared my throat, shutting up the lighter. "I believe I'll sit in the rear this time."

Harris pushed open the passenger door. "That's a good idea," he agreed. "You do tend to crowd me, you know."

"Do you think that it might be possible not to drive so fast?" I asked as I wedged myself in.

"Right," he said. "We've plenty of time—needn't rush." No sooner had these words left his mouth, when the accelerator was pressed to the floor.

I held on, gritting my teeth, and prayed that we'd encounter no Yanks on the road.

The sky brightened by the time we neared the circus grounds, and it had grown light enough to see the activity already under way. At that moment, the big top was coming down, massively descending its poles, and settling to earth. Teams of men and boys bustled about, some hauling lines or carrying gear. Horses and camels were led by, and I could see at least one elephant being put to work handling the immense tent poles. A local farmer sat by, gaping, on a tractor with a rope trailing from it with nothing attached. His head pivoted continually as he followed the activity all about him, and he seemed comically out of place.

As soon as we'd parked, Harris and I went to work straightaway. Joining Boris, we each took five boys and set about pulling down booths and stalls. Robert went about directing us, mucking in himself where needed. It was amazing how efficiently we worked together, and my doubts subsided about the boys being suitable for shipboard duty. They were strong, wiry lads with not an extra ounce on any of them. It seemed odd that these were the "children" of the orphanage. The eldest one looked about the same age as young men I'd known who'd already had their own homes and jobs. I knew that the legal school leaving age had recently been raised to fifteen. I wondered how O'Connell managed to justify funds that would maintain boys obviously older.

Once we had the canopies and timbers neatly stacked, we sat down to rest and catch our breath, not realising the hours that had passed. Robert went off to see if the tents had been laid out and were ready for folding. He came back a few minutes later with the welcome tidings that lunch was nearly ready, so we might as well go and have ours before we began on the tents. He led us to several massive charcoal braziers where some nice fat sausages sizzled on the grill. The sound was music to the ears of the ravenous workers. A queue was already forming, so we took our places behind and settled in to wait.

Eventually the sausages were done. We collected mugs of tea and tin plates, and then moved along as each received a generous helping of bangers and mash. It did my heart good to see how the boys tucked into the meal. Robert and I looked on in wonder as a minor Everest of sausages and potato vanished down Harris's throat. I'm sure he was equal to another such, for he gazed longingly at the still-busy grill, but Bowman came up and engaged him and Boris in quiet talk. I couldn't make out a word of it, and presently Bowman went off again, taking Boris with him.

One of the boys, the red-haired one named Larry, came up to Harris and stood respectfully, plate in hand. "Mr. Harris, sir?"

"Yes, Larry?"

"Are we allowed to go back for more?" Larry waited in anticipation for his answer. He was the focus of many pairs of eager eyes.

Harris appeared to struggle briefly with some strong emotion. "You bloody well are!" he roared.

A cheer went up from the boys as they ran off to join the end of the queue. I felt like cheering myself.

Harris abruptly rose and strode off. I followed, hoping to learn something of what Bowman and Boris had been discussing with him. He went along the railway tracks and paused. A few animal cages still sat by the tracks, waiting to be loaded into cars. Strolling by the cages, he stopped at the last and stood gazing through the bars at a large brown bear. He seemed lost in thought, so I hesitated to disturb him.

After a while he turned about and stalked back over to the lunch area. I saw his tall figure rove into the vicinity of the grill, bend down quickly behind the serving counter near it, and then just as quickly move off back to the cages, this time carrying a substantial-looking paper packet in one hand. I watched curiously as he sat down on a bale of straw and looked in through the bars at the bear, which lay at the back of the cage, showing no interest in him or its surroundings. I usually felt rather sorry for circus animals, endlessly dragged from city to city, living in cages without proper room to move; a circus didn't seem the best of lives for them.

Now I saw the bear raise its snout, sniff the air, and turn its head to look at Harris. One could tell it was old; its muzzle was silver with age. I decided to take a closer look. Drawing nearer, I could see that there were broad calluses on its shoulders and elbows from long years of lying caged up. I wondered what a circus could want with such an ancient specimen, for no one was pampering this bear. It looked ill cared for, its coat dull and patchy.

All at once Harris noticed me standing by and smiled sheepishly. "You know, when I was younger, I used to spend time watching a bear at the zoo." He shook his head, chuckling a little at the memory. "A brown bear it was, and they had him by himself in a big stone compound that had a pond—he did so love that pond. And he was a *dancing* bear. I've no idea where they got him. But if I held up a bit of food and said dance, brown bear, he'd come up front and stand on his hind legs. He'd make a full turnabout, and then come down on all fours again. At that point I'd throw in the food to reward him. There was a Do Not

Feed The Animals sign, but I managed to escape the notice of the attendants most of the time. God, that bear fascinated me. I really loved that animal. And he liked me too. Who else brought him so many treats and sat by talking to him for hours on end?" He turned his gaze back to the grizzled old fellow before him and sighed. "I always was soft on bears," he said.

The bear, with a great wheezing and grunting, now raised itself stiffly to its feet and shuffled up to the front of the cage, the shackles on its hind legs clanking. It stood looking at Harris. Then, with no prompting, it tried to rise up on two feet. On the third attempt it managed to stand and started to turn about. We both stared open-mouthed as it laboured halfway round, and then with a groan came down onto its front paws with its great furry rump towards us. It whimpered, then looked back round at Harris with a mournful expression.

Harris was wide-eyed with astonishment. He swallowed, then opened the paper packet and pulled out a sausage. He held it up. "Dance, brown bear," he whispered.

The bear tried to stand again, but after several attempts gave it up and slumped to the floor of the cage, where it lay with a mournful expression and its sad eyes upon Harris.

"Oh my God," said Harris huskily. "It's *him*! Brown bear? Here, here, brown bear." And he threw the sausages in through the bars. The bear eyed them in surprise, then gobbled them up, licking its chops. A dim light began to kindle in the bear's dull eyes. Harris, with tears trickling down his cheeks, was murmuring, "Brown bear, poor old bear," while throwing in the sausages, which the bear devoured with obvious relish.

It was truly the most touching reunion I've ever witnessed. Soon, it was spoilt by the intrusion of one of those people who don't seem to know that there are times to enforce rules and regulations, and times to let them slip by a bit.

"Here, what d'you think *you're* about? You've no business meddling with that animal!" It was one of the managing assistants, who quite disproportionately was annoyed and probably for no more reason than his own bad temper. "Just clear off now," he ordered, "this isn't a zoo."

Harris, rather uncharacteristically, tried to reason with him. "But I know this bear. He's a friend of mine."

"Right, it's your dear old schoolmate," said the fellow. "Now sod off!"

Behaviour like this was quite uncalled for and I could see the turn the situation was taking.

"Now, Harris," I put in; of course it was pointless.

The managing assistant now noticed the near-empty packet of sausages. "Oh, pinching bangers into the bargain, eh? A bear-feeder *and* a thief!" He launched into a general tirade on the subject of the presumption and dishonesty of casual help. "Hire 'em for a day, and they think they own the whole operation!" he ranted. "Let 'em out of sight for a minute, and they're stealing everything they can lay hands on *and* abusing the animals into the bargain…"

"Shut your bloody face!" Harris thundered, "or I'll shut it for you!"

Harris rose looming, with anger terrifying to behold. He put one giant hand over the fellow's face and began shoving him backwards at arm's length. They proceeded thus for about fifteen feet, until they were stopped by a dustbin, into which Harris propelled him, arse first. The sight of a pair of feet and the top of a head protruding from the bin would have been richly comical had not Harris been so dreadfully angry and distraught. Squirm as he would, the hapless manager could not free himself from the bin, and his cries for help went unheard amidst the noise and bustle of work and lunchtime.

Harris had resumed his seat on the bale, and was now hunched over with his head sunk in his hands, his great frame shaken by sobs. It was unnerving to see the normally self-assured Harris like this, and I tentatively made a move to approach him, but was stopped by Bowman, who had just come up. He led me away.

"I've known Harris since he was a wee lad, and *never* have I seen him quite so undone," Bowman said in a hushed voice. "I recall he long ago told me about spending much time at a zoo. I hadn't any notion that he was mates wi' a bear, not that it isn't fitting if one thinks on it. Perhaps they're related. Now, that would be living proof of evolution," he added, trying to inject a lighter note into what was obviously a sad situation.

Harris now went to crouch by the side of the cage, the bear tilting its head to watch him. Holding the bars, he spoke to it in a low voice. The bear, pulling round to face him, replied with soft moans. This great mountain of a man began weeping again, with the same intensity I'd seen during the war when so many were losing homes and loved ones. It was a sight to tug at the hardest of hearts, and I could see that even the rusty old heartstrings of Bowman were getting a good pull. Not knowing what to do, we sat on a bale and waited quietly.

Meanwhile, strangled curses flowed from the dustbin, which rocked and quivered with the vain struggles of its human contents. Now that lunch had finished, young Larry came up and halted, absorbing this entertaining spectacle with a quizzical eye. Seeing the weeping Harris, he stared in dismay for a time. He turned to Bowman.

"Cap'n, we're ready to go back to work," he ventured. "Is Mr. Harris coming, sir? What's the matter with him?"

"Never ye mind what Mr. Harris is about," said Bowman, rising. He took Larry by the shoulders and faced him back the way he'd come. "Just ye go and work with Robert and Boris, we'll be along presently."

The boy went off reluctantly, casting many worried glances back at us. As Larry went off, one of the circus workers happened to pass. He spied the animated dustbin.

"Mr. Moorland!" he cried, "what's happened to you?" He hastened forward, then saw the still-disconsolate Harris huddled against the bars. "Here, what's all this? Do you need any help mate?"

Harris looked up, "This is a dancing bear, you know," he said.

"Well, of course it is, this is a circus," replied the other, probably supposing him to be drunk.

Harris went to the bale and took up the few remaining sausages. "Here, I'll show you." Then his face darkened. "And if you say one word about feeding the animals, that bear's next meal will be *you*!" The man backed away as Harris turned to the cage. He held up the sausages and softly called, "Dance brown bear!" Again, the poor old bear tried to perform, but was unable to stand. "No, no, don't try, don't dance," sobbed Harris remorsefully, and tossed in the sausages. "Have your bangers, brown bear, I won't torture you anymore."

While this was going on, the circus worker was trying to extricate the livid Moorland from the dustbin. He succeeded in overturning it, but couldn't manage to free the imprisoned man. For a time a sort of hermit crab or turtle effect was achieved. At last, a furious managing assistant was released among the living and went rampaging off to return with two burly chuckers-out.

He pointed a shaking finger at Harris. "Hold that man," he snarled. Harris stood and loomed.

The two looked at Harris, at one another, and then at Moorland. Shaking their heads, they walked off. Moorland glared, and then shifted his gaze to the other circus worker, who turned pale and lifted his hands in protest.

"Don't look at *me*," he cried. Moorland marched off in disgust, and the other, relieved, made his departure.

Bowman came up to Harris, "So ye really know that bear, eh mate?"

"Yes, of course I do. Or I did years ago. I don't care to go into it just now." Harris turned and walked away from the cage, wiping his eyes on his sleeve. The bear watched him go, then with a rattle of chains, crawled to the back of the cage, and relapsed into inertness.

Evidently, Larry had spoken with others of our company regarding Harris's unusual behaviour, for Boris and Robert had come up and witnessed some of what had transpired. When I did become aware of their presence, their heads were together in a suspiciously conspiratorial-looking conversation. I worried that Robert was hatching some crazy scheme. In the Navy he'd been notorious for his rash plots, but I hoped that Boris would be the prevailing, cooler head. They soon separated, and Boris looked at us with hands on hips. "Come on, work," he called.

We proceeded to the lads of our Orphan Brigade, who were ranged about the huge expanse of precious canvas. It took hours to fold the huge tents. What a dusty, sweaty job it was. It may sound simple to say that we'd folded that canvas, but it was hard work and needed proper co-ordination, as each piece was at least thirty yards by twenty. Mercifully, there'd been no rain, and the canvas was dry and light. At first we had another circus worker overseeing the operation, but eventually he left us in Robert's hands. Harris had evidently thought it best to keep out of view, which I'm sure *was* best, though we did miss his muscle. We could see another crew occupied at folding tents, so we worked with frantic haste lest theirs be packed into another lorry before we could intervene. As it turned out, they were simply stacking the folded canvas neatly and leaving it to be loaded by others. Well, this time we'd be the others.

There were enough lorries about that little attention was paid to ours as it was backed up to load the first tent. The lorry looked as roomy as a house to me, but we filled it. Such a huge lot of canvas! Then I noticed this wasn't the same lorry Harris had before. Bowman only hinted it was "on loan" from the Chatham Dockyard, so I didn't ask more.

Bowman was now giving orders, and pointed in disgust to one bundle with bright red and yellow stripes. "We won't be needing that one."

Boris gave me a wink and as soon as Bowman's back was turned, in went the striped piece, to be quickly concealed beneath a plain one. There were quite a few pieces Bowman rejected on the basis of colour, but every bit of canvas was whisked into the back without his knowledge. It became quite a game, and the boys entered into it delightedly.

Once the tents were neatly stowed, I went to see who was at the wheel. Not surprisingly, it was Harris. Boris and Robert were with him, looking like the cat that just got the canary. I was relieved to see that Harris appeared his usual self, and I asked what else I should do.

Harris smiled, "Since you asked, you can take my car and follow me at a distance. Unloading will be just as heavy and we won't have the boys helping us on that end."

"Me drive *your* car," I sputtered, clapping a hand over my eyes, "without the benefit of brakes?"

He reached out the window and dropped his keys into my hands. Good Lord, I thought, this is like going into combat again. That old Morris took at least a hundred yards to come to a halt by brakes alone.

"I had them mended somewhat," he said. "You'll be perfectly safe."

One of the workmen came up, puzzled at seeing Harris at the wheel, and cast a look of displeasure over the lorry. He halted by the driver's window.

"You there! *I'm* supposed to be handling this lot," he said brusquely.

My heart was in my mouth, but Harris met his gaze levelly. "No, you're bloody well not!" he fired back. "You didn't make much of a job of it last time you put these tents away. If I have to talk to your supervisor one more time, you'll not be working for us next year. In fact, you should be expecting to get your cards, and start looking for somewhere else straightaway."

The man stepped back in surprise. Harris sounded very convincing. "You've talked to my supervisor?" the man quavered.

Harris started up the engine and shouted over the roar, "You get back to work and see that the rest of those booths and stands are properly loaded up. I'll take charge here."

Without further ado, he began driving away. As I made for the car, I could see the man take off his hat and scratch his head, trying to make out what he'd done wrong. Of course he'd actually done nothing to warrant such a reprimand. I hoped he wouldn't be sacked over this.

Harris's car might have had the brakes mended, but there were other causes for anxiety. For one thing, it kept popping out of gear unexpectedly and had a chronic wobble at low speeds. This never bothered Harris, who didn't believe in low speeds.

It was dark by the time we approached Tower Bridge. In the traffic, I lost sight of the lorry once we had crossed over. I pressed on, although the only way to avoid collisions was to go at an excruciatingly slow pace, which won me no friends amongst the other motorists. It took a bit of prowling about to find my way, as I'd only been to the tailor's workshop once before by daylight. Harris waited at the main road, and again took the lead once he spied me. Soon we reached our destination, and he backed up to the loading dock.

Harris's pounding brought Brian out. He was apologetic—no canvas yet. Without a word, Harris pointed to the lorry, where Robert drew back the tarpaulin to reveal the densely heaped takings of the day's raid.

"God in heaven!" the tailor exclaimed, "where did you get all this?"

Harris waved a hand dismissively. "No need for you to worry about that. Right now time is of the essence! One ship is being taken off the day after tomorrow and ours the day after that. We'll see how far we can hold them up before they take ours. All I ask is that you work as fast as humanly possible! The two spankers and eight of the big sails for the fore and mainmasts are priority. Get the sail-makers to help you get two jibsails done, the two spankers and eight of the big sails for the fore and mainmasts, as priority. We hope you'll have time for more but we definitely need those straight away!"

Brian raised his eyebrows at Harris's urgent manner. "For you, God knows, it's a small enough favour." He turned and called to those inside. Out came two more men and Brian's son, David. We set to work unloading the entire volume of canvas into their warehouse. It seemed to have grown even heavier during the drive up. How they were going to deal with it all was beyond me, but handling cloth was their business. Boris produced drawings and measurements necessary for cutting each of the sails and gave them to Brian. The tailor looked them over with a practised eye, and then nodded his approval.

We were all exhausted after emptying the lorry, and Brian tendered an invitation for dinner. Harris shook his head, "Again I have to say sorry." He took a deep breath. "Now then, Robert, you run the lorry back down to the circus so you can drive Bowman and the lads home again. I'll return the lorry to Chatham later."

"Aye, aye," said Robert saluting smartly, and climbed back into the driver's seat with Boris beside him. As they rumbled away up the street, I saw that a thick fog was closing in, one of the real London fogs with that metallic taste to it.

I was becoming anxious to leave, and equally nervous about the drive back. Harris went to the car and wedged himself in behind the wheel. "Well, let's be off," he called out to me.

I walked around to the driver's side and crossed my arms. "Out of it, Harris! It's the passenger side for you, or even the rear. *I* have the keys, remember? Let me treat you to a chauffeured ride."

"Then we'll *never* get there," he said impatiently. "Flynn, you drive like an old lady."

"And how could you possibly know how I drive?"

He looked petulant, "Well, it took you enough time driving here. I don't usually let anyone else take the wheel."

"Ah yes, but without the keys, you'll be going nowhere in a hurry."

"Oh all right!" he conceded, "but on your head be it if we're never seen again." He got back out and went round to the other side. Opening the door, he looked in with a critical eye. "Not much room in there," he grumbled, and squeezed himself into the seat.

I pressed the starter and we moved off slowly and uncomfortably into the fog. I prayed I could find the A2 and the right turnings in the fog and darkness. *Anything* was better than having him drive. I was glad of Harris's direction as we crawled, wobbled along. It felt as though the car would fall to pieces at any moment.

"It wouldn't wobble that way if you'd make your foot a wee bit heavier," my passenger hinted.

I bit my lip. "I think it's about as heavy as need be. After all, I drove this thing up to London. I think I can drive it down to Kent." At this point I had to envy Robert, who was driving something more substantial, and wasn't being tyrannised by an aspiring rocket pilot sitting next to him.

With a deep sigh, Harris subsided. I wanted to ask him about the bear, and he appeared to be quite himself again, so I felt sufficiently encouraged to bring it up.

"So," I said casually, "what was it Robert said to you back at the circus before we left?"

"About the bear?" said Harris. "I can't believe I made such a fuss over it all. It turns out that brown bear wasn't *with* the circus. They were just transporting him. You see, his old trainer, another Russian, had found out where he was after many years of looking. He wanted him sent down to Sussex so they could spend their retirement together. I'm glad that our paths crossed again. Dear old brown bear. Of course I'd like to have a word with that chap too. Those were rotten conditions under which to transport that ol' boy."

Well, it was a relief to know that there was a happy ending to it, and I felt a little easier as we jittered along, narrowly avoiding lamp-posts and other vehicles. Finally we came out of the fog well and were able to make better headway.

When we reached the inn, instead of leaving me off, he directed me down to where the ships were moored. I managed to bring the car to a stop without getting too many more grey hairs. Mended brakes—ha! It appeared that the lorry had already returned from the circus, for Bowman came down the gangway to greet us rubbing his hands together.

"So," he nodded, "the canvas has gone up to London. A very sweet bit o' work that was! Well done. Boris has just gone to take the young lads back up."

"That's fine," said Harris. With an unexpected lightning movement, he seized my hand and plucked his keys. "Many thanks, Flynn, but I can handle the driving from here."

Now I could get back to the inn. It seemed like weeks since this morning.

"A good night to you both then." I turned to go.

Harris took hold of my sleeve. "Ah, one moment there, Flynn. We'd best go aboard. There are a few things we should attend to."

"Damn you, Harris. I've done enough today," I said wearily.

"Oh very well, run along. I don't *own* you," he replied.

"One would never suspect it," snorted Bowman as he headed back up the gangway. "Good night!" he called out.

Tired and a bit light-headed from hunger, I began the walk to the inn. It was infinitely preferable to another few minutes in the dreadful Harris-mobile. Seeing Katherine's welcoming smile at journey's end, I would happily have gone ten times the distance.

I walked into the heat and noise of the pub, and nipped into the toilet to clean up a bit. When I emerged, I looked about eagerly for Katherine, but didn't see her. To my surprise, Mrs. Beasley now came into view bearing a tray laden with glasses and foodstuffs. She looked flustered. It wasn't the usual thing for her to serve customers as well as prepare food, since her cooking was vastly more agreeable than her manner.

"Ah! Mr. Flynn, you're back," she said. "Did all go well today?"

"Everything went splendidly, Mrs. Beasley. We made a good day's work of it and now all the boys have returned safe and sound."

"Well, that's good then." She bustled off, and returned not long after, the tray now piled with dirty dishes. "I suppose you'll be wanting your dinner. Go on into the kitchen—you'll find plenty about. You'll be serving yourself. I'm busy. I haven't time—Miss Katherine has gone missing. She never showed herself this morning and left me to do all her work in addition to mine." She sniffed indignantly. "I find it quite extraordinary. Well, get along with you…wait! Take these dishes with you. And don't touch the roast beef. That's for customers. Have the mutton stew." Leaving me with the tray, she smoothed her hair and made her way in the direction of the bar.

A moment later I was in the kitchen doing mighty work among the eatables, and puzzling over Katherine's disappearance. I wasn't overly concerned. She was a capable lass and had probably just gone up to the village for the day, though it was odd that she'd left no word. It occurred to me that she might be in her cottage. As soon as I finished, I went out and strolled by her door.

Still not seeing her, I walked back to the pub and asked Martin. He'd seen her at breakfast, and she asked about me. Martin hadn't heard about the circus, so he couldn't tell Katherine anything. "No one tells *me* anything," he shrugged. "She'll catch hob from Mrs. B. when she gets in!"

I drifted back outside, wondering if there was cause for alarm. My body cried out for rest, but I was too unsettled to sleep just now. I began to wander along past the garden and onto the path that led down to the ships. I hadn't realised until now how much I'd been counting on returning to find Katherine in the pub, kind-eyed and ready to minister to a weary tent-thief.

Before I knew it, I'd come in sight of the ships where a flurry of activity was under way by lantern-light. All three vessels appeared to be involved. I stood on the bank at the bottom of the gangway, uncertain as to whether I should make my presence known. A light bobbed above on deck, and revealed a familiar face. "Robert!" I cried, "I thought you were back at the circus."

He peered at me and shone the lantern onto the gangway. "Hello there, Flynn, what brings you down here again? Word had it that you were completely knackered and couldn't lift a finger."

"Oh, I am," I assured him, "Don't expect anymore work out of me tonight."

He laughed, "After the lorry was filled with boys, I put in my bicycle and hopped in with them. There was nothing left for me at the circus. I got my last wage and one for each of us for today. After *borrowing* those tents, I figured I had a vested interest in clearing out and coming aboard with your mates."

"True enough," I said. "I wouldn't care to be around in the spring when they open the store and find that the big top is the big open sky."

"Flynn, those tents have seen a good deal of wear. I caught a rumour that there might be new ones in the making."

This made me feel better about the whole enterprise. Now I was concerned the canvas might be too worn to take the winds. I joined Robert on the deck. "Does this mean that you're along for the voyage?"

"The circus work wasn't bad, but Scotland is beginning to sound more interesting all the time," he said.

"That's great," I responded, with an involuntary yawn.

He looked at me reproachfully. "Try to sound a little more enthusiastic, can't you?"

Boris appeared and waved a brief greeting, then got into a bo'sun's chair with his lantern and drew himself up the mainmast. I watched in awe as he swung from mast to yardarm. He was amazingly agile. At one point, he made a flawless trade-off in order to swing directly to the foremast without descending. "Just look at him," I exclaimed in admiration.

"Aye," mused Robert, "I used to watch monkeys do the same thing."

"Here, if I were you, I wouldn't speak that way in Boris's hearing," I said warningly.

He looked abashed. "Oh, I didn't mean it the way it came out. I promise I'll not wave any bananas at him," and we both laughed.

Above in the dark, the rigging issued a jovial carolling in Russian as Boris went about his work. He clearly knew what he was doing up there and was enjoying himself into the bargain. I felt heavy footsteps approaching and looked round to see Harris's great face beaming in the lamplight.

"So, you've come back to us," he said genially. "Good. I've plenty of work to keep you occupied."

"No, no," I protested, "I was just on my way back to the inn."

Harris said, "Speaking of the inn, there was a young lady here not long ago, enquiring as to your whereabouts."

My heart skipped a beat. "How long ago?" I asked urgently.

He shook his head. "After I told her you weren't about, I had to finish hoisting some gear with Boris."

"Are you certain that you didn't see which way she went?" I said.

Harris sighed. "I told you, when I looked she was *gone*."

I made my way back to the inn, with the moon helping to light my way.

When I reached the inn, the pub was about to close. I looked in at the window, but Katherine was nowhere in sight. Glancing in the kitchen window, I saw only Mrs. Beasley, grumbling over a massive wash-ing-up with the wireless blaring cheerful music. I carried on round to the cottages. Martin's cottage had a light showing, but I saw, with a sinking of the heart, that Katherine's was dark. I was at a loss as to where I should look next.

Suddenly, from the garden I heard a faint cry. It was a voice calling my name. I looked up, but could see no one. Then the voice called again.

"Flynn, Flynn," came the call. "Here."

I turned back and peered up into the darkness, wishing that I'd brought my torch. I still couldn't see anyone, until I raised my eyes to the top of the rock. Silhouetted dimly against the stars stood a dark, hooded figure. I knew at once it was Katherine, and an instant later I was dashing up the slope. Once I stepped on the rock, I held out my arms and she came straight into them. We clung to each other word-lessly, wrapped in a moment perfect with relief and joy.

"Where have you been?" I said finally, not loosening my hold. "People are asking for you at the inn. I was beginning to worry. And Mrs. Beasley…"

"Oh hang Mrs. Beasley!" she burst out, pulling away a little. "I'm sorry if you've been concerned about me. I've just been walking about, watching people come and go at the inn and watching the men at the ships. I've been thinking about life, and what's come and gone…just generally feeling rather down in the dumps." She sighed bitterly.

I felt helpless in the face of her sadness. "Is life really so bad here?" I asked gently.

She sighed again. "Oh, it's a reliable enough situation. I've no real expenses. I've a roof over my head and regular meals. Compared to the past few years, it's been a real change. Mrs. Beasley would be quite happy to see me continue till I'm grey. It's not someplace I can stay, Flynn. I'm thinking I'll give my notice tomorrow. After today, she may want to sack me anyway. If I don't take the money I've set aside now, and try to make a better start somewhere else, I'll be living out life as a maid-of-all-work, waitress, and barmaid, with the occasional thrill of some drunken lout pinching my behind while my back's turned."

I took hold of her shoulders. "You're not serious, Katherine? It's not the right thing to do."

"How do *you* know it's not the right thing?" she said, meeting my eyes defiantly in the dim moonlight. "I've bloody well put in my time in plenty of places, and still have *some* dreams. I do have relatives up in Scotland, and back home in Ireland. There's got to be a better life for me *somewhere*. There are too many memories for me here in the south—mostly bad. I have to do something better than this. I don't mind being a drudge, if it's in the right place. I just know it's time to leave." Her voice was trembling.

We stood there for a time. After I'd helped her down from the rock, I could think of nothing else to say that seemed appropriate, so I linked my arm in hers and was relieved to find that she made no objection. All too soon we came up to her door.

She turned the key and then faced me, her hand on the latch. "You've been a real friend, Mr. Flynn," she said.

"Oh? I hope you can call me more than a friend now," I protested. "And see here, it's just Flynn, and you can drop that Mr. permanently. We're not exactly strangers."

She took hold of my hands, then looked at me and smiled wanly. "I could call you something else, if you'd rather."

This was taking a better turn. "Katherine, you can call me whatever you like, so long as you didn't hear it from a sailor," I smiled.

"Oh, I'd never use that sort of language, sir," she said, playing the wide-eyed colleen. We both laughed. She surprised me with a hug, which I returned with interest.

"Look," I said earnestly, "if you really need to be moving along, would you...well, might you consider coming with me?"

She gazed at me, her face a pale oval question mark. "Go with you? But Flynn, I hardly know you...! And where is it you'll be going?"

"Blast! I'm not at liberty to discuss things at the moment," I said reluctantly, looking down and scuffing my foot on the doorstep. I looked up. "Have you seen all the work that's going on at the ships?"

"Yes, and I've heard that those ships are to be towed out and scuttled."

I adopted a serious tone, "Well, that's true for one, but not the other."

She gazed at me perplexed. "There was a good deal of work going on there tonight when I came by," she said thoughtfully.

"I'd like to tell you all about it, but somehow this doesn't seem the best place."

"Well then, come inside." She opened the door and stepped in.

I glanced back at the pub. "What if Beasley catches me in here? There'd be hell to pay!"

"Then let *her* pay it. I don't care a fig for what she thinks. As far as I'm concerned, she can take her nasty old boyfriend and her nasty old cat and go jump in the river!"

"All right," I laughed, "You needn't preach to the converted!" I went off a few steps and peered over the kitchen garden at the window. I could see the landlady still washing up within, and I could hear faint music playing. I returned feeling slightly reassured. "Well, I don't think she knows we're out here."

Katherine seemed amused. "If you're so worried, I'll go in now, and you come back and hoot like an owl. I'll let you in at the window."

I chuckled, "Get on with you, girl, I've come calling." I followed her into the tiny cottage. Once the door was shut and the curtains drawn, she lit a candle on the bedside table. It was just a one-room cottage that had been converted from various outbuildings and hers was the smallest. A bed, a wardrobe, a worn armchair, the table, and a small pot-bellied iron stove made up its modest furnishings. It was certainly humble, but very tidy, and exuded a general air of comfort. Perhaps it was only her presence that made it seem cosy.

"Quite like home, don't you think?" she said. "Modernised too!" She gestured towards the single light bulb hanging by its bare wire. "Won't you sit down? I think we deserve a drink, don't you?"

"That sounds right," I said as I sat down in the chair.

She produced a bottle and poured out a tot for each of us, then shivered. "This should warm us up. I'm chilled from prowling about in the cold. Let's have some heat." She pulled open the door of the stove.

I started to rise, reaching towards the scuttle. "Here, let me do that."

"Sit down," she ordered, slapping my hands away. "I think I can light my own fire. You'd be surprised at some of the things I know how to do, Mr. *just Flynn*."

"Fine," I said, and settled back. I was watching as she crumpled up newspaper; then noticed a photo of the three ships on one page. "Hold on a minute. Let me have that one." I pulled the page free and smoothed it out on the table. The story dated from a week before and detailed the impending disposal of the two vessels yet afloat. I read it to Katherine as she started the fire. It was all familiar news, and went so far as to report some local opposition to the proposed removal by "retired Sea Captain William T. Bowman." Unsurprisingly, there were no direct quotes from him—they would have been unprintable.

She blinked at me in affected awe, "Well, aren't you lot the celebrities now."

"Never you mind. Do you want to hear more about it?" I asked.

"Perhaps a little more, but I really ought to go over while Mrs. Beasley is still up and explain about today. If I'm still working here tomorrow, my day is going to start *very* early."

Just then there was a loud rapping at the door. We both jumped. Then the dreaded voice called, "Katherine, Katherine!" We looked at one another in horror. Mrs. Beasley!

Quickly, Katherine opened the wardrobe door and motioned me in. I heard her go to the door, and then Mrs. Beasley's heavy tread as she entered.

"Katherine, well! So here you are. All the livelong day, and never a word. You could at least have told me you'd be away so I could get Jean from the village, but by the time I rang her she'd gone up to Stoke. No one knew if you were dead or alive. I almost had the police out after you! I hope you realise that I've had to do all your work as well as mine. I haven't had an instant's rest, and all due to you. What have you to say for yourself?"

"I'm awfully sorry about all this, Mrs. Beasley. I wasn't feeling well today. I've been quite ill. I felt I needed some air, so I walked a bit and then the sun came out, so I sat down for just a moment, and I must have dropped off. I didn't mean to let the whole day slip by and never say anything. By the time I got back, I was too exhausted to think about it."

There was a pause. I wanted to see, but I dared not betray my presence.

"Well, if it was no more than that," said Mrs. Beasley less sharply, "Will you be back at work in the morning?"

"Oh yes, I'll be quite myself tomorrow," Katherine replied.

I heard movement, and the door creaking open. Please go! Good night, I pleaded silently...run along to bed now!

"You should have some hot tea or Bovril, you know," the landlady went on. "Whisky won't put you right—corrodes the stomach."

There was silence for some time. Why didn't she go? The whisky! Did Katherine hide the second glass? The answer was soon apparent.

"Oh, so we've been entertaining, have we? I suppose it was the doctor!"

"No, it wasn't the doctor, Mrs. Beasley," Katherine sighed. "I must have forgotten pouring the first."

"Don't come the innocent young thing with me my girl," Mrs. Beasley sneered. "I've seen a bit of life in my time and I know what's what. You little trollop! I give you a good position, and then some worthless man comes along, and off you go with your skirts flying up. I know what young girls are these days! Well, if you want to play the merry widow, at least *I* won't be saddled with the consequences."

I was seething with indignation. How dared she say such things? I was aching to jump out and take Katherine's part, but I knew that I'd only make it worse for her by doing so. I could see us being sacked on the spot, losing our free lodging and going off with no pay. It was maddening to stand idly by and hear my poor Katherine insulted by that old shrew!

"I *should* dismiss you here and now," she continued, "but I've been quite satisfied with you until all this. It would be very inconvenient to replace you at this time. So if you can promise to be prompt and industrious tomorrow, I shall let it pass this once."

"Yes, Mrs. Beasley," said Katherine tonelessly.

Footsteps approached my hiding place. I was unnerved at hearing the landlady's voice scant inches from my ear. "Don't keep her up too late young man," she said. Of course she was only guessing, but I was relieved to hear the door shutting after her.

After a moment the wardrobe door was opened. Katherine wore a blank look, but her cheeks were wet. "Well, she's gone."

"That foul-mouthed old witch! If she speaks to you that way again—"

"Oh, never mind. Just look at me, smuggling a man in, and trying to cover up with feeble lies. So much for not caring what Mrs. Beasley thinks! What a miserable hypocrite I can be. I didn't want to risk getting you sacked as well."

"Don't be hard on yourself." I sat down. "You can get out of this, you know."

She gave a short laugh, "Oh right, go sail off on one of those old wrecks. I don't know how they even stay afloat." She took up her glass and sat on the edge of the bed. "Are you really suggesting I do that?"

"Yes, I am," I replied seriously.

She stared. "You must be mad!"

"Katherine, look, I'm not mad. Just let me explain something. One of those ships is quite sound and seaworthy, but she's been made to *look* like a decaying wreck." Here it went; she'd not come without knowing the whole scheme. "We're taking her up to Dumbarton, Scotland, where she was built. What I'm offering you is passage on that voyage. It won't cost you a farthing. You can do what you like once we dock."

"You are serious," she said, deep in thought.

"But there's a catch to it, I'm afraid."

"Ah?" Her eyes were wide and enquiring, with a curious perilous glint.

"You'd be working your passage as ship's cook." I hastened to explain, "Some of our men imagine they can attend to it themselves, but I'm afraid their ambitions far exceed their ability." I put on a mournful expression. "Oh please, we'll be living on salt pork and ship's biscuits if you won't take the position, Miss Katherine."

She laughed. "I suppose these are the men you've been huddling with in the pub. Exactly how many mouths are we speaking of?"

"Well, there's me, Harris, Bowman, Boris, Edward, and Robert. That's six."

"That's not so many," she said.

I held up a hand. "That's not quite all. You've been to the orphanage?"

"Oh yes, a few times," she said. "Mrs. Beasley sent me up with odds and ends for the boys. She seems to think the place is full of dear little toddlers and sends them baby clothes. Most of the boys are too big to be in an orphanage. That nasty O'Connell thinks he's fascinating to women, and anything in skirts is fair game. I suspect that Beasley must be the only woman he's ever got, and she's welcome to him!"

"What?" I exclaimed, incensed. "Did he try something with you?"

She waved a hand dismissively. "It was nothing. You don't want to know."

"Oh yes, I do!" I cried, leaping up and nearly knocking over the chair in my haste. Appalled at having been so loud in our delicate situation, I righted the chair and sat again. "Well, I do."

"The first time I went up there, he offered to give me a ride back in his big shiny car, with *extras*. He promised me dinner, the horrid old troll! Now what were you going to say about the orphanage? Are you taking along some of the boys?"

"Yes, was it that obvious?" I said.

She smiled, "Flynn, you're the most obvious men I've ever met. I need some time to think it through. It's moving rather quickly, you know."

"Not as quickly as O'Connell," I growled. "He needs to be taken down a peg or two! What an absolute bounder. He's no more than a dirty old man and a sneak into the bargain. I've swept more appealing things off my boots."

She laughed, "That's a common sentiment around here, and I've heard worse from some of your sailor friends. That old charmer seems to bring out the beast in all of us."

I hadn't shared the rake incident with her yet, so I told her, and we both roared. She had some wonderful tales of her customers to relate, and for a time merriment reigned and the whisky flowed while the little stove put out a cheerful heat. We even managed to laugh about me in the wardrobe. I wished the night would go on forever, but at last she rose and stretched her arms.

"I do think we both need *some* sleep," she yawned.

She walked me to the door. "Now then, I'll be thinking over your interesting offer. You want me to dash off to Scotland with a man I scarcely know, toil as the ship's cook on a condemned vessel, with no idea of what's to happen when we arrive? Isn't that about the gist of it?"

"Well, yes." It didn't sound terribly sensible, put that way. "Oh, and about the orphanage, there'll be twenty boys coming."

"Twenty?" she asked in astonishment.

"Yes, they'll be our crew for the ship. They've been training for quite some time. I can tell you more another time, but that's the way it stands at this point. Do give it some thought, but keep it to yourself."

She gave me an inscrutable look.

"Not a word to anyone. If Harris or Bowman knew I was discussing this with an outsider, I might suffer a worse fate than the bloke who went overboard the other day." I then told her about Thursday's thrilling "Thames Invasion of the Government Officials," with a high diving demonstration and umbrella duel. We roared with laughter.

"You know, I think I've met those two. Came in for a pint, didn't tip, and pulled my apron strings as I walked off. Lovely fellows." she said.

I growled, "Just let me catch them at it!" Then I said wistfully, "This could be a right cosy place if only it weren't in Beasleyland."

"Yes," she sighed, "It's a shame I can't just pack it up and take it all with me."

"At least it's better than living upstairs over the inn. What heat I get comes from downstairs and it doesn't always seem to have the strength to climb all that way. Unlike the noise from the pub!"

"Oh, but you're lucky, you're under the same roof as the loo. A bit of modern plumbing never hurts, now does it?"

I laughed. I hadn't thought of that.

She nodded, gave me a soft kiss on the cheek, and pushed me closer to the door. "I'm leaving! Really, I'm leaving!" I said as I put on my cap. I opened the door and said good night.

"Good night," she whispered.

Drifting off into the night, I was buoyed by the hope that Katherine was coming with us! She hadn't said as much, but she was thinking it over. Up the stairs and ladder I floated. After kicking off my boots, I fell exhausted onto the bed. What a day! I kept turning these thoughts over in my mind. I drew aside the curtain, and peered out into the darkness towards Katherine's cottage, where a light still glowed. A few moments later the light was extinguished. I trusted that my ship's cook was on her way to dreamland, where I dared to hope there might be room for me.

Chapter 9
ANOTHER DAY, ANOTHER GOOSE CHASE

My head had scarcely touched the pillow when I was jarred into consciousness by the screams of Mrs. Beasley, punctuated by the honking of a goose.

"Mr. Flynn! Mr. Flynn! Do come quickly!" sounded in urgent tones beneath my window.

With a sense of dread, I arose half-conscious and hastened into my clothes. Next, I launched into my daily round of hunting for my boots. By sheer chance, last night's kick had landed them neatly together on the other side of the room. Mastering the sudden urge to open the window and hurl them at her, I pulled them on. Being at the beck and call of that woman had become more galling than ever. I descended the stairs to the kitchen where I found Martin finishing his breakfast.

As his eye lit upon me, he clasped his hands together in tremulous supplication. "Oh Mr. Flynn, you big strong man," he cooed, "Mrs. Beasley needs you. You must render aid and succour to the frail and fair!"

"Leave off," I snarled groggily, "or I'll give you frail and fair." He laughed as I crossed to the door and stood blinking out the window. I couldn't believe it! There was Purdy back up in the same tree with the same goose rampaging below. And once again there was Mrs. Beasley frantically hovering, beside herself with distress. Nursing another bitter thought, I opened the door and prepared to play the hero of the hour once more. Before going, I turned and fixed a narrowed glance on Martin, raising a warning finger. "You're not out of this yet, mate," I said ominously, and went out.

"Oh, there you are, Mr. Flynn," exclaimed the landlady as she hurried over to me. Her dressing gown of bright magenta mercifully concealed whatever lacy nighttime confection presently adorned her form. "That dreadful goose waits for poor little Purdy when he goes near the pond!"

I held up a weary hand. "Purdy should have the sense to stay away from the pond, don't you think?"

"See here, young man," she snapped, wagging a finger under my nose, "don't you *dare* speak about my Purdy in that fashion. He's a wonderful sweet-natured cat, and very, very clever. And what a wonder he is with the mice!"

"He seems to like his mice with feathers," I muttered, trying to conceal my mounting resentment, which was especially sharp after remembering the way she'd spoken to Katherine last night.

"None of your cheek now," she scowled. "Can't you see we've an emergency here? Purdy is up the tree again. I want you and Martin to get him down straightaway, by whatever method you used before.

The great bird was now proceeding back towards the pond at a stately waddle, but Mrs. Beasley remained. I had the distinct impression she intended to watch the proceedings, and that would never do. "I'll fetch Martin," I said. I turned to find him descending the kitchen steps.

"Ready for my expert assistance?" he asked cheerfully.

"Yes," I said, rubbing my eyes. "But I think she means to watch us."

Martin grimaced, "That complicates matters."

The outlook did seem questionable, so it was plain that a diversion would be needed. My mind ran over desperate and impracticable schemes, but just then came the welcome sound of the telephone ringing within.

Mrs. Beasley glanced impatiently in the direction of the inn as the ringing continued. "Why doesn't Katherine answer that? Where *is* the girl?" she grumbled. "After all I've done for her, and this is how she repays me! Oh, I'm coming, I'm coming…" and she scurried back inside. She really was a beastly old slave driver! "Beastly" seemed just the right word for her, so I made up my mind that henceforth she'd always be Mrs. *Beastly* to me.

I realised I was wasting precious seconds. The phone was in the windowless corridor connecting the kitchen to the pub, so there was no chance of her glimpsing Purdy's descent if we acted quickly. I leapt for the hose and turned on the tap. Twisting the nozzle full on, I sent a vigorous stream into the upper branches of the larch. This time Purdy didn't wait for the water to reach him, and may have carried no more than one or two stray drops with him as he streaked down and into the haven of the rose bramble.

"*Flynn!*" I jumped at the wild shriek, and turned to find Mrs. Beasley poised upon the kitchen doorstep, her fists clenched. I remembered tales of the frightful attacks suffered by people who came between wild animals and their young.

"Yes, Mrs. Beasley?" I said sheepishly.

She glared. "Did I tell you to turn a hosepipe on my cat? *Did* I?"

"Really, it seemed much safer than pulling him down by hand. The water never intended to touch him, just to frighten him into moving." This didn't mollify her in the least. "What a horrid trick to play on an innocent creature! I suppose this is how you got him down before!"

I looked over at Martin, who was doing his best to pass for invisible.

I coiled up the hose, thinking quickly as I did so. "You see, Mrs. Beast...ah, *Beasley*, it's all a matter of the water. If Purdy were only a bit more shy of water, he wouldn't go near the pond and the goose. It was only to teach him the dangers of water that I turned on the hose. He could even fall into the pond, you know." Pure invention of course, but it did sound quite logical.

She knitted her brow. "It was a very ill-conceived plan, Mr. Flynn," she said at last, "and you should have consulted me before proceeding. But I suppose you meant well. However, don't you *ever* turn the water on Purdy again. Is that understood?"

"Yes, of course. I'm dreadfully sorry." I was only sorry I didn't catch him full in the spray.

Martin and I nipped back into the kitchen. As I made for the inner door to wash my hands, Martin spoke up, "Dreadfully sorry? Well, you're dreadful, but not a bit sorry, I'll be bound."

"Oh, shut up," I said.

"I can't think why people take on so over cats in trees," he went on. "How long have you been gardening?" Martin asked.

"I couldn't say exactly. Nearly twenty years on and off, I suppose."

Martin stroked his chin, affecting an air of sagacity. "Tell me then, when was the last time you found a *cat* skeleton up in a tree?"

I had to chuckle. "I never looked at it that way."

From behind the scullery door came a peal of feminine laughter, and Katherine looked out. "I was sorry I missed the first goose adventure," she smiled, "but this one must take a near second place. I saw it all out of the window. If only I'd had a camera!" she giggled.

I was relieved to find her in such good spirits. There was nothing in her manner to suggest a person pondering a weighty question, which I took as encouraging.

"You'll be wanting your breakfast now, won't you?" she asked.

"Yes, but not unwashed and unshaven," I replied. "I went direct from bed to back door with no stops between. I'm not fit for polite company."

"Not to worry," Martin laughed, "we ain't polite!"

Katherine flapped her apron at him.

As I made for the inner door, Mrs. Beastly bustled in and button-holed me again. Katherine quietly withdrew back into the scullery. "Now then, Mr. Flynn," she said in brisk tones, "I've a new list for you. Today I want you to start work on the rockery."

A rockery? That was news to me. I'd just finished repairing the old cucumber frame; it was perfectly serviceable. I began to suspect that she intended keeping me on until her "young gardener" returned, which might well never come to pass. Well, she was due to be disappointed, and she'd lose her maid-of-all-work when she lost her gardener-cum-cat-retriever, if I had any say in the matter. After a few more instructions she went back out and left me to my own devices, and to her list. I hurried to wash and get myself to breakfast, for there was much to do, and most of it wasn't connected with a rockery.

Thinking of the approaching voyage brought my Uncle George to mind. He had often told me of the days when he'd lived in Scotland, not far from Dumbarton. Perhaps Uncle George had tired of New Zealand and gone back to his old haunts.

I sat down to breakfast with busy thoughts, while Katherine scrubbed and clattered nearby in the scullery. Once I'd finished eating, I peered into the pub where Martin was sitting with his feet up, industriously polishing glasses while he listened to the wireless. As I went back through the kitchen, I paused on the doorstep surveying the garden.

"Mrs. Beasley, about this list. Would you object to my taking some half-days? I promised to help some friends." I followed this request with my most appealing nice-young-man look.

"Well," she said, "As long as you finish the job by the end of the week."

I set to work collecting stones for the rockery, which was to occupy much of the slope below the Ornamental Rock. By midday I had amassed an impressive heap, and called it my half-day. It was time I looked in on my future shipmates.

Chapter 10
A HUB OF ACTIVITY

As I came within sight of the old vessels, I was dismayed to see the same official car that had visited last week, but then all those official cars do tend to have a sort of shiny resemblance. Nearby stood two bowlered, striped-trousered, black-coated bureaucrats, engaged in a conversation with members of the local constabulary whose workaday police car was drawn up behind theirs. Bowman stood on the deck of the *Bonnie Clyde* watching them. As I came within earshot, the policemen approached Harris who was casually blocking the bottom of the gangway.

One of the policemen said, "Beg pardon, sir, but one of these gentlemen tells me that on Thursday last he was assaulted by you aboard one of these ships, so we've come to enquire into the matter."

Harris straightened his coat and looked blankly in the direction of the two officials. "Those gentlemen? You mean those pathetic excuses for human beings over there?" he asked in tones of the greatest incredulity, nodding towards the men standing against the car. "Assault one of them? Not likely! If I had, he'd scarcely be standing there neither bruised nor bleeding, and looking fresh as a daisy."

The officer said, "He told me that you threw him into the Thames."

"Threw him into the Thames?" Harris exclaimed. "I did no such thing! I was holding him up while he was sitting on the rail. That was after he kicked *me*, quite without provocation, which I admit caused me no small annoyance. He demanded that I release him, so I did. He went into the water entirely at his own request, and all here witnessed the event." Harris gazed at the officer levelly. "Well, Inspector?"

The constables looked at one another, then over to where the two stereotypical instruments of British bureaucracy stood by their gleaming black car, with suits, hats, and umbrellas all neatly polished and fitted to a nicety. They then looked at Harris, whose imposing figure made a clear argument that had any serious assault taken place, the effects would have been more apparent and more lasting. They were obviously growing uncomfortable trying to make sense of this situation in the absence of tangible evidence, and had little choice but to terminate the investigation.

They returned to the two officials. "Well, sir," said the officer, "I'm afraid we have no grounds for making an arrest here. It's no more than your word against his, and he has witnesses. I *am* sorry." Then the policemen got back into their car and left.

The two officials shot back many a black look at Harris, Bowman, and the ship as they got back into their car and roared off.

I daresay we all breathed a sigh of relief as they drove away.

Later, another black car came into view, and I thought at first that last week's officials were again returning to the fray. I joined Harris at the gangway, and we watched as the car rolled up and came to a halt. It was a *second* official vehicle. We watched as two different policemen stepped out. With them were two naval officers, one a full commander. Harris looked up at Bowman, "Heads up Uncle Billy, here we go," he murmured.

The police followed as the naval officers came over directly to Harris. He and the commander shook hands, so it was obvious that they knew each other. "Well, Harris! It's been some time since I've seen you back at the scrap yards," said the commander, gazing keenly at the old ship.

Harris was the very soul of amiable politeness. "Oh, I hadn't much left to do there and I haven't been recalled for another shift, else I'd gladly pop by, Commander."

"The reason we're here," the commander began in a cautious tone, "is that it appears as though quite a bit of gear has gone missing from some of the old rust-buckets and war-horses. We thought it best to come and have a look round the area and see what we could find."

I was horrified. If I wasn't pale before, I surely looked white as a ghost now. Knowing that I could be of little help here, I stood by and kept quiet.

The whole party made their way on board to be met ungraciously by Bowman. "What the bloody hell d'ye want here?" he snapped. That was scarcely more than the typical Bowman greeting.

"Request permission to come aboard," the commander said in proper naval protocol. "We'd like to have a look around," he added mildly. "Please step aside." Once on deck, they walked around, then slid open the hatch and went down the ladderway to explore below. This yielded no more startling discovery than a few empty glasses. They'd little knowledge of the ship's real condition and commented as they came back up the ladderway that it didn't look half bad down there, and surely when she was broken up some of that nice panelling could be salvaged. Wouldn't it look famous in someone's den? Then they walked over to Harris, who was sitting on the hatch of the main cargo hold.

The commander looked expectantly at him. "I hope you'll pardon me, Harris, if I have a look inside there."

"Whatever for?" said Harris, appearing surprised.

"Now don't be coy with me. You know I need to see what's inside. Oddly enough, the inside hatches seem to be jammed."

Harris slid off the hatchway and rose to his full height before the commander. "Yes, sir," he replied in a flat voice giving a crisp salute, and then turned away towards me. I knew what they'd see in the main hold. It was a bo'sun's gold mine and virtually everything we'd need for the voyage. When they looked in that hatchway and discovered everything, we would be lost!

They wasted no time throwing back the hatch cover. They looked in, I looked in, and we all looked in, and then at one another as a terrible smell drifted out. I was astonished, as were they. For the entire hold was filled nearly to the top with the most putrid, evil-smelling rubbish I had ever seen or smelt in my life! How on earth had my shipmates put it all in?

The commander walked over, pushed his swagger stick into the reeking mess and gingerly stirred it about.

"Harris, this is nothing more than a damned old rubbish scow," he said, holding his nose and shaking off his stick. "Ugh, look at it! Here, close this up," he said to the police officers, who did so with all possible haste, while trying to hold their breath.

"Well, what did you expect, the bloody Queen Mary?" growled Harris. The other naval officer spoke up, grimacing. "So this is what you lot do, just bung all your muck in there?"

Harris smiled, "Would you feel better if we'd thrown it into the river and had it wash up somewhere? The ship's already condemned. What could it matter?"

"What indeed!" the commander agreed. "Well, let's look at these other hulks." He turned and led his party onto the centre vessel, but there was nothing to be found. A glance was sufficient to show that the sunken coal barge beyond held nothing of value. "Very well, Harris, I've seen your little exhibit. But I know those things taken from the yard went *somewhere*."

Harris pointed out that there were plenty more docks at Sheerness and plenty more men there who also worked in the scrap yard. The commander shook his head. He was certain that Harris was either in possession of some of the missing items, or at least knew something about where they had gone, but this served him no good purpose. They weren't where he'd expected to find them, and he was not going to devote much more time to hunting for articles that had been marked for scrap.

"A good day to you, Harris," he said with a wry look, "till we meet again." And he led his little entourage away while Bowman glowered. Harris made no reply, but waved cheerily as they left the ship. He said not a word as they got into their car. As they backed away, his smile turned to a snarl of defiance. "You bloody Admiralty bastards, may you rot in seven shades of hell!" he muttered.

I turned to him, baffled. "How did the hold get filled with rubbish since yesterday? And what's become of all our line, tackle, and the lot?"

Bowman was laughing now. In fact, I don't believe I'd ever seen him laugh so wholeheartedly before. Edward emerged grinning from some corner. Harris joined in and was slapping Bowman on the back as they stood laughing and shaking hands, obviously congratulating themselves. I stood by feeling very left out. "Here, will someone please tell *me* what's going on?"

"Aye," said Bowman. "Have a look here, lad." As Harris opened the hatchway again, he took a very small belaying pin out of the rails and used it to stir up the rubbish. The stench was overpowering. "Ye see, it appeared to me that if ye wanted to make this sort of arrangement convincing, it would have to be deeper than an Englishman's riding crop, or swagger stick, if you will." He then replaced the pin in the pin rail and brought out a stick nearly as tall as himself. "But," and he poked it down through the rubbish, "no deeper than a Scotsman's walking stick." He tapped. I could clearly hear the hollow sound of a wooden surface under the rubbish. A false bottom. What a bloody great trick!

"Now then," said the old man, "We've got to move this nasty lot into the hold of the other ship so they'll deep-six it along with her. So, lend me your backs, boys! Let's have at it."

I balked at this. "Now? But I've been moving rocks all day..."

"Oh come now, Flynn, it'll be done in no time," Harris cajoled. Done in no time usually meant that *we'd* do it, and he'd supervise. I'd not let him get away with it this time.

"Boris!" Harris roared down into the hatchway. "Give us a hand here with the rubbish." Boris raised his head through the hatch. "Sahmi nagadili, sahmi ubirayte. Yah ne sobirayus vam pomogat! *Nyet!*" (You made this stinking mess, you clean it up yourself. I'm not going to help you with it. *NO!*), he yelled and disappeared just as quickly.

"What was that?" I asked.

Harris looked at me. "I don't know, but that last bit, *nyet*, was no!"

The rest of us set to work together at this unsavoury task, trying our best to avoid breathing deeply. The afternoon sun shone down upon us with unseasonable heat, which of course brought out the full bouquet of this vile "cargo." One had to admit that Bowman knew what he was about doing when he thought of this. It was the perfect deterrent to a further exploration of the hold.

Luckily, Bowman thought to lay out a sizeable tarpaulin before loading in, so once we'd taken off half the stuff, the rest could be gathered up into one great malodorous bundle and hauled out. As we tugged and wrestled with the beastly thing, I fancied I could hear the faint sound of a man singing from underneath. I turned to Harris. "Listen! What's that?"

He cocked an ear for a moment, then poked his head into the hatchway and shouted down through the half-exposed false bottom, "Boris, give over that noise!"

Quite a wealth of muffled words in Russian came back in reply, none sounding like an expression of delight. Harris shrugged. "Well, no matter now," he chuckled, "I'm just thankful he wasn't singing when the Navy was here. Silly old sod, he does enjoy singing."

After all the rubbish had been loaded into the cargo hold of the other ship, I sat down to chat with Harris.

"Here, what's this? Sitting down?" he cried. "You get yourself up straightaway and get back to work!"

"Damn your eyes, Harris, I've *been* working all day. You've been giving more orders than working yourself. You're forever interrupting any rest I'm trying to get. You're a bloody insomniac!"

"Oh, I'm the bane of your existence, poor fellow. I'm sorry, Flynn, I know I do go on a bit, but there's so much yet to do," he said.

I sighed. "Well, what's it to be now?"

"Ah! Since you ask, that lifeboat over there is fair rotted out and collapsed. Let's see how much of that we can pitch onto the next ship. Whatever we can't toss over there will have to go over the side and piled on shore for burning." He rose and stretched his giant arms.

We set to and found we could manage no more than to simply drag the thing about. There was no way of lifting the lifeboat over the gunnels. It turned out to be more difficult than Harris had anticipated, since the old boat was disintegrating in our hands. At last, we were able to fling the better part of it onto the *Auld Lass*.

It was getting dark, and we'd done enough for now. It was interesting that the patch of deck where the lifeboat had lain showed no trace of decay. It had been part of the stage setting, carefully arranged to help make the ship seem in far worse shape than she really was.

"The Navy was certainly repulsed by your little show," I remarked, "and weren't you the centre of attention with the men in uniform today?"

"Oh, you should've been here a week ago when Fleet Street had a go at us. Uncle Billy gave those reporters an earful," Harris laughed. "Called them spies and libellers. Told them, 'Go write yer story and be damned, ye dirty muckraking scribblers!' Let's hope he's not quoted verbatim in the press. I found out from one of them that he has a local acquaintance—Martin from the pub no less. I suggested he keep in touch with Martin just to see how things go with the scuttlings." Harris paused as if in thought. "Actually, for a newspaper-man he wasn't half bad. I hope we can rely on him later for some good stories." He added sombrely, "We'll need as much good news as we can get when the Navy and Whitehall start filling people's ears with half-truths and lies."

I had seldom seen Harris so serious. It was obvious that this whole venture was of great importance to him. I realised that everyone considered this a sacred cause. I was now drawn in closer to this improbable venture and to the men committed to its successful outcome.

We washed our hands and wolfed down some bread and cheese. That brought to mind a certain issue at hand. "So, Harris, who do you fancy as ship's cook?" I asked casually.

He said. "Oh, Robert says he can cook."

I gasped, "Robert is a tip-top seaman, and can manage anything to do with sailing, but for God's sake keep him out of the galley!"

"That bad, is he?" Harris shrugged. "Ah well. It seemed better to use him than to have Uncle Billy running amok down there. You couldn't have him in the galley and on deck as well. Lord knows he'd want to do both. I'm afraid the old boy is…" He was interrupted by an "Ahem!" behind him, and looked about to see Bowman, his narrowed eyes gleaming. Harris sank back in embarrassment, giving a feeble laugh, and threw up his hands.

"Now, Uncle Billy, let's face facts, your place is here on deck or in the navigating room where you're properly in charge. A captain's place is not in the galley."

"Oh aye, is that so?" said Bowman. "That's yet to be determined as to who does what." He helped himself to bread and cheese, then moved back off into the twilight, calling out to Edward below as he went, "Light's failing, Ned! Look lively!"

Edward brought up some lamps, which I viewed with dismay. So it was to be night work as well? I sighed. I was longing for a proper bath. I must have smelt rather as the hold of the other ship did. And a little sleep wouldn't do me any harm either. Rubbing my weary eyes, I helped Edward fill some of the lamps with paraffin. By their light Harris and I began to knock the false bottom out of the main hatchway. Beneath was Boris's prized bo'sun's locker. Boris abruptly emerged on the main deck screaming at us in English and Russian, one hardly more intelligible than the other. We understood not one word. Evidently he hadn't known about the tarpaulin, and had visions of a horrible avalanche descending upon him and his gear. A glance into the main hatchway satisfied him that everything was in order. Without further comment, he climbed up into the rigging and set about his work without further comment.

I gazed up after him. "There's an amazing chap," I said to Harris. "By the way, have you any idea what *mudak* means?"

"Not the least," said Harris. "He says it from time to time. It must be some choice bit of Russian profanity. He's welcome to be offensive in any language he likes so long as he honours us with his presence. He'll certainly be kept busy for some time to come. And speaking of being busy, how early can you be ready for me to fetch you tomorrow?"

I groaned. This had been another long day. "I can't really say now. I still have work at the inn all week, but I've arranged half-days."

"'Twould serve better if you took one full day off tomorrow. Do see what you can manage. When this hulk alongside tows out, we'll be on the tug." He shook his head mournfully. "It's a damn shame to see another one go. The old girl is in such a sorry state, the only thing keeping her together is the rats holding hands. Boris is bending all that old canvas from the forward hold onto her yards, and we'll unfurl just before she's breached and cut loose. She'll sail till she's too deep and then go down with all sheets set for the next world."

"That's rather touching," I said.

"Touching?" Boris said. He came into the lamplight shaking his head, carrying a block and tackle. "Touching? No touching. No one touch anything."

"I wasn't going to touch anything, Boris," I assured him, "I was just making a comment."

Boris scowled. "Ah?"

"Conversation," said Harris, "he was making *conversation*." Boris's face brightened in comprehension. "Ah good!" And he went off.

Harris sighed. "Sometimes I don't understand that chap one bit."

"Sometimes he may not want you to," I put in.

"Oh, he knows. He just likes to be contrary," he snorted. "Well, be off with you. You'll arrange for tomorrow off, right?"

I didn't much relish making new arrangements with Mrs. Beastly, but I told him I'd do my best, and bade him good night. As I set foot on the bank, he called after me, "As early as you can! I'll be driving the lorry." I waved him off limply and trudged up towards the inn, dreaming of a hot bath and a warm bed directly after.

When at last I stumbled in the door, the hot water, always inadequate, was long gone. What came out of the nozzle was cold enough to freeze a penguin's pecker. Real brass-monkey stuff. It was discouraging, but I was choking on the smell of myself. I gritted my chattering teeth and had a cold scrub. Afterwards, shivering so violently that I expected to hear my bones rattle, I conceived a sudden heartfelt yearning for the warm fireside of the pub. But I'd forgot to bring down any clean clothes from my attic, and of course I could scarcely present myself there wrapped in a towel. My appallingly soiled garments, with their rank exhalations, now reposed in the laundry basket, and I was not about to touch them again. Then I remembered that the pub was closed by now, so I'd have no witnesses if I should venture in to avail my chilly self of any remaining embers in the fireplace.

Emerging cautiously from the bathroom into the corridor between the pub and kitchen, I tiptoed up to the pub door and listened. All was quiet within, so I gently pushed it open and slipped through. I blinked in the comparative darkness, but the gloom was happily relieved by the welcoming ruddy glow of still-burning coals, a beacon that soon led me to a blissfully warm nest in one of the armchairs. After a few minutes there, I shivered no more, and a delicious drowsiness crept over me. I thought mistily of nipping over to the bar and drawing myself a pint, but it seemed too much effort somehow, and it was so nice to be curled up by this lovely fire. I floated away on rosy clouds.

I awoke with a start, aware that something was not as it should be. Why was I so cold? Where were the bedcovers? I sat up in shock to find that I wasn't in bed at all, but before a dead fire in the pub, naked in a towel. Thank God it was still dark! Clutching my towel around me, I groped my way to the door. I peeped through. Damn! There was a light in the bathroom, and its half-open door faced the stairs. I then realised that both the door and the light were just as *I* had left them. I picked up my boots and fled upstairs.

I was soon snug in bed, nearly asleep, when I became vaguely aware of someone climbing the ladder. Martin kept some of his stock up here and needed to fetch it occasionally, but one wouldn't expect to find him doing so in the early hours. I heard a thud and a faint "Ouch!" I decided to ignore it, and sank once more into the arms of Morpheus.

An instant later, someone took hold of my shoulder. I turned to see who could be so heartless as to be keeping me from my slumbers. Much to my surprise and delight, that dark figure bending over me was Katherine.

"Some staircase," she said, holding her forehead.

"Oh, it's caught you, has it?" I mumbled solicitously, trying to hold onto consciousness, and half fancying that it was all a dream. "Are you hurt? Can I do anything? And whatever are you doing here at this hour?"

She sat next me on the bed. "My head's all right, on the outside at least. I suppose this sounds dreadfully bold, but I really wanted to spend more time with you, even if it's while you're asleep. I suppose I just need to be held."

Here was any man's dream come true, but I found myself unable to reply to this very attractive proposal. After waiting a moment for my response, she took the lead and stretched out next me on top of the covers. I gently put my arm over her and she clasped it, pressing against me. Her hair tumbled about my face, smelling of lavender. We lay thus for a space, until she began to shiver.

"Do you think there's room for two under those covers?" she whispered.

Did I? After all, she just wanted to be held, right? But a man's only human! I felt caught between the fact and fantasy. I'd often dreamed of her lying by my side. I'd fallen hard for this girl, and the temptation to give into fantasy was overwhelming. In my upbringing, I'd been taught to think of girls as either good or bad; the good ones one married, the bad ones one paid. These ideas where a bit old-fashioned. The war had changed the attitude to courtship for so many of us. After all, we'd been living from day to day not knowing what the future would bring, or whether two people in love could ever find each other again once parted.

"I'm not wearing anything, you know," I pointed out dutifully.

"Oh hush," she scolded, "we're only bundling," and she removed herself from the bed with a bounce. I hesitated briefly, then threw back the covers and she crept in beside me still clothed. She nestled her head on my shoulder. It seemed an absolutely perfect fit, and we lay cosily wrapped in one another's arms as we drifted off to sleep together.

Chapter 11
THE SCUTTLING OF AN OLD SURVIVOR

I awoke at the first hint of daylight. Katherine had slipped away without waking me. I lay there drowsily drinking in the memory of her warm sleeping body. Feeling as though I was parting with some vital organ, I sternly forced my protesting body out of bed. I dressed quickly, intending to get in a little work on the rockery before Harris showed. With a last longing glance at the place so recently occupied by that sweet form, I made my way quietly downstairs. After breakfast, I started setting the rocks, keeping an ear cocked for a lorry passing down on the road.

When at last I heard the rumble of a large vehicle, I turned and hurried to the front of the inn. I was surprised to see a lorry backing right up to the storeroom doors—not Harris's, but the local victualler's. The driver got out and stood looking about expectantly. A moment later Martin came along yawning from the direction of his cottage, looking very disgruntled at such an excessively early delivery of supplies. He cheered up somewhat when he saw me.

"Flynn, just the man I need," he cried. "With the three of us, we'll have this lot unloaded in no time." I opened my mouth to protest, but thought better of it. Kegs and crates and sacks made their way from lorry to pub at a fair rate, as I pushed the others into working at my pace. I was anxious to have this job out of the way and be off before Mrs. Beastly caught sight of me.

We had laid a plank over the pub steps as a ramp, and up this we rolled the kegs of beer and ale. One keg suddenly blew out its bung halfway up the ramp, spraying Martin from head to toe with dark bitter ale. I laughed as he sputtered and floundered about, finally letting it roll down and take its own way towards the front drive, still gushing a fountain of beer as it went. He gave me a sour look, but then chuckled at the absurdity of it, drying himself with his apron. We hurried to finish binging in the goods, leaving the rogue beer keg where it lay.

Freed at last, I'd just begun walking towards the road when I heard the dreaded voice.

"Mr. Flynn! Oh, Mr. Flynn." I halted reluctantly and looked round. "You can fetch that keg later," the landlady cried. "Come to the pond and look at this." She pointed to the ground. "Look what he's done! Oh, the poor bird!" There on a bed of its own scattered feathers lay a freshly killed mallard duck. Preening himself on a rock nearby sat Purdy, looking very complacent. Our eyes met, and he prudently vanished. What a splendid rapport we'd established. I looked back at the duck. It was plain to see what took place.

She wrung her hands. "Oh, it's all from this wretched pond. How could any good come of something that began with an enemy bomb? Vicious geese attacking little Purdy! It's such a shame this bird dead, but it probably provoked him. These wild birds have a savage nature. Why, I remember when…"

"So what do you need me to do?" I asked in a patient voice.

"Ah!" She pointed to the rockery. "You'll have to fetch those stones back down, as we'll need all we can find." I listened as she outlined her plan for a nice wall about the pond. "We need to keep out whatever doesn't fly, and to keep in what does." It sounded daft to me, but I didn't want to argue with her. I wasn't planning to linger in these parts long enough to be involved in the building of her Great Wall, so I nodded an affected agreement with whatever she proposed. "Right, then," she said at last, "now, if you'd see to this duck?" I gingerly picked up the limp bird by its feet.

"I'll dispose of it right away."

"*Dispose* of it?" she cried. "I should say not! Let a nice young duck go to waste? And in October! Ducks are at their best in November, you know, and October is very near November. Ducks are at their best this time of year."

"Cook a bird that's been killed by a cat?" I couldn't hide my distaste.

"A duck's a duck my lad. Just take it to the kitchen. Katherine knows what to do with it."

"Yes, Mrs. Beasley," I said, and hurried away. I went into the kitchen, where Katherine was busily attending to some steaming pots. I presented Purdy's trophy.

She looked at it with vexed dismay. "What a pity! I just saw that bloody cat stalking it not ten minutes ago. One would think that a full-grown duck would be safe from a cat. Not that it hasn't happened before, mind you. Oh, I should have done something. It's such a shame."

"I quite agree," I sighed, "but here's the duck and Mrs. B. intends it for the pot."

"Oh, she does, does she? And I know who's expected to do the plucking and drawing. Well, give it here and I'll hang it up. Duck should be aged a day or so or it's not tender."

"She'll really eat that, then?"

Katherine drew herself up huffily. "A duck's a duck," she said, exactly as Mrs. B. had said it.

"What!" I laughed.

She made a rueful face. "I told you it wasn't the first time. The dirty part of it always goes to me."

"Perhaps I could help you with it tomorrow," I ventured.

"Oh, would you? That would be lovely," she smiled.

I could have looked at that smile all day, but duty called. I imagined Harris fuming as he waited for me.

"Now," I said awkwardly, "I really must go." I rushed out of the door and got to the road, just as Harris's old lorry was passing. He slowed, nodding at me. I ran up and clambered into the back with Edward as we headed upriver towards the Royal Terrace Pier and the tugboats at Gravesend.

Upon arrival, we found the crews from several different boats standing huddled about a scrap-wood fire in a steel drum nursing mugs of hot tea. One of the tug captains came over to talk with Harris.

"I still don't understand why so many of you are going along," he said. I wasn't exactly surprised by his curiosity, and tactfully chose not to participate in the ensuing conversation. Harris explained that we needed to see the operation as preparation for the next one.

There was Bowman, Harris, Edward, and myself. Representing the other side were two specimens of what Bowman called tap-dancing bureaucratic nitwit twits. I hadn't seen this pair before. Their bowlers, umbrellas, and suits were speckless. Each wore an identical Burberry, for one can't go to sea without a stylish raincoat. They made no effort to speak with Harris, only to avoid him, which was probably the wisest approach. Another chap came dressed more sensibly in warm clothes and with a camera. Presumably, this was the press.

We crowded onto the tugboat, and with a great stink of diesel engines began our slow cruise downstream to where the ships lay. The two different factions—government officials and ourselves—did our best to ignore one another and the efforts of the tug captain to try and make small talk as we went. It was a chill grey morning, its dullness all too apparent for our dismal purpose. At last the masts of the condemned vessels hove into distant view, looking helpless and desolate in the grey light.

The photographer started taking photos. He kept to himself as the tug laboriously manoeuvred into position off the bows of the three derelicts. The captain began grumbling over the inconvenience of avoiding the sunken barque on the outside in order to pull out the *Auld Lass*.

Boris was on board her waiting to take on the towlines with the heavy steel hawsers attached, to make them properly secure. His responsibility was to stay aboard and man the helm, steering the old ship behind the tug. He wore an uncharacteristically grim expression, looking for all the world, like a man unwillingly assisting at an execution. I think we all felt a bit that way.

I turned to Harris. "By the way, I've never asked you the real name of that ship," I said.

"That's the sad part," he said soberly, "I just don't know. The letters were so eaten away by time and salt that there was nothing left to read. Nor were there any legible papers on board to give one any clue. A damned shame, it is. But *Auld Lass* has served well enough so far, so it should do for her funeral, don't you think?" He rubbed his hands together. "Well, at least this scuttling gives us the opportunity to refine our plan of action for when they take the *Bonnie* off. It's easier to bear this one going down when one thinks how her end will help another escape. We'll be ready when they come. Have no fear." I wondered if he felt as confident as he sounded.

While Boris didn't much care for his part in the operation, he knew he must comply because it was part of the plan for the *Bonnie*. He was especially disheartened at the insistence that the ship's wheel be dismounted and taken off before she was finally sunk. The officials could see no reason why such a decorative artifact should go to the bottom.

As the tug took up the slack in the lines, Boris cast off the doomed ship from her last mooring. Slowly her nose swung round to meet the open sea as she began her final voyage. Every line, every inch of standing rigging and mast seemed to be groaning in protest as she was drawn out into the waterway.

It was a long journey, well over four hours, before we reached the spot where they intended to scuttle the old vessel. During that time everyone aboard the tug was very solemn. Even Harris had little to say. The photographer discreetly readied his camera for a candid shot of our glum faces, but thought better of it after Harris shot him one meaningful glance. Once we'd reached our destination, Boris made ready to unfurl the pathetic remnants of sails he'd bent on the day before. The canvas was not in good shape, most of it mouldy and without much strength. He had made it possible to set it all from the deck below by an ingenious system of lines without going aloft.

There were eight sufficiently intact sails, and Boris soon had them all flying, tied down to the deck at the pin rail. The wind pulled at them and the *Auld Lass* began to stir as though awakening from a long slumber. Boris watched the straining canvas for a few minutes, then headed back to the helm and grimly removed the weathered ship's wheel. Treasure-hunters and scrap dealers had already made off with her compass and everything else of value before Bowman could put a stop to it. Boris said he found it appalling that the old ship should be looted of this final remnant of her glory days.

Boris threw a rope ladder over the side as the tugboat drew alongside, then lowered the ship's wheel to the deck of the tug below. He switched off the pumps that had helped keep her afloat and transferred these and the generator to the tug as well. He then vanished below to set the detonator on the explosive charge that would breach the hull. Finally, just before climbing down her port side, he cast off the towline and jumped onto the tug. He turned away at seeing one of the government men running his hands possessively over the old wheel, remarking on its picturesqueness. He joined us as we watched the last voyage of the *Auld Lass*.

Now freed from the towline, the old barque began to move away. The tug captain seemed alarmed momentarily, unaccustomed to the sight of a dying ship moving off silently under her own power. She started to turn, began to heel over, then caught the wind and righted herself. Steadily gathering momentum, she ploughed off bravely through the waves, seemingly set for a far-off port. But then came the dull report as the explosives burst, opening her bilges. We watched her sail on, riding ever lower for approximately fifteen minutes. At last her mainmast snapped, bringing the crumbling yardarms down, and smashing through the decaying deck and gunnels. She drifted to a near-halt, and then toppled over slowly onto her port beam much like some great beast collapsing onto its side, brought down by a well-aimed shot. The camera clicked.

Bowman and Harris removed their caps, as did I. The tug's captain, seeing this, likewise bared his head. Harris reached over and smacked one of the officials on the back of the head, knocking off his bowler. The fellow wheeled indignantly, but noticing the rest of us with hat in hand, felt compelled to follow suit, while the other official prudently did likewise.

As we watched, the water around the *Auld Lass* appeared to boil as her hull filled. She settled deeper into the water, finally slipping beneath the waves, as she vanished forever from the sight of men into the dark

waters of the North Sea. The camera clicked again. Boris spoke briefly
with the photographer and pocketed his card.

We replaced our caps and went below for some hot tea, as the tug
turned back towards Gravesend. We were all feeling rather moved by
what we had seen and took our tea in silence. I suppose that most people find the sinking of a ship a thought-provoking and emotional sight.
I'd seen a few vessels go down during the war, but surely no seaman
ever becomes accustomed to the sight.

Now the *Auld Lass* was gone. It remained for us to wonder when
they'd be coming for *our* ship. We were very close to readiness, and it
seemed as though we'd need at least another two or three days to have
the *Bonnie Clyde* seaworthy.

The government official, who'd been unhatted by Harris, casually
remarked, "Ah well, one down and one to go."

Harris affected unconcern. "Yes, of course. How soon was that,
again?"

The fellow waved a hand airily. "Soon-ish." He obviously relished
keeping us in suspense, and was not likely to volunteer any real information. Well, we'd not give him the satisfaction of seeing us scramble
after his vague hints. As one man we moved away and pointedly ignored him. Soon-ish? What the devil did he mean by that? Perhaps
nothing. Perhaps *tomorrow*! We sat silent, agonising over this possibility,
and I daresay presenting a very downhearted appearance.

The tug captain assumed we were sorry about the ship we had just
scuttled and tried to lift our spirits with friendly chatter, but his efforts
were wasted.

Harris remarked to the captain, "I see you've a nice wireless, but no
key. Don't you have to use one anymore?"

"No," the captain replied, "I never learned Morse code, there's no
reason to use it on the river."

After a while we sighted the dim coast of Essex, then made out the
Southend light as we neared the mouth of the Thames. Passing through
the estuary, we strained for a view of our own masts by the Kentish
shore, but saw only haze. At last we docked at Gravesend, hastily dis-
embarking as soon as the tug was secured. Boris stayed to have a word
with the captain.

We watched as the government officials directed the securing of the
ship's wheel atop their car, being careful to have it well padded with a
blanket. Mustn't scratch! "Aye," growled Bowman bitterly, "a quaint
little knick-knack for some landlubber's wall. Lord knows where it'll finish up." He turned away.

"Give me five minutes alone with that twit and I'd make him talk," Harris muttered darkly. We all relished the mental images evoked by his words.

It was after two, and well past lunch. None of us had thought to pack any food, but no one felt hungry. We were too worried. Uppermost in every man's thoughts was the matter of our sails. We decided that a trip to Whitechapel was warranted. The canvas had been there for two days already, so perhaps we might come away with a few completed pieces. What if they *should* come for her tomorrow? We were certainly not beaten yet, but there was a perceptible flagging of confidence, and we knew we must do *something*. We all needed to see for ourselves. I hoped that this errand wouldn't simply turn out to be time thrown away.

Harris and Bowman climbed back into the cab of the lorry, while Edward and I resumed our places in the rear. The motor was already running when Boris hastily joined us. We sat silently, enduring the long rumbling ride, each absorbed in his own thoughts. When we arrived at the tailor's workshop, Boris and I hopped out. We trooped up to the door, which was opened by a decidedly hollow-eyed Brian without waiting for Harris's unnerving knock. Behind him we could see his son David, dwarfed by vast canopies of canvas. Scattered pieces hung about the ceiling and rafters, some furled and tied with bends and pulls, looking as though they were ready to go. Everywhere the long cutting-tables were swallowed up under great expanses of stacked sails in progress. It was an encouraging sight.

"Brian, you are fantastic," Harris said. "This looks miraculous, but how are you getting on?"

Brian shrugged, rolling his eyes upwards. "My friend, my friend we are doing the very best we can. I have never in all my life broken so many needles, and my hands and fingers are no longer on speaking terms with me."

"And?" prompted Harris.

Brian turned to his son David with a gesture, and father and son walked around, reviewing their work. Boris followed watching keenly, then wandered on alone and poked amongst the canvas heaps. After looking over the list of specifications and comparing notes, Brian came back to Harris. "I'm sorry I must disappoint you, but we must have at least two days more to complete all you asked. I assure you we have been working around the clock."

Harris put his hand on the tailor's shoulder. "I know you're doing your best. Anything that's ready we'll take along with us now, and a thousand thanks to you, Brian. We may need a miracle to see this through, so please carry on as fast as you can."

"The day for removing the ship is so soon then?" asked Brian. "The sail-makers have been very helpful, and stay long hours to make sure everything is done right. Do you know when the day is?"

Harris grimaced. "That's just the trouble, we don't *know*. Now that they've taken the other ship, there's precious little we can do to prevent them coming at any time."

"Harris, you are always full with ideas. Is there no way to delay this?" asked Brian.

"There must be," Harris muttered, "there surely must be."

Leaving Boris inside, we returned to the lorry to find Bowman pacing impatiently. He had decided not to come in case the lack of progress was too depressing. We were glad of it, for much of the canvas on display sported gaudy circus colours and had been included against his express wishes. He marched up to Harris. "Well?" he asked.

"Two more days for the whole suit of sails, Uncle Billy." The loading doors creaked open. Boris and David along with several helpers went to and fro. Rolls of completed sails made their appearance on the platform. Fortunately none of them were showing colour, so Bowman oversaw their transference into the lorry with apparent satisfaction. Brian waved encouragingly as he pulled the doors shut again.

"Any sail is better than no sail," Bowman grunted, "but far better is more time. How are we to make sure of it?"

I turned over implausible schemes in my mind, while Harris leaned against the platform lost in thought. Boris was still in the back of the lorry fussing over the proper arranging of the precious bundles. After a while Bowman spoke up, suggesting we board the tug at night and pour saltwater into the carburettors and engine to muck it up. Harris dismissed this idea out of hand because if just one tug were out of commission, it would be too obvious that someone was engaged in deliberate sabotage.

"Well then, what's it to be?" cried Bowman. "I'll nae give o'er! I don't care if I have to strip every clothesline in London. I'll fly everything, including my nightshirt, but I'll see that ship sail to Scotland!"

"No one is asking you to quit. No one is asking anyone to quit," Harris said.

Boris tapped his shoulder, "I have speaking with tug captain."

Bowman looked at him suspiciously. "Oh aye?"

"I ask him, is he taking other ship tomorrow?" replied Boris.

"Of course! Why didn't I think of that?" groaned Harris, clapping his hand to his brow.

"Ye were busy wi' yer temper, ye great oaf," snorted Bowman. "And what did he say?"

Boris replied, "He is saying he has no towing of ship tomorrow. For this towing today he was arrange in advance one week almost. I ask can he find out if other boat perhaps is taking the *Bonnie*. He say no."

"By God, this is just what we need," said Harris.

"We can ask what he hears when we pass Gravesend," Boris added.

Bowman doubled his gnarled fist under the Russian's nose. "Ye sly bolshie bastard, why did ye nae mention it afore?"

"What? When?" Boris said, throwing up his hands. "Noise too much for talking in back of lorry. Noise too much when you all yelling! Is not sly, only logical to ask."

Harris shook his head, chagrined. "I was too bloody clever for myself, always thinking to get word from higher up."

"Then up the mast you look," said Boris impatiently. "I am *always* higher up!" There was no point arguing this logic with Boris; he was surely right about that.

"Aye, well right now the word from higher up is lunchtime and well-nigh teatime into the bargain," Bowman said. "We'll be wanting to take the road again once we've got something inside us."

None of us cared to argue with that. Our breakfasts had been long ago and our appetites had returned with a vengeance. A short while after, we were rolling along on our way back from London stopping at the Leather Bottle Pub in Gravesend, and were now full of pints, fish, chips, and curiosity over what the tug captain might have to tell us.

At the Gravesend docks we were disappointed to find that our tug had gone out again. The captain left word with a messenger that it would be his own tug coming for the ship. There was heavy weather predicted, and nothing was apt to happen till Saturday at the earliest. We all became a bit giddy at that. Harris gave the surprised messenger two bob and energetically shook his hand. The poor lad went off looking from the shillings in the one hand to the limp ruin of the other hand.

"Let's stow these sails and get around some pints," laughed Harris. Feeling light-hearted, we piled back into the lorry and took our way towards the old barque we were once more feeling confident of saving. There was plenty left to do, and plenty that could go wrong. As long as the storm didn't pass us by, we'd be fine.

It was seven o'clock as we came to a halt by the remaining ships. The space left by the departed vessel gaped eerily, and revealed a different view of the sunken coal-carrier. At low tide much of her hull stood out of the water. I followed Boris as he walked out on the sand spit for a closer look. One could still see the sleek lines of the once-proud tall ship in the battered rusted ruin before us.

Boris shook his head in regret at the sight. "Terrible" was his only remark. He wheeled around and headed towards the lorry. "We bring sails now."

We finished wrestling the bulky canvas bundles from the lorry onto the *Bonnie Clyde*'s deck when Larry and Todd from the orphanage came down to enquire about our day. Harris recounted the story of the scuttling and the sails and how we were still determining our day of departure.

"Everything depends on the weather," said Harris. "Have you kept a good watch on it as we agreed?"

"Aye," said Todd. "We're at the wireless everyday."

"Todd's a dab hand at the short wave," said Larry. "We can't tell half the languages we get, but we listen to every word on the weather that's broadcast."

"What's that about weather on the wireless?" Bowman asked.

"Well sir, according to the bulletins, we should expect a bit of a storm tonight. In fact it might well be pissing down rain for days," said Larry.

"Here here, who taught ye words like that? Mr. O'Connell?" Bowman frowned.

"No sir, Cap'n," said Larry innocently, "it was Mr. Harris."

Bowman shot him a nasty look, as Harris pointedly looked up at the sky.

Larry hastily resumed his report, "There are storm warnings out for the Channel and the North Sea. It's very unlikely we will see ships going in or out of the Thames for a few days. No one expects a break in the weather till Saturday or Sunday."

Harris rubbed his hands. "And we're only standing by for that break. We could go Saturday."

"Saturday, if the weather's agreeable?" Larry cried. He and young Todd exchanged excited glances.

"Will you be ready?" Harris smiled.

"Will we?" Larry cried out, "We're ready now!"

Harris chuckled at their enthusiasm. This was everything they'd dreamed of: going on a great sea adventure, escaping O'Connell's stifling repression, and maybe finding real homes. It was certainly easy to see why they were so excited.

I knew this delay was a godsend, but then again it could be very awkward. We must be attentive to the timing of our disappearance. After all we'd literally be emptying the orphanage, and some of us had jobs.

"We must be on our keenest watch with the forecast lads, for we don't want to be caught by heavy weather once we're under way," warned Bowman. "'Twould be a sore trial for such an old vessel." He squinted up at the bare yardarms. "I'm much afraid that we'll not be using all of those yards, the skysails in particular. Boris has been over them all, and advised me that some don't look over-sturdy to him. If one of the masts should snap high up, there'd be the lot coming down and through the deck. It could ruin our lifeboats, and then where would we be?"

"What lifeboats?" I asked in surprise. We'd cleared away all the old rotted ones that sat in a heap on the sand next to the ship with two others waiting to join them still on deck that we couldn't move when we took the rubbish from the hold. Were there new ones I hadn't seen?

Bowman glared at Harris sourly, "Oh we could have got a number of proper boats. Harris decided that he wasn't going to be fetching anymore goods out of the shipyard, so he brought us those damned things." He pointed at a canvas-shrouded heap.

I had a look underneath and found there were three large cork ellipses, as big as rafts and with netting all over them. They were easier to launch than standard lifeboats, and would hold just as many people. I'd seen them on quite a few ships during the war, but luckily I'd never had occasion to use them myself.

"It's the best idea imaginable," Harris pointed out. "Lash them down in a stack on top of the hold, then they'll be at hand if they're needed."

They looked satisfactory to me. I had to agree that further raids on the scrap yard would be ill advised with the Navy sniffing about. Larry and Todd looked over the rafts with glistening eyes. I think they were beginning to entertain hopes of a chance to try them out. They were at that reckless age when young men are convinced of their own imperviousness to death and disaster, and apparently the years of German bombardments had neither persuaded them otherwise nor dulled their taste for danger.

"Well," Larry said, "we'd best get back before we're missed. We'll keep a good weather eye, and everyone's standing by for your word. You'll have no delay from Starke's Raiders!"

"Saturday Saturday, could be Saturday," they chanted, and off they went into the dusk with jubilant laughter.

I was anxious to get back to the inn, but Boris wanted to see the sails safely into the hold before the rain started. Bowman and Edward were engaged in one of their heated discussions. Harris said he'd drive us all up shortly, but I politely declined and set off on foot, which had me in at the pub door before the others.

Katherine looked round from across the room and our eyes met. I had news, but couldn't discuss it in company. I sat down and sipped at the pint she brought me. A few minutes later I heard the rumble of a heavy vehicle on the road and glanced out into the dark. It appeared that another lorry was en route to the ship. More deliveries perhaps. When it came time for Katherine's dinner break, we repaired to the kitchen where we'd have a bit more privacy. I told her of the brief, glorious, and heartbreaking final voyage of the *Auld Lass*. We arranged to meet and continue the conversation after closing. I wondered if she was ready to give me her final answer. It couldn't possibly be no.

When I got back into the pub, I found Harris, Bowman, and Edward comfortably installed at a table near the fireplace. Bowman and Edward were embroiled in one of their unending disagreements. Harris gestured me to another table nearby where he joined me. We began discussing the matter of the sails. We'd given Brian dimensions for the full rigging of a three-masted barque, but since we stood in some doubt of using every piece, given the questionable state of the upper yards, it might be wise to speed completion of our sails by leaving the useless ones. Boris was the best judge of which to forgo and what to use. He'd be arriving shortly with final recommendations to tell Brian as soon as possible. We could only hope that he hadn't wasted much precious time over some of those unwanted pieces already.

We looked up to find Katherine standing over us with her tray. "Oh, three's a crowd," winked Harris as he began to rise.

Katherine gave him an uncompromising smile. "Sit down Harris!" she ordered. His eyes widened. He sat.

"You keep right on with your important matters," she went on briskly, "and don't ever let me catch you putting on that naughty-boy smirk on my account again!" She turned to me. "And I'll be seeing *you* later."

We both stared as she went off. I was grinning with delight at the matter-of-fact way she'd mastered Harris and her unashamed manner regarding the two of us. Harris seemed stunned, and for once, at a loss for words. Bowman and Edward were still wrangling, as they had been since I first met them. It was quite amusing that this seemed to be the only way they could communicate.

"I swear, those two are always at it," Harris said shaking his head. "Anyone might get the impression that they don't like each other very well. They're really quite devoted friends—they just never seem to agree on much."

We listened in awe as explosive bits of Irish and Scots invective flew, to a lively musical accompaniment of Gracie Fields on the wireless. This, along with the general evening noise of a well-attended pub, muffled all sounds from the outside.

When Robert appeared at the door, I assumed that he'd come on his bicycle. He said he'd just finished delivering some "surplus" circus goods to the ship in a borrowed lorry. I wasn't about to ask him where he borrowed it from, but I assumed Harris had a hand in it since he had borrowed many from Chatham and returned them by leaving them short of the gate to be found.

"Well," he said cheerfully, "I loaded things we might need and they will never miss."

"Let's hope those *things* are of some practical use, whatever they are," I muttered. Suddenly I realised something about his appearance. "Robert!" I cried, "You're bloody soaking wet! Did you fall in the water?"

He gave me a quizzical look. "Well, either I've taken up showering in my clothes, or it's pelting down with rain outside."

We ran to the window and looked out. Sure enough, just as the boys had told us, there was our hoped-for rain. And not just rain, but quite a squall blowing in. We trooped outside and across to where the road overlooked the river and stood there laughing like idiots in the pouring rain. Of course it was too dark to see anything, but it had all the taste and feel of quite a storm driving in off the North Sea. I don't think any of us could have been happier!

Harris and I began dancing about and waving our arms in glee. Even Edward and Bowman kicked up their heels in a creaky jig. We were acting like schoolboys just let out on holiday, cheering and splashing through the growing puddles. At one point, Edward lost his footing and fell flat into a huge puddle. Bowman chortled at that, offering a hand to pull him out. As soon as Edward had got a good grip on Bowman's hand, he pulled *him* into the puddle as well. I decided I should go inside again before this turned into a real dust-up, as entertaining as that would be. Happily, Harris now moved in to restore order as I fled back to the pub, feeling that I'd really had all the wetting I could enjoy for the present.

Robert was waiting inside the door having had his dose of rain already. He must have thought we had all gone mad. Apparently Boris hadn't briefed him on the magnitude of the much-needed weather, so our behaviour seemed a trifle surprising to him. Katherine studied me with wondering eyes, but she was so busy with customers that she hadn't much time for speculation. Harris now brought in the two soaked but grinning old men. Robert alone had dressed for the weather, but even his mac and wellie-boots hadn't kept out all the wet. He began industriously piling logs onto the fire—there went tomorrow's measure of wood, I thought, but for now it was needed to prevent us all catching our deaths while I explained to him how this rain was the saving of us.

Bowman and Edward were installed as close to the blaze as they dared be. Soon they began to steam like a pair of hard-ridden horses on a winter's night. Harris and I turned round in the heat, wringing out the excess water. Katherine came up with mugs of hot tea, ignoring our pleas for something stronger, and muttered something about great stupid daft fools.

Edward scowled into his mug, his lips quivering. "Saucy bit of stuff, denying a grown man his wee dram," he grumbled aside to Bowman.

Katherine had a good sharp set of the ears. "A *grown man* knows better than to go out in the rain without so much as a coat," she retorted and flounced away.

"She's a terror, nae doubt about it, just like my Meg," Bowman said thoughtfully as he watched her go.

Shortly after, Boris came in looking for something to eat. "Is ugly weather," he remarked.

"But it's *beautiful* weather," Harris smiled, "The loveliest weather that ever was!"

"Aye beautiful," Bowman agreed with a crooked grin, raising his mug. Boris stood looking confused.

Boris's thick accent caught the attention of one of the locals at a nearby table, and he now began to stare at the Russian in a very unfriendly manner. He was obviously deep in his cups, and not quite in command of his senses. "Whole bloody country's overrun with dirty foreigners," he declared rather too loudly. As an attempted insult this was a dismal failure, for Boris simply turned away with scarcely a glance in his direction and sat down with us. The man wasn't so easily put off and continued to stare sullenly. We did our best to ignore him, but when he unsteadily rose and presented himself at our elbows, he had to be dealt with.

"You've the wrong table, lad," Harris said mildly, rising to his feet and looming. Friends at the other table now urged the rash challenger to sit down and not act like an idiot and get himself killed in the bargain. Boris tactfully removed himself over to the bar in the interests of international amity. I was now certain that I recognised this unwelcome chap as one of the players in last Friday's dart incident. He'd evidently not learnt his lesson, for he stood there swaying and heaping uncomplimentary remarks along with intriguing but biologically improbable speculations on our parentage.

His mates couldn't be bothered to come and remove him bodily, and in fact found much of his discourse hilarious. I might have thought the situation amusing as well, had I been unaware of the ominous significance of the beatific smile now blossoming on Harris's face as he stood taking in the drunken performance. The fellow waxed incoherent, working himself up into a fever of indignation. He finally decided that he was going to take the first swing at the nearest target: Harris. Needless to say, this constituted a severe error in judgment. Not only did he miss his mark completely, but Harris gave him three good knocks while he lurched about trying to keep his balance.

The drunk's two friends now took offence at this and made for Harris, only to be restrained by Robert and myself. This action was met with disfavour by some other locals who then leapt into the fray. A further contingent now imagined this to be a dispute over the relative merits of rival football teams. Suddenly we were in the middle of a first-rate, full-scale absolutely pointless brawl. There seemed to be no one, save for Boris, discreetly sitting this out, so I joined forces with Harris and Robert to see how quickly we could make an end to it. After we, mostly Harris, had cleared the tables next to us, we moved out into the room to subdue the main troublemakers.

As matters escalated, Mrs. Beasley peered round through the inner door then quickly pulled it shut as a glass shattered against it. She was not about to enter the pub under these circumstances and doubtless went off to ring up the police. Martin called to an old friend who, from time to time, served as a chucker-out. He was a big strapping lad who often spent his evenings here; unfortunately he'd been coshed with a chair at the start of this and was rendered unfit for immediate service.

Harris was more than holding his own, occasionally pausing between assailants to restore himself with a drink from someone's pint, usually a different one each time.

Meanwhile, Boris got his food and drink from the bar and was making his way back to the comparative safety of the table where Bowman and Edward sat, repelling all comers with the fire irons. I marvelled as he wove in and out of an obstacle course of thrown punches, hurtled furniture, and flying bodies without ever being touched or spilling a drop. I was doing my best not to get involved, but pushed a few would-be troublemakers away from my side of the table.

Harris, standing over a heap of the fallen, finally lost patience, deciding that he wanted no more part of this. Leaping onto a table, he gave a roar, "RIGHT—THAT'S ENOUGH!" Heads turned, fists froze in mid-swing. "Let's have this over with right now before *I* start getting angry!"

There was a general consensus of opinion that Harris *not* angry was quite enough and that Harris *angry* wouldn't be necessary. The violence quickly subsided after that, and a sort of a post-hurricane quiet prevailed. The door to the ladies' opened cautiously, and the female contingent returned amongst us to rebuke or commiserate. Katherine emerged from behind the inner door with a disgusted look.

Returning to our table, we looked about and discovered that we were among the few combatants still standing. At first no one seemed able to locate the drunken fool who'd started the fight in the first place, but at last he was found looking very peaceful stretched out under one of the tables.

Katherine approached us with a decidedly stiff manner. "The whole World War and the male of the species still hasn't had his fill!" She looked about the room in distaste. "Luckily for *you*, Mrs. Beasley hasn't managed to get hold of the constable yet."

"Could you tell her it's safe to come in now please?" I said humbly. "*We* didn't start it!" followed by a despairing, "We'll help clean it up!" Now that the dust was settling, I was chilled by a gnawing fear that this little affair had scotched our developing closeness. I sat feeling miserable, watching patrons limping out into the storm, some being lectured by wives or girlfriends as they went.

A little later the landlady stood near the bar surveying the carnage. None of this would sit well with her, and I was resigning myself to immediate expulsion. When she came over and halted before us with hands upon hips, I was prepared for the worst. She fixed me with that all-too-familiar accusing glance.

"So," she said, "Katherine tells me that you and your sailor friends subdued the troublemakers and sent them on their way."

"Well, yes," I faltered. Her eyes travelled coldly over Robert, Harris, Boris, Edward, and lastly, with obvious revulsion, Bowman. "Imagine this group being good for something! I do appreciate your breaking up the violence tonight. I understand that you've also volunteered to put the room right again. Certainly a reward is in order." She turned. "Martin?"

"Yes?" he replied from his refuge behind the bar.

"Please give these gentlemen a drink apiece for their contribution." She looked about. "I wish I knew who was responsible for this."

"He was!" we cried together, and all pointed to the outstretched body under the table.

She peered down at him. "It's Lottie Pilford's boy, Giles. He always was a bad lot. Even as a baby, he was an ill-tempered little brute. Of course, what could one expect? I know there weren't many marriageable men after the Great War, but I do think Lottie could have been a bit more selective. There's *no* accounting for some people…It was surprising enough to find him fathering children. Perhaps if Lottie had sent him away to school, he could have learnt to pass for a decent human being. Well! Young Pilford won't be enjoying *my* hospitality again soon, I can assure you!" She paused to take a breath, then turned to go. "Just throw him out," she finished with a dismissive gesture and vanished back through the inner door.

"My God," Harris laughed, sitting back in his chair. "I never thought I'd live to hear a kind word from her Royal Hind-Arse. Dare we accept praise from such a quarter? Dare we accept free drinks?"

"We dare!" Robert and I chorused stoutly.

Soon we were enjoying our welcome, but far-from-princely payment for services rendered. Harris had his nose deep in his glass when he suddenly frowned and set down the drink.

He looked over at me. "Did I hear us volunteering to clean up?"

"Well," I said awkwardly, "it would be a nice gesture." He continued to regard me reproachfully. "Never mind Harris, I'll do it myself."

I finished my drink and set to work. I swept up broken glass and other debris and went into the scullery for the mop. When I returned, the others were busy attending to the rest of the job. That miserable Pilford bloke had been removed and lay just off the walkway. Damaged furniture was set aside for later attention, and the room was speedily restored to order.

"Right," Harris said, sucking a raw knuckle, "It's back to the *Bonnie* for us, lads." The crew struggled into coats and macs and made ready to venture back out into the storm, which was steadily increasing in violence. As they battled their way out the door against the buffets of the wind, I was thankful that I hadn't any need to stir outside.

The storm continued to grow quite violent with flashes of lightning closely followed by deafening peals of thunder. People were concerned with getting home before it grew even worse, although closing time was yet a while off. I sat at the fire, watching somewhat anxiously for Katherine to come back in. When she did, however, she only added to my unease by pointedly ignoring me. And all because that bloody Giles Pilford didn't like a Russian accent. It just wasn't fair. Eventually everyone had left, and I was happy to put the day behind me and think about the future, which I hoped would start just about the time Katherine got off work, if she'd only acknowledge my existence!

Getting tired of the silent treatment, I decided to go upstairs for some dry clothes. As soon as I'd switched on the light, I noticed that someone had come in and tidied up the place. I knew it must have been Katherine. There she'd been trimming up my humble nest, and I'd repaid her by helping break up the pub. I wanted to go straightaway and thank her, but I had a feeling that it would be best to leave her alone for the moment.

I changed out of my damp clothes, wondering if I should just pack it in and go to bed. I glanced out the window to see if there was a light showing in Katherine's cottage, and switched off the lamp to better see out through the wind-driven rain. I paced and fretted in the dark for what seemed an eternity, listening to the groans and clattering of the old inn, till at last I saw her window was lit. I wanted to apologise and resume the thread of our dinner conversation, but now I hesitated to approach her. I paced and fretted for another eternity, unsure of how to proceed. Despite the noise of the storm, I heard the unmistakable sound of someone coming up my ladder. As I strained to hear, there came a soft thud and a gasp. I put the light on just as Katherine appeared, holding her head.

"That's the third time today," she groaned. "They didn't make this any too spacious," she groaned.

"That sounded like quite a smack," I said. "The damned thing lies in wait for the unwary. Can I do anything?" I held out my hand uncertainly, and was relieved when she took hold of it. I gently pulled her towards me and gave her a hug. "I saw your light go on, but I wasn't sure that you'd care for me popping by."

She drew back enough to look me in the eyes. "I wasn't so sure myself for a while. But after all, knocking heads is what men *do*, isn't it? It seemed safer to collar the brute in his lair than to have him running about loose in the storm and scratching at one's door."

"Here!" I protested. "Brute indeed! I didn't start the trouble and stood off mostly."

"We need not worry about interruptions in my room tonight, the Beasley is otherwise occupied."

I raised my eyebrows. "Oh?"

"Ah-h," she nodded.

"Ooh!" I shuddered. The lightning and thunder suddenly burst in approved haunted-house fashion, as though to emphasise the horror of it.

We sat down on the bed together laughing. "So, what do you think?" she asked, with a wave at the room.

"I *thought* it was you," I grinned. "It's quite an improvement, but I'll miss my cobwebs,"

"Honestly, Flynn, I can't believe you've actually been living like this. By the number of spiders in the ironwork of your bed and in every crevice of the rafters, one would think you were breeding the things. Had I caught sight of them the other night, I might have been a bit more selective as to where I chose to lay my head."

I looked at her abashed. "Yes, well, I never claimed this place was fit for polite company. Anyway, what with not knowing just how long I'd be staying, I wasn't over-anxious to make a serious assault on the Empire of Dust here." I peered out the window, and noticed a spark of light still showing in Katherine's cottage window. "You've left a candle burning, you know."

"Actually I was planning on returning there," she explained. "One shouldn't be wasteful by leaving a candle burning in an empty room."

"But here it's so snug and tidy now," I coaxed.

She shook her head with a little laugh. "Now really, Flynn! I'm sure you could do with a nightcap after the soaking you had this evening."

I couldn't detect a bottle on her person. "Is Martin still down in the pub?" I asked.

"No," she answered offhandedly, "but not far away there's a nice little cottage we could go to."

"Do I take that as an invitation?" I asked.

"Oh I should think so," she smiled, "but just for a nightcap."

I got my coat, switched off the light, and quickly descended ladder and stairway, pausing at the kitchen door as Katherine threw on her cape. We stopped and looked out the window at the pelting rain.

"Well, that's not letting up soon," she said, "and it's just as well. We'd best have the torch off. No point in attracting attention."

I switched off the torch and opened the door, taking her hand. "Oh, kind lady, it's awfully dark out there. You'd best keep hold or I might get lost along the way."

"Oh hush," she laughed, and out we went into the deluge. We took the short way through the kitchen garden and splashed across the lawn to her cottage. We slipped inside, where the candle's mellow glow combined with the heat of the little stove to create an atmosphere of comfort that struck a responsive chord of hearth and home in me. I gave an inward sigh of wistful longing. Think of coming home to this every night!

Cape and coat were hung up to dry. Katherine looked out of the window as she drew the curtains shut and shivered. "What a miserable night," she observed.

Bringing out the bottle and glasses ready on the table, I sat down and poured us each a tot. I raised my glass. "To the weather, long may it rain," I toasted.

"What, you really want this?" she asked incredulously.

"It has to do with our sails not being ready yet. This storm is supposed to last a couple of days. This should buy enough time for our needs, so cross your fingers and pray for more."

She sat on the bed and sipped at her whisky. "Well then, I shall try to cultivate more pleasant associations with rainy weather." She looked about at the spare but sturdy little room. "The war didn't end for all of us when the shooting stopped. I can remember some very cold desperate nights in the wet." She took another sip and gazed at the ceiling.

"I'm sorry," I murmured. I didn't want her to get depressed again tonight, especially as I hoped to hear her decision about coming with us.

She went on. "Some people simply aren't very chivalrous towards young girls on their own. The sort who offer one a place to sleep, and then in the middle of the night when it's got good and nasty outside, surprise! It's more than sleep that's offered. I'd wind up huddled in some wretched corner many a night after refusing an invitation to share a bed. It's been such a luxury having my own little place, and feeling a bit *safe* again. You're quite sure that this," she waved her hand around the room, "wouldn't fit on the ship?"

"I'll find you something better than this up north," I said reassuringly.

"We'll see. And how are your salty friends taking to the idea of having a woman on board doing their cooking and supervising their eating habits?"

"Oh. Well, I haven't got that specific as yet," I admitted. "You really should come down to the ship and get better acquainted with them in their natural habitat. They do like you already, you know."

She made a face at that, then rose and squeezed in next me in the old chair. I put my arm around her, and we sat nestled together in the warm candlelight by the fire, listening to the wind and rain. I burrowed my nose into her soft chestnut hair, drinking in the scent of lavender, with a subtle something that was all her own.

"I've something to show you," she said, going over to the wardrobe. She opened the doors. It was almost empty of clothing. "Nearly everything that was here is packed up in my suitcase and my trunk as well. Now, I still haven't made up my mind whether I'm going along on your mad voyage, but I'm ready to be off at a moment's notice."

I could have done a little dance then and there! "Well," I advised her, "a moment's notice may be all you get."

Katherine sat on the bed looking thoughtful, "Though I don't anticipate using her as a reference in the future, I'd hate to leave Mrs. Beasley with no one to help her. I should ring up Jean in the village and put in a discreet word for her to be standing by."

I agreed that we shouldn't be heartless about this. I didn't feel too badly for my own part, since the garden was really in splendid shape now. "Let's not worry about Mrs. Beastly. It's bound to be a shock when we disappear, but she'll have Martin. Of course the gallant O'Connell will be here to comfort her."

She laughed. "Exactly my own thoughts. But *should* I decide to come, I'll need to have a look at this galley of yours. I can just imagine what that's like. It's sure to need some work. Can I see it tomorrow, do you think?"

I smiled and kissed her on the forehead. "You're an angel," I said. "We'll walk down there tomorrow when you're off work. But now," I continued as I reached for my coat, "since we're both to be up early, I must be off, so I'll be fresh for Mrs. Beastly's morning hysterical fit."

Katherine positioned herself between the door and me. "Not yet, me lad," she said. "There's a little matter of talking about the future which we promised ourselves the other night. Tired or not, I want to feel sure of more than just a job as the ship's cook!"

I hadn't really thought of just when we would talk but now seemed as good a time as any, better in fact, with the firelight and the warmth and the whisky to help move my stubborn tongue along.

"Yes, I can see how you'd be anxious," I said as I hung up my coat.

She wagged a finger at me. "Despite some dusting and de-cobbing, your room still has certain deficiencies. Don't you think this is a much more romantic place to be spending the night?"

"Spending...? Well, that all depends..." I began.

She sighed. "Flynn! You needn't pretend such innocence with me."

"Here! I don't pretend a thing, especially innocence. It's just that I'd rather know I was welcome than assume something and find I'd assumed wrongly."

"Well, if you don't know you're welcome by now—oh, make yourself useful. Bung some more coal onto the fire," she said disgustedly.

"Yes, ma'am," I said humbly, tugging at my forelock. I took some lumps from the scuttle and threw them into the little stove, then went over and sat next to her on the bed. I still felt awkward, and I'm sure Katherine could sense it.

She gazed earnestly into my eyes. "I suppose one can never really know how another feels. But I hope you feel as I do." She looked down. "I just need to be sure."

This took me by surprise. "I certainly never meant to seem distant. I just didn't know how to...I mean...Damn it, Katherine, this is all coming out so wrong," I said in frustration.

Her eyes were ever so soft. "Just say it, Flynn."

Come on, Flynn! This is the moment of truth. You *want* to say it. You're *trying* to say it. Be out with it! I drew her towards me. My tongue still seemed tied, but just holding her and looking into her eyes was working magic, and I said, "Katherine, I care for you more than I could have believed possible, and more than my words can express. I do, you know."

Her face lit in such a smile, that I was well repaid for that supreme effort. "I daresay we've both had our rejections in the past, but that doesn't mean one should go through life expecting them."

"You're quite right," I agreed, and kissed her. Or rather, *we* kissed. And kissed. It was a kiss that I knew went through both of us. Didn't Shakespeare say something like eternity was in our eyes and lips? I knew what that meant now. Somewhere in another time, our mouths parted briefly, breathlessly.

"Flynn…" Katherine whispered, "you manage to say so much in so few words that a girl can be bowled over without thinking. We've known each other such a short while. I still can't help being afraid…"

"Don't be," I put in gently. We sat for a time just holding one another, listening to the storm.

We turned and watched as the candle guttered and went out. The rain drummed on the roof, and the wind sang to us through the trees as we two joined the night.

Chapter 12
MUCH ADO AND THE PIES THAT BIND

Katherine's alarm clock seemed to ring only moments later. At first I thought it must be a mistake, but when I rolled over to shut it off, the hands stood at six o'clock. Katherine stirred beside me in the dim light, her hair spread on the pillow, looking like some old master painting come to life. Outside, the storm had settled into a steady downpour. Though it was a blessing for us at the ship, there was much to do and we wouldn't be comfortable doing it in weather like this. The rain seemed to have a pulse to it, chanting lie abed, lie abed, lie abed— sweet torture, when one couldn't heed its siren song.

I gently smoothed the hair back from her face and kissed her sleeping eyes. "Katherine, the alarm's gone off, time to get up." I whispered.

She groaned. "Oh, can't we just stay in bed till spring?"

"Wicked temptress! Trying to lure a poor sailor to his doom?" I said.

She laughed. "Your bones will be discovered a hundred years hence with a great big smile across the skull."

I had to kiss her then. Nature would surely have taken its course once more had not less sublime urges intervened. "I've got to go over to the inn," I said regretfully. "Shall I wait the bath for you?"

"No, you go on, I'll be in presently." Her face took on an impish expression. "I might even join you." And she pulled the covers over her head.

What a girl! God, my heart was bursting with her. I put my mouth close to her covered face. "Does this mean you'll be our ship's cook?"

She uncovered just her eyes and peered at me. "Some people will do *anything* for a decent meal. Your clever campaign has succeeded. I'll follow you to the ends of the earth now. What a simple creature I am." Then her eyes grew serious. "But you must take very good care of me."

"The best care, the *very* best care, Katherine," I promised. Oh, it was hard to tear myself away, but I crept out of bed and quickly dressed. Katherine lay watching me, only her eyes showing. "I'll see you soon," I called softly and slipped outside. I darted across the lawn and through the kitchen garden. No one was about as I passed the kitchen and fetched down some fresh clothes. Soon I was gratefully showering under warm water, being careful to leave plenty for Katherine. When I emerged from the bath, she passed me going in, not the least bit shy. She gave me a quick kiss as she went by. I felt ready to take on the world and wrestle lions!

To add to the perfection of this morning, the Beastly One hadn't shown herself and we were left to ourselves in the kitchen. We lingered over a breakfast seasoned with kisses and were fighting the temptation to return to the cottage when Martin came in. He took one look at us, then rolled his eyes.

"Good morning, children," he said, making his way from the pub through the inner door. I was glad Mrs. B. was not there to spoil things with one of her snide remarks.

"Good morning, teacher," we chorused.

"And where is Mrs. B. this morning?" asked Katherine.

Martin put down his cup with a smile of pure pleasure. "Well, you know, I woke up in the middle of the night and saw her and Mr. O'Connell staggering in completely inebriated—just blotto! They were utterly sodden with rain. I believe the elegant Bentley had broken down and the poor things had to walk all the way back in the storm."

There was a moment of silence, and then we all burst into wild laughter. The picture Martin conjured up was so richly graphic. We were having such fun that I had to remind myself there was much to do, and I should be at it.

I heaved a sigh, "I'd best take myself down to the ship, and see what's afoot." I rose from the table and kissed Katherine's hair. "Don't you go away! I still half think I've dreamed you." I got my wellies and mac from the cupboard by the scullery door and made ready to brave the wet. A long kiss at the door made me begin to reconsider my purpose, but Katherine was equal to the test, and heartlessly shooed me out into the rain. I made my way to the lane and began walking briskly.

As I splashed through the puddles, it was hard to imagine there'd ever be another dry day, but we'd be wanting one soon. Dear old rain! Rain was helping save the *Bonnie Clyde*, and it was rain drumming on the roof that would always make me think of last night with Katherine. It seemed that all that had gone before in my life was only preparation for what was to come. Yet where would it have all gone had I not come here?

There came a rumble amidst the roaring hiss of the rain as a lorry came up from behind. I moved over to let it pass, dimly visible through the unending curtain of water. I forged on. Finding a bit of tree branch along the way, I began to use it as a walking stick. After a few minutes a second lorry went by, then a third. That struck me as unusual, for the only lorry that should be passing this way was Harris's. Discarding my walking stick, I picked up my pace to a steady jog and soon reached the moorage.

The three lorries stood side by side, with men busily carrying sacks and crates up the gangway onto the ship. The winch was also grinding away. Boris had several types of block and tackle rigged up in makeshift fashion to lower these goods into the forward hold, where scant days before had reposed only rotted canvas going to mould. Seeing Harris at the rail with his back to me, I went up the gangway and put my hand on his shoulder.

He jumped and whirled to face me. "Damn it, Flynn, don't creep up on me like that! We're trying to get these things loaded and the lorries out before raising any suspicion. It's unsettling."

"I didn't creep up at all," I said innocently, suppressing a smile.

He relaxed, "Perhaps we're all just a little edgy today with this storm, much as we need it."

"What's all this?" I asked, waving a hand at the loading.

"Provisions, me boy!" he answered. "All this lot is what we've been storing up for the voyage. We'll need plenty of water and food, plus a few other necessaries," and he held up a flask of aspect both familiar and welcome.

"Don't you think it a bit early for that?" I asked.

He raised his eyebrows and regarded the flask solemnly mouthing his pipe. "Well, perhaps I'll let it age a little more, say, until lunch."

I laughed, shaking my head, and turned to watch. Crates, boxes, sacks, and jugs were being lowered into the hold, many shrouded in glistening wet oilcloth. There seemed a great deal of it, enough it appeared for a world cruise. Were we expecting to reach Scotland by way of the Antipodes? Then again, it wouldn't hurt to have something left for our new beginnings up north. People *do* eat in Dumbarton! And winter is coming.

Harris looked round the ship and sighed. "When Bowman, Robert, and Edward stop fighting over who's captain, navigator, and cook, we may actually get somewhere with this."

"Well, Harris, I'm glad you brought that up. I don't know how to put this, but I've found a cook for the voyage, provided everyone agrees."

Harris's mouth dropped open. "You don't mean to say you've actually been telling anyone else what's going on here?" he cried.

"No, no, not at all. I've done nothing to endanger the project," I reassured him. "Each of us should keep to the jobs we know best. By bringing in a proper cook, we can be done with this squabbling. I get the impression that neither of those old salts knows much about cooking. Bowman should concentrate on being ship's master. As to Edward, he may be a fine navigator, but I doubt he could find his arse with both hands in the galley."

Harris regarded me rather coldly, and then turned away, as he weighed the danger of a possible security leak against our need for a cook. He looked back, fixing me with a keen eye. "Well, whoever you're thinking of as cook would have to keep very quiet about this. Everything will be happening here very suddenly, and we don't want any last-minute complications. I'd really like to know who this fellow is you've seen fit to include amongst us. Do you know for a fact that he can cook an edible meal for over twenty? I know we'll not be eating as well as we've been up at the inn, but I'm also not fond of salt pork and ship's biscuits. So, do you suppose you could indulge me by divulging the name of this mysterious person?"

"Well, yes, I could, but I won't right now," I said evasively, using his own conversational tactics. "I can tell you this, though, there's no reason whatever that you should be eating any poorer than you've been at the inn."

"And what the devil is that supposed to mean?" said Harris.

This time I quoted Bowman. "All things in good time," I said airily. "Come by the inn tonight and we'll discuss it further in private. Perhaps I can introduce you to the party in question." I'd found that employing Harrisisms and Bowmanisms often brought compliance—either that or instant rejection.

"Oh very well," he said grudgingly, "There's a good deal doing here with the loading, and plenty more to do after that. Well, off with you now." With a last measuring look at me, he moved off to lend a hand at the hatchway.

This seemed dismissal, so I made my way down the gangway and started back towards the inn. The contents of the lorries were being piled on the bank to speed unloading, and get the vehicles out of the vicinity as soon as possible. I started back up the lane, thinking of how quickly everything would be happening. I hoped I'd be equal to it all. This was a new and different life coming, for better or worse. I hoped it better for Katherine's sake, as well as my own. Lord knows I'd had enough from a demanding old battle-axe, but I had to thank her for Katherine.

The driving wind was blowing even harder as I approached the inn. I looked in the kitchen window and was gladdened to see Katherine bustling about. The next instant Mrs. Beastly came into view. She didn't appear to be enjoying one of her rare good-tempered mornings. Thursday was baking day, and storm clouds always hung low over the Beasley ménage on that day. My poor Katherine was trapped in there with that harridan. I watched until the Beastly One went through the inner door, before I darted inside. I was met by a rush of warm air laden with the heavenly odours of baking.

Katherine looked up from the breadboard, flushed and floured to the elbows, but apparently bearing up very well. "There you are," she smiled, "and looking half drowned, I must say."

I looked down at the muddy pool forming about my feet. "Perhaps I could be more presentable." I glanced at the inner door.

"She won't be back for a few minutes at least," she said with amusement. "She's seeing her *visitor* off, and this time there's no Bentley parked by her door."

I made a face. Disengaging herself from a great mound of dough, Katherine came closer. "I suppose we'll have to wait and see each other in the pub later, since things are going to be lively in here with Mrs. B. for some time yet. Oh, she just has to moan! This time she's moaning over such a late start to the baking. But don't worry, all her fussing means nothing to me. I'm far too happy."

"And me too," I said. "It's such a comfort to know I can just drop in and say hello to you when I feel like it. But I've plenty to occupy myself. Would you think me a coward for avoiding the Beastly?"

She laughed, "Not at all. I told her you're outside working. I seem to recall you promised to dress a duck for me?"

"Oh, there's a nice grisly finish to my morning," I groaned.

"Well, it could be worse. It could be Purdy." She quipped.

I put on a snarl. "I wouldn't mind plucking and gutting Purdy in the least. *Or* O'Connell!"

She laughed. "Isn't he a savage creature?"

"You don't know the half of it, my dear," I said. "Now where's that wretched duck?"

"Oh, you can't do it in here. You could use the scullery, but Mrs. B. would be over your shoulder all the while. I hung it in the shed. You can do the deed out there and not worry over the mess." With a quick look at the inner door, she put her face up for a kiss, and I wasn't slow to oblige. Now I felt equal to any bloody duck. Show me a bushel of 'em!

Warmed by this, I went off to the shed. Some time after, I presented myself at the kitchen door with the naked fowl in hand, having first looked to be sure the landlady was out of the room.

"Oh that's splendid," said Katherine. "Men are good for something after all!"

"What shall I do with it now?" I asked.

"Put in under Mrs. B.'s pillow," she grinned. "Oh, give it here, I'll see to it."

I handed it over, "I'll see you tonight?"

"Tonight." She kissed me quickly and hurried into the pantry.

As there was some time yet before my lunch, I thought I'd see how the garden was faring with all this wet weather and forced myself back out the door. Pushing against the wind and lashing rain, I made my way around the property finding nothing worse than some lesser-fallen branches and flattened perennials. The pond was doing its best simulation of High Seas on the Broad Atlantic, with the surface a veritable maelstrom as the rain beat down on it. The birds were huddled amongst the shrubbery. Coming closer, I noticed the intended rockery had migrated downhill in the storm, including all the stones I'd carried up the small slope. The whole lot had formed quite a mountain at the edge of the pond. There was the start of Mrs. Beastly's Great Wall. I felt much easier abandoning this project. Whoever took it up after me wouldn't have so much to do.

I'd earned my lunch by now. The pub had just opened, and I had myself some soup and bread—not new bread, worse luck—it was too early. Afterwards, I stood by the fire and got myself thoroughly dried and warmed. Katherine was a prisoner in the kitchen, whence issued the muffled sounds of Mrs. Beastly in full cry. I decided to nip back down to the ship and make myself useful. Back into the rain I went.

My timing was near perfect. There were just a few things left to load. Boris showed me the fresh vegetables and eggs, generously donated by a farmer friend of Harris's. These were the most perishable goods, to be stowed in the galley for ready access, along with sacks upon sacks of potatoes and onions. The boys would be stout fellows by the end of this voyage.

I set to work and hauled in potatoes, onions, and assorted vegetables. Most of them went into the forward hold, which I was pleased to see was well stocked, scrubbed clean, and properly shipshape. When I had a proper look at the galley, I immediately felt uncomfortable. It needed work to have it fully ready for operation. It seemed that in general one could account for everything needed: pots, pans, cutlery, mugs, dishes, and such, some still in boxes. I hoped that Katherine wouldn't find it too daunting a task. It seemed rather grubby.

I went up on deck and found Boris ready to close up the hold for the day. He shouted something to me from his position on the opposite side of the hatch, but I couldn't make out a word of it because of the wind and rain. Finally, I realized it was about a load of ice that was to come in at the last. Evidently a quantity of fresh meat was in the offing. This was welcome news, for the green boys from Starke's must be forged into working seamen. We'd all be needing our strength. I thought how lucky I'd been with the rationing going on. I almost felt guilty because of the rationing coupons I'd saved. You'd never guess all the rationing everywhere with what was in stock here and at the inn.

Boris looked in and thanked me for coming back to make sure there was enough help. I thought I'd put in a fair day's work and was preparing to leave, when I encountered Robert coming out of the chart room with mop and bucket in hand.

"Robert, I keep bumping into you with no time to talk," I said apologetically.

"Damn talking, Flynn. We'll have plenty of time for talk later. Right now I have all this rubbish to deal with. Just look at this!" He set down his bucket and produced a list which he waved before me. "I can't do all these bloody things in a few hours. And I rather think that my skills should put me above some of the jobs on this list. What am I, no more than a slavey, for God's sake? I'm a damned valuable crew member!"

I had a look at the list, which did in fact mention some rather disagreeable custodial tasks. I was heartened to see that putting a good finish to the galley was included. "Well, mate, we're not in the Royal Navy anymore," I pointed out. "After all, someone must take on these jobs. We're all doing what we must."

Robert continued to grumble over the offensive list.

"Complaining won't get the jobs done," I put in cheerfully. "Time to put your shoulder to the wheel, old boy!"

Robert sniffed. "Oh indeed? And what wheel are you looking to put your shoulder to just now?"

I replied, "There are a few things I'm seeing to elsewhere that should make this voyage a little more pleasant."

"Pleasant?" Robert cried, slapping the paper. "Well I'll just get back to my *pleasant* chores. I feel like a bloody scullery maid! A bloody scullery maid I'll tell you! Can you fancy that?"

Behind Robert, Edward was sitting at ease looking over a map, with his feet propped up on the chart table. Robert looked at the old man peevishly. "Here, what are you doing?" he demanded.

Edward glanced up at him impassively. "Thinking, young man, thinking. Someone has to," he said and returned to his map. Robert gave me a look.

I shifted uncomfortably. "Well, I'm sorry. I'll talk to you later. Must be off."

"Aye, you must be," Robert muttered sarcastically.

"Now see here, I've been doing my part here, plus at the inn," I protested. "Why, I've even got us a cook!"

He seemed unimpressed. "Oh, that was hard work I'll wager."

"As a matter of fact…" I began stiffly. Robert was studying my expression suspiciously, unable to fathom what I was trying to conceal. Obviously a hint of guilt was showing.

"Yes?" he prompted.

"But now that you mention it," I gulped, "I suppose I could help you put in some time in the galley."

Boris was waiting to close up the hold for the day, and was growing impatient with us. He finally gave over trying to shout above the roar and closed up the hold. Giving us a wave, he moved off after making certain everything was secure.

I went down into the galley. Behind a basket of well-watered celery, I made a discovery that might not sit well with our new cook. Edward had seen to it that tradition was served by the presence of some ominous-looking casks of pickled fish and salt pork. There was also a box of one of his personal favourites: that malodorous dried fish known as Bombay duck. Anyone who's lived through the stench of this particular delicacy during its preparation, has my heartfelt sympathy. There are certain foods I regard as a dare, this being among them. I made a note to warn Katherine.

Three hours later, feeling a lot less guilty but a lot more tired, I was striding through the rain back to the inn, having done penance by playing galley slave. I'd made a visible difference. Perhaps now Katherine wouldn't be utterly taken aback by the contrast between the well-ordered, spacious Beasley kitchen and the cramped little chamber the ship's cook would command. Between the gardening and helping out down at the ship, I was now fitter than I had been for some time. It had been a long while since the soup and bread of lunchtime.

When I arrived back at the inn, a few hardy souls had braved the wind and rain to come to the warm pub. With the heavenly scent of

Baking Day in the air, tea was uppermost in their thoughts. I took off my mac and cautiously peeked through the kitchen door. Happily, the Beastly One was not in evidence. Katherine, looking beautiful but wilted, glanced over and asked where I'd been.

"Oh, down at the ship for the second time today," I sighed feeling wrung out. "Can we meet later? I've arrangements to make, and I'm thinking of a good way to introduce you to the ship and crew. You've met most of them, but I haven't told them who I had in mind."

She smiled. "Mr. Flynn, I place myself in your hands," she said softly. That stirred up such an interesting train of thoughts, that only a cry of Katherine! from the scullery saved me from attempting some indiscretion on the spot. I gave her a yearning wave and retired back into the pub in search of sustenance. Suddenly, I discovered the delicious baking odours were making me quite ravenous.

Behind the bar Martin was in rare form, regaling a village couple with tales that sounded entirely pointless to me, but had them roaring with laughter. Martin's sense of humour wasn't for the masses, but he could talk two people to death with ease, but I may have been under-estimating him. When he saw me, he sidled off from his listeners, who looked grateful for this, and jovially waved me over. I went up to the bar, and he drew me a pint.

"What do you say to a meat pie then?" Martin asked.

"What do I say? Lie still and think of England. I'm so hungry I could make short work of a dozen."

"You're in luck. We've quite a few just out of the oven," he chuckled and set a platter of warm pies before me. "They're Katherine's pies too, not Mrs. Beasley's. I know that makes a difference to you," he winked.

They were things of beauty, those pies, and smelt divinely of well-cooked meat and potato. One almost hated to destroy them by vulgar ingestion. Mind you, I said *almost*. I picked one up and admired it as Martin looked on.

"Katherine's outdone herself this time," I said with a measure of pride. She was *my* Katherine after all, which somehow made these pies flesh of my flesh. With that thought in mind, I hastened the family re-union with a succulent mouthful. Maybe I was just peckish and love-struck, but I swear that little pie was the most exquisite thing I'd ever tasted. The meat was tender and delicately spiced, with just enough potatoes and vegetables, all wrapped in the most butter-flaky crust. Martin laughed at my ecstatic expression.

"Martin," I said solemnly, "this is food of the Gods. Have you tasted these pies?"

He blinked at me in the most curious fashion. "No, their aroma was quite enough treat for me," he chortled.

I couldn't concern myself with his vagaries; there were pies to be eaten! Soon my mind began ticking. No mortal could resist these pies. Therefore, no ship's company could resist the cook who'd baked these pies once they'd tried them. Armed with this platter, I could wave aside any and all resistance to Katherine's appointment as cook. I fixed Martin with a look.

"Martin, I'll give you ten bob for the lot," I said. For some reason that sent him into gales of laughter.

"Done!" he said, wiping his eyes, "and I'll throw in a pot of tea to help wash them down."

"What on earth is so funny?" I asked as I handed over the payment.

"I'll tell you later," he replied, still tucked over quivering with merriment.

"Oh, never mind," I snorted. Not being in the mood for anymore humour, I took my pies and my pint off to a table near the fire.

Without delay I set about the absorption of this delicious meal. After three pies, I'd had my fill, but it was very tempting to go on. I reminded myself that I must leave enough for my shipmates and carefully counted the remainder. There were thirteen yet, a full baker's dozen. That should be enough to win over the most recalcitrant among them. Sipping at the last of my pint, I breathed a long sigh of contentment and lit my pipe. I sat gazing out the window. After a time I realised the rain had slackened to a light drizzle. With little daylight remaining, this would be an opportunity to have another look about the garden I'd soon be abandoning.

Groaning, I damped my pipe and rose. Sounds issued from the kitchen indicated that it would be unwise to enter there, so I carried the plate of pies up to my room and carefully placed it on the highest shelf, laying a sheet of newspaper over it. Thursday was baking day, and legendary amongst the local populace. The lighter rainfall had encouraged others to come out, so more tables were occupied now. For years the locals had been coming to the village to buy buns, pies, and pastries. Some would stay to have tea or a full meal, but a good half of the oven's fruit was for home consumption. This had gone on long before Katherine's arrival. The enterprising Mrs. Beastly found her new helper so capable she soon entrusted her with upholding the kitchen's reputation by her own efforts. Well, the old slave driver would soon be back to doing her own cooking! Katherine deserved better. And she certainly deserved better than the bedraggled figure I cut at this moment. I made my way upstairs and found fresh clothes, casting a solicitous eye over the pies in their nest. They had work to do, after all. I went off for my bath.

A little later, clean and tidy, I was ready to join the living once more. A small but contented-looking dinner crowd were enjoying their meals, among them Harris and Bowman. Katherine passed me on her way back to the kitchen, beaming. I almost followed, but I knew that my two shipmates wished a word with me. I approached and was hailed. I joined them at their table, noting that they were dining upon mere steak-and-kidney pudding. I had a surprise treat for them! A newspaper-wrapped bundle sat by, waiting to be taken back to the others still on the ship. Harris seized the opportunity to speak up first. He launched into the latest report.

"Well, Flynn, we're still in the running. We've almost everything but the remaining sails on board now. I've been getting reports from Brian, but it's still hard to say where we stand. I'd hazard that we've an even chance of having our full suit of sails before we go. If it's not all ready, we'll have to take what is. The rain hasn't finished yet, but once it has, there's at least one tug standing by to commence operations when the weather turns. We'll want you early tomorrow morning, right?"

"Right!" I agreed.

Bowman reached across and seized my arm in a surprisingly strong grasp. "What's all this about you hiring on a cook?" he snapped. "Ned and I can see to the mess."

I looked at him earnestly. "Surely, Mr. Bowman, it's beneath a captain's dignity to be messing about amongst the pots and pans. You'll want your strength for command. Edward is the most valuable to us as navigator and I'd sooner see him pilot us clear of dangerous waters. I've heard some dark tales of his cooking."

Harris rolled his eyes. They'd obviously been through this many times before. Bowman snorted and returned to his meal. I excused myself and dashed upstairs, laying hold of the newspaper-wrapped bundle of pies still on the platter. I carried it back to the table in triumph.

"What's all this?" Bowman growled, eyeing the pies suspiciously.

"These were baked by my cook. I swear to you that Mrs. Beasley had no hand in them. Have a taste!" I set one on Bowman's plate. He scowled at it.

Harris, however, was never coy where food was concerned. He quickly had his teeth into a sample of his own. His eyes closed in bliss as he chewed, and only his face told the story as the pie vanished in a flash to be swiftly followed by another. To Harris, good food was almost a religious experience. He was reaching for a third when Bowman grudgingly took a nibble at his.

His eyes lit up at once at the taste, and he then took a whole mouthful. He chewed it well and long to extract the most enjoyment out of it. He swallowed it, then licked his chops and gazed at the remainder of the pie almost fondly. I felt a thrill of paternal affection myself. Our little pies...

"Mr. Flynn," said Bowman at last, "that's the finest thing ever I've tasted since my Meg passed on. Who wouldn't want such fine food for his crew? But we can't afford to pay a cook."

I smiled at that. "Captain Bowman, this cook will work for passage alone." Bowman and Harris exchanged glances. Noting the dwindling pie population, I hastily pulled the platter out of their reach. Still chewing, they followed its course with longing eyes. I needed the rest as ammunition for Boris, Edward, and Robert.

"Right," Bowman said, "I think we can accommodate this cook of yers. Bring him down to the ship later tonight and we'll have a look at him. I'll be happy to take on anyone who can make such food as this."

I thought it prudent for now not to correct his assumption that the cook was a man. Boris, Edward, and Robert must become converts by taste alone. Then I'd have their support in the debate that would surely ensue about having females on the ship. Having made a satisfactory end to this subject for the time being, we now proceeded to go over our speculations and plans for the coming days.

Harris grumbled over Edward monopolising the charts. "We'll want a look at those, you know. Unless our Ned stops being such a damned stickler over protocol with those charts, I'm going to roll them up and feed them to him, and I don't care which end I go at."

"Now, steady on, Harris, he knows exactly what he's about," Bowman said evenly.

"Oh aye? Then why are you two always fighting over details?" cried Harris.

Bowman fell back on his favourite maxim. "All things in good time."

"Bloody hell!" Harris laughed. "You've said that once too often, Uncle Billy." He rose and strode off, waving goodbye over his shoulder.

Going out the door, he slammed it so vigorously that I thought it would come off its hinges.

Almost immediately we could hear the voice of Mrs. Beastly. "Will you please not slam that door! You'll pay if it's got to be mended again. I'll have the police on you!"

Harris gave forth a lion-like roar. "Bring on your Bobbies, I'll have 'em for supper! I'm a slammer, I am, as my dad was before me!" and he laughed fiendishly. Not quite the approach I would have taken. I heard the landlady's own door slam as she retreated inside, probably worried that there was a lunatic at large.

Bowman got to his feet, chuckling. There were eight pies remaining. I parcelled up seven of them in newspaper. I couldn't let them *all* go! I added the packet to the other bundle as samples for the others.

"Please make sure that the others get these, and mind that Harris doesn't get his great paws on them," I cautioned Bowman.

"No fear o' that," Bowman said stolidly, and set out with his precious burden.

I sat looking wistfully at the last pie. I was well in the toils of serious temptation, when I glanced up to see Katherine approaching. She sat down across from me and looked at the pie, all alone on that big platter.

She smiled. "I understand my pies have made quite a hit."

"Haven't they just?" I laughed. "The general opinion seems to be that they're the best thing on the planet. Can you really make them again? And what was in them? Some kind of poultry, wasn't it? Or maybe rabbit?"

She turned her head and twinkled at me. Then I knew. I gasped. "The duck!" I cried in horror.

Now, I've always liked duck. The only thing that put me off about this particular duck was the fact that Purdy had a romp with it and mauled it to death before it was cooked and served up. I found the idea distasteful, shall we say?

"A duck's a duck," said Katherine. "Forgive me?"

I had to grin. "All right, a duck's a duck...and I'm a goose for ever making a fuss over it." It wasn't like conditions during the war, when some soldiers had eaten a dog or worse because there was no meat or rations. All supply lines had been cut off, while they tried to hold a beachhead until support could reach them. And here I was squeamish about a duck caught by a cat. They would have eaten the cat too and been glad of it.

I looked at Katherine. "I love your duck pies. I'd eat them every-day, even if they were all brought in by the cat."

The smile she gave me was worth eating *worm* pies. My heart did a two-step. "I'm off at ten," she said.

"That's perfect. We'll go down to the ship and make your ap-pointment official. Bowman has already sworn to take on the cook who baked those pies. Harris agrees, and everyone else is being *pied* into submission. I suppose we really owe Purdy a vote of thanks."

She looked at me askance and rose from the table. "Well, I'll leave *you* to deliver it to him, then. I've work to do."

I stared at the last pie. Perhaps I should get the thing bronzed.

Taking the pie into the kitchen, I tucked it into the larder. I went and busied myself cleaning the mud from my wellies. I pottered about in my room, tucking various items into my duffel. It occurred to me that I might need to retrieve my soiled clothes from the laundry basket if I wanted them along on short notice. I reached into the back of a drawer and pulled out a photo of the woman I was courting before I sailed off years before. She looked lovely in her nurse's uniform. I took that along with a bundle of letters tied in a ribbon and hurried down-stairs into the empty pub. The top shelf behind the bar had a multitude of photos of various people from years before. I carefully took her pic-ture and placed it with the others, then carefully pushed it back so that no one would notice something new had been added. I then rushed over to the fireplace, removed the ribbon that bound the letters I'd read many times, and watched the hot coals turn them to flames. With a final glance at the photo, which I couldn't bring myself to burn, I re-trieved my clothes from the hamper and dashed upstairs. At last the longed-for hour struck, and I came downstairs, full of anticipation.

Katherine was waiting. She'd discarded her apron and was putting on her cape. She waved happily when she saw me. I ran to the kitchen, retrieving the lone pie which I carefully slid into the pocket of my mac. We set off into the night, which wore an inky darkness under its blanket of water-heavy clouds. I'd brought my torch so we'd not be tumbling into any ditches or puddles along the way. A chill wind was blowing up, and Katherine shivered and drew on her hood. I put my arm around her as we walked along the lane, picking our way amongst the puddles and streams. As we walked, we talked of different things, mostly of the past and our dreams for the future.

As we passed the churchyard, its old gravestones looked like ghostly aberrations in the darkness.

Katherine told me of her marriage, which had lasted one short month. Her husband had been a casualty early in the war. Looking back now, she thought they'd married too young.

"He was a nice boy," she sighed, "but being a nice boy doesn't mean that life will be kind. I hardly even knew him. It seems a hundred years ago, another lifetime. Since then, I've met so many men who were anything but nice boys, the kind who don't care a bit for what's inside a girl's head, only what's inside her knickers." She squeezed my hand. "But don't think for a minute that I ever classed you with that lot. You're not just a nice boy, you're a good man, and something more beside. You're just different from anyone else I've ever met."

I'm sure I was blushing by now, but the dark mercifully hid it from her. I didn't quite know what to say, so I stopped and gave her as eloquent a kiss as I could muster. It must have spoken volumes, for the conversation went on for some time, and Katherine met me word for word! We were oblivious to all else for some time. At last we parted lips, aware that we couldn't simply stand kissing all night on a muddy road with the rain threatening, though it seemed a splendid idea. We had the future to think of, and we had to get to the ship if we *were* to have a future together. We continued on at a brisker pace.

When we reached the *Bonnie Clyde*, I helped her up the awkward gangway. Although Katherine said she'd never been on a full-sized sailing ship before, she seemed quite at home on the uneven boards of the ramp and didn't need help at all. I was glad to find her so agile, for I'd only thought of her as graceful and feminine. No hothouse rose, she! Well, she'd be using that agility soon enough.

As we came on board, the hatchway was immediately thrown open, and there came a murmur of voices from below. I could see Harris's looming silhouette against the lights below. "Who's there?" said a great booming voice. I trained my torch's beam on his face.

"Flynn here," I responded crisply, "bringing our cook aboard for inspection, sir. Are all hands present?"

"All of us, and we've eaten all the pies. Did you bring more?"

"Just the baker," I laughed, pulling Katherine forward.

Harris craned his neck, squinting at the muffled figure curiously. Seeing this, Katherine threw back her hood exposing her long hair and smiling face. Harris gasped in astonishment, and then grimaced, shaking his head.

"Well, I'll be damned," he said.

"Perhaps," I taunted. "But not if you behave yourself. Anyway, we're not here to discuss the state of your wicked soul. Now be a good fellow and stand aside so we can come below and get down to business."

Harris looked uneasy and a bit worried. He took a couple of steps farther up the ladderway and slid the hatch shut behind him. "I should warn you, there's a bit of a dust-up, or rather a full-scale war going on down there. Uncle Billy, Boris, Edward, your friend Robert...they're all daft and talking complete bollocks."

"Oh? The continuing debate over who does what?" I asked.

Harris nodded, "They'd had their sausage rolls, and then Uncle Billy brought out the pies. We were doing well till the pies ran out," he said. "They seemed to drift into the same old arguments. More pies would be a great help just now." He fixed a soulful gaze on Katherine, who giggled.

I took her hand. "Here, let's go below." I laughed, "If there's an all-out war, we certainly wouldn't want to miss any of the action."

He raised his eyebrows. "Oh yes, you would. It's no place for a lady."

"Nonsense," I cried, "lead on, MacDuff!" We descended the ladderway into the cabin, and there sat the combatants at the chart table, conducting their own on-board storm. Bowman and Edward were wrangling over the course, Boris was holding forth about the rigging but had lapsed into Russian, and Robert directed advice at all three and was ignored by all.

"But there are the currents and winds to consider, man," Bowman shouted. Edward was opening his mouth to respond when he spied Katherine. His mouth remained open. Bowman, Boris, and Robert looked up. A hush fell over the cabin.

I put on a bold face. "Good evening, me hearties," I said in my best hail-fellow-well-met manner, "I would like to introduce our cook."

A stunned silence prevailed. I cleared my throat. "She baked the pies," I added.

Robert was the first to break the shocked hush. He came forward with a delighted smile, holding out his hand. "Welcome aboard, Madam Cook. You're a brave creature." And he shook her hand warmly. Not to be outdone in courtesy, Boris made a deep bow and delivered a flowery speech in English and Russian. Katherine nodded and curtseyed, with a mischievous sidelong glance to me.

Bowman and Edward wore identical glowers. They were seamen of the old school and plainly rejected outright the idea of having a woman on board. "That's no ship's cook," growled Bowman.

Now Katherine showed what she was made of. She drew herself up, and planted her hands on her hips. "Is that so? I can serve up a banquet out of a *real* kitchen ashore, but when it comes to your nasty little galley, you'd rather live on tinned beans than let a woman taint the premises, coming on board to bring bad luck with whatever else she's supposed to bring! Ha! Of course, you have no objection to us working in factories and turning out the guns you lot have used to blow each other up. You're more than glad to have us nursing your wounded, but when it comes to some simple cooking for a crew of orphans and raggedy old codgers, oh no, a woman *couldn't* do that!"

"And just who d'ye think ye're calling *old codgers?*" Bowman cried. "I have legitimate and *serious* objections to having any woman on board this ship wi' me," he declared, his face flushing a deeper crimson by the moment.

Katherine faced him squarely. "That's easily settled," she said reasonably. "We could go up on deck and I could push you over the side. Then we *wouldn't* be on the same ship together."

That set us all to laughing, and Bowman gave a glare all round. "Just what I need, another quarrelsome mick like Ned," he ranted. I couldn't tell by Edward's expression what he was thinking, but his lips were getting ready to form some words.

I hastened to speak up. "Now see here, everyone, let's be practical about this. Of course it flies in the face of old-fashion tradition to have a female on board. Neither is it customary to have sails sewn from circus tents in a tailor's shop or to make up a crew with green boys who've never been to sea before. We must make do if we're to do well, isn't that what this is all about? Katherine's a great cook and tough as nails into the bargain, as you can well see. She wants passage to Dumbarton. Don't you think we're all best served by having her along?" I was looking at Bowman as I said this, and I could see his common sense wrestling with his stubborn nature. Edward looked thoughtful.

I had a thought, and quietly retrieved the last pie from my pocket, passing it to Katherine. She drew over near Bowman, and placed it before him with a dazzling smile, folding back the paper to expose it in all its nicely browned glory.

"I hope you'll forgive me for being sharp," she said gently. "It's me Irish blood."

He stared at her, then a smile stirred in his whiskers, and he laughed heartily. Thank goodness! The day was won. To show his good will, he held up the pie as if toasting her and took a bite of it, an action witnessed with naked envy on the part of us less fortunate.

He swallowed, then took a sip from a bottle of stout and wiped his mouth with his pocket-handkerchief. "Young lady, if everything ye cook is as good as this, ye're sent from heaven. I did say I'd take on the cook who'd baked these pies. Well, ye've made me eat my words and like it too." He had another bite. "I can't quite place the meat in it—it's not rabbit, I think." He took a further mouthful and chewed thoughtfully.

I had a sudden premonition of doom, though I couldn't think why. Duck is a great delicacy, and no one but Katherine and I knew how that duck died. I tried to signal Katherine, but it was too late.

"Why, it's no mystery Captain Bowman," she piped up blithely. "It's duck."

I thought for a moment that Bowman was going to choke. He gagged and sputtered as if poisoned.

Harris turned to me in horror. "Of course you didn't know. He hates duck, always has." Bowman seemed ready to spit the now-loathsome bite of duck out across the table, but he managed to swallow it down, followed by a long draught of stout. He sat gasping for some time, glaring at Katherine, who returned his gaze with honest concern.

Finally, Bowman's expression softened and colour returned to his face. "I never fancied duck," he said gruffly, "but it was rare fine eating till I found out what it was. So there's no harm done. After this Mistress Cook, don't tell me what's in my grub. If it's good, I'll eat it. Just no duck!" he put out his gnarled hand for her to shake. She took it gladly, and there was general rejoicing. Even Edward gave her a grumbling salute.

Once the laughter and congratulations died down, Katherine looked round and squared her shoulders. "Well, let's see this galley of yours. I want to know what sort of disaster I'll be contending with."

"The galley's shipshape and Bristol fashion," retorted Bowman, "You'll find everything you need and more."

I stepped into the breach and took her arm. "Here, I'll give you the grand tour." Glad to have her away from Bowman before more trouble could brew up, I led her to the galley and proceeded to light the lamps. I felt confident of her approval, for I'd made a tidy job of it.

She first looked over the aged stove and gave a sigh. "I suppose it could be worse. At least it seems fairly clean." I beamed proudly. I had done well. Then she opened the oven door and peered inside. This time the sigh was much deeper. "Good God, someone's been baking mud-pies in here! Well, this will want a thorough scrubbing out. A bit of blacking wouldn't hurt, either."

My assurance evaporated as she worked her way around the galley, sometimes exclaiming to herself at what she found. At least I'd hidden the Bombay duck. She could find no spices of any sort and pointed out other omissions that had escaped our mere male attention. I brought her the lists of provisions already on board. Gazing unbelievingly at these smudged and rumpled scraps of paper, she pulled a small scribbling book from her bag and set to work. Once she'd made up a single legible list, she went over it with me, ticking off the items as she read them to me and I nodded agreement. I remembered a few things she hadn't found on our lists, and she added them on. She frowned over the finished inventory and appeared to be calculating.

This was all a bit unsettling. "It's only for about a week, at most," I ventured.

She made no comment, but turned to a fresh page and began writing. When she'd finished, she tore off the page and handed it to me. "Here's a new list. I know time is short, but see if you can have some of this brought in. We'll be wanting proper meals three times a day for twenty growing boys and six grown men, though I'm sure Harris counts as two or three and I've been known to have the odd bite myself as well. Do be sure of getting the tinned milk and plenty of sultanas. I can bring some herbs from the inn." She looked at me quizzically. "About a week? You really can't be more exact about it?"

I shook my head. "There are a great many factors involved."

"And three meals a day! Hmm! I've only been doing two on my hardest days back at the inn. This should prove to be quite a challenge." She was smiling as she said this, so I took heart. She wasn't bothered and she looked ready for the task. I was proud of her. We returned to the chart room, and Bowman looked at me enquiringly.

"Well, the galley might need a bit of work yet," I said cautiously.

"And ye're just the lad for the job, Mr. Flynn," he replied cheerfully. "The best of luck to ye." He tipped his cap with a hint of mockery. Katherine smiled.

I saluted, "Aye, aye, sir," I said chagrined.

Katherine said she'd be down to help the next day as early as she could manage. Since our departure depended upon the weather, we couldn't be sure of when we'd sail. It wouldn't serve to have her go missing too soon, and raise any questions at the inn. With the baking behind her, she'd have a bit of time in the morning, barring any Beasley emergencies. She bade the company a pleasant good night, and we made our way up the ladder and down the precarious gangway off the ship.

We'd only taken a few steps along the bank when Harris leaned over the side and cried, "Flynn!"

I looked round with a sigh. "What now?" I called back.

He shook clasped hands over his head. "Well done, the pair of you," he boomed, "Bloody well done!" And with a wave, he turned and vanished below.

Katherine and I laughed, and I swung her in my arms, while the cold wind surged about us. I'd felt a drop or two of rain, so we hurried on.

She shook back her hair and took great breaths of the brisk sea air. "It's so refreshing to be out in the wind after that smoky pub. I can't tell you how awful it is to be in there with everyone puffing away at pipes and cigarettes. It makes me feel quite ill sometimes. The place smells like an ashtray, and my clothes and hair are full of it as well."

It hadn't occurred to me until that moment that I'd never seen her have a cigarette. "Well, everyone seems to smoke," I said uncomfortably.

She poked at the pocket where my pipe lay. "Don't they, then?"

I stopped for a moment, and then I pulled out the pipe. Upon reflection, I realised that I chewed on the thing more than I ever lit it. It was a creature comfort, but not a necessity of life. Now my Katherine, *there* was a necessity of life. "I had no idea you found it so unpleasant," I mumbled.

"Well, after all, it's something I suppose I'll just have to live with on this voyage like I do everyday at the inn as well," she sighed. "I didn't like to mention it."

I handed her the torch, and took out my tobacco pouch. I emptied the contents onto the road, wincing at the terrible waste of it. Then I took the pipe and threw it into the darkness as far as I could. I turned to her. "Well, you'll not be having that from me again." I hoped it was true.

"That's it? You've chucked it just like that?" she exclaimed.

"As of now, as in I quit!" I declared with conviction. "I was never terribly attached to it and this is a very reasonable time to give it up."

She put her arms round my neck and gave me such a sweet kiss that I knew it would be well worth the effort. "You *are* a good man, Flynn. And whenever the craving for a smoke should strike you while I'm nearby, you're to come and have a kiss instead. Not that you need wait till you want a pipe!" she laughed.

I held her face between my hands. "Then you must never be too far away," I whispered, and staved off Demon Tobacco with another kiss. Then we hurried back to the inn.

As we came up the drive, we could make out Headmaster O'Connell just exiting the landlady's door. He was easy to see in the glow of the little light above the door. He looked both ways, straightened his coat, smoothing back his thin hair, put on his hat, and strode over to the sleek Bentley. I indicated to Katherine that I was going to give him a little fright and we giggled like naughty children. I couldn't help feeling a bit devilish. Once he'd got into the car, I stepped up and rapped as hard as I could at the window. He started violently and straightened in his seat, staring about in every direction like a gun dog whose quarry has just flown up in his face. Seeing me, he wound the window down partway.

"Wha...what...what do you want?" he asked nervously.

"I was just saying good night, Mr. O'Connell, sorry to have troubled you." We strolled on by in a casual fashion, hearing him mutter something unintelligible as he wound the window back up.

A moment later we heard the roar of his engine starting up. We turned to watch the big car set off at high speed up the road. Our eyes met and we both sputtered, holding on to one another as we laughed.

"Flynn, you're a heartless dog, frightening that poor old stinker. Did you see the look on his face! It was as good as a play. But what will you do for an encore?" she gasped.

"Oh, I don't know...shout out fire during one of their little trysts," I suggested.

She was seized by another fit of laughter. "Come on," she said, trying to compose herself, "let's get round the back before the Beastly one hears us." It was sound advice, and just to spur us on, scattered raindrops started pattering down.

When we reached her cottage door, she turned breathlessly and smiled up at me. "It's been a lovely evening. I really enjoyed meeting everyone."

"Thank you," I grinned. "I never thought anyone could tame Bowman, but you played him like a harp, or perhaps a hoarse old bagpipe."

"It was your plan," she said modestly. "He's really a dear old duck. Oh my, perhaps another word would've been better." She giggled.

"The others couldn't believe their ears when you suggested pushing him over the side. They loved it! You certainly have them all on your side," I said. "I take my hat off to you."

"If you do, you'll get your head wet," she pointed out, stroking the side of my hair. She gave me a short kiss and sighed. "I hate to say this, but it's the attic for you, my man. We both need sleep and tomorrow's going to be very busy. Do you mind awfully?"

She was quite right, and I knew I'd be better with a full night's rest. I needed it, but there is such a thing as too much common sense! I would have thrown it away in an instant but for her blasted common sense. I gave her a quick kiss in return. "Thank you for being so wonderful," I whispered, then dashed off through the rain to my own bed.

Chapter 13
ANCHORS, SAILS, AND MORE SURPRISES

I awoke to the busy chatter of the waterfowl in the rain and stretched luxuriously. I'd slept like a top and felt ready to take on the world, Mrs. Beastly included. Cheerful morning sounds and savoury breakfast smells filtered up from the downstairs kitchen where Katherine and Martin were chatting as they began their day. I lay a little longer hugging my pillow and thinking of Katherine before I forced myself out of bed and shivered into my clothes. It was a chilly one today! Glancing outside, I saw that the smoke from the morning fires was weighed down by the cold air. It rose only a few feet above the rooftops while the rain beat the smoke plumes apart.

Hustling downstairs, I had a quick wash. When I came out into the corridor, I bumped into Katherine and bade her good morning with a kiss. "I hope you slept as well as I did, even though I missed you every minute," I said, holding her tightly.

She smiled playfully and punched my arm. "Hush, I think I hear the Beasley. Come and have some breakfast."

We went into the kitchen where Martin was at table reading his paper. I sipped my tea while Katherine bustled about setting out a nice meal for me. There came the rumble of a heavy vehicle and I looked out, wondering why the victualler would be coming again so soon. Just passing the drive on its way down towards our moorage was a large lorry with a crane mounted on its bed, towing a flat trailer freighted with a big canvas-covered cube.

This alone was potential cause for alarm, and then it suddenly dawned on me that it wasn't raining anymore. I quickly opened the door and had a good look from the step. Oh, it was dark and cloudy, but the rain had stopped. I knew there were government personnel standing by with a tug for the first hint of a dry day. I snapped up my coat from the hook and told Katherine to hold breakfast as I'd be back shortly. I was ready to dash straight out, when I had the bad luck to be spotted by Mrs. Beastly. She hailed me.

"Just a moment, Mr. Flynn, I've got your list for today."

I stopped in my tracks and turned round, "Could it wait for a little while, Mrs. Beasley? I was just going for a short run. I'll be back in half a tick."

"A run?" she said, puzzled. "With breakfast on the table? How odd."

"Yes," I babbled, "I like to let it cool, you see." I began running in place. "Very stimulating to the appetite and digestion, having a run before breakfast. Do have a look at all the work I've done on your new wall. I've carried all the rocks down from the rockery."

As she turned to look, I seized the opportunity to escape. Flinging my scarf about my neck, I dashed out the door with a last look back at Katherine. I made for the bottom of the garden, swampy though it was, and pelted down the footpath. If only I could have overtaken that lorry! I shivered despite my exertions. It was a cold world today, even for a long-distance runner. I took my watch cap from my pocket and pulled it over my ears as I went.

Panting and gasping, I came in sight of the *Bonnie Clyde*. The crane was in operation, lowering the great shrouded crate down into the main hatchway. I relaxed and slackened my pace as I saw that this was being done under Boris's supervision. The others were paying little attention to it. It seemed that I'd been alarmed over nothing.

Then to my horror, I saw the crane operator's mate attach the hook to one of the ship's anchors that was secured to the bow. Bowman set up an exceedingly loud and outraged protest at sight of this. The worker in attendance on board, a laconic fellow in a battered trilby hat, tried to reassure him.

"Shouldn't go to the bottom, guvnor. It'll make a better remembrance put up safe on shore."

The crane operator shut off his motors to hear what was said. After a moment's listening to Bowman's ravings, he put in a word himself. "Look here, the suit-and-bowler brigade says these anchors is coming off and off they're coming. You don't want this nice lot o' scrap gone to waste—think what it's worth by the pound."

I wondered if I should step in, but as Boris was standing by looking calm, I concluded that this unfortunate development was part of the plan and must be endured. Bowman was nearly beside himself with rage. His face was that familiar beet-red, and his language would have scorched even the most callused ear. But Mr. Trilby Hat signalled his mate to start up again, and followed along as the anchor was hoisted off from the ship and laid on the trailer. Then the chains were cut away. "No need for these now," remarked Trilby Hat. The crane swung back round and hooked onto the second anchor to the discordant accompaniment of Bowman's invectives. The last anchor was pulled unceremoniously off her bow and laid against the other. Once the last chain was cut and both anchors stowed on the lorry's flatbed, Trilby Hat started up the gangway.

"Ye'll not be settin' foot aboard this ship again," shouted Bowman, shaking his fist. There was a tense moment. Then I heard heavy footsteps behind me, and turned to see Harris approaching at express train speed. He passed me without a glance and went straight to the gangway. Taking hold of the end of it, he lifted it from the bank and then let it slam down again, sending Trilby Hat flailing into the rope handrails, where he clung on for dear life.

Harris marched past him up the gangway and joined Bowman at the rail, from which position the old man was treating the struggling figure to his opinions on the antecedents of both Trilby Hat and the crane operator. Harris tried to calm him, but with little success. Disengaging himself from the ropes, the unwelcome visitor adjusted his trilby and continued up the gangway onto the deck.

"I don't know who you are," he said, looking at Harris warily, "but we've a job to do here."

Harris looked him up and down. "And I don't know who you are, and I don't really care. I'd say you've done your job. You've already taken the things left of real value."

"That's as may be," the other grunted. He then walked back and up to the bridge deck stopping at the ship's double wheel. He tugged off the canvas that covered the binnacle in hopes of finding the ship's compass. A glance showed him that the binnacle was untenanted. Looking no further, he replaced the canvas and took himself to the wheel. Leaning a hand on it, he called down to shore, "Hoy, Sam! Can you bring a couple of wrenches up here?"

"Belay that order," Harris barked, taking hold of Trilby Hat by his lapels. "Now *you* pin back your lugholes and listen to *me*. You may not understand this, but when towing this ship out, someone has to be manning the helm to keep her on the straight course, otherwise she'll yaw all over the place and probably part the towline. So make up your mind that there's nothing else here you'll be taking."

The fellow looked at the old wheels regretfully, but he saw the logic in Harris's words and relented. Harris released him. The man started down forward on the main deck, but paused at the aft hatchway and slid back the cover to have a look. His eyes met those of Edward, climbing up from below.

"What is it you'd be wanting here?" the old Irishman growled.

Trilby's persistence or stupidity was astounding. "Well, guvnor, I'm going below to find out if there's something else worth salvaging, if you must know."

Edward scowled, his eyes burning slits. "I don't believe that it's any of your bloody business. Whatever else is left down there belongs to the ship, 'tisn't your concern."

Trilby stood his ground and begged to differ. Bowman, never one to miss a good argument, now joined in.

Harris doffed his coat as though preparing for action. "The next step he takes down that ladder will be the one that takes him over side," he muttered to no one in particular.

It was dawning on the fellow that he was decidedly overmatched. Looking at all of us, he shrugged his shoulders and walked down the gangway to the shore. The lorry departed up the road with its plunder.

Bowman was still fuming over our loss. "Look at that! They've got the bloody anchors! I can't believe it." He sat down, suddenly looking alarmingly pale and weak. He put his hand up to his heart and leaned back against the mast.

"Are you all right, Uncle Billy?" Harris enquired anxiously. "Is that ticker of yours playing you up again?"

"Nay, nay, I'll be fine. These frays just wear down my patience, that's all. What I wouldn't give to be able to sail out and never see any of these thieving bastards again!" One could see that he was having difficulty breathing. Harris wanted to open his coat and have a listen at his heart. "Give over wi' that nonsense," Bowman said, and waved us off.

Harris tried to console him by pointing out that losing the anchors wasn't really a problem since we weren't making for an anchorage. Since we would be docking, there'd be no real need of them.

"Small comfort," sighed Bowman, "when they'll be taking us off with hardly a bit of sail. The sails aren't ready, and that's that." He brushed his hands off wearily as though finishing with a long and hopeless task. He looked up at the barren yardarms. "This is a wind-ship without lungs, and soon we'll see her drowned. Aye, scuttled and gone down to meet those that went before her."

Harris's broad jaw was stubbornly set as he patted Bowman on the back. "Here here, that's no way to talk. We're not beaten yet! You sit tight. I'm going up to Whitechapel and bring back every finished sail my old wagon can carry." Wasting no time, he dashed off down the gangway and ran for his lorry. A moment later he was roaring off with me running after, hoping for a quick ride up to the inn. I was too late, and all I got was a pelting of mud and gravel thrown up by his tyres. I retreated back to the *Bonnie* and was relieved to see Bowman looking much improved. Boris and I saw him below out of the cold and Edward passed him a hot toddy. He seemed in good hands.

"Is there anything I can do for you here?" I asked.

Bowman said, "I don't think so. I'm going to stay here with Ned. Take yerself back to the inn and we'll send word when ye're needed."

"Right," I responded, and started back for the inn. A sharp wind was rising up as I walked, and it began to blossom into a real gale. The weather always seemed to turn while I was en route between the inn and the ship, probably because I spent so bloody much time out on this bit of road! Looking up, I could see several figures moving on the path that led to the orphanage but at this distance couldn't make out who they were. The wind increased steadily. At least it was at my back, though that made it no warmer, and I still had to battle for control of my course. The peaceful wet morning I'd awakened to had well and truly fled. At last I got back and struggled through the kitchen door, pulled off my coat, and sat down at the table with a sigh of relief. I looked up at Katherine. "There, half a tick," I quipped through chattering teeth.

She shook her head smiling and set a mug of hot tea before me. "I kept your breakfast warm for you." She went to the oven and brought out my plates. With this restorative array before me and Katherine looking on, life brightened. I still couldn't help being worried at the uncertainty of our situation.

"Thanks very much," I said.

She detected the sober tone to my voice and my expression. "New developments?" she enquired alertly.

"I'm concerned," I said. "We still don't have our sails, and Bowman's got a dicky heart. Harris has gone up to the sail-makers and he'll fetch back whatever can be used. I hope there'll be enough. There isn't anything we can do for Bowman, except try to keep him calm. I don't see any point in you having to rush down there this morning. We'll need to see how Harris fares."

She put her hand on my shoulder and squeezed it gently. "Well, we'll just wait and hope for the best. I'm sure Harris will accomplish whatever he sets out to do."

"Of course you're right," I replied, sipping my tea. Outside it was turning out a harsh bit of October gale and there'd be no towing anything out to sea today. No tugs would be active but for emergencies, and there'd be little but the bell buoys and the Southend light to greet any incoming ship this day. All the tugs were snug at their moorings, and I knew we'd be safe from them for the moment. I wondered what would come of Harris's visit to the shop in Whitechapel. He intended to come back with sails, but the gales that would keep vessels in port today could also present a grave hazard to a large vehicle. There was nothing to do but wait, so I tucked into my breakfast.

I was finishing my last bit of scone and began to long for my pipe when the landlady bustled in, a bit like a gale wind herself. She told me I'd a good start on the wall and when could I be back at it? After all, wind should be no deterrent to piling up stones, now should it? I told her that I'd exhausted the supply of stones in the vicinity and needed to cart them in from farther off. I took the opportunity to ask if she could pay me today, pointing out that tomorrow was my usual day off. She saw no problem with that and insisted on paying in cash. Having handed over the bank notes and coin with her customary ill grace, she then led me off on a round of minor repairs, one after the other: loose shutters, leaky pipes and such. I was paid up through today, and she wanted her money's worth.

When lunchtime came, she went back into her parlour to take her meal in private, and I returned to the kitchen. Katherine guided me to my chair and gave me a heartening hug from behind. "No lorry passed by yet," she said, "though with all the howling and rattling of the wind, one could very well miss it." We both kept an ear cocked for Harris's return.

Something occurred to me, and I pulled her galley list from my pocket. "I don't see how I can attend to this. When the sails come, I won't have a moment to get away. Can you take it?"

She nodded her head, "I know what's on it."

"Then you'd better have some of this," I said, pressing some money into her hand. "I'll have little use for it while bending on sails down the road."

Before long, the Beastly One was back among us with plenty of bright ideas for more chores. She was carrying the fascinating subject of warped floorboards when a movement outside the window caught my eye. As I watched, a black-visored cap rose up into view, followed by a set of dark eyes, nose, and moustache. This repeated itself three times. The next instant, a familiar face appeared under the visor. It was Boris, and my worries immediately multiplied. "Bloody hell," I muttered under my breath.

The landlady broke off her discourse. "Did you say something, Mr. Flynn?" she said testily.

"No, Mrs. Beasley, I thought I saw a slate or something blow down." She glanced halfway round, then back at me. There it came again: first the cap and then Boris's eyes. As soon as our eyes met, he beckoned to me to come outside, then sank back out of sight. I went for my coat. "Yes, I do think I should go have a look. One can't be too careful."

"I do hope you'll be able to put it right in short order," she said as I went to the door. I glanced at Katherine on my way out. She gave me an encouraging nod.

I found Boris sheltering near the cucumber frame.

"What's happened?" I asked, anxious to break the suspense.

"Sails! Harris saying come now." So, Harris was back. I was ready to dash off down the footpath straightaway, but he led me towards the road.

"I have car," he said, and pointed to Harris's car. This really was urgent, then.

"Here, just a moment Boris, come into the pub." I hurried round the front as he trailed me protesting, and we went inside. "Wait right here," I told him and went to the inner door. I looked in. The corridor was empty, while from the kitchen I could hear the landlady in the thick of some lengthy lecture. I ran upstairs and dragged out my chest, wrestling it down the ladder. The voice in the kitchen still droned on, so I hefted my burden and bore it quickly into the pub. Boris raised his black eyebrows, but he saw the sense in seizing what might be my last opportunity to avoid carrying it all the way to the ship. We were just able to wedge it into the open boot of the little Morris. Then I ran back in the kitchen door.

Katherine and Mrs. Beastly looked round as I came in. "Well," I panted, "I'll need to be out there for a good while yet. There are a number of things that need my attention." I gave Katherine a look. "Things are simply *sailing* about in this wind."

"Oh, well, that's very industrious of you," said my soon-to-be-former employer. Katherine watched me as I went back out, her eyes full of hope and enquiry.

Between the gale and the state of Harris's car, I don't know if I'd have made the trip with anyone else but Boris at the wheel. The car laboured along against raking headwinds, and I began to have my doubts as to whether it would reach the mooring. I could probably have walked it as quickly, but not carrying that chest. At last we sighted the masts of the *Bonnie Clyde* and drew up near Harris's lorry at the water's edge.

The yardarms were already tilted down towards the embankment, and facing them was the open back of the lorry that was crammed to the gills with sails. I walked over and eagerly examined the fresh stitching on the sails. It looked firm and even and built for the ages.

Harris's voice came over the roar of the wind. "Flynn, what's kept you?" he bellowed. "Let's have some of that strong back you advertised."

Boris came up and shouldered me aside. He laid hold of one great roll of sail canvas and tugged it part way out from the load. From nowhere, a whole group of the orphanage crew materialised and bore it onto the gangway. Fortunately this was wide enough to permit us to roll it up. When we'd heaved the roll onto the deck, one young man brushed off his hands and faced me. I knew that red hair.

"Mr. Flynn!" he cried. "It's me, Larry."

I shook his hand heartily. "I remember you very well, Larry. It's you and Todd who are the short-wave experts, as I recall." He nodded.

"So, are you ready for the great undertaking?" I said.

"You'll find no shirkers amongst Starke's Raiders," he replied stoutly. Another lad came up, with flashing dark eyes and a pockmarked face. "Here's Ted. He's a real one for hard work." Ted made a rude noise at Larry, saluted me, then loped off down the gangway. More boys appeared, and the operation was in full swing. The wind was less of a gale now, though it still tore about us as the lorry was emptied of canvas. Most of the sails were laid out, ready for hauling up. Thank God the rain had stopped. Once Boris was satisfied that all was in order, he went quickly aloft and directed the hauling of sails onto the tops of the yardarms. Boris had already decided which of the upper yards to trust and signalled here yes, there no to their critical placements. It was backbreaking work handling the vast rolls, but at least there was no rain soaking them to add more weight.

Harris paused in the hoisting of a great mainsail onto the deck, wiping his brow on his sleeve. He pulled his cap back on firmly and resumed his labours. The back of the lorry now gaped empty. "Harris," I shouted, "is that everything?"

"Everything but a few scraps," he yelled back. I looked at the bundles lying on deck and those along the bank. It scarcely seemed possible that so much could have fitted into the lorry.

"Now we are bending on with these," announced Boris. If it was hard before, now it became even harder and dangerous. We'd be handling the canvas unrolled, which made it even more unwieldy and gave the wind more to take hold of. I could see the potential of a real accident in the offing unless we were very careful. As we hauled the expanses of sail over the gunnels, they'd never felt heavier.

I groaned. "At times like this, we could make good use of those circus elephants."

Harris cast me a sour look and kept doggedly to his task. I saw Bowman emerge on deck, looking on with shining eyes. He seemed to have dropped twenty years, but none of us would let him lift so much as a finger. He was content to be witness to this great day. He left the task to Boris's supervision and kept busy with Edward. It was just as well that he didn't see the gaudy striped tents now fitted as sails.

We kept on steadily until dusk, when the wind at last died down allowing us to work that much faster. The sky had almost cleared by the time the sun went down, and there was a splendid scarlet and golden sunset to cheer us into dusk. Red sky at night, sailor's delight! Lanterns were brought out as the car and lorry were turned and angled to direct their headlamps onto the rigging. Bread and cheese were passed round, and then we were back at it.

Later that evening, I felt the job had progressed enough so I could go back to the inn and let Katherine know how matters stood. It was drawing near the time for her to be coming along herself. I stopped for a moment to marvel at it all. This was really happening! I asked Harris if he could spare me for a short space, and he waved me off.

He told me in no uncertain terms that he wanted my arse back at work as soon as I could manage it.

"And bring the rest of you with it!" he added in parting.

As the car and lorry were occupied, I was the intrepid hiker once again. I was glad I brought down my chest when the chance offered, and wondered how many more times I'd walk between the inn and ship before it was all done. It couldn't be many, I told myself happily as I set out, scarcely noticing my sore muscles.

As I reached the inn, I saw the last customers were departing as the pub was just closing. I looked to see if Katherine was in the kitchen and narrowly missed being seen by the landlady. She'd come round outside from her door to the pub entrance calling for Martin, who responded with a weary grunt.

"Are you quite sure Mr. Flynn isn't in here? Well, I can't think what's become of him. Do you suppose he could have been blown off in the gale? You should get the ladder and have a look on the roof. I've heard of instances where people vanished and were found months later in the chimney. Now what's become of that girl? She was here but a moment ago and I had a recipe I wanted to discuss—" This oratory was mercifully cut short by her pushing the door shut as she went inside. Poor Martin! I felt bad about leaving him to her, but he'd worked here for years and was accustomed to her tiresome nattering. Now that Katherine wasn't in the pub, I went back round to her cottage. To my disappointment, all was dark. I peered in at the kitchen window, but couldn't see her there either. I didn't like to go inside till I was certain Mrs. B. had retired for the night. It would certainly be awkward for her to catch me there. I wasn't sure what explanation I'd give her for my absence, and I really didn't care to deal with her at all tonight. Or ever again, for that matter! Now *there* was a thought.

The wind had died, and it was a crisp still night, with only faint stirrings from the pond and the nearby hooting of an owl. The owl seemed very close. Hoo…Hoo, it called softly. I looked round and then spotted a hooded figure emerging from the shrubbery.

It was Katherine in her cape, trying to get my attention. "I'd just got off, and I was about to come down and be sure everything was all right at the ship," she whispered. "Then I saw you creeping about and wanted to catch your ear. Couldn't you tell it was me?"

"At first I thought it was an owl," I said.

"They say the owl was a baker's daughter," she breathed in a little-girl voice.

She came to me and clung round my neck. "Oh God, I am glad to be leaving this place! I'm quite giddy with it and I don't care if I have to cook for a whole battleship."

Suddenly we were startled by headlamps as a car came down the hill. We crouched down, watching as it turned in and stopped at the roadside. O'Connell! Well, having him here would certainly make matters easier for the boys and us! We made our way back to Katherine's cottage and sat on the bed in the dark for fear of a candle revealing our presence.

I spoke softly, "We've been rigging up the sails, and so far it all looks fine. We expect to be ready to move out on the morning tide. All the old barque needs now is a pretty young cook, if one might be available."

"Carry me off and I'm yours," said Katherine, "Oh…me and my luggage. I did a bit of shopping from the list. I persuaded the Beasley that we were dangerously low on certain items and she sent me off to the village."

"Out in that windy gale? The heartless old witch!" I cried.

She laughed. "It was my idea, silly. I took her car, so I wasn't really out in it."

"You drove that death-trap?" I said.

"Very slowly," she said. "I didn't care for it, I assure you. But I'd set myself to do it, and do it I did."

"You could have been killed!" I cried in horror. "Don't you ever do such a foolhardy thing again! I can see I don't dare let you out of my sight for a minute."

She patted my cheek. "Lucky thing for me then, I'm just going off on a nice safe voyage."

"Well, that's different. You won't be alone," I quipped. "Now where's the luggage?"

She stood and looked out. "Beasley's light is out." She struck a match and lit the candle. "I've got my suitcase, trunk, and this hamper. I put the new supplies in with my other kitchen gear. Wait till you see my granny's pudding basin. We dug it out after the bombing and it wasn't even cracked."

I surveyed this assemblage with dismay. "This is a lot to carry."

"Well, I don't intend coming back for them. How much do you have?" She asked.

"My trunk's down at the ship." I added, "All I have here is my duffel."

"I saw it in your room when I took up clean clothes earlier," said Katherine.

"I'll fetch them down so we can be on our way." Alert to any sign of Beastly activity, I went through the kitchen garden where Purdy hissed at me from the shadows. "That's your last hiss at me, mate," I muttered and hurried to the kitchen door. The light was on and Martin sat at the table reading *The Times*. He looked up as I entered and set down the paper.

"Oh," he said, "here's our wandering boy."

I hardly knew what to say to him. "Hello, Martin," I managed at last, "ah...I'll be back in a moment." I went upstairs and retrieved the duffel bag, stuffing the clean clothes into it. I took a last look at the room with the memories of Katherine in it and went back down into the kitchen.

"Well, Martin, I'm going off and Katherine with me."

He nodded. "I thought as much."

"We haven't known each other a long time, but you've been a good friend to me, and I appreciate it. We may yet be calling on you for more indirect assistance. I hope you'll be able to manage, though I can't tell you more until you hear about it."

"Well, that sounds mysterious enough to keep me speculating until I do hear, but I'll help if I can," Martin replied in his usual amicable way.

I put out my hand and he shook it warmly. Another thought struck me and troubled my conscience. I reached into my pocket and pulled out some money. "Mrs. B. overpaid me for today, so if you could give her this when you think it appropriate…" I counted out a half-day's pay and set it on the table. "That's it then. I'll be off," I finished awkwardly.

"Goodbye, Flynn," he said, "And best of luck to both of you."

I took my leave of him then. Back at the cottage, we tried to devise the best way of carrying the luggage. We carried her trunk between us, with the hamper riding on top of it, holding my duffel on my shoulder with a hand free for her suitcase. We tried this and got as far as the front drive before it became too painful and difficult. We had to set down the lot. This would never do. If we only had some kind of cart…"Wait!" I said. I ran back to the shed and brought out the inn's wheelbarrow. I'd kept it well oiled so it never squeaked, and on the damp ground, no rumble should betray us if we went carefully. Katherine gave me silent applause at the idea.

"I can bring it back easily enough," I whispered.

We loaded up as best we could and found we could take it in one trip. We both took a deep breath and pushed off. We went carefully until we were clear of the inn and then settled into a comfortable pace. It made a nice walk for us, just me and Katherine on the road, trundling our worldly goods into the future. It would be our last time alone together until we tied up at Dumbarton. I wondered out loud where my pipe was so that I could claim a kiss. I could foresee these being few and far between on this voyage.

The ship was a hive of activity when we came up, and the work would be going on far into the night. Quite a few of the sails had already been tested and then furled up along the yardarms, secured in place by the gaskets. As we reached the bottom of the gangway, Harris greeted us.

"Oh, there you are, Flynn!" he cried impatiently. "We need you up here. Get busy!" Noticing Katherine in tow, he smiled, doffed his hat and bowed. "Welcome aboard, milady," he purred.

She gave him a smile, and we brought our luggage up the gangway from the wheelbarrow. We were carefully setting down the hamper when Harris reached out his long arm and took me by the back of the collar. "We need you *now*," he said. Katherine stared at him indignantly, but held her tongue.

Bowman put out his head. "Keep yer voice down, ye great bully, and be about this quickly!"

I smiled and put my best face on as Harris led me down the gangway where the last rolls of canvas were laid out. "These are the sails that'll be used on the jib, and we'll need those up near the bow. The other ones are the spankers and will be needed aft."

"You don't say! I never knew spankers went aft! Tell me more," I said with heavy sarcasm. He talked to me as if I were a raw recruit, and I rebuffed him.

He continued, "Get these on board, and then we'll have everything we'll need, except for a few odds and ends."

I gave him a nasty look, "The odds are there's no ends to it."

"Well, there are things and then there are more things, but I've kept a very important thing for you to do! It's important, very important, but—" and he struggled to suppress a laugh, "no one could call it a rest cure!"

As I listened, I couldn't believe it. Even an enemy surely would have been more lenient, but Harris was adamant. He had no one to spare except Robert and me, who were agile enough to do the job. Our job was to arrange for the acquisition and application to the furled sails, of a quantity of *mud*! Then, when suspicious eyes would be looking during the tow tomorrow, the sails would look like mouldering rags, just like those of the *Auld Lass*'s final voyage.

While I found the prospect of this messy task unappealing, my mind was active as Harris outlined the plan. I could immediately see the difficulties of it. Hauling the mud up to the yards in buckets was going to be a picnic compared to the job of slopping around in the dark to find the right consistency of mud close to the ship.

Of course, it was an essential job, if we were to keep up our deception. I went to find Robert, who was more than happy to leave his current job of showing two of the lads how to clean the heads for something less pungent. We got Boris to show us a spare sheet belayed to the pin rail at deck level and which, at the top of the mast, was already travelling through a pulley. We then had our hoist as we each took turns at either staggering about in the mud or swaying along the yardarms applying mud. At the end of three hours, we were covered with mud from head to foot, but so were the sails that now looked old and ugly. I noticed that Brian had the colour covered on the outside of the rolls with white canvas, so Bowman wouldn't see them till they were set. I knew this was Harris's doing but thought to ask at another time.

The boys were busy handling lines and canvas under Boris's guidance and folding the jibs so they could be raised quickly and easily. Nearby, Harris, Bowman, and Edward seemed to be having an argument held in whispers. As I started towards them to find out what the problem was, Harris and Edward turned away. Bowman, who seemed to have settled his point, started to walk in my direction. Suddenly his eyes closed and he clutched at the lines in the standing rigging for support. He turned quite pale and one hand came up and clapped to his chest. That was twice in one day. This was more than alarming. It seemed that all this activity was really too much for the old man, tough as he was.

I ran up to him. "Can I help you, Captain Bowman?" I said.

"I'm in nae need of help," he gasped. "I slipped, that's all. I suppose ye think I'm too old to go to sea. Too much work—isn't that it?" he gasped."

I didn't dare say so. "Well, you look a bit green about the gills."

"Thank ye very much, Dr. Flynn," growled Bowman. "Next time I get a medical examination, I shall endeavour to have ye present to give yer expert opinion."

I watched worriedly as he went off slowly towards his cabin, but had to suppress my concerns for the moment. Surely once we'd gotten under sail and away from interfering officialdom, he could relax a bit and take some of the strain off his labouring heart. I had a feeling that Katherine's presence would have a tonic effect on him. How could it not?

I set to work again, completely exhausted and covered with mud, but with my enthusiasm undampened. When everything on the yardarms was furled, tied, and muddied, Harris assembled the boys around the mainmast and addressed them.

"Now then," Harris said. "You boys know what you have to do, and do it quickly and quietly. You bigger lads help out the smaller ones. Remember we're a crew now, and a crew works together. We must be set and ready to go before the first ray of sunshine even thinks about coming over the horizon. Bring everything you need, we'll not be returning."

I got close enough to whisper something to Harris and he turned back to the boys with a grin. "I've just been informed that the headmaster is...er...otherwise engaged this evening and so you'll not need to be so quiet. Get some rest and pack it down. Off with you now!"

The boys all hustled away together and vanished without question or complaint, running into the night to the orphanage one last time. I sagged, taking hold of a line in the standing rigging and clinging there.

"Whew!" I said, looking at Harris. "Where do they get the energy?"

Harris replied, "You forget we were young once. We used to leap about like hares that way."

"Yes," I said with a weary sigh, "I do remember, but it seems a lifetime ago."

"It *was* a lifetime ago, before Hitler. There were millions that didn't get another lifetime. Perhaps what we're doing now is saving a little of our heritage, which is what we fought to keep, after all, and which will honour them for what they sacrificed. God!" he pounded his fist thunderously. "Damn those butchers. May they all rot in hell!"

We stood in silence for a time. Harris went ashore and shut down the lights on the car and lorry, which were growing dim despite periodic running of the engines, while I went down and brought up my chest. The wheelbarrow still awaited returning, but there was plenty of time before it would ever be missed, and I felt sure of getting it back right enough. But right now I had to clean myself up a bit and change my clothing, even if it was not a full wash.

When we at last went below, the lovely aroma of baking enveloped us. Katherine had already put the galley in order and had tested out the stove with a pan of golden shortbread. She'd raided the coal-bunkers and tamed the ancient appliance all on her own. It would see some real cooking now. Bowman sat nearby, sampling the shortbread. She enquired as to how many there would be for breakfast in the morning. I told her there was much to do, and so much critical timing to be observed that I doubted we'd be sitting down for meals at all tomorrow. We simply could not risk even the faintest trace of smoke rising from the fire from the stove.

"Well then, I'll just keep a good supply of sandwiches and cold snacks coming up," she said. "They may not be hot meals, but you'll be eating, make your minds up to it. Is that quite understood?"

Harris and Bowman both straightened, looking at one another as if a superior officer had given them a direct order. I had to laugh. Harris gave me a look.

"Now then," Bowman said, "we've only a few more things for the doing this night. Miss Katherine, ye'll remain here."

"Indeed?" she said. "Well, it happens that I have cooking to do anyway."

"Then that's as should be. But mind, no smoke must show after daybreak." He rose from his seat. "But first, put yer carcass in the chair and take what rest ye can for now."

She softened. "Thank you, but I've no time for sitting just yet."

Robert and I probably looked like something that had grown out of a swamp. We were still covered with mud, and Katherine was understandably appalled. "And just what have you two been doing?" she said, looking us over disapprovingly.

"You wouldn't believe it if I told you," I groaned, looking down at my muddy clothing. "I'm off for a wash."

I went to my cabin for some clean clothes, then to the bath where I had a quick cold wash. I returned to the galley, and after passing cook's inspection, was permitted to seat myself in a chair by the stove while Katherine went on about her business. I'm ashamed to say that I actually dozed off and was happily dreaming when a cry came from above, "They're coming!" By my watch, it was nearly four o'clock. Boris and Harris stood at the rail. "There!" Boris pointed. And there came the boys back from the orphanage, a dim company in the pale starlight, some carrying mattresses, some with great bundles of blankets and linen, and each with a small bag of personal things. It was an orderly and quiet procession, as Boris pointed out. He'd rigged up a little pulley system with an old cargo net to hoist all the bedding on board. After having borne their belongings all the way on foot, the boys gladly piled their burdens into the net. Once their load was on deck, they stood waiting.

"Now then, boys, up to the fo'c's'le with these," Harris directed. The company moved forward and arranged the bedding on the empty bunks. After a good deal of joking and jostling for the best bunks, they put their pitifully few clothes in the lockers fixed to the bulkheads. After all, this would be home for a time, and they wanted to make the most of it. One of the boys opened the stove, and finding no coal within, pointed it out to Harris.

"Sorry, boys, but there will be no fires till we're under sail. Don't worry over the coal supply, we've plenty in storage. Damned near stripped the old barge clean." He pointed over the side at the dim remains of the former four-master.

We also saw fog had come up over the dark water, which would soon be filling the estuary from shore to shore.

Given that nearly everything was tucked away properly, Bowman went up and had a brief man-to-man chat with the new crew regarding their duties. They'd now wait in the darkness and silence for the sound of the bo'sun's pipe summoning them on deck. They would be sent to the same mariners' tasks no doubt performed by their ancestors. As that would be some hours off, they were best off getting any rest they could in preparation for the grand moment of setting sail.

It had been decided to wedge the fo'c's'le doors shut before the authorities arrived. No one would have any need to go up there, but it was a precaution. As their beds were now tenantable, the boys retired into their racks for a rest, excitedly anticipating their first call to stations.

Bowman stepped up and cleared his throat. "I know it's going to seem forever, but ye must all lie quiet until ye hear the sound of the bo'sun's pipe. Each of you knows his job. So do it well, and by all means, do it carefully." We left them then, but I wondered just how many would be able to get any rest.

Harris went below to start up the pumps. The bilge wanted a good clearing out, and when the tug came in the morning, this would look like preparation for towing and not arouse suspicion. Bowman grumbled again over the loss of the anchors. "At least Boris had the good sense to have the compass out of the binnacle before they could get their greedy mitts on it, or we'd be having a fine time navigating," he snorted resentfully.

That reminded Boris of something important, and he held his finger up saying "Ah!" He went over to a pile of mouldering dirty canvas that shrouded an old lifeboat and pulled it back. There beneath the canvas sat the compass. He lifted it and tenderly carried it up to the bridge deck, setting it in place inside the binnacle. When he finished, Edward ran a couple of quick checks on it and covered it with the filthy old canvas again.

"Looks right enough," grunted Edward. "My chronometer is in my cabin. I'll make sure of its setting now," and he stumped off heavily.

Robert pointed to the rotted wood and old lifeboat parts that we'd dumped on shore. Some was rubbish that had never made it onto the *Auld Lass*. There was even some of it still on deck with us. "Are we going to leave this mess?" he asked, "or should we attend to it?" I looked at Robert in dismay. Here he was proposing yet another job.

"That's a good question," Harris said thoughtfully, "You and Flynn come with me." We followed Harris down onto the landing. He went to his car and returned with two shovels, handing one to each of us. "Now make a small dig, say about eight feet across."

My mouth dropped open. "Eight feet is a small dig?" I cried.

Harris frowned, "I didn't say dig till we struck oil, just make a shallow dig! These are customary rituals when scuttling ships."

We started digging, scraping away the sand and pebbles and mud. With all the demands I had made on my poor body these last few days, I didn't think it would hold up a moment longer, but soon Harris was satisfied with what little we'd done.

We piled the debris in the centre of the pit. There were pieces of the old lifeboats, cracked oars, rotten belaying pins, every piece of rotten wood and all the other things we'd used to make the ship look bad—whatever you'd care to name, it was most probably in there. If we couldn't use it, it went onto the pile. Harris brought some paraffin and poured it over the lot. Soon we had a splendid bonfire going, only a couple of weeks early for Guy Fawkes Day.

The last thing onto the fire was the old gangway. We cut the ropes and broke it loose from its supports. Then we dragged it over the sand and unceremoniously flung it onto the pile. The fire now leaped high into the air and kept the chilly fog off as we sat poking at the wood to keep it blazing.

"Aren't you afraid someone's going to notice us?" I asked.

"I don't care," said Harris, "We're supposed to be watching for them to come and take the ship away. Any informed onlooker might think it very strange if no one's in attendance. Disposing of the scrap by burning makes a declaration that we're putting an end to anything connected with the *Bonnie*. Soon we'll have officials here poking about as well as the tug captain, and no doubt a reporter or two. But there'll be no more than a pile of ashes on-shore for them to gawk at or loot, and no gangway for them to use to get aboard. Any inbound waterway traffic that might be passing and needs a beacon in the fog would surely find it a welcome sight." He stretched out his hands to the blaze. "Besides, it's nice and warm."

Exhausted, we sat gazing into the flames as the pre-dawn twilight paled about us.

Chapter 14
AN ACT OF PIRACY

It seemed that I'd closed my eyes a scant few seconds when they were rudely snapped open again at the sound of Harris's voice.

"Now then, men," he barked in his best officer manner. All that remained was the lurid smoke looming over us making Harris look like some sinister lord of the underworld.

I blinked and looked about. The fire had burnt down, and the fog had taken on the glow of growing daylight.

Robert sat up. "Oh my head! What time is it?" he groaned.

"It's *Now*," boomed Harris, "and NOW HEAR THIS! Up with you! Time to be on the move!"

I looked at Robert. We were thinking of breakfast and made a quick scamper back to the ship with him in the lead. He seized one of the lines we'd rigged to the shore and went up hand-over-hand to the rail where Boris helped him over. I followed a little less nimbly and turned to see Harris regarding me from the bank below.

"*Now* what?" Harris demanded.

"Just getting some food and checking on Katherine," I called back.

"Don't you be long," he admonished, wagging a finger.

I gave him a crisp salute and pulled myself up the rope. Katherine had a cabin aft on the 'tween deck, where the officers usually stayed. Mine was across from hers, and then came those of Robert and Harris. Bowman kept the old captain's cabin above, below the bridge deck. I thought of knocking at Katherine's door, but instead went directly to the galley.

There, all was light and bustle as Katherine loaded trays held by two of the boys with plates of food and teapots and mugs to be borne back to the fo'c's'le. It made sense to have both meals and bunks in the same place. When a seaman isn't working, he's generally sleeping or eating. Today the food would have to be snacks, but that meant plenty of Katherine's famous pies. We wanted our crewmen where they could be found when the whistle sounded, so they were treated to breakfast in bed. Quite the pleasure cruise, thus far. Robert stood by absorbing tea from one hand and egg pie from the other. By his manner, it was apparent he'd just been snatched back from the brink of starvation.

The boys took their load and moved off. Katherine looked at me, hot-faced, through tired but glowing eyes. "Why, can it be morning already?" she yawned. "I must have overslept. I think I've been making breakfast while sleep-walking." And she gave a smile. Now we were alone but for Robert, who soon noticed his position as odd man out.

"Oh, pardon me," mumbled the still-masticating Robert, and considerately exited.

I lost no time gathering her into my arms, where she clung for a moment, then drew back and looked into my eyes. "My goodness, we're *really* doing this, aren't we?" she laughed.

I held her face in my hands and kissed her. "And there's nothing else in this world I'd rather be doing."

She smiled and tapped my nose with a fingertip. "Back to work!" she cried. "And here's some chamomile tea to have along." She noticed my surprise at this unconventional beverage and put her hands on her hips in exasperation. "It's good for you," she said and handed me a thermos flask. I collected the pies and tea in the vacuum bottle and took my leave.

I paused as I passed the chart room where I could see Edward still poring over tide charts, with a series of maps laid out completely covering the table. I watched him at his calculations for a moment till Harris came up, carrying a tray of breakfast, and addressed him impatiently.

"Damn it, Ned, haven't you figured out that rubbish already? How many times do you need to go over it?"

Edward squinted at him, his lips quivering. "Don't you be bad-tempered with me, you great lump! I have to check these figures like a carpenter—measure twice and cut once. How would you like to wake up and find yourself fifty miles or more off-course? That wouldn't sit at all well with Bowman. Hah! One could scarcely picture it."

"Oh, *I* could," Harris confided. "Trust me. I could picture it *quite* vividly." He looked thoughtful. "You know, it's about time I looked in on Uncle Billy. Come on, Flynn."

We two proceeded to Bowman's cabin and knocked at the door. "What?" came a testy voice from within. "Well, come in if ye're coming."

We entered, and Harris set tea and pies before the old man where he sat at his desk. He took little notice of this and seemed distracted.

Harris leaned down to look at him. "You will eat, won't you?"

"Aye, in good time. Don't fret over me. I'm just thinking of our crew. They're unseasoned. They haven't worked aboard any sort of ship before. We've taught them what we could with our classes at the orphanage and on board here, but it's no substitute for experience. Why, we've one boy here who's only thirteen years of age," and he shook his head.

Harris grinned. "But Uncle Billy, you went to sea when you were thirteen years old. What makes that any different from now?"

"A good many things," he said. "Now is not like then, just as then is not like now."

"Well, one can hardly argue with logic like that!" Harris snorted. "Here, it's getting light, come get a breath of air on deck and see what we've done. All those old lifeboats and other scrap are gone now. All were burnt up in a bonfire from hell during the night—you should have a look."

We proceeded out and looked over the port rail. Bowman nodded approvingly at the now-tidy shoreline, or what could be seen of it through the murky air.

"At least they'll not complain we've left any rubbish behind," he grunted. He turned to Harris with a scowl. "Now, *that* was bloody stupid," he growled.

"Here, *what's* stupid?" said Harris.

"Ye've burnt the gangway, ye ignorant blackguard! How in blazes d'ye think—"

Harris held up his hand. "Wait, wait! Before you go any further let me just say that first of all, we shan't need it for the voyage. Second of all, having it gone will prevent any outsiders coming on board. And last, should we reach our destination, I'm quite sure that *someone* can supply us another. At Dumbarton they're hardly strangers to the needs of ships, after all."

"Well, ye could just as well have brought it along and then burned it for fuel later on," fumed Bowman.

I heard a chuckle and turned to see Boris looking on in amusement. Bowman also wheeled and glared at the Russian who casually drifted off out of view. Harris began to look uneasy. We all knew we needed to avoid upsetting the old man, but clearly that was no small task.

"I'm sorry," Harris said quietly. "I never meant to cut you off that way, but we will be going out in a few hours' time."

"Aye," grumbled Bowman. "And it's just as well."

Harris turned to me. "Well, let's be off," he said. "It's time to go to Gravesend. I've asked Robert along because I have a little job for him to do later, perhaps one of the most critical jobs for this voyage!"

"Oh? And what would that be?" I asked. Harris was not forthcoming with any details, but hinted darkly that if any violence should erupt to "stay to your place and don't involve yourself. I'll take care of the rest. I'll tell you more later." It was all very mysterious and none too reassuring.

After sliding down the ropes to shore, we got into Harris's car and were preparing to depart when we heard someone coming down the lane, whistling a tune, accompanied by a clinking noise that was oddly familiar.

"What's that?" hissed Harris, switching off the engine. We quickly jumped out of the car, and positioned ourselves behind bushes on either side of the lane. We waited quietly, listening while the sounds grew louder as the intruder approached. It could be anyone, but at this late stage we didn't want strangers snooping about. We tensed ourselves, prepared for anything, when round the bend came Martin from the pub, pushing the Beasley Inn's wheelbarrow. In fact, the Beasley Inn's one and only wheelbarrow, which I'd left at almost this spot some hours ago. I'd quite forgotten about it until this moment. In the barrow sat a case of whisky, two crates of stout, some brandy and several other bottles.

Harris stepped out and held up his hand in approved highwayman fashion, as if holding a pistol. "And where would you be going with all them bottles, my fine fellow?" he boomed. Martin jumped in surprise, then grinned and obligingly raised his hands.

Robert and I came out of the bushes. Scratching my head, I asked wonderingly, "Martin, what on earth—?"

Martin lowered his hands and laughed. "Well, I'd best stand and deliver, hadn't I?" He cleared his throat. "Flynn, I've been tending bar practically since I can remember, so I can make a sentence out of a few words. You gents used lots in my hearing. Be glad that it's me you're seeing here now and not someone less welcome. This is a bon voyage gift," and he indicated the barrow.

Harris looked from him to me narrowly, doubtlessly wondering how much Martin knew. I shifted uneasily. "Martin, we're more than glad to have it, but isn't Mrs. B. going to be missing all this?" I asked.

"Actually no," he said. "Most of this is what's called barman's perks in the trade. Retailing spirits by the tot, you actually sell using one measure, and record using another. The difference builds up over a time. It's legal, but only *just*, and the bar owner can do what he likes with the perks. So, here you are."

Harris didn't say anything and was still trying to make out what Martin might know, so I thanked him.

"Now *this* bottle," said Martin, removing one, "had been sitting back in the storeroom for longer than I can remember. I believe it was actually ordered by *Mr.* Beasley before the Great War."

Harris and I exchanged astonished glances. "You mean this has been lying about for over thirty years?" cried Harris, reaching out to touch the old bottle reverently.

"Our Mrs. Beasley never was one for keeping a close inventory, so every time she wanted something I ordered it, whether we'd plenty or not. That has stood us in good stead during all the lean times. I'll leave you gentlemen with this. But I do need the wheelbarrow."

"Here," I said, taking the handles. "Let's unload it on the bank."

Martin and Robert followed as I pushed the barrow next to the ship. We piled the crates and bottles on the ground while Boris looked on wide-eyed from the deck above. Martin had his first close-up look at the *Bonnie* rigged and ready.

"Get these on board and stowed, would you, Boris?—there's a good chap," joked Robert. Martin lifted a bottle in each hand and squinted at the labels. "Here are two bottles of Vodka for your Russian friend. Who else would touch the stuff?"

"So you came all the way down here and took the barrow and we never even noticed?" I said in chagrin.

"You were fast asleep and I'd no reason to wake you. I just went to fetch the wheelbarrow and had to go a little farther than I expected," he said with a shrug.

We walked back to the car where Harris asked Martin, "How long can we count on your silence?"

After all, the secret was a precious one. The people on board were determined to get away and didn't want any last minute hitches. We'd burnt our bridges and were pulling together for a common purpose.

Martin just laughed, "Harris, you have my silence for as long as it takes. I don't intend to do anything but go back and set up my bar for the day…even if my barmaid should disappear, and Mrs. Beasley goes raving to the police." He seemed to know just about everything already, but it really didn't matter. I knew *he* could be trusted, and Harris seemed to have understood it as well, for he relaxed visibly.

Martin's only connection with the inn was the pub, but all this made me wonder anew: what *would* the landlady do? And O'Connell— it would be only a matter of time before he returned to the orphanage to find it deserted. Time would tell.

Martin took one final look at the ship. "I do hope you know what you're doing," he said, shaking his head.

"Time to go," ordered Harris.

We shook hands all round.

"Well, then, I'll be on my way," said Martin, and went off with the barrow.

"Thank you, Martin," I called after him, and he turned to wave goodbye.

I looked at Harris as he pressed the starter, and was struck by an agreeable thought. "By God, this is the last time you'll be chauffeuring me about in this wreck, isn't it? I shan't be sunk in melancholy over it."

"Oh, leave off," he returned, and we started with a violent lurch. "I haven't killed you yet."

We passed Martin, and then the Beasley Inn one last time. Robert made himself as comfortable as he could in the back and closed his eyes. We proceeded for some time in what passed for silence in the clattering old vehicle when I asked Harris, "By the way, what are you going to do with this car once we get to Gravesend?"

"I'm leaving it to Brian and his tribe. They haven't one, and it's surely better than nothing. Also, I'm leaving them the keys to the lorry, which they can pick up where I've parked it along the road. This one was written-off as wrecked by the Chatham yard."

I shifted in my seat and tried to stretch, but there wasn't enough room. I was aching all over from my long night's toil.

Harris glanced at me in amusement. "Here, what's all this?" he asked.

"Drat! I feel as if someone crept up on me while I wasn't looking and broke every bone in my body."

"Well," he said, "working all night and napping on the ground will do that."

"And riding in a broken-down relic driven by a madman doesn't help," I added.

He applied the brakes—mended, ha!—, downshifted, and came to a halt largely by virtue of our heading partway up a hill at the time, which lessened the drama of the gesture considerably. "Right, then! If you don't like the way I drive, *you* do it," he pouted, and climbed out.

"Really? I thought you said I drove like an old lady," I said as I scrambled from my seat and round to the driver's side. Harris got into the passenger seat and left me in possession of the field. In my eagerness, I rolled back and then stalled the engine as I started off. Harris drummed his fingers on the back of my seat irritably, then pointed to my feet.

"Flynn, it's the pedal over there," and he pointed to the accelerator.

"Well, I simply haven't your talent," I retorted and re-started the motor. He gave a sniff of disdain as we unsteadily set off once more.

When we came into Gravesend, he directed me to the car ferry where we found Brian's son, David, waiting for us.

Harris said, "Here's the Morris and the key to the lorry as well. Tell your Dad how much we're still in his debt."

We watched him install the old Morris on the ferry and turned our steps towards the tug docks. As we walked, Harris said, "That son of Brian's is an ungrateful sod—complained that the shop still smelt of elephant dung." We had to laugh at that.

The morning was still cold and Harris took in a great breath of foggy air saying, "Now then, let's walk the last mile."

"You make it sound like a bloody execution," Robert groaned.

"You never can tell, any given day," Harris replied.

"Oh, belt up and give it a rest! How did I ever fall in with the likes of you?" I asked.

"By coming to the just reward of a blameless life, m'boy," he returned with a cherubic smile.

I concentrated on keeping up with his long strides and Robert fell in alongside. As we walked along the docklands, there didn't seem to be a soul out in the yards as yet, only a few signs of life from the early-rising maritime working folk along with maintenance and security men.

We were in good time for it looked a while yet before departure.

Already in attendance at the tug were the two government officials, standing primly by. I heard a low growl from Harris as we approached.

"Good morning, Mr. Harris," one of them said, touching the brim of his bowler, "and where is the delightful Mr. Bowman today?"

"He's not feeling well," Harris replied, "but he sends his love and hopes you won't miss him too much."

"Oh, not *too* awfully," said the official representative, tilting his bowler with a well-bred little laugh. "I say, it looks as though everyone is here. What do you say we just push off now and go down a bit earlier than we'd planned, eh?"

Harris eyed him speculatively. "I have no objection, but I think you'll find the tide's not entirely in agreement as of yet," he cautioned.

The tug captain had come up and caught some of this conversation. He looked the government officials up and down, then took his pipe from his mouth and spat. "It's just about on the turn," he said, "and the engines need a bit of warming up anyway."

As we were about to board, one of the officials looked at Harris earnestly. "I hope you'll not be making one of your celebrated scenes over this," he said in a clipped accent.

Harris returned his look coldly, "No, it's just a bloody shame that you lot don't know what to do with a good ship. She's been sound, sharp, and right in her time. But now you think she's nothing but a worthless wreck. We'll certainly never see eye-to-eye."

"You know," the other said lightly, "as with everything, it's out with the old and in with the new. Besides which, it's well past time we cleaned up that area down-river."

Harris began to heat up now. "Another of your pat little excuses, is it? Well, if you're so bloody interested in tidying things up, you might well have a closer look at the Beasley Inn. I have my doubts whether the sanitation there would bear up under close scrutiny."

I caught Harris's eye and shook my head warningly. One by one we climbed aboard and were treated to the ugly stench of fumes from the tug's funnel as we cast off from the dock. Hearing shouts, we looked back to see a reporter with photographer in tow, both of them running frantically. The tug captain was all for leaving them behind. Luckily we were still close enough to the dock for the tug to be manoeuvred against the side so the two men could jump on board. Harris said quietly that we needed their publicity for the start of our voyage. I wasn't sure what he meant. Harris simply repeated the formula: all things in good time!

The tug sounded one loud blast of her horn, the international signal for getting underway, and we began our slow cruise past wharves, docks, and warehouses. Many were in ruins, bearing the enduring tokens of the Luftwaffe's regard, and loomed eerily in the fog like some landscape from a nightmare. It was a gloomy and dispiriting ride, making it hard to believe that there was to be a glorious break for freedom at the end of it.

As we passed into the estuary, the water started to get a bit choppy. We slowed our speed and crept along through the pitch and yaw. We strained our eyes for a sight of the shoreline in the fog, and at last we recognised the dim smoke of our bonfire. In the end it was the tall masts of the *Bonnie Clyde* that guided us in as we spotted them above the low-lying billows of fog. The tug captain now slowed us down by putting the engines in reverse to aid in negotiating the turn that would bring us up to the bow of the *Bonnie*, carefully avoiding the hazard of the sunken coal barque.

As we drew alongside the ship, we could see Boris standing there. In his hands was a line ending in a heaving weight. He swung the heavy knot and flung the line over onto the tug, where it was taken up. This line was attached to a large hawser which was then drawn over to the tug. More lines flew, and were exchanged and pulled across while the tug's engine was put ahead to take up the slack. The tug captain walked out onto the stern of his boat, looking the *Bonnie* over with a practised eye.

Then an ominous bag containing explosives and timer were carefully hauled aboard.

"Here, looks like a fair bit of salvageable material there. Why, some of that line looks rather new." He craned his neck this way and that, trying to see more.

One of the officials made a dismissive gesture. "That's of no consequence now," he declared. "We don't intend to spend all day chipping away at bits and pieces."

"Well, that's as it may be, sir," said the tug captain, "you'll not want to be forgetting to save the ship's wheel after that fellow's done steering her to where we're going to do the scuttling."

"Aye," put in Harris, "You've already taken the anchors and whatever else was worth having."

"That's right then," said the tug captain. He turned to his deckhand, "Let me know when we're secured," he cried. Then he went into the wheelhouse returning a moment later with a mug of what must have been month-old coffee. The stuff looked as if it could eat right through the bottom of the cup.

We watched as Boris deftly got everything in order. It was amusing to think that everyone imagined Boris was the only hand on board the *Bonnie Clyde*, when a full outlaw crew was quietly hiding below.

"Do you need any help?" one of the deckhands called out.

Boris looked at him. "No, no help. Boris not needing help. Everything much under control."

The deckhand looked round with a baffled expression. "Here, who's this Boris?"

"That's him you're talking to, you bloody fool," said Harris impatiently.

"Now, now," one of the government officials chided, "We can't know everyone's name here. We're just doing a job. I hardly think that anyone sensible will grieve for this old hulk once she's gone. Why, the shoreline will look much better straightaway."

Harris was preparing a retort, but just then the deckhand returned to tell the tug captain that all the lines were secure and she was ready to go.

The tug captain went out for one last look. "Since we're not pressed for time, I believe I'll just go aboard for a bit of a look around." Then he realised that there was no way onto the ship from the bank. "Wasn't there a gangway there only the other day? Who in blazes took that down? And what on earth for?"

Harris and I looked at one another out of the corners of our eyes. "Oh, that was gone days ago, probably stolen like everything else," Harris said casually.

"It was? Those bloody scavenger bastards!" yelled the tug captain. "I'm sure they've picked her clean by now. Well, let's not sit here and mope. It's time to be off."

The rumble of the tug engines got louder as they met the strain on the hawser when the slack was fully taken up. A long slow turn to starboard would bring the bow of the ship around. We watched as her nose came round and she was carefully eased past the sunken barque. All the lines and rigging groaned a protest as if the ship were a bit arthritic and didn't care to stir out of bed. I looked carefully, but could see nothing visible about her to arouse any suspicion. Harris's mud idea seemed to have done the trick.

"There's a lot of canvas on those yardarms," one of the deckhands remarked.

"Yes, but it's all old worn stuff we came across," Harris responded. "Surely we owe her that much. After we put a hole in her, we'll set the sails, and let her go down on her own, just as we did for the last one. Surely all the tug operators must have heard about it."

The tugboat captain nodded in agreement, and everyone settled in to await the pull out to sea.

It was at that moment I realised why Harris had called the other scuttling a rehearsal. The tug crew and the officials would be expecting the same procedure this time, so no one was the wiser. Harris pointed, and we looked to see the *Bonnie Clyde*'s old commission pennant being run up the mainmast, ostensibly for the last time.

"Right then, we're off," the tug captain cried out. "Take her about easy."

He pushed on the throttles, and the tug moved forward with a roar, easily pulling the ship from her mooring. A single gull circled, seeing her off with plaintive cries.

"It's sad when you think about it," Harris said sombrely. "This good ship giving decades of service, all those years of usefulness, and when she's finally going, only one single seagull shows up."

I put my hand on his shoulder in exaggeratedly solemn consolation. "Do not despair, my friend," I said in a theatrical voice. I muffled a yelp as he pushed his elbow into my ribs.

"Let's not put it on too thick," he hissed.

As the ship bobbed along behind, we could see Boris at the helm, keeping her on an even course behind the tug as we worked our way out over choppy waves. I watched in admiration at the way he handled the great vessel, expertly compensating for resistance and slack in the hawser. The fog had nearly gone, giving us average weather for these waters.

"Good thing it's not raining," one of the deckhands said.

Now that we'd started on the long haul to the scuttling site, Harris beckoned Robert and me to go aft of the tug's cabin as if to watch the *Bonnie Clyde* straining at the tow behind us. He then told us a bit more of the plan that had been hatched to give us as many hours' head start as possible.

Harris said to me, "Your part is to back me up and make as much noise as possible when I pick a fight with one of the tug's crew or one of the officials. I'll signal you in some way when we start our part, and then just do your best."

"Fight?" I asked.

"It won't escape your notice!" he assured me.

To Robert he said, "Your part is critical. You have to be quick, and make sure that none of the others sees what you're up to. Your signal will be when the fight starts. You'll be waiting for the chance to get into the wheelhouse." Harris took a small magnet from his pocket. "Place this magnet on the east side of the binnacle, so that magnetic north will appear to be north-east or worse, and the boat will be steered in a more northerly direction, pointing to Clacton or Harwich. Use this tape to be damned sure it stays put and out of sight." He went on, "Next, while you're in the wheelhouse, you have to remove the handset from the radio and hide it on yourself. Once you're done, you must get to where the fight is so I can see you. Then you and Flynn are to get up the rope ladder to the *Bonnie* as fast as you can, and I'll be as close behind you as I can manage."

Now we were really burning our bridges—with a vengeance! Suddenly Robert and I were the key players. Robert wanted to know what to do with the handset. "It's to land on board the *Bonnie Clyde*," Harris said.

"I want to know how I can help," I told Harris.

"Just make sure no one tries to clobber me with a belaying pin or something from behind," Harris replied with a wry look.

I was angry that Harris had not discussed these details with us before we set out. This way we had very little notice to accomplish something so critical. Harris insisted that all would be fine if we did as he said. Harris and Robert went to scout out the wheelhouse while I sat quietly and waited.

Now every passing minute seemed like an hour, and an hour all but an eternity. The two officials were having a jolly time. It was like an outing to them.

I went up to the wheelhouse after Harris and Robert had finished enquiring as to our position. It seemed we'd be arriving at the spot they selected for the *Bonnie's* grave in less than an hour. I went back for my vacuum bottle and poured myself a mug of tea.

"What's that you're drinking?" Harris asked with a hopeful expression.

"Oh, it's a type of tea."

"Tea?" he said, with obvious disappointment.

"Yes, tea." I showed him the cup.

"What are all those bits floating about in there?"

"That's the tea—it's chamomile tea."

"Well, I don't know what the devil that is," he snorted. He took the handle of the cup, smelt it, and shrugged. "At least it's hot." He took a sip and then handed it back to me. "By God, that stuff tastes just like lawn drainings! That's no proper drink for a sailor. Why, when we'd set out for the day, I'd have a mug with me that size filled with Scotch or brandy. Even in port," he sighed. "Yes, that was fine for keeping the blood warm."

"Right," I said. "And had it not been for those large cups of Scotch or brandy, you probably wouldn't know what lawn drainings taste like." At that, he muttered something unintelligible and walked away.

The sky was growing clearer by the minute, and the sun was coming out. We took off our heavy woollen coats, staying warm in our sweaters as the morning wore on.

At last the tug's engines slowed to a rumble and the towrope to the ship behind slackened.

The tug captain came out. "Now lads, cast us off that line and we'll take the tug alongside."

"Alongside?" I whispered to Harris.

"Not to worry," assured Harris.

The tug moved along, circling the *Bonnie Clyde*, while Boris stood at the helm like a figure of stone. As we got closer, he threw down the rope ladder that was fixed amidships on her starboard side to make it easier to climb aboard. A deckhand threw him a line so he could tie off the tug to the ship.

The tug captain returned, "It's now time to go disconnect the pump and take away whatever else needs removing. If you want to set that last bit of sail, you'd best go and do it now." As he squinted up at the rigging, he noticed that more sail had been bent on the arms than he had previously seen. "Where did all that come from?" he puzzled.

Being noticed at this point made no difference whatsoever, for the die was cast, and everyone on board was anticipating the call to stations. As the photographer made ready for his pictures, all hell was about to break loose.

Harris turned about and in a whisper asked, "Ready?"

"Yes," I returned nervously. I turned to Robert who gave me a wink and a victory sign with his fingers. There was no turning back now.

Harris then wheeled, seized one of the government officials by his collar, and slammed him against one of the bulkheads of the tug. "What was that you said?" he roared in his great deep voice.

"I didn't say anything!" the man squeaked in alarm. This was in fact quite true, but Harris was brewing up a storm.

"I heard what you said! Asking me how I even know *who* my father is? Because my mother *told* me? You bastard!" He now roughly put him up against the derrick. Everyone came running out of the wheelhouse in alarm. I was sure Harris was going to kill this fellow; he certainly had *me* convinced. Suddenly it came to me that *this* was the diversionary tactic designed to get the attention of everyone on board, and it worked! Feeling stupid about not picking up on this at the outset, I immediately sprang into action.

In keeping with the imaginary grievance, I now spoke up as a witness, confirming that this man had rudely questioned Harris's parentage. I also kept an eye open in case anyone should try to help the official by trying to subdue Harris. At the same time, out of the corner of my eye, I saw Robert sliding into the wheelhouse. Harris now yelled at his victim, "I don't know why I'm even bothering to touch someone like you. You and your kind just make me want to vomit." And he lifted the man clear off the deck and dropped him in a heap next to the aft winding gear.

The captain intervened, "All right you two, break it up!" he commanded. The other official went and knelt by his colleague. "I say, that was bloody awful! What was it you said to him?"

Harris's victim, still trembling from the experience, found it hard to say anything. "I didn't say...I...I...didn't...I...," and he leaned back against the windlass, trying to compose himself. Luckily for him, Harris wasn't actually angry.

Just then Boris cried out, "Coming down! Coming down!" Looking up, I saw that he'd swung one of the ship's booms over the side and was lowering one of the pumps down to the tug.

"Wait a minute!" the captain yelled out. "I don't know where I'm going to stow that."

"Best to find a place fast," Boris cried, "or I give a little suggestion." The deckhand cleared a space on the tug's deck and the pump was then lowered carefully into place. I was wondering how we were going to get by less a pump, then I saw that the pump that had been lowered was one that didn't work. We still had two others aboard the *Bonnie* of which I was very glad. The thought of using the antiquated hand pump method was not something even to consider.

Robert now appeared at the *Bonnie*'s rail, having left the tug's wheelhouse, and got himself on board the ship by way of the rope ladder. He was wearing the smuggest smile, like a kid who'd just put a drawing pin on the teacher's chair. Later he told us that the helmsman was so anxious to find out what was happening that he'd practically begged Robert to steer for a little while as he rushed outside. "Well, of course I *couldn't* really refuse, but at the same time, I know as much about tugs as I do about catching tigers. At least I had plenty of time to fix the magnet in place and pull out the handset."

Harris quickly climbed up to the deck of the *Bonnie*. I hustled right behind him, but before I could lay hand on the rope ladder, the captain got between, crying out, "Here, what the bloody hell is going on?"

"Here, nothing!" Harris replied. He waved at me to hurry up the ladder, but one of the government officials got there first and started to climb in my place. Suddenly, it came crashing down onto the deck of the tug. Apparently Harris's weight had weakened it just to the breaking point.

"What the devil?" the captain sputtered with a curse. I stood in surprise. Without the ladder, how was I to get on board? No one had thought we might be doing without it. Everyone seemed puzzled for a moment. Then the line that had been used for the pump was lowered from the same boom, with Boris yelling, "Grab on, grab on. Hold

tight!" I jumped, and was pulled on board so quickly that when the
boom swung, it nearly threw me over the port side, but thankfully I was
none the worse for wear. Once I was on board, Robert and Boris cast
off the towlines.

No one on board the tug had yet realised what was going on, and
one of them yelled, "Throw down that rope. We'll tie the ladder back
on." But just as the words were leaving his lips, the bo'sun's pipe rang
out its shrill tune in the wind.

Immediately there came the thunder of feet from the fo'c's'le and
decks below. Boys were swarming up the standing rigging, all the way
up the ratlines and out to the massive yardarms. They were full of pent-
up energy and rushed to their stations with cries of excitement. Harris
was keeping an eye over the side just in case anyone should try to get
aboard, but the party on board the tug were all standing there completely speechless.

"Cast off foremast gaskets!" Bowman yelled. The ties holding the
furled sails to their yards were untied, the buntlines and clewlines slackened, and the sails bellied out from the yards. Some heated discussions
had been about how to set the sails; some in favour of all at once, others
mast by mast, and this is what we were now doing. After the foremast
came the main and then the mizzen. I think if we had tried to explode
all the sails out at one go, the strain on the ship could have caused one
of the masts to come dangerously close to breaking a yardarm or worse.
As it was, the ship groaned as the canvas on each mast was lowered
and caught the wind that dug the bow deeper into the water.
Finally all the strongest topgallants and topsails were set. What a sight
the ship was, as she heeled to meet the wind and surged away from the
tug. The crews on deck were then turning the huge yardarms to match
those already set to take the wind.

As the circus tents took their first breath of sea air and began to unfurl, the mud that was used to conceal the fact that these were not old
sails came to life with what looked like a magician's illusion. As they bellowed out, the dried mud gave off a cloud of dust into the wind and the
sails appeared as from a magic cloud. None of us, however, had given
any thought to the mud that dried in larger bits, which now rained
down upon the deck with Bowman receiving a generous dusting.

"Bloody great idea of yers, *Harris!*" He roared, as he brushed some
away with his hands and reached for his neckerchief, but the immediate
task of sweeping the deck or thoroughly brushing clothing would have
to wait—we had a ship to get underway.

Those aboard the tug watched this, but as we left its side I could hear one of the officials shrieking, "Piracy, they're making off with the ship! Piracy!"

The tug captain immediately went into his wheelhouse to radio in his status and report this completely unforeseen turn of events, only to come out a moment later shouting and waving his fist. We could all hear his words clearly. "You bastards! You've stolen my handset. I'll get you!" He ran out on deck and proceeded to treat us to the longest string of obscenities and profanity I've ever heard anywhere. Not only were insults heaped upon us, but upon every relative we ever had, ancestors and generations yet unborn. This chap was definitely a professional! I doubt anyone could beat him in a swearing contest. Even Bowman and Harris were suitably impressed by his expressive abilities, and we could hear snickers from the boys. No matter what the crew was hearing; the captain went back into the wheelhouse after exhausting his expletives. We could see black smoke pouring from the funnel along with the water boiling at the stern of the tug. She was going to give chase! The photographer started clicking as events unfolded before his very eyes, and the reporter was taking everything down as quickly as he could.

Now all that our boys had learnt and practised would have to pay off. After the initial setting of sails, Boris continued at the helm. The boys started to walk the capstan in earnest, bringing the yards round to capture the maximum wind. In all, we had set sixteen of the largest sails. I heard that in a half-gale a three-master set like that could do fifteen knots. Unfortunately we were not in a half-gale, but by the skill of Boris's steering and the response of the boys to his orders, we would soon be seeing twelve knots. But what of the time till we built up speed?

The tug captain, thoroughly enraged at all that happened, was capable of ramming us. We didn't want him to get athwart our bow. This would slow us down by forcing us to veer and tack, which would quickly exhaust the boys as they laboured to reset the yards at each manoeuvre. For a while it was really touch and go. The tug caught up and slowly started to overhaul us down the ship's length. This went on for what seemed like hours. At one stage, the tug's bow was level with the foremast. The tug captain's deckhands threw lines trying to grab a stanchion or a cleat so they could reverse their engines and slow us, but these were caught or cut before they grew taut. Then very slowly, we started to draw away. Tugs can manage twelve knots for a short distance, but are more comfortable at nine or ten. Their engines aren't designed for racing.

As we drew away, Harris walked aft waving something in his fist that had a long curly tail. It was the handset. His voice thundered across the gap, "You son of a wharf rat, call yourself a sailor? Never, unless you served aboard one of these." Harris picked up the bag containing the explosives and lowered it to the tug's deck. "Tell the Admiralty we won't be needing this." He laughed at the sight of the captain jerking about in his frustration, while obscenities flew across the ever-widening gap.

Edward now pulled the canvas hood off the binnacle, and there sat the ship's compass gleaming in the clear light of day. His spreading smile told all. Boris handed over the steering to Harris and went aloft to check on the boys' work. I could hear him praising and damning, but on the whole, more of the former than the latter. He came down to show the deck crew how to coil and stow the ends of the sheets and lines holding the yards and sails. This was something they hadn't been able to practice before for lack of rope. There was much to learn from practical experience that we had no opportunity to teach them before.

Bowman and Edward were poring over charts and taking sightings of the sun to determine our exact position. The wind was set fair for us, blowing from the south-west and fresh. Soon all we could see of the tug was a smudge on the horizon.

The whole thing suddenly hit me like a blow on the shoulders and I had to hold fast to the gunnel. We'd done it! We were on our way. The most dangerous part was to come, but we were all together in our purpose, come what may. I went below to find Katherine, to share the sheer sweetness of this time with her. She was in her element and had been able to get a fire going. Soon I found myself sitting comfortably with a mug of hot tea in my hands. I looked on drowsily as Katherine busied herself preparing our first meal afloat. This must be close to absolute bliss. And the real adventure had only just begun.

Chapter 15
SAILING AWAY

There was no time to sit about idly dreaming, now that the *Bonnie* was once more alive and doing battle with the sea! The crew was busy wrestling and trimming the sails as they slapped in the breeze. I went on deck to find Bowman looking over the stern as if half-expecting to see the tug reappear. He slapped his knee and rubbed his hands together in obvious enjoyment of what had happened.

He turned back to Harris and Edward with a smile. "Well, lads," he began. His attention was suddenly drawn to the sails now stretching from the mast. At least three of them were decoratively displaying the broad stripes that had once enlivened the circus tent. His smile faded as he turned to Harris, pointing aloft at the striped canvas.

"What the bloody hell is that? I told ye we weren't going to use those things. I told ye they weren't necessary!" Bowman shouted.

"Now come on, Uncle Billy," Harris said, putting his hand firmly on the old man's shoulder, "we're using everything possible to catch the wind. If I remember correctly, you said you'd even fly your nightshirt. So go and fetch it, will you?"

Bowman was not to be cajoled. "Bugger it!" he cried. "There's not much I can do about it now, but it'll be damned embarrassing if anyone sees us looking like this."

Harris threw up his hands and shrugged. After one more look, Bowman walked away shaking his head.

The boys were running round the deck carrying out Boris's orders. He was trying to get every ounce of power out of the wind. The boys were first on the brace winches, adjusting the lower yards, and then hauling the halyards to the upper yards to bring those in line. Having made a couple of corrections, Boris told the boys to stand down for a while as we followed our course south through the English Channel.

Katherine put her head up out the hatchway. "Can I come up now?"

Harris spoke up. "Yes, but be careful of all the coiled rope lying about."

I went over and helped her out of the hatchway and steadied her along the rail. We were still finding our sea legs, even Harris. It was too easy to miss the motion of the deck as the ship rolled and heeled even slightly to the pull of the waves and the push of the wind. Katherine gazed out at the expanse of waves, and I pointed out the faint trace of the tug's smoke disappearing in the distance.

"I hate to be the bearer of bad news," she said, "but what's to stop them radioing in to give away our position and which course we're taking?"

Harris nodded in agreement, "That's a very good point. However, they'd be needing this." He pulled out a long curly cord and a microphone with a touch-key at the top. It was the handset Robert had "borrowed."

Harris smiled, "Without this, no one's going to find out a single thing until they get back to port! Bear in mind, they don't know Morse code anyway, as I found out while chatting with the tug captain."

Boris had just come down from the rigging and darted up when he saw the handset in Harris's hand. "This is it!" he said excitedly. "This is last part we need for radio." I realised that Boris had not seen the theft, nor Harris taunting the tug captain.

"That's right," Harris said with a knowing smile, "I couldn't find a whole radio anywhere in the scrap yard. By the time I started looking, most of the radios had already been removed and others had parts missing. But, Flynn," and he turned to me, "I heard that you have some experience using a radio. I hereby appoint you Chief Signalman and Radio Operator, acting unpaid, in addition," he laughed, "to your regular duties as watch officer and general dogsbody. That should keep you busy and out of mischief," he added, with a swift look at Katherine. Harris held up his hand as I started to protest, "What you don't know, you can learn by trial and error. I've also done a bit of sparks in my time."

"This very good, very good," Boris called as he hastened below to put together the rest of the radio. Now we could call whomever we liked! Use of the ham radio was forbidden during the war because of fears of spying and espionage, but its popularity now flourished.

Katherine had been taking all this in and looked doubtful. "All right, so he doesn't have his radio, but that tugboat captain is going to burst his boiler to get back and make his report. It was only a few hours to get out here, after all. It'll probably take them the same to get back to port and then perhaps there'll be something much faster trying to overtake us, or hadn't you considered that?"

"Katherine, you've a fine grasp of these things," Harris said as if deep in thought, in actuality trying to hide his grin. "You see, they'll have to use their ship's compass to navigate, and I'm afraid that magnetic north is not where it once was. With a little diversion, we managed to sabotage the compass. I calculate that by the time they realise they're not seeing the correct lights, it'll be dark. They'll be forced to heave to until morning or head for one of the Southend lights. The only place at Southend that could dock a tug is the end of the pier. I'm sure that captain won't want anymore publicity for this affair than he's already going to get. My bet is he'll put out a sea anchor off the shipping lanes, keep a lookout all night, and move in the morning when he can get line-of-sight bearings. Taking all this into account, I think we have a nine or ten hour head start before he's able to make his report. Surely someone will follow, but we've more surprises in store for them." Harris was definitely looking smug.

Bowman was jumping about and clapping his hands in delight that the plan had succeeded so perfectly. At least for now, he'd forgot about the striped sails.

"They've enough fuel to make it back, I suppose," Edward remarked to Harris. "If not, then we have even more time."

Harris shrugged his shoulders. "Any captain making a trip like today ought to have left the dock with a full tank. If he didn't, it's not our worry."

There was a momentary pause, and Katherine took advantage of it to ask if anyone wanted something hot to eat, as most had gone without since early morning.

Harris applauded. "Yes! I don't know about the rest of you, but I'm starved. Eating cold food at sea is something we should only be doing in storms. Come to think of it, that was most of the time, not so very long ago." While Harris was awake, hungry was his usual state. Katherine disappeared below to see about a proper meal for the crew, and Harris detailed two boys to go and give her a hand.

I suggested to Harris that he get together with Boris and take stock of the various boys' abilities so watches could be set up and chores could be allocated to each watch. That would leave one or two jobs, such as the helm, as duties for the rest of us. Edward was manning the helm, so an impromptu meeting between Bowman, Harris, Edward, Boris, Robert, and myself was held near the wheel.

The boys were split into two watches, eight hours on and eight hours off duty. Off duty meant if you'd just sailed the ship through a storm, you were entitled to some sleep, but you'd have to help out if the weather got bad, or if chores needed tending. The list was endless!

We finished the meeting and were about to go below when Robert asked us to hold a moment. "Well now," he said, "since we're all officially involved in this act of piracy, I felt it my obligation to contribute something as well. At first I didn't know what that might be, but then I thought of a little token that would remind us, and tell anyone looking at us, that we're not pirates. After all, at best we're merely thieves, taking property that doesn't belong to us."

"What in God's name are you on about?" Harris demanded.

Robert reached under his coat and pulled out the folded-up red ensign of the British Merchant Navy, the famous Red Duster. "I'll run it up at the stern, that's the traditional place," he said, but Bowman overruled him.

"No," Bowman said, "not at the stern. There's nothing usual about this voyage, so run it up the mainmast instead, there for all to see and know who we consider we are. We'll fly the British ensign at our stern."

We all stood by as Robert dogged the flag to its line and slowly ran it up the mast. Everyone saluted as it disappeared above into the vari-coloured expanses of canvas, which were now pulling us along at a steady twelve knots. Then we went below for a well-earned meal, leaving Boris at the helm and the starboard watch on duty.

As we stepped into the galley, we all sniffed appreciatively. The smell of good food was overwhelming. The main dish appeared to be in a huge cauldron steaming at the middle of the stove. Harris said to Katherine, "I don't like to think of that great pot going over in a rough sea. I've put ties on both those handles so you can lift it quickly if the sea gets too rough."

"Thank you very much," she replied, "that sounds like a fine idea, but why don't we take it one step further? What if we turn the pot into a swing by putting the ropes over the beam, and I can suspend it over the stove. This pot is going to be in operation most of the time, since the best and most warming food at this time of year is a good stew."

"Now, that's an even better idea," Harris admitted. He turned to me. "Why don't you be about it, while—"

"Oh no, you don't," I said. "You're always good at giving orders and then wandering off. This needs two to make it work." We set to work straightaway. Once we'd installed ropes to both handles, we were able to get our meal. The others had quickly piled a tray high and vanished out the door to our wardroom. Harris followed them while I stayed behind to get in Katherine's way by using part of her worktable.

"How are you coming along with all this so far?" I asked.

She turned with a smile. "Splendidly," she said, giving me a kiss on the cheek. "I've been working like a slave since I came on board and I've just made a meal for twenty-six starving men and boys. I'm enjoying every minute of it. Life seems to have taken on a bit of purpose, after a long time without it."

She paused and became a little pensive. "I never really liked Mrs. Beasley, but I do feel a bit ashamed about leaving without warning. With you gone as well, she certainly must be feeling the strain. But," and she brightened, "I'll bet she'll be so mad I pity all there. Still, Jean from the village should be there to keep up with the cleaning as I arranged with her yesterday."

"Stop blaming yourself," I said, and caught her by the waist, holding her comfortably to me. "You just said that you're enjoying yourself, so don't look for gloomy puritan reasons for not doing so."

She grinned up at me, "This is unquestionably the greatest adventure of my life."

I reminded her that although I'd seen active duty in the war, I'd never done anything quite like this myself. I gave her one final kiss and set off for the radio room.

The radio room was actually a corner of the chart room where the receiver and transmitter had been set up on a bench along the port bulkhead. Boris had already wired in the handset, using power from the same generator that worked the pumps. I then remembered Todd, Larry's friend who was good with a wireless, and thought I'd have a word with him later.

All that could be heard was a hum with occasional crackles. Since Harris had given me the job, I tracked him down and asked him to clarify my duties because I hadn't any real idea what was expected of me.

He pulled out his massive silver pocket watch and said, "There's time to tell you what I've arranged with friends of mine before they call. Let's get back to the radio and I can explain."

Seated in front of the machine, Harris took down the clipboard I'd seen hanging up on the bulkhead and started to tell me what the numbers and names meant. "See here, the *Grouse* is a powered three-masted square-rigger out of Harwich. The captain, Bob Freeman, is also the owner. He owes me a wee favour or two and is part of this adventure as well. I've arranged an innocent little diversion with his help. These two numbers are the frequencies for his ship. The same applies for the other names." He checked the time again using the ship's clock, whose brass glowed from the starboard bulkhead with its bell striking the hours.

Harris continued, "Bob should be calling in about five minutes, at 1100 as arranged. We've fixed our position by triangulation, using three radio beacons from old wartime aerodromes that the RAF hasn't used since the war ended. But when the aerodromes were abandoned, everything was left turned on. Now, when we talk with Bob, we'll tell him our position and he'll head this way for about a half-hour. Then he'll change course due north. This will take him back into the normal shipping lanes while we change our present heading of east-sou'east to sou'sou'west."

Just then, the radio broke into life, and Harris listened to the clock strike four bells before picking up the microphone to answer.

Bob's time was spot on. "*Calling Harris, calling Harris,*" called the voice over the radio's speaker, "*can you hear me, over?*"

Harris depressed the switch on the handset and answered, "You're loud and clear, Bob, you old bastard. How are you and the missus?"

"*Hey, a little less of the old, Harris. I'm all right and so is the old lady. Long time no see, but I'll have to make this short and sweet. The fish are running and every pair of hands is needed. Tell me what time you want me to change course. Sorry I can't stay and chat.*"

"Head due north at six bells and keep that course for about four hours. After that, just carry on about your business as usual. It should buy us a little more time when I report sighting a sailing ship heading due north, possibly a three-masted barque. I won't keep you, Bob, but we really owe you and thanks a million!"

"*Right, Harris,*" came Bob's voice. "*I'll look forward to a few jars with you next time, out.*"

Harris stowed the handset. "So now we're going to make a course correction. Where the devil is Bowman?" he asked impatiently.

"In his cabin, I assume," I said. "But now that you come to mention it, I haven't seen him for a while myself." We started down the companionway and along the passage to find the captain's door shut. Harris beat upon it with his fist.

"For God's sake!" said Bowman inside, "do ye think ye could beat on it any harder?"

"Not without breaking something, Uncle Billy. It's time for you to come up on deck. We're about to make a course change."

"Ah, right! I'll be there directly."

We went back up to the bridge deck and found Boris still in charge of the huge double wheel. It was so tall that there was a step built to raise the helmsman so that he could stand easily with his arms stretched sidewise just below shoulder height. There was another step on the other side so a second man could be added when the weather got rough. There was also a foot brake to help slow down the wild turning of the wheel during heavy weather.

While we waited for Bowman, Harris went into the chart room to speak to Edward about the exact heading. At the moment, we were heading away from the Essex shore as fast as we could go. Once we were far enough east to clear the Kentish coast, we needed to turn due south and head down through the Straits of Dover.

Bowman reached the top of the companionway and walked down the deck like his usual self. However stoutly he carried himself, I felt he was putting on an act and was actually in pain. Having learnt the new course from Edward, he gave the order to prepare to change course onto the other tack. This was going to test our boys and I could hear them chatting excitedly.

"Wouldn't Mr. O'Connell just die to see us now?" said one of the boys.

"Yes," said another. "All this time he thought it was a class in history."

The boys started laughing. One put his hand up on the guardrail quickly as his shoe slipped, and Boris scolded him, as much of a scolding as Boris was ever committed to giving.

"You boys pay attention! Down there, Big Splat! Over there, Big Splash! Doesn't matter, we can't stop and find you. It takes long time to turn about, and who knows what fish swim these waters?" he lectured. The boys eyed each other sheepishly for a moment and then set to their work with a more serious attitude.

Several blasts of the bo'sun's pipe sent one watch to brace the upper yards round, while the other watch manned the brace winches for the lower. We'd been travelling since noon with the wind abaft the port quarter. Now we were going to swing with the wind through an arc of ninety degrees, racing against the turn and brace the yards round, so that the sails would start to belly out again from the wind now blowing across the starboard quarter.

Everyone knew his station. Boris had prepared them well.

Harris sang out, "Let's do it!"

A couple more blasts on the pipe and the large yards started to turn slowly. Robert was at the wheel with Boris, alternately helping and then going off to check on the boys manning braces and buntlines. The ship seemed to hang there for a long time before she came round onto the new heading, heeling low over the water before the helmsman caught and centred the wheel. Now we were well and truly on our way. Having seen the operation through, Harris and I went back to the radio ready to report the *Grouse* as us, or rather to report an unknown sailing vessel sighted about eleven hundred hours near our "scuttling position," heading due north.

Bowman was beside himself with an almost unholy joy. He kept walking up and down saying good, good, very good! to everyone and rubbing his hands together.

He stopped to talk to me. "I can just see it, ye know. If they send anyone out to try and locate that ship, they'll probably follow her for miles, and all the while," he laughed hard and long, "they'll be trying to call her using the *Bonnie Clyde*'s frequency and she won't answer because she's the *Grouse*. The best part of the joke is we'll be able to hear all that's going on. If they do manage to get close enough to read her name or try to question anyone aboard, the *Grouse* is just an innocent by-stander." He roared with laughter and went on, "I'd dearly love to see the faces of those Whitehall twits when the news comes through." And off he went still smiling, which certainly made a difference to his earlier dour expression.

This was the first time I'd seen Bowman and Edward acting in tandem. That, in itself, was a major accomplishment. I wasn't certain how long that would last, given their previous history together. I always found it amazing that each of them could have such high respect for one another and yet fall into such bitter disagreements. For now they seemed perfectly satisfied to agree. I wasn't about to say or do anything that might jeopardise this accord.

Robert was now at the helm. Harris and I made our way onto the bridge deck with him. The ship seemed truly alive and pushed on as if there was no end to where she might go. The sails held firm, bellied out to catch all the wind available. The breeze lessened to where we were doing ten to twelve knots. It was cold, but it was the sort of night when one felt the fulfilment of the day.

I had a score to settle with Harris. I was tired of being treated as though I was some untrustworthy child. Today had been a last straw! I'd known nothing about the fight until the last minute, much less about the magnet, and I knew nothing about the *Grouse*. Yet I was supposed to take an active part in this whole enterprise.

"Now Harris," I began, "I want to know now what other little arrangements you have up your sleeve. I'm sick and tired of your 'all things in good time.' I want to know the rest of the story."

He paused and considered this and then replied, "Bowman and I decided from the beginning that the less people know, the more likely we would succeed. We knew quite well there were too many who would talk after a few pints, not to mention others who might be tempted to tell a girlfriend a thing or two." I started to protest, but then thought better of it. "However, there's one thing left. It's an unknowing decoy to give the Whitehall idiots a range of choices. It's the *Willow*. She's a four-masted barque, one of those that took part in the last great race from Australia in 1938 under a different name. She's a training ship now out of Gothenburg, and according to Bob, she's travelling between the North Sea and the Channel to give the apprentices some wet weather experience. She looks enough like us at a distance to be reported. And report her we will. All we need is enough time to muster distance if a pursuit starts."

The sails began making heavy flapping noises as the bow fell slightly, which Robert quickly adjusted.

Harris said, "This is just what we needed. We'll pick up a few more knots as soon as the wind increases and be farther away before they make the discovery. If they wait until the tug turns up, then we'll have an unbeatable head start. The trick with the magnet should ensure that the tug won't find its way home until mid-morning tomorrow."

"That's if it works," I remarked.

"No reason why it shouldn't," Harris went on, "There'd be no reason for the tug captain to doubt anything was wrong until he was in sight of land. Then he couldn't be deceived any longer by what he originally thought were the right landmarks. I suppose the skew we put on the compass will bring him somewhere between Clacton and Harwich, which is far enough north for him to probably not know the landmarks. He's damned sure to notice how much time it took for him to get nowhere! It'll be right about dark by then. Having to heave to till morning will just set his arse on fire. Well, there you have it. Have you anymore questions now, Mr. Must-Know-Now-Instead-of-In-Good-Time? Time is here, time has come, and time is passing away," he roared. "Let's get some work done, even if we have to pull this lady all the way to Scotland!"

"And to that," I said, "some of us need sleep. If we don't get it, we start doing funny things like falling over and walking sideways. I suggest we call it a day and get some sleep so we will live to fight another day, like tomorrow!"

Harris gave me a sidelong grin. He went to the chart room to go over some things with Edward. This probably meant more arguments over the course we were to take, and I was just as glad not to include myself in the discussion.

I made my way down to the galley where I found Katherine sitting and nursing a mug of tea.

"Long day," I began, "I don't think I've ever had one this exciting."

"You never cease to amaze me, Flynn," she said, giving me a hug.

"But I think if I don't get some sleep, I'll surely fall on my face," I whispered.

We headed for the officers' quarters, and I kissed her once more at her door, then entered my cabin slowly sliding the door closed behind me. I wonder when it is that I shall awake peacefully, with a cup of tea placed just to hand and the chance to contemplate a long slow day with little of urgency in it. Not this morning anyway.

I was awakened by the sounds of a hundred squawking seagulls, before I realised it was only the boys gathering in the well deck, standing around chattering. I sat up, still in my clothes of the night before when I'd fallen on the bunk and gone out like a light. A quick shave and a light wash at the corner basin made me feel more alive. I could still hear the sound of the boys' voices and went out to join them. I decided to get to know some of my fellow crew members. After all, these were the ones we'd have to rely on for the voyage.

"How long have you been at sea, Mr. Flynn?" one of them asked.

"Too long, or not long enough, depending on your point of view," I laughed.

At that moment, Boris came on deck with Robert. Both of them were carrying large bundles under their arms.

"Right lads, come and line up," Robert called. Once they were all standing ready, Robert and Boris started to undo the bundles. Inside were woollen uniforms, oilskins, jerseys, hats, and boots. It was called Navy surplus, but was actually the clothing taken from sailors as they were demobbed. "When you get uniforms that fit," Robert explained, "I want you to get your pocket knives and cut off all the rank stripes, badges, and Royal Navy shoulder flashes. We don't want anyone saying that we're desecrating the King's uniforms or any nonsense like that!" Now they'd have something designed for the weather.

Robert was giving out more instructions. "Larry will be in charge of things. I want you to take this lot to your quarters and sort out the uniforms as close to your size as possible, especially the boots."

Here Boris broke in. "Boots most important!" Boris said emphatically. "Last night I see boy slip. I know I said before, but boots very important!"

Robert continued, "There'll be some items left over and you'll look after them, Larry, for extra issue when anyone's clothes are too wet. All the rags that you're wearing now are to be bundled up and ready to go over the side by tomorrow. Just think of it as where you'd like to see

Mr. O'Connell go." At this the boys gave a great cheer and, picking up the bundles, headed for their quarters.

I was pleased for them. Soon they'd discover what I'd learnt years ago before I became an officer. The Navy bum-freezer with its long back collar was one of the best all-weather uniforms I knew. If you couldn't get out of the wind—as who could while a hundred feet in the air setting sails?—the flap, pulled over the top of the head and held by a cap, kept you from freezing. Besides, wool's the only thing that will keep you warm even when it's wet.

As the boys disappeared, Edward came stumbling along from the chart room. He was distracted and muttering to himself. At one point, he stopped and sniffed, looking about as if trying to find whatever he'd smelt. He turned to Boris. "This damn place smells like a bloody circus. Like a bloody zoo, it does!"

Boris pointed up at the sails. "Circus!" he agreed and nodded, grinning. Edward just growled and carried on with his walk.

After a while the boys reappeared, and what a difference! The clothes helped give them bulk, so they looked more like men than weedy children. It was the way they held themselves that really made the difference. Even though the clothes were castoffs and musty, they were real uniforms. The boys now looked like seamen on a voyage. I think this had really now come home to them. They weren't solemn in any way, but their talk was not all bright and birdlike; it had more meaning, sincerity, and seriousness about it.

Boris made a quick inspection and separated out those boys who would be a danger to themselves aloft. They were to form the deck party whenever the sails needed furling or setting. "You good boys," he explained. "Nothing wrong with you. Just clothes and boots not fit." No doubt he'd already begun thinking of a solution to this.

I saw that Bowman was standing near the wheel. A smile of quiet satisfaction was on his face as he saw the boys looking and acting like sailors. He had a word with one or two, glancing every now and then at his watch and compass. Suddenly Boris's bo'sun's pipe shrilled out, sending all the boys to their stations.

"Right, lads!" Bowman called out. "'Tis time to turn the yards again, but only a little. This will bring us around just a bit more to the west, and if we're lucky, we can beat along close-hauled for the next fifteen hours."

The pipe sounded again, signalling the deck party to put their weight to the capstan bars and walk the yards round. Others on deck and aloft let out the lines cleated to the leading edges of the sails, while other boys hauled in on those to the trailing edges. With the wind abaft our port quarter, the ship continued close-hauled to keep the maximum of her wind power.

I went to speak to Edward who was in the chart room, with maps and charts spread over the big table. He always had a pipe in one hand and a map in the other. His glasses, which he wore for this, made him look rather like the mad scientist at work.

"I thought we'd already made a course correction last night," I said.

"It was really only partial," Edward replied. "If you're interested, I can show you where we are on the map."

I should say I was interested! After having to pry information out of the others with the mental equivalent of a pick and shovel, anyone volunteering information was to be listened to with great attention. Seeing me eager, he went on.

"This is how it is, then." Pulling one chart to the centre of the table, Edward pointed to the first of a series of crosses marked in the Thames Estuary about midway between Clacton and Margate. "This is an exact position which we got by triangulation. It's about halfway to the scuttling point. While you were sunning yourself on the tug, we were working up here, being very careful to keep out of eyeshot of anyone on the tug. This cross here was our position last night when we made our big course correction to head south," He pointed to the last cross heading almost due east. "You can see from these sandbanks that we had to go far enough east to avoid going aground. Having come far enough due south, by my calculations, I've put her sou'sou'west. As Bowman said, with any luck, we should go through the Straits on this tack, and won't need to change course until we get to this point," and he slapped the chart south of Brighton.

I made up my mind to get to know Edward better. He was willing to keep me up to date about the ship as long as I wasn't going to be as argumentative as Bowman and Harris had been with him. As long as I didn't question his judgment and seemed eager to learn he was very happy to answer questions—as long as he felt he was teaching.

Chapter 16
CLEARING AWAY AND MESSAGES FROM HOME

Boris had been finishing up splices and extra work on the lines, and then he checked the grommets on the sails. He exclaimed, "They did very good job! Never making sails before, they did very good." He nodded, tipped his cap, and disappeared below. Shortly thereafter, we heard quite a bit of banging and thrashing about, but this was Boris's way. He liked being alone, and he didn't like people irritating him while he worked. Everyone stayed clear of the main hatchway, for this was Boris's domain.

"What's he doing down there?" I wondered aloud.

"Don't ask!" Harris said. "It's his place, and if you venture down there, you'll gain nothing but his wrath which I assure you can be formidable at times."

After a while Robert went forward, saying something about stores, and left Harris at the helm. It was unusually quiet and I asked where the boys were who were off watch.

"Down below, 'tween deck forward," Harris replied. "Maybe you can go and help."

I gave up on my intended assault on the dreaded radio for the moment.

The 'tween deck was an upper hold just under the main deck, about five feet high at its low end and as wide as the ship, with the aft section divided into our cabins. It stretched from the foremast and ended at the main hold. We weren't carrying much, so Boris used this forward hold as a store for anything in the way of food and extra sail. The main hold was reached through the main hatchway where all the lines and serviceable equipment used for running the ship were stowed. This was Boris's private domain and served double duty as his sleeping quarters.

In the rush and tumble of getting everything on board, many things were put down anywhere there was room and left unsecured. I was glad that we'd not had a storm our first day out. With all the hatches battened down, the 'tween decks is a dark place and one needs plenty of light to avoid falling down through the tonnage openings under the hatches. I had my own method of avoiding these openings and walked as near to the hull as possible. However, with twenty boys dashing around excitedly, I made a note to talk to Harris about putting some sort of covers in place for these traps.

I went down through number two hatch and could see the boys further forward. They'd found some lanterns and had two suspended over the great mound of stores.

I could hear Robert giving instructions, "All this stuff was accumulated by Harris and Boris over quite a period. We might not need all of it on the voyage, but we'll never know if we don't sort it out. Now what we're looking for is paint, and anything to do with cleaning, such as tools, soap, and disinfectant. If you sort those out and put them here," he showed them a space between two of the ship's ribs, "that'll make it easier to see what's left."

Robert moved some things and came up with a blanket. "As you're looking for cleaning supplies, make another pile for any bedding or clothing you find, including life jackets and life belts. Eventually, we'll need to make things secure during bad weather so they don't get thrown about."

I congratulated him on handling the task, to which Robert blew a quiet raspberry. "I didn't tell them what their next job was going to be," he said. I raised my eyebrows questioningly. "And that is cleaning and painting as much of the topsides as we can, without getting paint everywhere. You remember what the Straits are like, don't you, Flynn? If we get caught in a headwind, we'll be tacking back and forth for ages. We don't want wet paint all over the place. Painting aloft is a stupid idea if you ask me. I'll ask Harris to get free of that notion."

I agreed and suggested we should explore lockers and other spaces to find out what they contained and to get to know the ship. I'd never been on a three-master before, and I knew that Robert's only experience had been on a schooner. As we were the lowest-level officers on the ship, we needed to learn about the ship before an emergency found us short on knowledge and unable to carry out orders. We found another couple of lanterns and went into the gloom and smell of the area under the fo'c's'le head, deck, and forepeak.

The forepeak was piled high with coal, so I knew where Katherine needed to send her helpers when the galley ran out. The coal-store was fragrant compared to the rest of the area, which consisted of the crew's head, washroom, and a store full of grease drums.

"Ah!" exclaimed Robert, "just the place to store the paint. We should be able to tie it down in here."

We came back to find the boys hard at work sorting the pile of soft-goods. Walking aft, we came to the area below the poop deck and found a large locked door marked Galley Stores. Having seen the way the boys could eat, locking these doors was simply protecting our interests. On our way through the 'tween decks, I'd shown the tonnage openings to Robert and asked him to keep an eye open for something we could use to cover them.

By the time we got this far, I knew I had to get on with my radio studies. I said to Robert, "Before Harris starts shouting at me, find out how to reach someone in the village or near it. We need to know if there's going to be a pursuit. And if I can find a way to reach Martin, I'm sure he can make some discreet enquiries." I made off to the chart room.

To my surprise, there sat Harris. He was sitting in what was supposedly my chair, although I'd laid very little claim to it as yet, with headphones on and guidebooks open everywhere. He looked up as I came in and motioned me to sit in the other chair. He had the handset up to his lips and was listening very intently to someone at the other end.

After a while, he clicked on the handset and said, "Right then, I'll be expecting your call in about two hours. Be careful how you make contact. Just make damn sure nobody is listening. And thanks for agreeing to go out straightaway. We do need to know as soon as possible, over."

As he turned towards me, I put up my hand and said, "Wait a minute! I wasn't at the radio because you told me to go and help Robert."

"Feeling guilty, are we, Flynn?" Harris grinned. "Not to worry. I've been filling in for you since this morning." He laughed and feinted a cuff at me. "It's just me, lad. It's the way I am. I've been a sparks in my time, but the equipment was very old-fashioned and we didn't have microphones, only a Morse key," he said with evident nostalgia. "I suppose I could still use one of those. By studying these books, I discovered that we can do a number of things with this machine. Most importantly, I found we can call a ham. I remember about Martin being a good contact for the newspapers, and after he brought us such a nice going-away present, I thought we should contact him." I didn't tell him that only a moment ago I remarked on the same thing to Robert, but listened as he went on.

"I'm sure there'll be some sort of investigation started in the village when they can't find the boys. Amongst these books is one that tells you how to find the call sign of someone you don't know. You need an address, and I thought that Allhallows wouldn't be enough since it's so miniscule." Harris chuckled, revelling in the excitement of the chase.

Harris continued, "Would you believe it? There are two in the area, one in the village and one at Cliffe just down the road. With a little more investigation, I found out how to broadcast the call sign. In short order, I had the man himself on the speaker, but I found I could hear much better using the headphones. His name is Richard Samson, though he prefers Dick, and he knows Martin well and most of the regulars too.

"He told me that he heard the police had been round asking questions, but I was able to reassure him that nothing had happened to any of the boys or to you or Katherine. At first he was a bit worried about that because he didn't want it to be found later that he'd aided and abetted a suspected felon, as they say in the newspapers. I had to tell him very briefly what we'd done, and he was all for it. Apparently, like most of us, he'd had a bellyful of government interference from wartime regulations, and so long as nobody was hurt or likely to get hurt, he was willing to help us. I think there's something instinctively British or maybe exclusively English about what we consider right and wrong. We'll obey a hundred regulations blindly, do as we're told at every step, but give us a whiff of injustice or unfairness, and we'll be on the other fellow's side against officialdom like a shot.

"All Dick had heard is that we'd proposed to the government a feasible solution to what they regarded as a problem, but that they wouldn't consider changing their course of action. He's going out to fetch Martin, who should be able to get away for a couple of hours, and have him tell us the latest news." Harris said smugly.

"You've outdone yourself this time," I said. "Even if you can't drive, you can certainly make the radio work. I still want to be the radio officer, however."

Harris said he'd be back in an hour, but I could find him with Bowman if Martin called earlier. I settled down to wait with the pile of guides in front of me, eager to do my part in our kick against authority.

I was just starting to grasp emergency procedure when the radio suddenly started to crackle. I could hear someone speaking, but too low for me to understand. Then it came to life with a high howl.

I called to Boris, "Tell one of the boys to go and find Larry or Todd."

A system of blasts on the pipe were signals for different orders and different operations to be carried out. They were often all that could be heard over the wind. The pipe gave its shrill call, and soon Larry came running.

The radio was squealing like a pig going for slaughter, and then a voice suddenly broke clear, *"Calling Harris, calling Harris, are you receiving me?"*

I picked up the handset. "Harris here, Harris here, receiving you loud and clear." I released the switch and waited for a response. It seemed a long time coming. Meanwhile Harris strode in and I told him I was still waiting for some response. Taking the handset, he pressed the switch several more times, as he took his seat.

There was a loud click from the speaker and Martin's excited voice came over. *"Is that you, Flynn? Ha! This is fantastic to think that we're talking like this. Is everything all right with you, Katherine, and everybody?"*

"We're all right," I replied, "but unfortunately I don't have all the time in the world to stop and chat. What we'd really like to know is what's been happening at the inn and in the village. Have the police been round? Any lackeys from whatever ministry is responsible for forcing us into this action? Has anyone—"

"Hold on there," Martin came back cheerfully, *"that's far too many questions for me to remember. Let me tell you what's been happening, and then you can ask questions."* After the crackling and howling, the radio settled down to a more or less even tone as we listened to Martin's story.

"This morning, as you can well imagine, Mrs. Beasley was doing exactly as I thought she'd do, going mad before my eyes. She was ramping about trying to get things cooked, tidying this and that, suddenly remembering something in the bar or kitchen and such. She was at full steam, trying to do everything at once.

"'I will never understand what people are about,' she said to me, 'Flynn and Katherine disappearing like that, and here I'm left with all these things to do.' I suggested that we could do with some extra help. At that point the lady from the village still hadn't shown up and I did feel a bit sorry for Mrs. B. I suppose it serves her right. After all, she should be a bit more understanding of people, and then she might not be surprised by their reaction to her. Just when I thought she'd start screaming in frustration, there was the hooting of a car's horn and that grey face of O'Connell appeared round the door. He looked terrible and about to collapse.

"'Oh, Bertha,' he said, and I thought he was going to cry, 'when I got back...' and he looked at me, wondering, no doubt, if I knew where from, but I pretended I was seriously studying a menu. He carried on, 'When I got back to the orphanage, everyone had gone. Not a single soul to be found anywhere! That wasn't all', he said, and took her arm and shook it. 'Their belongings were also gone. Everything, even down to the sheets and mattresses!'"

Martin was laughing heartily, but it was a tinny sound over the radio. "*You can picture it: raised eyebrows and incredulous squeals from Mrs. B....Then she said it was odd, everyone around here seemed to have disappeared too. O'Connell asked her what she meant by everyone.*

"'*Well, I can't find the woman that works here. You remember Katherine and our gardener, Mr. Flynn? They both seem to have vanished.' O'Connell thought this was too much of a coincidence, and he rang the local constabulary. He also called Scotland Yard. 'All the boys and your two helpers gone sounds like a case for the police,' he said. She agreed and must have said a dozen or more times, 'Something odd is going on, something very odd.'*

"*I could hardly believe my ears*," Martin went on, "*She agreed without endless argument. I was quite surprised when O'Connell said Scotland Yard was sending somebody down. Later O'Connell met the local police, including the CID from Gravesend. I was told by one of the local Bobbies that when the CID inspector asked him how many boys were missing, he didn't know precisely! Can you beat that? Apparently he first said that seventeen or eighteen were gone and when the inspector asked which figure was right, he got angry with him! I'm surprised he wasn't arrested on the spot!*" Martin was laughing delightedly and I could see why.

Here was a man in an official position, receiving government funds, openly admitting to a police officer that he doesn't know how many boys were in his care. Although I laughed at how ridiculous it sounded, I knew from what I'd seen of the boys that he'd neglected them shamefully. Several boys were seriously malnourished, and I didn't like that one little bit.

"*Later*," Martin went on, "*the police came down to ask me some questions, and I started to sweat a bit not wanting to get caught in any lies. The inspector found Mrs. B. still in a tiff about her barmaid and the gardener who had vanished without a trace. He looked at me and made the comment that this was not making a great deal of sense to him. It was too much of a coincidence. If the disappearances were connected, he couldn't see why these two people would run off together with a whole lot of young boys. Still, he asked Mrs. Beasley to show him your room and Katherine's, but that told him noth—*" The radio started to fade and whine, but after a few crackles Martin's voice rang out again, "*then things got a bit unpleasant when he asked me if I'd seen anything unusual that morning.*

"*I told him that any activity early in the morning would be unusual. I went on rubbing down the bar and polishing glasses as if I hadn't a care in the world. Then the inspector asked what I meant by unusual. I told him that I would consider it odd if I'd seen a number of boys strolling about with mattresses and such, but that I hadn't seen anything. He finally said very well and walked out.*"

I could hear the relief in Martin's voice that he'd not had to lie to the police. Of course, he had told the truth. He never saw the boys at all. The only people he'd seen were me and my mates down at the ships. He volunteered nothing. It's an old adage of mine learned painfully in the Navy: don't answer what you're not asked!

"*Anyway*," Martin continued, "*the police talked among themselves, then O'Connell turned up again and went straight to the inspector, and said he'd had an idea. 'That damned boat down on the shore! They were supposed to be towing it out today. Maybe everyone went down to watch it.' I got a bit of a shock, I can tell you. Where could he have got an idea so close to what actually happened? Then Mrs. Beasley added her bit about always seeing lots of people going down there and talking with those dreadful people.*" Here Martin broke off to imitate Mrs. B. "'*Oh! You dreadful, dreadful people, you!' I could guess that she and O'Connell will enjoy a good gossip, after whatever else they get up to behind closed doors.*"

We were all riveted to our seats by Martin's story. "Have the police decided to alert the ports and Coast Patrol?" I asked.

Martin's next words seemed to confirm it. "*Well, things started to get interesting, because at that very moment, the CID from Scotland Yard walked in! The inspector seemed a nice friendly man compared with the grim-looking pair who came with him. These two introduced themselves as Detective Inspector Weaver and Detective Sergeant White.*

"*After they'd had a conference in the corner, Inspector Weaver said, 'Let's go down and have a look at the shore. Perhaps you, Mr.—?' 'O'Connell,' says the old rogue. 'Yes, Mr. O'Connell, if you could show the way, I can ask you more as we drive.' I didn't hear anymore until midday, when O'Connell came back with the inspector and sat with Mrs. Beasley in the bar.*"

There was a long pause and the radio went quiet. I began to fidget, when Harris reminded me that talking on the ham radio was different from proper radio protocol and not to worry.

Martin continued, "*Sorry about that, but all this talking is thirsty work. So, the inspector and O'Connell started going on about your funeral pyre, and he'd told the police that scuttling the ship had been planned long ago. He knew, because he got to know those black-suited bureaucratic vultures. O'Connell lowered his voice as he told Mrs. B. that the police had asked him what time he'd discovered the boys missing. 'I told them that it was about seven a.m., and that I hadn't heard anything unusual.' Weaver then said he'd go back to the station and write up what they had so far in his report. Customers started arriving and I didn't hear what else was said.*"

I pressed the switch and said, "Martin, thank you for taking the time to help us. It's really appreciated here I can tell you. I hope you can continue to keep us up to date."

He responded, "*No problem for me, as I can get free with advance notice in the morning or afternoon. I'll work something out with Dick, but now I must get back to the inn.*"

I nearly forgot about Dick. After all, it was his house we were crashing in on, so I quickly called out, "Hi there, Dick, my name's Flynn, and of course you deserve a good deal of thanks from us. We'd be very grateful if Martin can carry on bothering you and use your radio to get through to us for a few days, so we can plan for eventualities."

Dick's voice came over clearly, "*No worries here. This sort of situation is just what we hams love to get mixed in, and we're committed to helping when we can. However,*" he began laughing, "*if you're really a desperate kidnapping mob of crooks, they'll probably take my licence away!*"

Harris joined in, taking the handset from me. "No need to worry about that, Dick, we're just a bunch of average blokes—plus one lady," he added hastily, as Katherine looked on. "All we're trying to do is save a bit of our heritage against the wishes of our so-called government, and we certainly aren't out to hurt anyone."

"*I'm naturally agin the government ever since that twit Chamberlain and Churchill thought they could treat Hitler like a human being. But let's not get on to that! Just to say that Martin can come here any time, even when I'm not here. I'll give him a short course on how to call you and how to close down. I'll be ready to pass along any messages.*"

Harris was impressed. "I couldn't have asked for more. We really owe you, and I look forward to meeting you some time. Just for now though, it's goodbye to you both."

We all added our thanks as the connection faded out.

For a few moments we sat and digested what we'd just heard. I thought Katherine hit the nail on the head when she summed it up. "The police may think they know where we are but they can't do anything about it until they get confirmation from an independent source, which means the tug first thing tomorrow at the earliest." After thinking that over, we all agreed that there was no sense trying to get more information at this point, as we might give ourselves away by doing so.

It was late afternoon, about twenty-eight hours since we'd cut loose from the tug, and we surely would hear something soon. If the tug had done as Harris guessed, then she should have reached the dock within the last few hours. I pictured the government men looking the worse for wear—unshaven and blowsy—haring off up to London, where they might very well be in the middle of a meeting trying to get someone to decide what action to follow.

We were just about to get back to our posts when the radio let out a loud squawk and began wailing up and down the scale. In its usual way the speaker suddenly blasted out, "*Calling Harris, calling Harris. Are you receiving me? Over.*"

"It's Bob on the *Grouse*," Harris said and shouted for Edward, who came crashing in nearly knocking Harris over as the ship heeled over in the wind.

"Get back your sea legs there, old man," Harris teased.

"Oh piss off, why don't ya!" Edward snapped indignantly. "What d'you want, anyway?"

"Here's the *Grouse*. She's waiting to talk to us." Harris took the handset and shouted into it, "Harris here, Harris here, I am receiving you clearly. Hello, Bob, you delinquent. How are things?"

The tinny voice crackled forth, "*I'm travelling due north away from home with a hold full of herring, so you could say, middling. I haven't had a challenge or even a sighting since I started on this course, and I should really be getting back with this catch. But the reason I'm calling is that I've got a bit of news for you. Among my friends are a couple tug captains based in Gravesend, and one of them was on to me for a bit of chat earlier this morning. He, of course, knows nothing of my arrangement with you, but he happened to mention in passing that George Wiley seemed to be missing from a routine tow job. Not only missing, but also the 'subject of enquiries by the police'! Apparently several of the skippers were waiting near the dock office, when up drove a police Wolseley, a flying squad car no less, and out got two men, who introduced themselves as CID from Scotland Yard.*"

Bob continued, "*The CID wanted to know who had the tow job for that seconded derelict sailing ship on the Thames, when they'd departed, and who was on board. The Gravesend captains managed to piece together the information and were very interested to know that you and others were on board. They also asked about a group of boys, but you know George can't abide kids. There you are. I thought you'd like to know. Over.*"

"Bob, you're a prince!" Harris cried. "And by all means head home now. Before you go, can you give me the name of the other ham you know and his call sign? This way, I can get in touch with him directly." After exchanging information and a few more words of thanks and banter, Harris signed off.

After thinking about Harris having that additional call sign, I thought I'd better sound a note of warning. "Harris," I said, holding up a finger, "you start calling too many people on the radio, and you won't know who's on our side. For now, let's chat with the people we know and no one else." After thinking about this for a moment, he reluctantly agreed.

"Still, so far so good," Harris said confidently. "I think you're right about protecting our call sign. George Wiley's tug must be back by now. I reckon that we've got a real head start. Even if they send someone after us tonight, they'll have a job catching up, even if they knew where we are. They'll be searching east for some time, for no one would think we'd run such hazardous waters." Harris should have touched wood after such talk because, within twenty-four hours, we would be in the middle of a small but annoying storm. The wind was blowing directly from the west, and forward movement was gained only a mile at a time, after doing two long legs of a tack.

For now though, we were travelling sou'sou'west. The sails were thrumming, the shrouds whistling, and all was right with the world. A late sun was catching the starboard beam, glancing off the spray as the bow rose and smacked back into the water. The clouds were touched with red and pink as night slowly gathered in. Boris was on every mast and yard to double-check everything. Once satisfied, he moved off to arrange the navigating lights. He showed the boys the mysteries of the huge navigation lights on the fo'c's'le head. The two big copper and brass bell shapes were now lit, and the lookout posted. From below, the smell of fine cooking came up the passages and companions, promising more comfort. The world was all right indeed, and I was prepared to take it at its fairest face.

Chapter 17
THE UNKNOWN OBSERVER

After as good a dinner as one could hope to meet anywhere on the seven seas had been tucked inside us, I made Katherine leave the skivvying to the kitchen helpers. "You're now the official Cook," I said, "and aren't expected to do the cleaning as you were at the inn. Get your lovely self out of the galley, and we'll find a quiet spot with one of the bottles Martin donated."

Soon we were safely huddled in a lee on the poop deck, warmly dressed and snuggled under a large blanket. I'd found two glass tumblers, and Martin's brandy was warming inside. A quarter moon shifted between scudding clouds as the *Bonnie Clyde* ploughed her way through the dark sea, with only the sound of fluttering sails and the splash of the thrown bow wave as she met each seventh swell.

I said, "There's a belief that the sea runs quite deep for six waves, and the seventh can catch you out if you're not careful, throwing twice as high with an occasional twist in it. I tried counting many a time during my training days, but I had enough trouble with the six in between for me ever to find out if that story was true or not."

Katherine's voice was drowsy. "The only thing I know about the sea is that it tastes bitter and salty. When I was little, I remember going to Sandymount Beach at Howth near Dublin with my brothers. It was usually raining and the wind was cold and I hated changing under a towel." Her voice drifted off as she nestled deeper into my arms, her head pillowed on my chest. Her fatigue wasn't surprising when I thought of how much work was involved in feeding twenty-six people. She deserved the sleep, and I was perfectly content to feel her cradled against me.

I don't know how long we were sleeping, but I was woken by a rough shaking of my shoulder. An excited boy's voice shouted, "Wake up, Mr. Flynn, wake up! Mr. Harris wants you in the forepeak straight away. Oh! You'll never believe..." but seeing us awake, he rushed off without finishing.

I could hear a lot of voices coming from forward as I left Katherine and made my way over the flying bridge to the forepeak. Harris spotted me and boomed out, "Flynn, I hope your Morse is better than ours so you can translate what we're getting here." I stepped up to the rail near the bowsprit and looked ahead into the darkness where Harris was pointing.

The moon had gone and the night was completely black. Without some sort of reference, it was difficult to judge distances, but I would say that a light was flashing about a mile away. I tried to make some sense out of the irregular pattern. Harris was telling me the light had been flashing since the lookout spotted it ten minutes before and had immediately called the alarm to the bridge. Even Bowman had come, leaving Boris at the helm. After watching closely for a minute, I determined that this wasn't any type of real communication. Try as I might, I couldn't make sense of it.

"That's not Morse, nor any kind of message. I'm pretty sure it's a fixed light on some kind of vessel, but the light is close to the water so I don't think it's a large one. The light looks as though it's flashing because it's being swung about by the wind and movement of the boat," I concluded.

Bowman growled, "So, now ye're one of those magician chappies with x-ray eyes, are ye? Still, I hae tae agree with ye, it's not a signal lamp, it's too fluttery and the beats aren't regular." Our course was taking us past the light. I was wondering if it represented someone who needed help when Bowman spoke up again, "Harris, bear away two or three points to starboard. We must go to see if anyone is in trouble."

Harris turned and called the order to Boris, who turned the wheel to line us up with the light. Luckily it was not so big a change that we needed to close-haul the sails any further. The move lost us a little of the wind, but this was all to the good. If there was trouble, we'd have to heave to, and the slower we went the easier that would be.

As we wore round there was a sudden change ahead. The light was still there but was now joined by a bigger one, higher out of the water. In fact, this was a proper signal lamp and it started to flash its message immediately: *What ship is that? Identify yourself. We need assistance.* Now I could understand the meaning of the first light's erratic movements and why we'd not been challenged before. Under repair, they would still have lookouts posted but our heading had kept the navigation lights out of sight. Turning towards them had brought an instant response. Our Aldis lamp was kept near the generator that operated the pumps, plugged in to keep its batteries fully charged. A boy was sent to bring it up.

Meanwhile, the ship in front of us, not receiving a reply, was again flashing: *Identify yourselves immediately, or we'll take action.*

Bowman and Harris could read well enough to understand this message, and Bowman shouted, "Action? What do they mean, action? I'll tell ye what they—" but Harris cut across him.

"Come on, Uncle Billy, just think what you'd be doing if you were stuck out here under repair and some stranger comes along who doesn't reply as per international rules. You'd also be ready to—" He broke off for a moment and said, "Of course, it's a warship. She's got a forward deck gun." Harris started yelling, "Where the bloody hell is that lamp? Hurry up or we'll be blown out of the water!" The boy with the lamp had just come from below and streaked across the forepeak passing it up to Harris.

Harris swung round, and supporting the lamp on the rail, started to spell out a message. I spoke over his shoulder. "Be careful what you say. Just tell them we're a private boat out of Dover, and can we approach to try to help?"

Again, the signal lamp from the other boat chattered: *Come ahead, slow. We are low in the water. Keep a good lookout.*

As we got within hailing distance, a powerful searchlight suddenly caught us in its beam, and a loud hailer came to life. "*My God!*" were the first words forced out of the speaker at the sheer surprise he must have felt in seeing us looming out of the dark—a sailing ship straight out of the past.

Then a voice came over, "*This is Captain Johnson of the* USS Shark's Tooth. *I presume you are not the* Flying Dutchman. *Please identify yourself.*"

Both Harris and I said it together, "It's a submarine!"

In the meagre light, the mention that the vessel was a United States Navy ship was certainly surprising. We could now see the long black rounded shape of a submarine in the reflected glow of the searchlight.

Harris took our hailer and replied. "Captain, you signalled for help. What is your situation?" I noticed an inflatable dinghy and a figure in a frogman's wetsuit and pointed this out. Seeing that, before Captain Johnson could respond, Harris called out, "You've a screw problem?"

Surprised by this accurate assessment, the captain replied, "*Yes, we have a fouled screw. How did you know?*"

"I'm First Mate Harris, ex-Royal Navy. My bo'sun and I have a fair amount of experience with tangled fishing nets and gear, some of it strong enough to take the true out of the shaft. Maybe we could come over and have a word with your people." There was a silence and I could picture the executive officer reading the book at him about not allowing civilians aboard a US Navy warship, especially alien civilians.

The other's loud hailer came again, *"I can't let you below decks, but if you would have a word with my men, it would be better than nothing. It's taking a coon's age to clear!"* All this time, we'd been drifting down towards the submarine. As Boris turned the ship more into the wind, the sails slapped against the yards. Understanding the submarine captain would need our help, Boris asked Edward to ready the stern and the forward mooring lines to await his further gentling of the ship closer to the other vessel.

Bowman now picked up the hailer. "This is Captain Bowman of the *Bonnie Clyde*. Stand by to receive lines fore and aft." Two clunks on the submarine's hull followed as our boys threw down the lines. They were picked up and used to haul us closer in.

Harris was now able to call directly to the captain, "I'll lower a ladder and we'll come down." After a brief conversation, Harris and Boris went quickly down to the submarine's deck and immediately went to talk with the crew at the stern. They looked in awe at this incredible apparition, a vessel seldom seen except in photographs. And those sub sailors were probably thinking the same about the *Bonnie Clyde*.

"Captain Johnson," Bowman called with the hailer, "I've nae doot that my men can put yer trouble right even if they have to go into the sea themselves. And I'd like to invite ye to come aboard for a dram or two when they've finished."

"I'll take you up on that invitation," was the immediate response, *"I'm really interested in having a look at your ship. There aren't many left."*

"Aye," Bowman replied, "that's part of the tale we'll like to tell ye." Bowman put down the hailer. "I'll get back to my cabin while Harris does his bit," he said. I walked back along with him.

"We need to keep that captain quiet about this meeting." I said, "If he has a special feeling for old sailing ships that should be easy enough to do."

"I hope so." Bowman replied, "We'll have to see what he's doing out here, and whether he can keep quiet without one of his crew telling their base everything."

I left him at his cabin and went to the poop deck where I could look down onto the sub's stern. Harris was examining some of the rope already cut away while Boris was learning how to use one of the goggle masks with a breathing tube attached. I'd heard of them, but had never seen one used before.

I couldn't hear everything, but it seemed that he and Harris had encountered this problem before on another vessel. It involved some technique they had devised to loosen the rope and netting, making it easy to cut away. Whatever was done, after the engine had been turned a few times, their frogman was able to go down and cut the whole mess loose.

On my way back aft, I told Bowman the problem was solved and to expect guests. Boris was already back on board and into dry clothes, ready to pipe the American captain aboard properly. We made quite a party in Bowman's cabin, which soon became noisy from Martin's donations. Bowman asked the sub captain what he was doing there without riding lights.

"Riding lights?" he asked, puzzled, then brightened. "Oh, running lights. Well for starters, your ship didn't show up on our radar, nor did any other ship for that matter, and we were well off the main shipping lanes. We're on an exercise of seek-and-destroy, and this involves complete radio silence and blackout except for very specific reasons. Running one of these exercises is a real pain, and I wasn't about to mess it up crying for help because my prop got tangled. So, I surfaced and you found me. Boy, I'll tell you, was *I* surprised!"

Bowman pressed for more information, "Now that ye're free, will ye radio a report anywhere?"

"Hell no! I'm going ahead with my part in the exercise and probably won't establish radio contact for the next two days as planned." I'd only heard the expression *hell no* from some Yanks and in a John Wayne movie. I was trying to picture our guest with ten-gallon hat and six-shooter, but the image simply didn't fit. I listened as he went on, "As for my report, that's going to take some explaining as to how we got ourselves into and out of this situation, so I'm not sure what to write up. It just isn't going to look good, getting my prop fouled and an old sailing ship coming to our rescue. I can just see my C.O. looking at me like I'm nuts." Johnson looked at Bowman enquiringly. "But why should you care about my report?"

"Oh, just curious. We've never met up with an American sub before," Bowman said evasively, "and it calls for a special dram." He poured out about half a glass of whisky for everyone. "Down the hatch and no heel-taps," he sang out, and setting the best example, swallowed his drink in one go.

The sub captain could obviously tell from our behaviour that there'd been something odd about Bowman's reply, but he wasn't apt to learn anything from that quarter. The old man, having collapsed into his chair with a smile, was taking no further part in the action. So, Harris, with a last appraising look at Johnson, seized the moment and recounted our story in its true light, highlighting the stubbornness of the government and the Admiralty against the common-sense solution that we'd proposed.

"But no!" Harris roared, "The bloody twits can't tell their arses from their elbows and insisted on scuttling the ship, which is still perfectly seaworthy. We weren't proposing that the taxpayers should have any cost in preserving her. We're going to present her to the original builders in Scotland, who agreed long ago to make her into a floating museum. So, when it got too late for talk, we arranged to relocate her anyway," and he related what had happened as the scuttling was about to take place.

Johnson was suitably impressed with this and promised that no one was going to hear anything from him about encountering any sailing ship. "You people are either smart or just plain crazy. This is one for the books. To seal it, though," he laughed, "I'd really like a tour of the ship, and then I've got to get back to my own, damn quick!"

"Done," Harris shouted and seized his hand for a hearty shake. Johnson was game but I saw him wince. The sub's executive officer or second-in-command was one of those conscientious types, taking care of every eventuality, but even he couldn't find anything to argue about in such a simple arrangement. Johnson told us that his executive officer had been stationed in England during part of the war and was glad to be back at sea. Apparently his time there hadn't left him with a very good opinion of our green and pleasant land.

Looking about, Johnson was fascinated by everything he saw. "You have a real young crew," he observed.

"These boys have been training hard on this ship," Harris said with pride.

"I'd love to be sailing with you," Johnson said. "I have a picture of the old *Cutty Sark* on the bulkhead of my cabin." We saw him off and his crew cast off the lines. They disappeared into the darkness and eventually from sight. We congratulated one another, for we knew we'd made a valuable friend. We made sure of getting his radio call sign, for we'd acquired another ally.

Chapter 18
THE TUG REACHES PORT

Once the excitement died down aboard the *Bonnie*, the boys got back to their routine with a yawn, as they headed for their bunks in the fo'c's'le. I took Katherine back to her cabin. She needed sleep more than I did as she had the harder day's work.

"I know just how you feel," she sighed, "but between work and the need for sleep, we haven't had much time to spend together. The only good thing about it," she murmured, "is that it's only going to last a few days. Then we'll have a lifetime to catch up." We held each other a little longer, not wanting to let go. With a final kiss, she went in and closed the door.

I could have slept, but it kept nagging me that we hadn't heard anything about a possible pursuit or other repercussions we might be held accountable for. Martin wasn't in an ideal position to hear about it, even if the police were still around asking questions. There was a chance they might let slip about what their officials were up to. Harris told me a little of his wartime experiences with Bob and felt he would contact us should anything came his way. If this developed into a full-scale affair, it was good to have Johnson as another outside contact.

Arriving at the chart room, I found it full of smoke and people. Martin's donations had included a few cigars. Harris and Edward were nicely ensconced in the only two comfortable chairs, each with a cigar in one hand and a brandy in the other. Bowman was doing the Edward bit, immersed in charts spread over the table, with one or two on the floor as they argued over details. Robert was leaning against the door and had to move as I came in. He was the officer of the watch but was keeping a weather eye open from inside the chart room, out of the wind. Boris wasn't a part of this snug company, for he was at the helm. He appeared to enjoy it, always giving a smile and pointing upwards as one passed, as if to say look at those sails. See how we fly.

As I moved through the room, there were one or two technical remarks about ports and storms and such like, which I ignored to have a word with Bowman.

"What do you think?" I asked him, "I just wish we had some way of knowing what's been happening in the Admiralty. Those two officials on the tug must surely have got back to Whitehall not long ago. If we're lucky, the decision to send out a pursuit craft has to be made by a committee and so there'll be a delay of at least until tomorrow morning, that's my best guess. However, it may just be the decision of the Admiral on duty and a boat is already after us."

"Never ye fret, laddie," Bowman replied, "and don't buy trouble. 'Tis my experience it comes free. We'll be finding out soon enough. But just now, see if you agree with me by looking at this chart. Edward is not being too helpful at the moment." From what I could see, Bowman's calculations were correct and that meant we had passed through the notorious Straits of Dover late last night without a headwind and without riding lights. Fortunately, we didn't see the night ferry from Dover to Calais. The wind was still steady, but I'd heard Boris ordering the boys to man the braces once or twice as the wind veered and backed, almost a sure sign of change coming.

Suddenly the radio came to life with its usual whines and crackles, which quickly developed into a voice: "*Calling Harris, calling Harris. Are you receiving me? Calling Harris.*"

Everyone had gone still except Harris, who was having difficulty getting to his feet, so I grabbed the handset. "We're receiving you. Is that the *Grouse*? Harris is unavailable at the moment. My name is Flynn and I'm the radio officer. He's a little under the weather at the moment, although we are having good weather here, if you know what I mean, over."

"*Hi there, this is Bob. Tell Harris I have no sympathy for him. It's all his own fault. I thought you'd like to know the latest that I heard here. You lot are really hot news. I'm getting no end of have-you-heard calls. You'd better tell Harris he's a celebrity with his picture in the paper no less!*"

Then it struck me; the newspaper reporter and photographer. We hadn't remembered them. We'd been so wrapped up in our plan that this hadn't entered into our calculations at all. Now Bob was talking about us like we were celebrities.

Bob continued, "*I haven't seen the London evening papers yet, but I'm told that one picture shows Harris with the evidence in his hand. Apparently you pinched the radio handset, you bad boy! There you are in the paper, waving it about in the air!*"

Harris had sobered up enough and now took the handset. "Now then, funny man, stop your noise for a while and tell us what else you've been hearing."

Bob came straight back, "*Oh Harris, so good of you to join us,*" he chuckled. "*Caught red-handed at last!*" As Harris started growling, Bob said hurriedly, "*All right, just a joke. I got a call from my Gravesend friend about two o'clock, telling me that your tug had returned. As you know, George Wiley is not the most popular character around, he's a scoundrel of the first water, so everyone was quite cheered by the way he arrived.*

"Apparently he'd been travelling a lot faster on the waterway than he should, because he was so angry at what had happened to him and that he'd have to file a report with the authorities. As he came to the dock he put the engines in reverse, gave the wheel to his crewmen, and jumped off while the boat was still moving quite smartly. This merely added momentum to his steps. He tripped over his feet, lost his footing, tried to grab one of the pilings, and ended up going straight over the other side of the dock. He was going so fast that he managed to miss the water entirely and land in a dinghy that was moored on the other side of the dock. He landed neatly—but rather heavily, for his feet went straight through the bottom." Bob was laughing fit to burst at all this.

"My friend got the news direct from one of the crew. The crewmen said the dinghy sank with George standing bolt upright in the middle! Eventually he got out and hared off to the dock office to complain about everything, desperate to use the telephone.

"Meanwhile," Bob went on, *"the government men got off in a hurry and ran for their car, while the reporter and his photographer took their time asking for names and other details."*

Harris sat silent for a moment and then asked, "Did your friend hear why the tug had taken so long to get back?"

"Oh yes," said Bob, *"the crewmen had become very talkative by then, having been sitting in the pub for quite a spell making up for loss of good drinking time of the night before. My friend heard it all. You were a very naughty boy, Harris, cheating a poor honest man like George in that way. A magnet, no less! I'm not letting you on my boat in a hurry again!"* Harris again started growling, so Bob moved on, *"Still, you had to give him credit. George discovered it—about four hours too late.*

"Apparently his language was spectacular, and the threats of mayhem against you and Bowman were flying thick and fast. After you got away, George had sat off by himself for quite a while, leaving the wheel to our informant, who followed the compass without thinking too much about it. Eventually George started to use his binoculars, looking for landmarks, and came in to look at the compass. By the time they did see some landmarks, which no one recognised, it was nearly dark. It was about then that George discovered the magnet. He was on an unfamiliar coast, without a radio to tell others his position, or to find out where he was. He was, you might say, between the devil and the deep blue sea. Apparently they realized that they were north of Southend, and for a while they headed south. After a near miss with a small fishing boat, George decided to heave to and throw out a sea anchor.

"They had a very uncomfortable night, having to maintain a good lookout the whole time. The government men were not happy either, swearing they were going to get you all for piracy. Our informant says he wasn't happy to hear that and suggested that the old boat was going to be sunk anyway. He pointed out that if someone should take the rubbish that another was throwing out, it could hardly be called piracy. But they weren't having any of that and it seems obvious that they're out for your blood, whoever they are. One of the funny parts is that George wasn't sure who to call, but he knew an admiral and tried to track him down. Someone told him he was in the Cabinet Room at 10 Downing Street and gave ol' George the number. Imagine, ringing up number 10! The admiral was extremely annoyed because you know how George tries to fit an entire story into one long run-on sentence. Anyway, I suspect they will talk at Whitehall because of the potential embarrassment this could cause the Prime Minister's Office. The admiral didn't wish one word leaked." Bob concluded, *"So there you have it: fame of a sort—and a price on your head!"*

Harris was now quite sober and said, "Bob, you're really being more than a friend in all this and we can't thank you enough."

At this Bob interrupted, *"Oh, yes? I'll soon think of something."*

"Never you mind," Harris carried on, "did you see anybody after you? Did you see a Navy ship of any kind?"

"Nothing on the sea, but we did see a plane, looked like a small spotter plane. It didn't try to contact us, but proceeded due east at the time. I had a casual thought that he'd better not go too far out or his fuel wouldn't last him to get back."

Harris was quiet for a bit, apparently thinking of what to say next, then clicked the handset and asked, "Do you know anybody based in London? We've got to know what sort of reaction there's going to be from Whitehall."

"Whew!" Bob said. *"That's a bit of a tall order, but I'll have a word around. Just one last bit, though. Someone's shown me the London paper while I've been talking and you needn't worry Harris. No one will ever recognise you in the photo— you look so fat!"*

Harris rumbled back, "Ha, bloody ha, but can you read? Tell me the name of the reporter who wrote the article. I suppose it's in the *Evening News?*"

Bob rustled the paper and finally spoke. *"It says that it's from the AP, so it's not the paper's own reporter."*

Harris replied, "That's enough for the idea I have, thanks. We'll be waiting for any news you get. I'll say good night from all of us." Bob sent the same wish to us and left the radio to its usual soft moaning.

We all sat looking at one another, not knowing whether to be pleased or worried. On the one hand, we had our answer to the tug question, but on the other, we still had no clear idea what was going on at Whitehall. It was all speculation at this point.

I had to ask, "How did we miss such an obvious thing as the reporter?"

"Well, miss it we did," groaned Harris, "and if we'd only thought about it we could have saved ourselves a lot of worry. I don't know too much about reporters, but I think we're going to find this one very useful."

The rest of us were doubtful, but Harris spelled it out, "Now, just think about this set of steps and see if you can trip me up. First step, we get in touch with Martin as soon as possible. Second step, we get Martin to phone up AP and find out the name of that reporter and his phone number. Third step, Martin offers to let him keep his world scoop so long as we can talk to him and answer his questions before he publishes anymore articles. We're lucky that it's an AP man. Every newspaper can pick up the story and we can get a lot of publicity. If the reporter is sympathetic, there's no telling what effect he could have on the public."

"Oh, I dinna believe ye can get much good out o' any newspaperman," Bowman responded sourly. "Most of them are looking for sensation and wouldn't write a fair piece about us. They never hae before. It serves them better not to upset the Whitehall types they depend on for their bread-and-butter stories."

"That's a possibility, I grant you," Harris went on, "but if he should do the dirt on us, by that time we'll be able to have our choice of papers—all of which I'm betting are going to see this as the small man against the system. Sort of a David and Goliath."

"Well," I said, "the proof of that particular pudding is only going to be in the eating. We could sit and argue it back and forth for the rest of the night, but we've got nothing to lose by making the first contact. I'm still thinking about what would really scupper us, and that's being captured by the Navy. Our side of the story would be lost as Whitehall tries to cover for letting the ship be taken in the first place." I felt brighter as the penny dropped. "The same reporter, or another, could possibly give us information he gets out of Whitehall as part of his job, don't you think?"

Harris became animated as I've ever seen him. "Now that's clever. I hope it would work so, Flynn." He turned to everyone, "Let's get some rest, except for those on watch, and we'll start the ball rolling tomorrow morning."

We'd made good way thus far during the night, but the wind had freshened and veered more northerly, blowing us on a still-southerly tack. There had also been a few tears in the canvas and Boris was fetching his sail-making equipment, intending to take the job aloft rather than strike a sail to mend it. He preferred to slacken the head right down and repair it on the spot if he felt it would be easier. Otherwise they'd have to be taken down, but meanwhile the worst ones had been furled to the yards. We had one or two of the old ones in store that were in reasonable condition but didn't want to use them unless we had to.

I'd been on the night watch and was looking forward to a good sleep, though the sea was running twenty-foot swells and was making the ship pitch much like a roller coaster ride, and Bowman ordered the riding lights lit again. Harris had come on deck and was walking about inspecting work done and seeing what needed doing. He suddenly called to me, "By the way, where's that Robert? I haven't seen him yet."

"Oh? I have," I replied. "He's aloft helping Boris." It was difficult to see to the top shrouds when we were under full sail, but I had seen Robert going up with Boris. Two pairs of hands would be needed if they were to make a good job of mending sails aloft. Harris and I were now standing looking up into the rigging. "Those two have been working together on quite a few things lately," I remarked.

"That's interesting," said Harris, "Boris is usually a real lone wolf, but then everyone on a ship should have someone to rely on, wherever they are when the storm really breaks."

I turned to Harris and added, "I assume that you're on the day watch. I've been on the night watch, so if you'll excuse me now I'd like to go enjoy my breakfast. Then I'm going to lie down in my cabin. If anyone needs me, *find somebody else!*" I said, hoping that Harris saw I was serious.

I was so tired that I could barely keep awake to eat my food. Once I'd had a little sleep, lunch at least could be taken in a conscious state. I told Katherine I was sorry, but I'd talk to her later and went to my cabin collapsing fully dressed onto my bunk. It seemed as though only seconds had passed when there was a knock at the door. The only thing I could muster was a feeble please go away. Instead, the door slid open and Katherine came in, shutting it behind her.

"Just checking up on you, Flynn," she smiled. "You looked like death warmed up when you came below today."

"I felt like it," I said weakly.

"Indeed," she responded with a sympathetic smile. "Now, off with your jacket and shirt while I massage your back." She had a bottle of embrocation which she kneaded into my aching muscles. They responded gratefully to every touch. I lay back down to rest while we talked briefly. Since I wasn't going to have the night watch again that evening I told her that I'd come by and help her secure things in the cabin. "That would be fine," she said, "I'll be waiting. However, the news I bring is that Harris would like to see you on the main deck, and that we seem to be proceeding according to schedule." I thanked her and did my best to sit back up. She opened the door just a bit to see if there was anyone in the passageway, then quickly disappeared. I put my shirt and jacket back over my tired shoulders.

I must have fallen off to sleep. I was awakened first by nearly being thrown onto the deck, as the ship seemed to stand on her bowsprit and then crash back onto a more or less even keel. An instant later came a terrible banging and clanging as if a set of steam hammers were working just outside my cabin door. A freak wave had obviously caught us, pouring tons of water onto the well and main decks, and was now running off through the freeing ports. These were heavy doors set in the bulwarks. Hinged outward at the top, they opened by pressure to release all the water, and then crashed back shut. I slid open my door and staggered down the passage on my way up to the main deck. I realised that it would be hard going unless I either grew more legs, unlikely, or got a few more hours of sleep, equally unlikely.

As I slid open the hatchway, daylight stabbed my eyes like a cruel pair of daggers. I felt my way up to the deck, squinting against the bright sun. The day was still clear, the winds were steady, but great dark storm clouds were building in the east. Everything was masked— shrouded in fog on the horizon. I don't believe the sun could have been any brighter without blinding all on board. I thought about the tinted glasses I had somewhere in my belongings, given to me by an aviator friend of mine, but alas, I had no recall as to where they would be at that moment.

As I squinted and rubbed my eyes, Harris walked over and handed me a mug of coffee. "Take a drink of this," he said.

"Thank you," I said, taking a sip. "Boy!" I exclaimed, handing it back, "what the bloody hell is in this?"

"It's coffee of course, a little milk, some sugar, and a shot of whisky," answered Harris.

I ran my tongue over my teeth a few times. "Isn't it a wee bit early in the day to start with that?" I asked.

"Keeps my blood warm," he said, "and besides it's already 0800, not so early. We're doing well—in fact so well that we're ahead of schedule near as I can tell, at least as far as we've a schedule to *be* on."

"Exactly what does that mean?" I asked.

Harris scratched his head. "Did you wake up in an interrogation mood there, Flynn?"

I held up a placating hand. "I'm still a bit tired yet," I groaned.

"I suppose that what I'm saying is that we're making good time and Edward seems happy. He and Bowman haven't had an argument for at least two hours. That in itself is a major accomplishment," quipped Harris.

I looked up at the boys working in the rigging, up on the yardarms, trimming out a few sails and setting full some others that had been furled when the wind had threatened them. They were replacing old rope and checking the stays that would be put to a serious strain by the approaching storm.

Harris went on, "While you were sleeping, I managed to contact Dick. He had read all about us in his morning paper and also got it from the wireless. He agreed to get hold of Martin as soon as possible and ask him to contact the AP reporter at once, get him out to the village, and then call us."

"Let's hope the reporter has word from Whitehall, so he can pass a bit of information to us at the same time," I said. "By the way, where are Robert and Boris?"

"Cleaning fish," Harris laughed. "Imagine my surprise, coming up and finding both of them fishing from the stern."

"Fishing?" I exclaimed.

"Yes, fishing. They'd caught three or four," said Harris.

"Three or four of what?" I asked.

"Looked like cod to me," Harris answered. "We've enough food to feed an army, so I don't know why they need to be fishing."

"Marvellous," I said, taking another big yawn, "it'll probably reveal itself eventually."

"Want more of this?" he said, extending the cup.

I held up my hand. "No thank you." Then, thinking about the time and how we were travelling, I added, "I should think we need to turn and head north-west or else we'll soon be looking at the French coast."

Harris took a long considering look at the clouds building astern, with swells being whipped white by the wind as the bow dipped deep into the water. This change came on quickly, as only moments ago Harris was expressing elation about the sun.

"I'll have a word with Boris, who I must say seems to be able to run this ship by the seat of his pants, and see what his instincts are," Harris replied.

Suddenly, we both pricked our ears at an unexpected sound. In the distance we could hear an aircraft, although we couldn't see it through the clouds, even with binoculars. It certainly seemed to both of us that there was no chance we'd been spotted, and when we saw Boris and Robert a few minutes later, they confirmed our thinking.

"I heard you two were up fishing this morning," I ventured.

"Yes, we caught a few," Robert said offhandedly.

"I hope you both understand that Katherine will expect you to clean and gut those yourselves, should you want them cooked," I warned.

"Oh, that won't be necessary," Robert assured me.

"Really? Are you planning on eating them raw?"

"Not exactly," he hesitated. "I'll tell you more about that later. But," he said, changing the subject, "this looks as if it's going to be rough going," and indicated the sky and sea with a sweep of his arm.

"Yes," I said, "it does looks like trouble and we really must be able to rely on the boys absolutely, even though we know they have almost no experience. All of us seniors are going to be needed as well, but first, all in all, I'm pretty sure we must get ourselves turned onto a new course."

At that very moment, the sails started to flap as the ship's head fell. Looking over I saw that the wheel was held by Edward with no back-up. With a nudge to Robert, I ran to stand on the other side of the huge wheel. Robert darted in next to me.

Between gasps as we all strained to hold the ship on course, Edward said, "She seems to have a life of her own and it's bloody difficult to hold her. The worst is that she gets so loose at the top of the wave, with the rudder at least half out of the water, that she goes deep into the trough a few points off course." She certainly was twisting, with un-known sheer forces beating against her length as she pulled out of each trough.

Suddenly Harris was there telling us we were relieved as he took over the wheel, telling Robert and me to go aloft to reef in the lower topgallants. Both watches were on duty and were already bringing in the royals. I was glad I wasn't up there with them. I didn't know what stamina I'd have left after tackling topgallants. I got a reprieve as Bowman appeared from below and called me in.

"Martin's calling," said Bowman. "He's got the reporter man in tow. I think ye can handle any questions while getting what information we want from the reporter better than I could. Do as Harris has suggested and keep him on our side feeding him *world scoops*. Just keep using that expression."

We sat down in front of the radio and I took up the handset. Even though the chairs were fixed and we could brace ourselves against the table, it was difficult to keep upright.

"Hi there, Martin," I began. The handset joggled out of my hand when my arm swung against the table.

Martin immediately replied, "*Flynn, how are you? Is the weather forecast correct and are you in the middle of a storm, over.*"

"Not in the middle yet," I replied, "but soon, unless we sink first. Before that, we'd like to talk to the reporter. Is he there?" The sound was surprisingly good when one considered what we had outside.

"*He should be here in about ten minutes. He's on his way from Gravesend in a taxi and I thought we should get our stories straight before he actually shows, if in fact there's any difference between them.*"

I said, "We have nothing to hide and want to get the truth known to as many as possible. What's this fellow's name? What did he sound like to you on the phone?"

"*His name's Richard Clark. He sounds pretty genuine to me. I phoned my friend who worked at* The Times, *and he said we can trust Richard absolutely. He's a veteran reporter who joined AP a while ago after a fight with his editor at* The Telegraph. *He was given the scuttling assignment as a test, or so my friend surmised. Richard is not only a good writer, but he has contacts in industry, sports, politics, and its civil service. My friend knows him personally and rang him up to vouch for me.*" Laughing, he carried on, "*I suppose I'll be the one to vouch for you bunch of cut-throats. How is Katherine taking to a life on the ocean waves?*"

"She's fine," I answered. "How she manages I don't know, but she magically produces food for all of us. She and I are aaah…a pair, but with the time we have alone together, you'd think we were wallflowers, we're that shy."

"*You know,*" Martin said seriously, "*I do worry about the two of you.*" He broke off, then said, "*Mr. Clark's just arrived, so I'll hand you over to him. Give my best to Katherine.*"

A new strong voice came over the speaker. "*Hello, Bonnie Clyde, this is Richard Clark, but please just call me Richard. Who's there?*"

"My name's Flynn. I was one of those aboard the tug. I've Captain Bowman with me. He's in command of the *Bonnie Clyde*. Harris, the big fellow, and Robert, the one with the dark hair, are outside steering and reducing sail and all that has to be done to counter a first-class storm, which is nearly upon us. If you hear crashing noises, that'll be from the gigantic seas all about." I caught myself having injected a bit of drama. "I'd like to ask you a question."

"*I don't envy you at all right now. I only hope I'll not be writing obituaries by the time this is done.*" He gave a laugh. "*How's that for a bit of tear-jerking? What's your question?*"

"I suppose you'd have to say we're at odds with the law, technically anyway, and there are rules about aiding such, and concealing such, and so on." I enquired, "If we talk to you, and you publish the information, will the police take action against you if you don't reveal your source?"

"*That's an easy one,*" he replied. "*You have no worries about me, or yourselves. You're just like a suspect in a crime whom the police cannot find, who telephones a reporter or anyone to tell his story or confess or whatever, and yet refuses to disclose his location. A suspect is very often expected to be trying to evade arrest because he knows he's innocent and wants to get evidence to prove it, which he can't do in a prison cell. We, receiving such a call, cannot be guilty of anything unless we do really know where the person is.*"

"I was told you're a reporter, not a lawyer," I said. "But that's the answer we'd hoped for. Now, another question is do you want an exclusive on the story and all the stories of each of us, which we're prepared to give you for publication, in exchange for any information you can give us on what *they* are doing and, maybe, plan to do? At the moment, we only want to hold back our destination until we've established a mutual trust, but we'll tell you everything else as matters progress. Now, in a sailing ship as old as this with a good head start and with weather such as we're getting now that will keep powered boats in harbour, we can continue on our way. So, if we can throw them off scent, trick them in some way, or just know their plans as soon as they know them, that will give us a bit of an advantage. Would you like the story on these terms and can you help us? Do you want an exclusive on the story in exchange for any information you can give us? We'll keep you informed, but we need to know their plans."

"*I'd love the story and the stories,*" was the immediate reply, "*but I don't know how much I can give you in return. I have good contacts in a good many places, particularly with the police and Whitehall, but I must be wary of losing their trust. I can possibly hear things through other people, that is, ask another reporter what he's found out behind the scenes and then use it while trying to avoid putting him in a spot. If the informant believes that any information given to me is being used for the wrong purposes, things could get sticky. The best I can do at the moment is to promise that you'll know any official announcement before any member of the public. And that when another reporter gives me permission to disclose what he's told me, you'll get it first, and of course if a politician or civil servant says I can use it, again, you'll be the first to know."*

"Thank you for your honest reply," I said gratefully. "We're going a bit crazy for authentic news out of Whitehall. Martin has told us about the police visit and what happened to the tug. Sorry about that, because I'm certain it wasn't a very comfortable situation, but we felt that there were only slim chances of an accident. By the way, you really hadn't entered into our calculations as to what would happen after we cut loose. I must say, I only remember you flying along the dock and the photographer occasionally taking pictures, over."

"It's all part of the job, so don't worry," Richard replied. *"Most of the while I was so ill, I had no interest in anything! I was seasick starting from the dockside and curled up out of sight with my head on the gunnel. I finally got used to the boat by the next morning when we returned. Plus, of course, there didn't seem to be much of a story in the scuttling and I didn't really realise who you all were. No excuse really. I should have asked even if I knew, but the seasickness stopped that."*

"Well I shan't describe present conditions to you, then." I laughed. "But where was I? Oh, yes, so we don't know what's happened in Whitehall, but we surmise they must have heard of the *Bonnie*'s escape somewhere about two or three yesterday afternoon. That's nearly twenty-four hours ago. Anything you know?"

"I've no trouble telling you all I know on that score because it's general know-ledge in Fleet Street, and it just shows you how stupid grown men can get when they have to admit that someone has outsmarted them," said Richard. *"My contact in Whitehall is a middle-ranking man, kept down by the lesser men above him. He's quite cynical about what they get up to, and apart from giving away state secrets, he usually provides me with the background on anything that happens. I met him yester-day evening after I got back from my…er…holiday and I had had a good bath and a stiff drink! He was very informative!"*

Richard continued, *"The first that the department knew anything of this was when their two men, the two on the tug, didn't return the night before. The duty driver had phoned in late complaining about being kept waiting and was told to find himself somewhere to sleep for the night. This was duly logged for the head of the de-partment and was on his desk when he got in next morning. Poor man, quite spoilt his coco that did—something real to worry about! The next development was the ar-rival of a pair of distinctly grubby junior officers who, so my man tells me, could be heard shouting something in the head's office—which is never done in such a place— that it was piracy and the pirates should hang. These two unfortunates were told to go away and get cleaned up. I expect they'll be licking envelopes for some time as punishment for letting you escape! My man said you'd set them a tricky problem. If they let you get away with it, without protesting or attempting to go after you, they felt that in the future someone would go right ahead and take something really valuable, and then justify it by the lack of action in this case. Of course the present case is a matter of losing something which they themselves had shown they considered value-less—an old derelict ship which they were prepared to scuttle. Why, it was enough to make all the Chancery lawyers rich for life. It was quickly decided that some action was needed. They didn't want dirty washing showing in public, so I'll have to be careful how I write my piece."*

"But what action?" I asked uneasily.

"The department controls most of what the Navy does, and there are various admirals sitting around giving advice. One of them couldn't believe that they needed to do anything at all. He also said, 'You should have listened to them in the first place, shouldn't you?' The admiral suggested that he and my contact form a committee of two to decide on the action to be taken as part of the normal routine of the department. Within seconds they were on their own! Twits do tend to do their worst in pairs, you know.

"First they got the admiral's aide, a smart lieutenant, on the phone to the Gravesend tug depot, and he very soon found the captain. He heard all about your iniquities, especially about a certain magnet, which was blamed for the captain not knowing accurately your last position. When he last saw you, you were headed due east.

"As there were still a couple of hours of light, they decided to send out an old Fleet Air Arm spotter plane based near Clacton. The pilot must have been dying of boredom and inaction, because he was back on the phone within three hours. Having flown out to the area, he carried on due east for a time, and then flew one square of a grid to cover all four compass points. He had seen two sailing ships. It was the one farthest east that seemed to fit the description best, and he reported her position and heading. The admiral seemed to know the disposition of every ship in the Navy, and eventually decided to send out a Motor Torpedo Boat at first light this morning to begin searching."

Richard's next words only added cream to the cake. *"From what I know of MTBs they're very fast, but they burn petrol quickly so their range is lim-ited."*

Bowman now thought he should say a few words to Richard and asked me for the handset. "Mr. Clark," he started, "My name is Bow-man, captain of this ship. I'm overseeing most everything here. I would just like to say that we appreciate, more than words could tell, the time and trouble ye've taken to tell us what ye know. This is of great value to us in our journey. Once again, thank you." He gave the handset back to me and made his way out to his cabin.

Richard answered, "*It's I who should thank you, because your story has everything: a sailing ship, a group of real sailors, a group of young boys with whom all the boys in Britain can identify, and a solitary lady, if my guess is correct.*"

"You're quite correct on the last," I said, "and you might say we're taking a long route to Gretna Green."

This first session Richard and I had was principally about the project, how we'd planned it, a small bit about who had put up what, details about the ship, and a good deal more, but eventually I had to call a halt.

"I'm sorry, Richard, but this blow seems to be getting much stronger and every hand is needed. I'll have to sign off for now. *Bonnie Clyde*, out."

"*Goodbye for now and I hope you all stay safe,*" Richard called finally. I heard Martin echoing this in the background.

Edward had been in the room all the while. He was never a great talker, but now spoke up, "We'd better keep an eye on old Billy there. He doesn't look right."

A few days ago, I'd witnessed Bowman having some sort of attack, but he'd certainly seemed fit enough since then.

Edward carried on, "He'll never say anything, but I can see it in his step. He's careful not to walk too hard, and he keeps to his cabin most of the time. The Billy of just a few months ago would never do that—he'd be halfway up the rigging shouting orders. I don't think he's on his last knockings, but it's a worry."

The old man sighed gloomily. I thought about their years together as shipmates and how much these two had been through. But Edward shook it off, "Mustn't borrow trouble. Whatever will happen, will happen. There's another thing, youngster. You can be after telling Boris and Harris not to bother about wearing ship at the moment. By tomorrow morning, we'll be sailing in sunshine under blue skies. Within twenty-four hours after that, we'll be hit by a granddaddy of a storm, coming in from the west. See here," as he pointed to the barometer on its gimballed support, "the pressure's too high to support a storm. What we're getting now is the result of the edges of two pressure systems meeting each other, the high from northern Europe and the low from the Atlantic. I've always had an interest in the weather and like to keep up with the latest thinking on it. British weather has ever been the great joke."

Edward beckoned me to the chart table. "This is a map I managed to *win* from the weather office in Chatham Naval Dockyard. One day, it'll have to come that every ship will be able to produce one of these everyday on board ship, using information coming in from all the weather stations in Europe." Seeing my perplexed look, he said, "All right, lesson's over. Just go out and tell them what to expect."

I was certainly mystified by Edward asking me to go to Harris at the helm and explain something I hardly understood myself, and, as I expected, he curtly dismissed my comments.

"Edward's had these notions for years and he's right as many times as we are. We'll continue to secure everything, but leave the galley fire until the corkscrewing gets too much!" I recounted what Richard told me. Harris replied, "An MTB eh? Well, he's not going to be out in stuff like this!"

The reefing had been completed while I was talking on the radio, but we seemed to fly over the waves, even with reduced sail. During the next few hours, the wind roared through the rigging and the rain squalls raced over the sea, pouring down so hard that we couldn't see ten yards ahead. As it grew dark, the force of the wind began to subside and the seas started to lessen. By midnight the storm had died down enough so that one watch could stand down. Under less sail we were making about eight or nine knots. It was decided that a change in course could wait until morning. The helmsman was Larry. He was told to steer as close as he could to the south-west. This would help make sailing into the west easier when we changed course the next morning. It was Larry's first solo chance at the wheel and he was holding up well.

Once I felt I wasn't needed on deck for a while, I went down to the galley and found a none-too-happy Katherine. The dinner she was trying to prepare had been repeatedly upset, and her galley helpers were having to re-wash the meat and vegetables before trying again. She was upset that I hadn't come down earlier. I explained that this was the first chance I had now that the storm was dying down. She didn't seem very excited about that and was just generally unhappy at seeing her work spoilt so.

"Next time you're making course changes you should be warning me. You wouldn't believe the mess we had to clean up," she pouted. Despite the boys working nearby, I caught hold of her hands and pulled her to me.

"Well, I'm here now and I'll do whatever you want just to be helpful. I know these storms can be unsettling," and I gripped the table edge to stop us falling. "They can be frightening too, but this old lady was built truly. She still has a sound hull and masts, so we'll come through it all right. Trust me!"

There was still some food on the table, so I sat down and helped myself to a quick bite. I laid hold of a pot that still held some tea. This was more to my liking than Harris's early-morning coffee. Katherine started removing other plates from the table.

"Hungry and tired, are you?" she said more gently.

"Yes," I said, holding my chin up with both hands. "I'm afraid I used up more energy on our first night at sea than I had ashore in some time. I believe I'll pass out right here," and I put my head down on the table.

"Oh no, you don't!" she cried, pulling the back of my collar. "I have a good many things to accomplish this hour."

"Very well," I said. Dragging myself to my feet, I staggered off down the passageway to my cabin. I had just stepped into my compartment when the door opened behind me. I turned round and saw that Katherine had joined me.

"Hello," I said. "I thought you were preparing something in the galley."

"It needs to boil more thoroughly," she said. "By the way, I get the feeling that it's always me who initiates our little interludes." She fixed me with an accusing look.

"Oh my, I am sorry. Please forgive this walking cadaver," I said. With that, I folded her in my arms. We fell back onto the bunk, trying not to get thrown to the floor as we undressed.

I whispered, "Who up top would guess what's going on below?" The wind was tearing about the ship with the shrill yelling of lads heaving lines, making our little nest seem all the cosier. Of course we both held very special memories of the sounds of a storm...

Some time later as I lay stroking those rich chestnut locks, Katherine suddenly giggled. "You know, you're not too awful for a dead man!"

I said, "Just you wait. One day we'll have time when both of us are fresh." She stood up, and untangling her clothing from mine, started to tell me about her day. At some point in the conversation, my eyes rolled back in my head and I fell off to sleep, never seeing or hearing when she went out. I was rocked soundly by the motion of the ship, and didn't wake until the sun had made its appearance on the horizon.

When I showed up in the galley later and found Katherine alone, she greeted me with a dazzling smile. I began to nibble at her ear, but she started giggling uncontrollably and couldn't hold still. I asked her what the great joke was. At first she said it was nothing, not really all that funny, but then told me Harris had come down looking for me. She had told him I had died off an hour before, which set us both laughing. He asked for a mug of coffee and she then set down a cup and poured Harris a coffee, asking if he'd take anything with that.

"No, well, I usually do it up myself," he replied. Evidently he wanted to keep his personal formula from her, but she knew better. He looked out the porthole and commented on how lovely the sea looked, but Katherine had responded she'd take his word for it, as she was too busy to go up on deck for a stroll and there was dough that wanted rolling out.

Harris next asked, "Am I in your way?"

"Constantly," she'd told him, no doubt with that mischievous gleam in her eye, "but that's never stopped you."

This took Harris completely by surprise. "Really?" he asked.

"Just now, really," Katherine retorted, and fetching her bowl of already-kneaded dough, she began to roll it out in large strips on the table.

"I'll have to learn how to do that one day," said Harris, watching her.

Katherine saw her opportunity. "Here, I can teach you now. Grab hold of the rolling pin."

Harris then held up his hand, looking horrified, and protested, "Oh, no, not on your life," then went on to point out how many more things he had waiting for him up on deck.

"If you have so very many things to do, perhaps you should see to them," she spoke up, pounding the rolling pin on the table for emphasis.

He'd seized upon this immediately. "Perhaps I should," he said hastily. After he scratched his beard in a puzzled way, Katherine asked in a louder voice, "Have you not left yet?" Harris jumped up and retreated up the ladder, holding his cup of coffee very carefully.

Katherine chuckled at her own cleverness. "That's one way to get rid of a man, tell him you'll put him to work in the kitchen. Works nearly every time." She seemed very pleased with herself as she went on about her chores.

I had a sudden thought. "Here, have you been getting round me that way?" I said suspiciously.

"Ooh, wouldn't dream of it, dearie," she protested in an impish tone.

After some time had passed, Robert came in. "Missed a right good watch, you did," he said cheerfully.

"Oh, I don't know. I did get some sleep," I said smiling at Katherine.

She held up a finger as if to scold me for telling tales out of school, although I never would have considered it.

"I envy your sleep," snorted Robert, "especially since I know your bunk's no softer than mine. Drat! I keep waking up in that hard damned thing. I must have pounded it with my fist a hundred times to soften it, and quite unsuccessfully. They always called those bunks the rack in the Navy—and for damn good reason! Well, when a man's tired enough, such things go unnoticed—at least by some of us."

Katherine gave me several choices of what was on the menu, even if a menu was only her telling me what was ready at the time. I still wasn't quite awake, and could barely stop myself yawning. Finally, she said, "Well, what'll it be?"

"One of each," I decided.

"Oh, so you're hungry, eh?"

"Yes," I said. "Somehow I managed to work up an appetite, even with all that sleep."

She just turned and smiled and started to heap bread and stew onto a plate, which she then set before me. Bowman and Harris now staggered back down, looking well worn.

"So, you gents having a good day thus far?" I asked in the midst of chewing a succulent mouthful.

"Lovely," answered Bowman, collapsing in the first chair available.

"Just grand!" groaned Harris. "I'd like to know when they started to get so young and I got so old. A bloody shame, it is. I must have missed something in passing." He sat down with a monstrous sigh and propped up his feet on the table. Bowman followed suit.

"Missed anything? Oh Harris, I doubt that. If there's anything missed, you've missed hardly any," said Katherine tartly. As she turned to face them, her eyes widened at the two pairs of boots on her scrubbed table.

"You two! Get your great filthy boots off the table!" she snapped.

"Right," Harris said sheepishly, putting his feet down with one great thunk and then another. Bowman followed. She took a cloth and wiped down the defiled section of tabletop with some asperity.

"Have pity on an old man," quavered Bowman, putting his head down on the table.

"Old man?" sniffed Katherine. "If I'd called you an old man before we were at sea, you'd probably have me flung overboard."

"No, no," Bowman cried, and raised his hands in surrender. "Harris is the one who takes on that task. He's good at throwing people over side. Why, just a few days ago—"

"Shut up, Uncle Billy," Harris interrupted.

"Oh dear," exclaimed Katherine, "how disrespectful to address your captain in that manner!"

"Aye, that's right. Listen to her," said Bowman with obvious satisfaction.

Harris put his hands on his hips. "A few days ago you would never have said that, nor listened to anyone in a dress either."

"Times change, but you don't," Bowman shot back. He then peered anxiously from my nearly empty plate to the stove. "Still some food out there?"

"Come and get it, and try not to wear it in the bargain. We've had a time keeping it upright," she answered.

They shuffled forward and picked up plates. There was delicious beef stew with potatoes and vegetables, new bread, and, of course, Katherine's legendary pies.

"Smells wonderful," said Harris ecstatically.

"And tastes even better," said Bowman, tucking right into his. Katherine took off her apron and smoothed her hair, giving a sigh.

"This is the last I'll be doing for now," she announced. "I'll start it up again later. If you'll look in those two barrels, one of them has apples and the other pears. You'll want to eat the pears first as they don't keep—and some kind of fruit I've never seen before."

"Oh?" enquired Harris. "I'll have a look at that."

"Here's one," Katherine said. She held up a leathery-skinned red ball the size of an apple. "What on earth do you call that?" I looked, but it was quite foreign to me.

"Well, I'll be. I haven't seen one of these in quite some time," said Harris, taking it from her. "This is called a pomegranate."

"I've had those," nodded Bowman.

Robert's eyes lit. "There are pomegranates in the *Song of Solomon*. You know, in the Bible. Let's see…was it her *brows* that were like pomegranates?" Then he held his two hands cupped one on each side of his chest, "Or was it her—" Robert suddenly broke off in embarrassment, finding Katherine's steely gaze bent upon him. His hands snapped back down. "Yes, of course, brows it was," he put in hastily, trying to change the subject. "How's it eaten?"

Harris cut the biblical fruit in half, showing its curious interior. "You pull back the peel and eat these red seeds inside. If one ever had the runs, you boil the rind and drink it down. Works like magic, it does."

Robert looked dubious. "Oh, I see. Maybe another time."

"Actually, they're quite good," said Harris, taking a bite of the ruby-juiced seed. "Hmm, hmm, not as ripe as it should be, but very nice."

I sampled one of the jewel-like morsels myself and found it tart but pleasant.

Harris looked perplexed. "Where did these come from?"

Katherine shrugged. "They were part of the food stores you lot brought on board."

"I don't remember a thing about it," said Harris, setting the pomegranate halves on the edge of his plate. He took his bread and got down to some serious shovelling of stew.

Robert and I got to talking about some of our adventures during the war. Harris and Bowman were a tired but attentive audience.

We talked about sailors we'd known and our adventures, not to mention pranks, which had abounded. Among them being Robert's great achievement of rolling a cannonball down the stairs of the barracks. This was actually a time-honoured tradition.

He'd managed to dislodge one from a pyramid stack that stood next to an antique cannon. They weren't explosive cannonballs, but rather large iron ones. Freeing one from its weld, he took it to the fourth floor of his barracks. He rigged it so it could be triggered by a long piece of string that ran out the window, over a tree limb, across the park, and near the front of the pub where we were sitting.

On Robert's signal, a young boy walked across the park, pulled the string, and then ran by the window. Robert gave him half a crown and he merely disappeared with his mates.

Meanwhile, on the fourth floor, the cannonball began rolling down the iron stairs, crashing into the walls at each turn, and hitting doors at random. It caused a considerable commotion within the building, but the cannonball didn't come to its rest until it reached the lower level where the residing officer lived. Hearing all the racket, he opened the door just in time to have the cannonball roll over his bare toes.

"Oh my God!" Harris roared, pounding his fist on the table, "I'd give anything to see the look on that man's face!"

I continued. "We did see the look on his face a few hours later, but there was nothing to tie us to the incident, since, of course, we were having a pint with friends. The officer suspected we had a hand in it, but couldn't prove it. He put everyone else in the barracks on restriction, hoping the perpetrator would fess up. We were cleared to come and go as we liked because we had witnesses that we were clearly a street away," I chuckled.

Robert interjected, "You don't know what real pain is until you've had to carry a cannonball in a satchel up four flights of stairs without any expression on your face." At this Harris laughed again.

"Ah, well, it was little things like this to keep from being bored to death between assignments." Robert went on, "Escorting the convoys had its dangers, but I never saw a U-Boat the entire time. Flynn and I did see a freighter hit and she sank fast. All the patrol destroyers never found the U-Boat to our knowledge, but we blew up quite a bit of ocean trying. I had my ears near frozen by the winds in that brass-monkey weather. God, I hated that duty."

Harris turned round and looked at him. "Do you have any idea where that term came from?" he asked. Robert's face went blank and he shook his head.

Harris began, "In the days of sailing warships they carried iron or brass cannons. Those cannons fired iron cannonballs. It was necessary to keep a good supply near the cannon. To prevent the balls from rolling about the deck, the best storage method devised was a square-based pyramid with one ball on top, resting on four resting on nine which rested on sixteen. Thus, a supply of thirty cannonballs could be stacked in a small area next to the cannon. There was only one problem: how to prevent the bottom layer from sliding around. The solution was a metal plate called a *monkey*, with sixteen round indentations. To prevent balls from rusting, the monkey was made of brass. Few landlubbers realize that brass contracts more often and faster than iron when chilled. Consequently, when the temperature drops too far, the brass indentations shrink and the iron cannonballs come right off the monkey." Thus, it was quite literally, cold enough to freeze the balls off a brass monkey! And all this time you probably thought it was an improper expression, *didn't you?*" he said, pointing a finger at Robert.

I saw Robert blink as though someone had switched on a torch. I often thought Harris could spin a great tale, so I said nothing. Bowman only smiled. Actually, ready service shot was kept on the gun or spar decks in shot garlands which consisted of longitudinal wooden planks with holes bored into them, into which round shot or cannonballs were inserted for ready use by the gun crew, but I enjoyed Harris's yarn so much I never did tell Robert.

Just then, one of the lads knocked on the inside bulkhead. "Captain Bowman?" he asked.

Bowman looked up. "Yes?"

"Can we see Mr. Harris for a moment? Mr. Boris has something to ask."

"Be right there," Harris answered, putting down his coffee mug. "Come along, Flynn."

What there was in the way of sunshine greeted us as we came on deck, along with blasts of cold wind. The sails were filled and we were making good time.

Edward was already on deck. "Do you believe it, we're perhaps four-and-a-half-hours ahead of schedule. That's amazing!"

"Well, I suppose it is then, if you say so," remarked Harris. "You're the only one that keeps a schedule nobody knows or understands."

"Oh, never mind," Edward snorted, waving his hands in front of Harris's face.

As we headed to the stern, I walked to midships. As I looked up at the mainmast, descending like a spider in a bo'sun's chair, was Boris. He freed himself from the chair, unclipped it from the halyards, and set it down on the hatchway.

"I trust everything's well in hand?" I said.

Boris looked at me rather peculiarly, then opened his left hand and stared at it blankly. He repeated the gesture with his right, and shrugged his shoulders. "Yes, everything well in hand," he replied at last.

Harris said, "One of the lads said you needed to talk to me."

Boris spoke up, "That was before, now I fixed what I was needing you for. Now I don't need to ask. I'm finished with the thinking of this." He then led the boys off to help him with trimming the sails.

Harris laughed at that. Me, well, let's say I was never terribly certain when Boris understood and when he didn't, but I found it amusing.

Chapter 19
THE PURSUIT BEGINS

I awoke, for once naturally, quite early the next morning. This was an achievement in itself, as the ship was ploughing along hitting solid seas. It managed to stay on an even keel, with an occasional pitch to add to the steady roll. I tried to calculate how far we'd gone and how many more days we'd need to get to the Firth of Clyde. My mind was also filled with thoughts of what our lives would be like after delivering the *Bonnie Clyde*.

I spruced myself up, hoping that Katherine would appreciate the beginnings of a beard, and went to get a mug of tea to start the day. Katherine was already there, looking lovable in the sweater and slacks she'd been wearing since she came aboard. She'd confessed to me that she wasn't happy about the same clothes everyday but that at least she was changing her long woolly underwear. I told her that she was very conscientious, and that I heartily wished the men would follow her good example.

She was busy with baking and could only give a quick wave, so I took my mug to the deck.

Boris was just finishing his turn at the night watch and was sagging a bit over the wheel. The ship was nearly steering herself in these quiet hours and he was bored. He brightened when he saw me. "Maybe you come fishing today? Sea not rough."

I told him what Edward predicted regarding the weather. He thought about that for a moment and said, "Forget fishing, still some from yesterday. Now we make sure everything tied down." With the weather being mild for now, Edward came out and took over the wheel. Boris sounded his bo'sun's pipe to bring all the boys on deck and prepare for a change of course.

We senior officers made the decision to swing more north-west and stay farther away from France after much ado with Edward. We were sure that the pursuit would be looking for us in this area after finding we'd not gone east because that would have been the easier channel crossing. We also wanted to gain a bit of protection from the storm Edward said was coming. So far, we had no backing of the winds to the west. The change in course was very simple in the end because the boys now had enough experience to know which lines to haul on and which to let go. Those on the braces had found the rhythm to make the turning of the heavy yardarms smooth and quick, while Boris brought the ship slowly round maintaining the full belly in the sails as we bore up on the new course. Boris then had both watches working to secure the *Bonnie* against the storm.

I'd only been in a big storm in steel-hulled Navy ships with internal passageways for getting from post to post. Now of course we had to get out into the middle of the weather to take care of our motive power, the sails.

Safety lines were rigged along all the exposed decks where lines needed hauling or braces turned. Belaying pins had to be fixed firmly in their rails, spare coils of rope taken below, and the battening of the hatch covers closely checked. Losing a hatch cover with tons of water pouring into the holds didn't bear thinking of.

Boris wouldn't allow any of the boys to stand down until he'd been over the ship completely aloft and below. "Only one loose pin can kill," he warned darkly. At last he was satisfied and released the watch off duty.

We officers had no idea exactly when to expect the pursuit, but we knew that now the MTB would be miles away on a completely false scent. We hoped we could put enough sea miles between us to keep a jump ahead; rather like the tortoise and the hare. If we could meet up with people who were sympathetic to our cause in the Irish Sea, we hoped their presence would give the Navy pause at trying to stop us.

We'd a good crew, with many responsibilities put on them, and they answered readily every time whether it was climbing the mast and hauling in sheets, making repairs, or coiling down lines. I hadn't heard a complaint yet. When I mentioned this to Harris, he pointed out that this was the most exciting thing the boys had ever done—or perhaps would ever do—in their lives.

Robert had also come into his own. His training had been the same as mine, only his was on a schooner. He was up and down the mast nearly as much as Boris. Robert was university educated, while Boris had trained in the universal school of hard knocks. Communication was difficult, but they were becoming thick as thieves. The two of them were often laughing over some joke or other, sometimes at our expense. Harris said he couldn't understand the bond between them. Half the day they had fishing poles over the side of the ship and actually made some pretty fair catches. Fresh fish was an intended item on our menu, although I didn't notice it in the galley.

Robert had just come down from the rigging and I went to have a chat. We always seemed to be going in opposite directions, so I suggested that we spell Edward on the wheel for a while.

"How's it all going?" I asked.

"Well, it certainly beats being a chambermaid on this ship, as I was before we sailed, or working at the bloody circus."

"I can well imagine," I laughed.

"I wouldn't be too sure of that," Robert said, sniffing.

"Oh, why is that?" I asked.

"I hadn't noticed you doing a lot of the same type of tasks I did before our sailing."

"That's true," I responded," but there were many more things I've had to do than you'd know."

"Someday you must tell me about them," he said sarcastically. Grabbing a great bundle of rope, he left me at the wheel while he worked with one of the boys uncoiling the mass, taking out the knots and twists. When he returned, he seemed more cheerful and began telling me that he was really very pleased to have been included on this journey, even if it meant stealing the circus tents.

"I think being at sea is what I was meant to do—here, what was that?"

We were standing one on each side of the wheel, concentrating on our heading, but we both felt a distinct tremor. Looking up, we saw all the sails start to shiver ever so slightly, and at first couldn't work out what it was. Suddenly, Boris came hurtling across, pipe blasting.

"The wind!" he shouted. The wind was backing sharply from its nor'nor'east bearing, and was already past north. "Must tack now or big trouble. I take wheel, you help boys!"

Boris blew on his pipe again and all the boys came and stood lined up in front of him. "Now boys," he said, "very important change of course. This time change tack. You do once already, remember? Turning yards and taking slack on sails together—other team let out sails and yards, ready to belay time, I whistle. To positions now!"

The boys moved and took up their posts on the ropes, stay ends, and on the braces. It was a little easier because the royals and topgallants hadn't been reset, but it was still a hard haul. I fitted myself into a brace team and followed round putting every ounce of strength into it. It felt as though we were trying to move several tons rather than turning a yard on its mast, but I'd forgotten that the sails were also heavy and were being beaten by the wind as we turned.

I could see Robert on one of the lines and it was plain he was having the same problem as I—lack of stamina. There was no doubt about it, the right age for anything to do with sails is eighteen to twenty; at that age I'd almost enjoyed myself aloft or on the braces and seldom noticed the energy I was expending.

Finally, Boris was satisfied with the position of the yards. He still needed the boys on the lines to fine tune the close-haul needed to maintain our course. The wind was now out of the north-west instead of the north-east, as it had been so short a time ago. I knew that this sort of wind change was possible in the eye of a hurricane, but I supposed that other weather systems can sometimes get the same sort of eyes. Such close-hauling now brought the ship heeled hard over to starboard, and it was only then that I remembered Katherine and winced guiltily. Once again she'd not been warned. Well, there was no help for it now.

When I got to the chart room, I found Harris and Bowman there with Edward looking over the charts and making calculations. After a while we heard the radio speaker give out the familiar whine and howl of someone trying to contact us, then a voice broke out, "*Calling the* Bonnie Clyde. *Calling the* Bonnie Clyde. *Are you receiving us?*"

I picked up the handset and answered: "*Bonnie Clyde* here. Receiving you loud and clear, over." There were several minutes of static before they tried again.

"*Hello there, Flynn, Richard here. How are you today? I was worried about the storm.*"

"No damage here," I replied. I suggested he carry on talking with Harris. "You know, that huge man on the tug? He and Bowman are really the leading spirits in this enterprise. He can tell you a lot more than I, and how we got to our present position which seems to be up the proverbial creek—with bells on! Anyway, here's Harris."

As he picked up the handset, Harris shot me a glance. "You're a bloody comedian, you are." He put the handset to his mouth. "Hello there, Richard, don't listen to a virtual landlubber like Flynn here. Yesterday's was just a little blow and today's doesn't look much stronger. You can never trust storms to behave. We may be in for a three-day blow, but let's get down to cases." Harris leaned forward in his chair. "Your summary of Whitehall and the tug was interesting. I consider planting the magnet and taking the handset the only remotely dangerous or illegal thing we've done so far. Still, it was my fault that you all spent the night hove to."

Richard cut in, "*Nice to talk with you at last, Harris. I wasn't at all worried about being stuck on the tug, just wishing I could get off the bloody thing. Being seasick wasn't my idea of a good time!*

"*Now before I go on, let me tell you the latest I've heard from the nerve centre—OpHQ shall we call it? Your no-storm must have been very local, for the weather was good in London and in the Home Counties. The MTB left Chatham Naval yard at dawn and returned eight hours later, empty-handed. According to their report, they headed east to look for the ship the spotter plane thought was a more likely bet. They actually found her to be a four-masted barque. At first they thought it was you because they could see a lot of boys and young men in the rigging. They were able to talk through a loud hailer and found she was an old grain ship now used for training by the Swedish Navy based in Gothenburg. The MTB turned back to a refuelling depot near Clacton before going out again, heading north. They went as far as they could, but found nothing. However, they did have a stroke of luck in Harwich while they were refuelling.*"

My heart dropped, for Bob would have told us of anything from his side if it had happened.

"*The commander of the MTB was attracted by the sight of tall masts on the other side of the harbour and sent one of his crew to ask a few innocent questions. The seaman came back with the information that the ship had been heading north following a shoal of herring and had returned to port late the night before with a full hold.*

"*OpHQ were now in a quandary. Having relied on one of those two vessels being the right one, they hadn't made any other plans and apparently told the admiral they were back to square one. You'd got a two-day head start and there were some mutterings about letting it be dropped, but the head, on hearing this, issued a note that every effort must be made to find and apprehend these criminals.*" Richard added, as an aside, "*I'll try to get hold of one of those notes for you, in case of need. Very incautious use of words by a head of department, publishing a libel like that! So the committee-of-two looked at the situation again, just as I've been cogitating over where you could have got to. I'm a little ahead of OpHQ there because of an incautious word that fell in my presence yesterday, something about Gretna Green.*"

Harris shot me a glance. He surely knew how to express himself silently, and I felt like crawling off into a corner, only to brighten at Richard's next words. "*But any surmise by me as to what that meant is just for my own information. The general consensus was that you hadn't gone east because of the information now held by OpHQ, so you must have gone south. However, there have been no more sightings, in particular by any Dover ferry. If you were already through there, you probably went through at night.*"

Richard continued, "*Finally it was decided they'd use another MTB, this time out of Dover. They would make a zig-zag search, north-south, so they could re-*

fuel at various depots along the South Coast on each return leg. A small blow on the east side of the Channel yesterday prevented a search until today. That's about it. I've got to be careful what I say, when reporting your side of the story. I'm too old to have MI5 or someone breathing down my neck. I purposely didn't file a follow-up piece last night because I wanted a balanced story, and without more detail from you about your reasons for doing this, I simply couldn't write it."

We'd all been following Richard's words with great attention. Harris's ruse with the *Grouse* had worked, but it left only the southerly direction open as an option after the eastern ship proved incorrect. It was bad news that there was a pursuit boat based so close, but he still had to find us and even if he couldn't operate in a storm, we could. Now we hoped, really hoped, for a three-day blow. We would gradually move towards the Irish Sea, and any further increase in our lead was welcome. When the MTB moved out, it was going to make a zigzag search, careful not to leave any gaps. Once the storm stopped, we could hope that the wind would bring us back round so we could get on without tacking as often.

Harris was very happy at this report. "Richard, it's obvious to me that you're not only a real reporter, but also a man keen to put our masters in their places when they're unjust or just plain unreasonable. We were fortunate enough to find others who agreed with us. Bowman has been the principal player from the beginning. He's the captain of the ship, and a long-time friend of myself, Edward, and Boris." Harris recounted the story I'd already outlined to Richard, this time with more detail about the offer and the refusal, and Bowman's attempts to get this reversed, and the preparations, including where some of the materials had come from.

"On this point," said Harris, pounding the table that held the radio, "I want to make it clear that a lot of the money was given to us by the people at our destination. Robertson's, the Dumbarton builder of this and so many fine sailing ships, made an agreement with us that they'd be happy to give the *Bonnie Clyde* a permanent home and to keep her as a living museum. They had no knowledge of our actions in fulfilling the agreement. We didn't even discuss it as a *might*."

"*I understand,*" Richard said, "*and I'll report it like that. I'd like to talk to them anyway. This sounds like a worthwhile scheme, so I'd really like to get their angle. No objections from your side, I'm sure?*"

"None at all," Harris replied. "Flynn's slip is only life-threatening to himself, but the storm that's brewing up now is a lot more dangerous to all of us. We are now in the English Channel, but as this storm is coming in on a very wide front, no one can guess where we are from what you may write. Our sails are in good order and Boris, our bo'sun, is adept with palm and needle. There's not much more I can tell you to-night, but I'd just like to mention the boys. Most of them are seventeen or older, no one was coerced, and all are having a cracking time. We've been feeding them up from what were surely just survival rations before. Thank goodness they'd at least been getting their free milk, orange juice, and vitamins as issued. I reckon we've as good a crew as any ship. All normal safety precautions on a sailing ship have been taken, fixed lifelines, and the lot. In fact Boris has come up with an idea of his own which will make life aloft much safer."

Richard came on, "*Do you want to make any comments about the orphanage or the headmaster?*"

"Oh, we'd just love to," Harris said with relish, "but most of it would be so libellous you wouldn't be able to print it! The only good thing he did, and that unknowingly, was to let us give lessons to the boys in seamanship as part of his Character Building History Class. Anyway, the man is in enough trouble already with the police—you just ask Martin."

For some time, the noise outside and the pitching of the ship had been increasing. Harris now said, "Richard, I hope you don't feel that we're always trying to get away because of a storm or something, but we're going to have to—"

Richard stopped him short, "*Not one little bit! You've given me plenty here, enough for at least two news pieces and an article. I've got bags of leads, including the builder, who I hope has some pictures from when the* Bonnie Clyde *was first built. Oh, no, I've got plenty and I'm sure this story is going to take wing. Just one more point before you go. I want to have a word with Dick here to try and find another ham closer to my office and home. Coming out here wastes much valuable time, when I could be making sure that the story has all the right ingredients to support the facts. Is that all right with you?*"

"No objections from here," Harris replied. "We would like you to be sure that this other ham operator is the same sort of person as Dick and not some scared little man running off to the police or another newspaper to line his own pockets."

Another voice came on very quickly. Dick replied, "*Pistols at dawn is what used to be the only recourse for such insinuations! But I'll forgive you this time, being as you're only a poor ignorant member of the masses who aren't ham operators. We've a strong, unwritten charter worldwide that cuts out personal gain unless a person we've helped wishes to make an award. I think with the contacts I have around the country, I should be able to find an operator who's prepared to reserve judgment on this situation until the entire story is told. We're a bit like reporters in this. Just don't tell us direct facts, which we don't need to know or report. The police and Whitehall will be quite busy after Richard's piece appears tomorrow."*

Suddenly there was a thunderous crash outside and the old ship shuddered all along her length, straining against the invisible bonds tying her to the sea. With a series of crashing bangs as the freeing ports opened and discharged the water she'd shipped, the *Bonnie Clyde* climbed out of the deep hole she seemed to be in. Through the chart room portholes we could see the last of an angry light edging the massed clouds all round the horizon.

Harris rose and made to sign off. "You must have heard that. It was a real mountain of water dumped on the foredeck. We must get on deck immediately. The wind's getting too strong! I do hope you can find a new ham, Richard, and speak to us tomorrow. Dick, this isn't goodbye because I think you're right about official activities, so I'd like to hear from Martin and you whenever they do come back to the village. Now, we really do have to sign off and will wait for you tomorrow, out." And he cut the connection without giving them time to say more.

"I'm sorry I was so abrupt, but it's all hands on deck!" he said briskly, and we went plunging out into the sudden squall that had hit us. The rest of us, officers and crew, assembled quickly on deck. Each, I'm sure, equally apprehensive about the night to come.

Chapter 20
THE STOWAWAY

Earlier in the day, while we were all relaxing and enjoying the lull between storms, I accidentally discovered the reason for the fishing activities of Boris and Robert, and where their unlikely friendship must have started. Although it was quite a shock at the time, I reasoned that it was something that would be disclosed later on. It clearly wasn't anything that endangered the ship. For now, their secret was safe.

I'd gone down to the 'tween decks hold, along the dark passage still crammed with most of the things that had been brought on board, and now all sorted and secured by the boys. I was rummaging at the forward end near the main hatchway looking for anymore galley items I could find and just enough light was coming through the companion opening for me to see. I happened to look aft and saw Boris with a lantern and a bucket preparing to go down to the lower hold. I was about to call out when I saw Robert as well, looking about, I thought, a bit furtively as though up to no good, and then he too disappeared down after Boris. Now, as far as I knew there was nothing in the main hold except the remaining line, tackle, and miscellaneous equipment used for the ship's operation. This also doubled as Boris's private domain and sleeping quarters, but then I remembered the large crate or box that I'd seen being loaded before the anchors were removed, the one covered in a tarpaulin. At the time I had thought little of it; now I was getting interested. What was it that these two were hiding?

I moved quietly through the 'tween decks, until I could see down through the companion opening into the main hold. Boris and Robert were sitting quietly next to a shrouded shape and were eating a bit of lunch, talking in low voices. Near them was a bucket full of fish. As I moved closer I heard a loud groaning coming from under the tarpaulin. Boris carefully peeled it back and there, looking out from its cage with weary, miserable eyes, was a large old brown bear with a grey muzzle. I could hardly believe my eyes! I guessed at once that it was Harris's bear from the circus. What it was doing here I hadn't the slightest idea. I moved closer and eased part way down the ladder to a ledge for a better vantage point.

Boris reached into the bucket for some fish and threw them into the cage. The bear sniffed at them, and took a nibble or two, but soon turned away and started groaning again.

Boris said, "I'm not understanding. He eating, but not very live."

"I think he's seasick," Robert said. "I've read that animals can get seasick too, but it usually doesn't make them chuck it up. They feel awful, just like people do."

Boris disagreed. "Maybe trouble here," he said, pointing to the hobbles on the bear's rear ankles. His legs were raw and chafed which was probably causing him pain. Robert agreed with Boris and suggested that they try to remove them. Boris said he'd tried several times with a lock-pick from a piece of metal. "When I tried before, bear angry."

Robert pressed on. "Let's try again, because this looks like it could easily get infected. I think if we give him a fish, I can talk to him while you work on the leg iron, and we might be able to manage it," he said confidently.

Giving the bear a fish, Boris managed to reach in and grab one of the leg irons. Exercising the greatest caution, he started to pick the lock. The bear lay still and stared out the front of the cage. Then without warning, he suddenly turned and nearly got Boris with a good swipe of his paw. Luckily Boris was quick and withdrew without a scratch.

Robert continued to talk softly to the poor old creature and the bear continued to eat. Boris resumed his work, when suddenly there was a loud click. The bear's ears went up briefly as Boris started to untwist the fastenings. It must have hurt because the bear pulled away each time. But this time he seemed to understand that Boris was there to help and pushed his leg back each time. He put his huge nose between his paws in an attitude of submission.

Boris now reached over and pulled the hobbles off, rather like stripping off a sticking plaster all in one go, so as to give one short pain. This brought an immediate response, with giant paws flying round. After a minute he sank back again and started to lick the two raw ankles, every now and then looking up at Boris almost as if trying to say something. Boris also now tried to communicate. He pulled the leg irons out from the back of the cage and went round to the front, holding them up in the air. After saying something in Russian, he flung the irons as far as he could across the cargo hold, where they crashed against the bulkhead. Boris walked over and kicked them to show his disgust, then walked back and sat in front of the bear. He reached into the bucket, pulled out another fish and placed it in the cage, but more slowly than he'd done previously.

This gesture did not go unnoticed. The bear made a soft sound and gave a look at Boris, then pulled the fish between his paws and put his head to one side. The gesture seemed to show that the bear now knew who Boris was, and knew that he could expect no harm from him. Boris seemed to enjoy talking to the bear in Russian, and it soon became evident that this bear was the only one on board who might actually know what he was talking about!

Robert said, "He seems to understand Russian. Do you think it's possible he had a Russian trainer?" Robert continued to watch the bear, who was resting much more easily now. "There'll come a time when we'll have to share with everyone what we have down here. I hope this cage is properly secured. We won't want it shifting, maybe breaking, and the bear on the loose. One thing we can do right now is get the big pot of Vaseline. He'll feel much better if I put some on for him."

"Maybe works for now, but I make medicine which works much better," Boris said.

Robert came running up the ladderway with the lantern so quickly that I was caught in the beam before I could react. Seeing me, Robert called back down to Boris, "We have a spy here. What shall we do with him?"

Boris came up to see who it was. "Come and sit with bear."

When we were settled around the bear, I heard the whole story. The bear really didn't belong to the circus and was in need of a good home. Even the circus owners seemed to have forgotten about him at the last, fully expecting that all the animals would be taken in by zoos for the cold season. But there was nowhere for the bear. Thinking how much this animal meant to Harris, Robert suggested to Boris that the bear could be taken aboard the ship and kept a secret until we were well out to sea.

"He seems able to take the bad weather, but we must make sure he's fed everyday and keep him supplied with lots of fresh water," Robert said, "and very often that's quite a struggle with just the two of us to catch the fish. We're still in two minds whether to tell everyone about him or not. There never seems to be the right moment. I rather dread the reaction of the others, especially Bowman and Harris."

Just now, with the wind rising and all the indications of the gale and coming storm, the time also didn't seem right. I agreed that we should hold off for a while. "The storm is going to keep everyone fully occupied, so the fewer worries, the better. Ignorance is bliss, at least in the short run," I said. We covered over the bear's cage with the tarpaulin again and returned to our duties and the storm on the horizon.

Chapter 21
RUNNING WITH THE WIND

We were now running truly wild and free before the wind, for we were one with the wind, and the sea was ours. The pumps below had been operating all night. We were fortunate not to have taken in much water, although both pumps had to run, and we were measuring every drop of petrol to make sure we rationed enough to keep us afloat. It felt splendid to be running free!

Seven days was Edward's calculation of our journey time from the time we took leave of the tug, but no one knew for certain. With a storm such as this one, we might not make forward progress at all, but we remained hopeful. After fighting the currents in the Channel, we'd be passing through extremely treacherous waters where many a shipwreck occurred at Lizard Point. After that, we still had to get round Land's End, another hazardous navigation point, where the lighthouse observatory station was. This would be the first possible place to sight us, and anyone who did would be straight on the phone to Whitehall. However, if we took a more southerly course to pass south and west of the Scilly Islands, this hazard could be avoided. We'd then be heading up to St. George's Channel, a bad place for contrary winds, before arriving at the Irish Sea. And if this was not enough, we still had narrow seas to get through before reaching the Firth of Clyde and the final run north to Dumbarton. We knew little of what fate awaited us once we finally reached Scotland. My heart sank at the thought of all the things that could go wrong. Edward was constantly reviewing his navigational estimates, although he admitted there were many things to be decided between each tack before the wind. He wasn't willing to talk about them except to Bowman, who of course constantly challenged each decision.

There were discussions about what would happen when we finally made port, but it was all strictly conjecture.

We knew there were people awaiting the ship's arrival who would give her a berth to secure her and keep her out of the hands of those who'd wish her scrapped. The question on our minds was what would become of us? It seemed somewhat unlikely that we'd be imprisoned, but I admit it did cross everyone's mind. From there, what? This was to be a new start in a place foreign to most of us. A new start was what this voyage was all about. I kept wondering if everything would turn out well enough for Katherine and me to make a go of it. This particular thought was all consuming. I wanted this to be the beginning of our life together.

Many things had happened since the days at the Beasley Inn. It was only a few days ago, but it seemed as though years had passed. None of the boys missed their charming headmaster, O'Connell. I'd only heard his name mentioned once in passing during the entire voyage. I hadn't spent much time around young people, but I spoke to them as I would any enlisted seamen. During the last few months of planning, this escape had given them new life. The experience brought them a sense of unity.

As we came from the hold Boris said, "Weather."

Robert looked round. "Eh?"

"Weather," Boris repeated, "weather is coming. Get boys on deck." Robert took his bo'sun's pipe and gave the call for all hands on deck. When everyone had assembled, Boris stepped forward.

"Boys," Boris called out, "this, everyone must have." He produced a length of rope that looked like a running noose with a large halyard snap in front of the harness he was tying.

"This," he explained, "is what everyone must wear, everyday, all day, every hour." We all paid close attention. "Works like this." He stepped into the triple noose, pulling it up his legs with the other two loops under his armpits, and adjusted the knot on the clasp.

"You take this halyard snap and when you climb the mast to work with the sails, you snap this clamp to the railing which runs across the length of the top of each yard. This is called the jackstay as I have told you before. If fall, only little way!" He jumped into the nearest ratlines, clipped the snap on and let go. He'd fallen as far as the loop slack went and hung there with his arms and legs outspread before pulling himself back to the rigging. In this way Boris was going to make sure that each boy had a safety harness while working aloft.

I'd never seen anything quite like it before, but then again, there were many things on this ship and about this voyage I'd never seen at sea. This was certainly going to make me feel safe when I had to help with the sails. Boris had even covered the deck crew. He told everyone to practise using the fixed safety lines rigged along the decks so that each one would snap onto them automatically, even when there was no sea running.

"You practise," he said, "then no wave come and wash you over side. Bad weather coming, look!" Everyone looked astern in the direction Boris was pointing. Dark clouds were gathering even thicker, over-piling each other, and coming our way.

"You each do this, start now. When you want change direction, un-snap and snap on next rope. Have ropes both sides and amidships. This way, you be safe," he finished, casting a fierce glance over the lot of us. After that we all practised, for we realised that our lives might depend on it.

Boris and Harris's class in seamanship up at the orphanage and on the ship had given the boys a good head start on how to put these knots together. They were making quick work of this new harness and after each boy finished his own, he'd start helping the others. This co-operation and camaraderie was displayed frequently among the boys, who'd been together so long, holding one another together at the orphanage, and now at sea.

With the storm almost upon us, we worked to shorten sail. So long as there were enough boys, I wasn't about to go up to the yards and was quite happy to man the capstan, winches, and downhauls. It was diffi-cult enough to stay upright on the pitching, yawing deck. I didn't want to think what it was like aloft, with the masts and yards swaying through the air. I knew those conditions well, having been in them be-fore, but I also knew that I couldn't remain on deck all the time. Soon enough I would need to go aloft. Bowman had stayed inside the shelter of the chart room and when we'd finished, I staggered in to join him.

"I've been thinking," I was eventually able to gasp out, "that it might be a good idea to radio the *Grouse* and find out what the weather is like back there. Harwich and Dover are on the same longitude, and I'm worried what the MTB has been doing since this morning. If they've been getting the edges of this storm, it can only slow them down or have them shelter in a port."

Bowman considered this and said, "Yes, the more information we have the better. Let's try it. But first, send Harris down."

I went up on deck and intercepted Harris making his rounds. "Bowman would like to see you in the chart room," I called out.

"Oh he would, would he?" he exclaimed, wiping his forehead with his huge forearm.

"Yes, it's regarding the weather," I began.

"Oh yes, yes. I seem to remember noticing there was weather. Uncle Billy wants us to change that, right?"

"Enough God-damn sarcasm, ye great lump!" boomed Bowman's voice from behind me, announcing his presence. I jumped in surprise, not knowing that he'd suddenly decided to follow me up to have a look at things for himself. "Now, from where I stand, it looks much like it will be upon us quite possibly before nightfall, or certainly by early tomorrow," he said.

Harris pulled out a pair of binoculars. He gazed through the lenses, studying the horizon and murmuring something unintelligible, a habit he, Edward, and Bowman seemed to have perfected. Harris and Bowman then made their way back to the chart room and I went for the radio.

It was very hard getting through to the *Grouse*. When there was a response, it had a lot of crackle and static. "*This is the Grouse, over,*" finally came through.

"This is Flynn on the *Bonnie Clyde*. Is that you, Bob? We're curious as to what weather you're experiencing, over."

There was a lot of noise from the other end, plus the usual atmospherics, and Bob replied, "*Satan's cesspool, and all bloody hell. Lovely weather wouldn't you say? The North Sea only gets like this when we have the tail end of some really bad weather from over the Atlantic. I should guess by now you're well into the thick of it too, over.*"

"We are, or are just about to be," I shouted back. "The other reason for calling was to ask if you have any experience of how an MTB handles in weather like this. I've only seen them on coastal patrols in the Royal Navy. We've been told that there's one based in Dover with orders to pursue us, starting this morning."

"*I just hope the captain isn't a death-and-glory boy,*" Bob came back, "*and got back into harbour as soon as he could see what was happening. Those boats can easily be swamped and capsized depending on how big a wave hits them. The waves are high and the wind is gale force. I'd say we're looking at forty to fifty knot gusts and we're—*" At that moment there was a slam on the other end of the microphone.

"*—experiencing heavy buffeting,*" said Bob.

"Can you give me your position?" I asked.

"*At the moment, flat on my arse,*" Bob replied, which gave us a short laugh.

"Well, I suppose we're both busy so I'll sign off for now. Thanks for the information and best of luck."

"*Thanks, but here's hoping we don't need it. Good luck to you too, out,*" and Bob broke the connection.

Harris had come in while we were talking. "Sounds like quite a blow. Let's take a survey of what still needs doing. I'm sure there must be plenty we've overlooked," he said looking thoughtful.

"Hmm..." I thought for a moment. "You go ahead while I go make sure that Katherine has secured everything in the galley."

"Right, you start there and then meet me back on deck. And don't you be all day about it," Harris barked. I didn't really feel guilty about not telling him that I knew Katherine had already put the galley in order. I just felt I deserved a few minutes alone with her, so I headed quickly down there. Not seeing her, I went back to her cabin. Her door was open and she was making the best of trying to move the dust from one place to another. Seeing me, she turned with a smile.

"Ah, Flynn, do me a favour." She handed me a broom, "Give that a shake-out, will you?"

"Ooh-h—I don't really think we have the time for that. This storm is moving in at quite a pace, and I need see that everything is secured and tied down."

"How much of a storm?" she asked, looking worried.

"I suspect that we'll be doing a lot of step-dancing just to keep our feet under us for a time."

"Hm-m, lovely," she responded, unenthusiastic.

"Yes, Harris's sentiments precisely. Just make sure that anything that *can* move, *doesn't*," I said. "How does that fit with things in the galley?"

"Everything here seems to be fairly tight, she said with a fair show of confidence, I'll have one more go round." Katherine sounded reassuring. We began to stow things properly in the lockers under her bunk. This was difficult with the ship leaping about like a live thing, and I suggested she should make sure everything was shut up tightly, as the storm was going to play hob with anything left loose. It certainly played hob with my try at kissing her just then, for we finished up flat on the floor by the bunk—since we'd been holding onto one another rather than onto some other support, as would have been sensible. Being down but not out, the next few minutes were pleasantly passed despite the jumpy deck beneath us, but I finally had to tell her that I really needed to find Harris before he came looking for me. I heaved a tragic sigh.

"Oh very well, off with you then," she said with a grin.

I climbed up the ladderway to the main deck and found it was growing even more blustery. The boys on deck were wearing their harnesses and were busy tying down everything that could get loose. Harris was checking the fixed lifelines by swinging his great bulk on them. Boris was supervising a group of boys going aloft to check the stays, buntlines, and clewlines. They were also making certain that the gaskets had been properly fixed so that if it was decided that more sail was needed in the middle of the storm, no one was going to have trouble releasing it. Nothing worse in a storm than a sail half set, threatening to be blown away or ripped to pieces because a gasket won't come loose!

I could see Edward going along the pin rails, inspecting each of the lines running up to the great yards aloft. He looked over at me and waved. "Maybe we should talk to Boris and suggest using the mechanical winches and turn those yards just a bit. I'd rather ride out the storm just a wee bit closer to the wind so we don't get pushed too far off course." He squinted about. "Where is Boris?"

I pointed towards the towering masts. Boris was doing his high-wire act, as he swung from yardarm to yardarm, making sure all was in proper order to withstand the strain of the oncoming wind.

Edward peered up at him. "Well, I've a thing or two to do. Could you be after telling Boris of my suggestion when he gets down? We still need to connect those mechanical winches to the masts. We've tried that once before and it seemed rather successful to me," he nodded in satisfaction and moved off.

Harris was occupied with piles of wet line that still hadn't got coiled down after furling the sails.

"Here, give a hand with this lot," he cried. "They've got into a complete mess."

I took one of the coils of line and began to untangle it from another and then another. Wouldn't you know, it was just my luck to get the one with the most tangles, twists, and kinks. In the end, I had to lay all three down along the deck to knock out the kinks before I was able to coil them down in the proper fashion.

As I stood up, the sound of the wind took on an ominous pitch, and with a roar came through the ship like an express train passing. I looked round the horizon but it had disappeared. Without warning a squall started beating down on us, filling the scuppers in seconds and drumming on my sou'wester and oilskin. It passed just as quickly as it arrived, but working aloft was going to be even more dangerous with water streaming on all lines.

It soon became evident that during Edward's wanderings, he'd decided to go by way of the main cargo hatch to check on things below. Harris had cautioned him earlier about this being Boris's domain, that he was very territorial about the compartment, but these words he'd clearly ignored and went on below.

Above the din of the storm, I heard an ominous cry of terror. It seemed so close that I said aloud, "What the bloody hell was that?"

I looked aloft and hoped that none of our boys had fallen. Then I heard the shout again sounding, if possible, more terrified than before.

Someone was yelling as if he'd just seen a banshee. I glanced round the deck but saw nothing. By now all work had stopped and everyone else was looking about for the source of the cries. Suddenly I saw Edward coming up through the hatchway from the main cargo hold with his arms flapping about before him and running pell-mell down the deck as if he'd seen the devil himself. In fact, in his view, I'm sure this was nearly what was happening, for directly behind him, there came lumbering out a certain very large brown bear who seemed not at all annoyed at finding himself free, but by God he was noisy!

Once on deck, he slowed down and then stood looking shortsightedly about. The noise of the storm, with the continual flying spray and the waves breaking over the gunnels must have been quite confusing, not to mention alarming, to him, poor fellow. He stood up as well as he could and gave a roar of mingled defiance and bafflement. With that, everyone made for the ratlines. The deck was now empty with the exception of Edward, the bear, and me.

"God Almighty, A BEAR!" came another roar, this time from Harris, who was still aloft. Looking at me dangerously, he started to clamber back down. The bear shuffled slowly round the deck.

"You had a hand in this, didn't you?" he growled.

"I swear—" I began, but just then I was interrupted by Boris.

"Wait a minute, wait a minute!" said Boris as he descended the mast Tarzan-like on a long rope. He glared angrily at Edward, who was crouched down behind a stanchion.

"I told everyone stay out my place!" Then he turned and walked towards the bear without a trace of fear. On the way he managed to unclip a boathook from the bulwark. Holding the boathook, he advanced cautiously upon the great beast.

As he came closer the bear gave a low rumble of disapproval, but Boris began talking to him in very kindly sounding singsong Russian. The animal clearly didn't know what to do. He shuffled round the deck, sniffing the air, trying to find something familiar. He stood up again, but then decided there was no land to run about on and began to retreat. He made his way back in the direction of the hatch from which he'd emerged. At the hatch, he sniffed about in a puzzled fashion, not seeming to know how to proceed.

Boris darted in and opened the hatch as far as he could, surveying the cracks and damage done by such a big animal getting through such a small space. Now the most immediate—and daunting—task was to persuade the bear that he was to go back down there. Harris came along the deck to assist. "Brown bear," he said softly. The bear turned, stood up just a little, and smelt the air. "Brown bear, what have they done to you?"

Robert spoke up. "Well you see Harris, Boris and I thought—" but Harris cut him off.

"Just what the bloody hell were you idiots playing at? Not only do we have sails made from circus tents, now we have a performing circus animal! What the bloody blazes is he doing here anyway, and who or what else do we have lurking down there? This isn't bloody Noah's ark," he roared in a crescendo of furious wrath. "So tell me, how many other stowaways have you brought along?"

"Only this one," Boris started to explain, "Your old friend, we bring him. They treat him badly, remember?" He fixed Harris with an appealing look. "All of us, fresh start."

"Yes, the bear is an old friend, but I don't expect him to come and share my bunk," Harris snapped in a rising tone.

"We couldn't exactly leave him in such poor conditions," Robert chimed in, "I mean, think of it, he could have died there. At least he has a chance with us. Clearly something needed doing."

Harris scratched his beard from one ear all the way to the other, looking thoughtful. "Well yes, it all sounds right, something needed doing. But it was you that made up that story about him being transferred back to his original trainer and all that bit. Oh, and I suppose that's why you two have been so fond of fishing as of late, eh?"

Edward looked up from his hiding. "Now I know why it smelt like a bloody circus here. 'Tis himself down there," he scowled indignantly.

Robert quickly added that they were keeping the hold extremely clean. The bear now had some broken-up straw bales serving as his bed and since Boris had removed his leg irons, the old fellow actually had it better than before. Harris didn't know whether to laugh or cry at that point. He muttered something about bloody madmen, and then he and Boris began walking round the deck. The bear followed like a friendly dog, attempting to satisfy his curiosity as to where exactly he was, having never seen the sea before. Boris and Harris spoke to the old fellow a good deal, but who could say exactly how much was understood by him? Still, when Boris started down the ladderway the bear tried to follow.

After much pulling, pushing, and coaxing, Boris managed to get the front half of the great beast down the ladder just as Bowman came out on deck. His eyes opened wide at the picture before him.

"And just what the hell is going on up here now?" he exploded. "Harris, is this yer doing?"

"No!" protested Harris, "but let's get him back down in the hold before we go into all that."

The bear's rump was now sticking out of the hatchway and it took the combined efforts of Harris, Robert, and myself to push him through the rest of the way. The cage had slid at some point and broken open at one corner where it had hit the bulwark. Since the bear had no intention of going anywhere at present, no serious restraint was really needed now. At least he was back in the hold again.

Harris drew himself up sternly and said, "This is one case where there's going to be a post-mortem, so everyone had better have his story straight!" Then he roared over the wind and crashing water, "To your stations, everyone! Get back to work. Be at it now!" The boys who were not supposed to be in the rigging quickly scrambled back down to the deck now that they were assured that they weren't fated to be dinner for the gigantic hairy beast.

For some reason, the storm wasn't increasing in strength. Maybe we were running before it on our diagonal course across the Channel. Maybe the air masses were simply jostling each other before fixing on the direction they wanted to fly. Whatever the reason, it gave us a respite and a chance to get some food for the boys before their watch came up. Robert and Boris had been sharing the helm for some time and doing a good job of it, despite the wind and the mountainous seas. Every now and then calls would ring out for the sails to be hauled closer or slackened out.

Harris was still looking dangerously agitated and it appeared he was looking for somewhere to vent his anger. He came up to stand by the wheel.

"Well, somebody had better tell me something, and quickly too," he said, looking menacingly at Robert.

"Just as soon as Boris gets back up on deck," Robert responded with his most innocent look. Harris walked over to the ladderway where the bear had disappeared. Inspecting it, he could see how the wood had been cracked in several places.

Harris returned and turned to me. "All right then, Flynn, go below and get some spare lumber and caulking because when water pours over the side, you know damn well it's going to go below. We've no way of knowing precisely how the pumps will manage with any extra work, so see to this immediately." He slid the hatchway open a few inches, "Boris! Get your arse up here instantly!" he yelled.

Noticing several lads observing him, Harris turned, "This isn't a sideshow. Get on with your work. *NOW!*" They very briskly got on with it.

A moment later Boris reappeared in the hatchway. Harris's face was red as a beet, a most alarming sight. "Well then," he began in an ominously gentle tone, "tell me about our newest crew member."

Boris just shrugged his shoulders, as was typical of his response to any questionable situation.

"I see you at circus, you are much unhappy your friend look so bad."

At this juncture Bowman came up. He glared at Harris, who took out a handkerchief and wiped his forehead. Bowman turned to Boris.

"Oh, and that's yer excuse, is it? So were ye planning to save him as a Christmas present, eh? That's the bloody stupidest scheme I've ever heard of!

"And you, Mr. Harris. What d'ye propose doin' about it now? That's your damned bear! Unless ye'd care to go shares with this daft Ruskie!" Bowman yelled.

Harris shifted uncomfortably, darting a resentful glance at Boris. "I'll go down and see him later. But Boris, I'd like to know just how you managed to get him on board without anyone knowing about it? Won't the circus consider the fact he's gone missing?"

"Oh, was easy." Boris said with an ingratiating smile. "They come with big truck to get anchors, I pay them bring big box. They are not knowing what was in there and they not care. You and Bowman busy about anchors. Nobody notice what I do."

Harris raised his arms with fists clenched, speechless for the moment.

Then Bowman spoke up, "So now we're not only the proud possessors of an illicitly procured ship, stolen circus tents, and a crew of orphan runaways, but we have a bear for a mascot into the bargain!"

"Never mind, never mind," Boris said, "everything will be all right."

"Fortunately for ye," continued Bowman in a more collected tone, "I don't have time to consider the best judgment on this just now," and he pointed towards the whirlwind of activity taking place all around them. Everyone was preparing for the storm and the bear only added to his worries. His first concern was the coming storm, and how his unseasoned crew members would fare. With a stiff nod to Harris and Boris, he turned and walked aft to join Robert at the helm.

Boris shrugged and went back up into the rigging, and I set to work repairing the damaged hatchway, while Harris set out on another round of inspections. As he went he passed Edward still crouched behind a stanchion, looking very sorry for himself.

"Are you all right?" Harris asked.

"Oh quite," Edward said bitterly. "'Tis not often one gets to be chased about by such a large beast aboard ship. Oh, but wasn't it invigorating, though," and he reached into his coat pocket, producing a flask which he upended and drank dry. He moved away very disgruntled with a wary glance at the hatch.

After I'd finished what I modestly thought a first-rate patch job on the hatchway, Harris came by and motioned me to follow him.

"Have you noticed that she isn't pitching so heavily?" Harris asked as we went forward.

I stood for a moment, adjusting my body to the heaving of the deck and said, "Not only that, the wind seems to be slackening as well." We both stood and concentrated. The smack of the bow into the waves was definitely less heavy and the spray was much finer now than it had been even half an hour before. We were so busy that no one was taking notice. We also became aware that we didn't have to shout so any longer in order to make ourselves understood.

"Let's get back to the wheel and see what Bowman thinks," Harris said. Robert called out he was sure the wind had slackened up because it was much easier to maintain course since the sideways kick of the aft section had died down.

"If that's the case," Harris said, "stand down the boys not on watch. If we need to reset the sails, I'm sure the duty watch can manage." Going below into the chart room, he asked Bowman the latest on the weather.

Bowman thought it had been too local in developing and probably there was no weather ship close enough to pick it up. "There was nothing on the radio," he mused, "unless ye take 'Storms are expected in the areas of Fastnet, Irish Sea, and Channel' as a forecast. It would help if they could be a wee bit more exact. The Channel's a big place. The glass has been rising steadily so I suppose we're moving out of this one anyway."

Edward came in at that point, a little flushed but much calmer, and showed us our position on the chart. To my eye we were getting too close to France, something we were trying to avoid, and it was already dusk. I left the others to decide the next move and went outside to stand with Robert. The break-up of the storm showed in the lessening sea and the clouds opening up. We could see some stars, and the moon appeared occasionally, casting a silvery light to the sea. The noise of the wind in the rigging had changed from its normal roar. Every now and then a sail would give a smart crack as it flapped from loss of the wind.

Robert said, "You'd better tell them that the wind is turning, and we can't hold this course much longer."

Boris got ahead of me as we went into the chart room. "Need more sail now," he said, "we get ready bear north-west when wind ready."

The storm had been beating in on us from the north-west and we'd been close-hauled on a sou'sou'west course, but it seemed as though the wind was backing round to the north-east, so we didn't need to change tack, only to turn the stern through the wind and brace the yards as we went. After more discussion, it was decided that in order to avoid the Cherbourg Peninsula, our new course would be west-north-west, but first the sails needed to be set.

Boris's pipe shrilled fit to wake the dead. From the amount of work they'd been doing the last twelve hours, the boys off watch must have been sleeping very much like that. Out they came tumbling, pulling on clothes and boots as they lined up in the well. Boris made a quick check to be sure everyone was wearing his harness and then detailed them aloft and on the deck as needed. Those sent aloft were to release the gaskets and overhaul the bunt and clewlines, while those below got ready at the braces and buntlines to keep the sails full-bellied. I had to marvel at these boys. Here we were in the night with a strong wind still blowing, with the sea sending us up and down an endless switchback, and they act like old hands. They'd become sure-footed on the rigging, needing only to know their assigned sails to get on with the job. I remember my own training, where I always found it hard to remember the name of every buntline or jackstay, and its place on the pin rail.

Boris now blew on his pipe again and they moved into action. Within minutes the *Bonnie* had a different feel as the wind took the extra canvas and Boris adjusted the wheel to meet each new pull. Once all the sails had been set, he swung the wheel to starboard and the head started to turn. I played my part on the capstan as usual. Bracing against the pull of the wind with the help of the sails is a lot easier thing than going round on a new tack. As each yard reached its new position, the ship seemed to jump forward until the final one was secured. Then we surged ahead as the sails, helm, and wind acted in complete unison. This is why men had gone to sea all through the ages. This was feeling the power of the elements and man's own strength to endure as one with it—a unified thing of rarely glimpsed beauty.

With the dying of the storm and the ship on her new course, the pursuit came to the forefront of our thoughts again. We were certain once the MTB captain felt he was not endangering his boat, he'd be out looking for us. A more dismal thought was a small spotter plane might be brought into play if their previous actions were any indication.

Talking about it only kept us going over the same points, and Bowman was thoroughly annoyed by this. He pounded his fist on the table, "We could talk till Doomsday but we'll nae get anywhere. We can't know what action anybody might take. I'd suspect very little, apart from us ignoring them. So, for those off watch, let's everyone get a little shut-eye, shall we? Tomorrow can bring us what it may, and that should be not worrying about an MTB, but about the weather." He got up from his chair slowly, straightening himself like a man with a kink in his back, before walking heavily off to his cabin.

Once he'd gone, there was a general feeling of concern among us at the strain this was putting on Bowman. His expertise was certainly un-diminished, but he wasn't as active, he tired easily, and he lacked his normal bounce. I mentioned what I'd seen when we were still tied up at shore; how he'd had some sort of attack. We found that each of us had witnessed similar incidents.

There was no question of Bowman's ability to command. He was the captain and this was his project from the first. We decided that we must each make sure that he had the least strenuous of tasks, and that he'd give the orders. We would try to keep him from taking the wheel or staying too long on deck. I think we all knew there was no stopping him if he had his own ideas about what he wanted to do, but we all thought it was worth a go.

We then broke up, some on duty and some to take a rest. I had other plans and I dared hope that Katherine had a similar idea. It was late but she was still in the galley. I thought of going below to tell her of the dying status of the storm and that we were changing course. She had started to get a fire going and was glad to be advised of our course change in advance, so that not everything in the galley would take a tumble while she tried to make some hot drinks.

"You see," I said, "I knew what a treasure I'd found as soon as I saw you in your apron at Mrs. B.'s. Always ready to serve your fellow man, and I decided that the one most in need of serving was me!" She threw a tea towel at me but gave in and let me catch her after a brief chase to the end of the galley.

"Oh, Flynn, if you only knew how much I want to be taking care of just you. What I mean is you and me alone in our own home. All my life I seem to have been at someone's beck and call, but that's all about to change."

We sat there quietly talking for some time, about our hopes and how it would be in Scotland. It got late and we were thinking of going off to bed when Bowman came in looking for a mug of tea.

"I'm going up on deck to have a look after a moment," he said, "but there's nothing like a good cup of tea to keep out the cold, unless you come over to Harris's way of thinking."

Katherine was looking at him with some concern, "You don't seem so well to my eye, you look pale." She fixed him with a stern motherly gaze. "Maybe you should get a good night's rest and leave the worrying to Harris for now. You don't look as though a walk on the deck will do you much good."

"It's just my ticker. Every once in a while it puts me off a bit. It'll be right as rain soon," Bowman added, taking a drink. "Ah, rain. With every good wind comes a bit of change. Ye'd best prepare yourself for a wild ride up and coming."

"Yes, I've heard that, but weren't the last few hours considered wild?" she asked.

"Well, we'll just have to see how we fare when the storm gets here," he replied, sitting down at the table with his mug. He sat for quite some time, abstractedly drinking his tea, until he suddenly came to himself. Noticing us still there, he said, "Come on, ye youngsters, time for sleep. Be off wi' ye now, I'll be going myself by and by."

So we said our good nights and went off to our cabins, leaving him looking rather sad and alone, but knowing that he wouldn't take kindly to our staying and fussing over him.

Chapter 22
ANOTHER MESSAGE FROM BELOW

I was awakened by banging on my door that seemed to reverberate inside my head. I made a mental note to knock more softly on Bowman's door in the future. No wonder he got so crotchety about the noise.

"All right, all right," I shouted, "I'm awake, shut your noise."

"Mr. Flynn, sir," Larry's voice came through the door, "Mr. Harris says come quickly to the chart room. We're getting a call from the submarine."

"I'm on my way," I said as I scrambled off my bunk and got into my heavy outer clothes. It must be pretty important for them to break radio silence. Even though he was only on a training exercise, the captain said he would keep us advised of any new developments. I threw on my coat, grabbed my cap, and ran up to the chart room.

When I got there, Harris was calling, "*Shark's Tooth, Shark's Tooth,* I've lost you again, come in," but the radio only replied with squawking whines and those eerie silences when you expect a voice and get some low muttering noise instead. Harris was obviously frustrated and turned as I came in, "Here, you'd better take this and I'll listen in." I saw Todd passing the room and called him over. The lad set right to work at the radio as we watched.

After more static and squawking, Captain Johnson was on and started reporting about ship movements. He then faded, and came back strong for two words before dying again, and I found myself waving at the noise coming from the speaker. As I clicked the handset, the radio made a sound like a mechanical throat clearing and Johnson's voice at last came over loud and clear: "*Hello, Harris, hello. Can you read me? I'm using an old emergency set here to keep us off the main airwaves and I've just changed course slightly, a little like moving my aerial. Is that any better, over.*"

I clicked the handset again and answered, "Loud and clear, Captain. This is Flynn but Harris is here. I'm glad to hear you're using an unknown wavelength, so no one picks up this transmission. I don't know how much was lost just now so maybe you'd better start again."

Johnson's voice continued clear, "*Roger that, Flynn. Reporting late for duty? I take it that you were up having a high time last night, eh? Excuses on my desk by 0800, in triplicate! Joking aside, I know you've been through a storm, so I wanted to check up on you. These sorts of training exercises get pretty damned boring and we're always picking up messages, plus we have our radar, which has become reasonably accurate since our last meeting. I still don't know why it didn't pick up your ship on our first meeting, though. Using this old radio set I can add a bit of excitement to my crew's day, not to mention my own. By the way, your Admiralty has been broadcasting a whole slew of messages telling—not even asking—anyone to report if you're sighted. Are you sure you haven't kidnapped the Prime Minister or something? Over."*

"It's just as we told you, but you know civil servants, always needing someone to blame when things go wrong," I replied. "This time they dug their own grave when they wouldn't listen to our offer. They now realise that a lot of people are going to consider them right twits for that," I laughed. "But now they're being discussed and further exposed at everyone's breakfast table and can't hide anymore!" I quickly explained about the newspaper story being read all over the country. "We were hoping that public opinion will be on our side. Regardless of that, the men in Whitehall are going to get nasty, over."

Johnson was laughing as he came back on: *"Roger that. I can see their faces as they read about it on the train to work. By tomorrow I think one of those faces will be in the newspaper too. Still, as you say, they'll probably get nasty. The most important thing I wanted to tell you is that an MTB based at Dover left this morning and is now on the first leg of her search pattern, somewhere near Dieppe. She's complaining of high seas and we have her on our radar at position,"* and he read out a list of numbers in a crisp staccato which Edward had no difficulty taking down. He went on, *"Your boys are using a spotter plane again, but the nearest suitable one is from an RAF base near Swindon in Wiltshire. His range isn't going to be too far, but his horizon is a lot bigger."*

"That is bad news," I exclaimed. "It's bad enough not knowing when we might see the MTB over the horizon, but to worry about the plane as well…"

"Oh hell, I don't think you have to worry all that much about the plane. I think this one's a single-seater, so the pilot is also the lookout. He can reduce his horizon by coming down low to see if he can spot you, or opt for a broader one by staying higher. Either way, it's my guess that he'll have a hard time seeing you, especially when his training is to look for smoke to lead him in. You have a dark hull and the sails at a distance could easily be mistaken for whitecaps. Believe me, I've got a bit of Navy flying experience myself." He stopped for a moment, then came back with a proposal.

"I'm sure there's something in the books about divulging information in the line of duty, but what the hell," he said. *"What if I give you an up-to-date report every twelve hours of all the ships in our range, with course and current position?"*

Harris cut in quickly, grabbing the handset, "I'd say that would be as fine an offer as I've ever had, but I'd hate to be the one responsible for you violating your regulations. You know the men at the top, only too glad to blight a career for breaking some rule that's only really meant to be enforced during certain circumstances in time of war. We could put your information to good use. Plotting those positions against our own could help us steer away from a possible sighting, over."

Johnson laughed at the idea of such a problem. *"I'll be handling it at this end. I have the emergency radio in my cabin and will take the positions off the charts as my navigator makes them. Later today we'll have to surface to recharge our batteries, so just before we submerge again I thought a little message to the MTB would keep her off your back for a bit longer."*

Harris protested that the risks to him were too high, and I must say I agreed. From what I'd seen of the military bureaucracy in action, I assumed that any wrongdoing would receive punishment all out of proportion to the crime.

On an inspiration, I butted in. "Are you a career officer?"

"No, I'm not, but that's not the only reason I'm willing to help," Johnson replied. *"As you remember I said I had a liking for sailing ships. To think that there are people willing to scuttle one, well…I'd do just about anything to stop it,"* he said. *"And then there's the sheer stupidity and injustice of their attitude! All in all, I'm with you boys the whole way, over."*

Bowman had now joined us and asked for the handset. "Captain, this is Bowman and I have to say I'm very grateful for all yer help."

"Roger that, Captain Bowman. Pleased to be of assistance," Johnson replied. *"At the moment I'm keeping our patrol very close to the mouth of the Channel, roughly a line from Boulogne to Hastings, to make it more realistic. I'm pretty sure that you're farther into the Channel, but with that MTB doing ten to twenty knots when they can, I estimate they'll be on their third leg by now. The commander keeps sending out messages calling for your surrender. You'd need a radio like my main one to pick him up. So my message will be a reply to him on our main radio on his frequency—and then we'll submerge."*

I was ahead of him. "Yes, and then he'll have a message, but no sign of you on the radar. He'll have to investigate no matter what else he believes, once he's got the message and his radioman's confirmation of the position of the ship that sent it. Very clever! I hope you can hear the applause." I held the handset out to pick up the clapping of the others in the chart room.

"I just hope it helps you get farther out of sight. He'll eventually come back here, but after finding nothing, his nearest fuel is back at his home base in Dover, over."

Harris chimed in, "This is going to give us the advantage we need."

"*No doubt about it,*" Johnson replied. "*Here's a list of positions we have on our radar and their courses.*" He read them out in the rapid clipped tones he'd acquired during the war, when clarity of vocal transmission was vital. Edward took them down without hesitation and got busy with his charts. I thanked Todd for his help as he returned to the deck and joined the crew.

"We've left the bo'sun to steer and run. Now we need to relieve him and get properly cleared up after yesterday's storm. Thank you again for what you're doing and the decoy idea. It's the sort of thing I'd love to have brewed up myself." We called our goodbyes and signed off.

Bowman spoke for all of us. "It really is a wonder tae find such good men nowadays, even though he's a Yank." After briefly watching over Edward's shoulder, he walked off slowly to his cabin.

Chapter 23
A HEAVY SEA APPROACHES

Edward had a brief word with Harris to acquaint him with the other ships' positions. Harris grimaced over Edward's calculations, and then turned to Robert and me. "As for you," he said, "I've got just the job for you. This time I'll give you some of the boys to help. We need to get this done quickly." He strode outside and pointed up to the sails.

My heart sank. I love sailing and I'll do whatever is needed, but I've never really got over the terrible nervous tension one gets when hanging one hundred and fifty feet in the air, bent over a yard with feet supported by a rope underneath. The rope moves as you move and cannot be said to give any support at all except spiritual. There you are being hit in the face by the canvas of a sail you're trying to furl, and even when you do furl it right down onto the yard, you then find you can't reach the gasket to tie the bundle down except by bending right over the top of the yard and furled sail, thus having to take your feet off the support of the rope. Then you must balance yourself on your midriff as you reach down for the gasket, and all the while the yard is swinging in an arc across the sky, coupled with a forward rotation to follow the pitch of the boat. I have to admit that I'll never get over that tight feeling from chest to scrotum.

"We've been grateful for those sails," Harris said, "but now we must pay our dues. With this spotter plane around, we need to have canvas with less colour. Take some of the boys off watch and get them painting over the stripes."

Harris went off on another of his inspection tours and one could hear various roars as he came round and found lines not coiled down properly, missing pins in the scuppers, or anything else that offended his critical eye.

Robert and I looked at one another and then up at the sails. "You have to admit they do look pretty gaudy," I said. "How are we going to tackle this?" We stood there contemplating the situation.

"To look on the bright side," Robert commented, "Brian only used them on the smaller topsails, the royals and topgallants, but that means they're farther up and the paint has farther to fall, and I don't agree that it will dry on the way down," and he laughed.

Harris now came back and asked why we weren't at work yet. I told him we were still thinking of the best way to manage it.

"I think this will go much faster when you get aloft and rely on Boris's supervision in bringing those smaller sails to the deck where they can be painted one at a time. They can dry aloft but they'll be painted right here," he said, pointing to the deck with a firm gesture. "Once they're down, we'll call all hands and do the job more quickly and less dangerously."

After climbing the first mast, I awaited further orders from Boris. We were spread out preparing to lower the sails to the deck below. Gingerly we let them down, encountering only a few flaps of resistance before each came to rest on the deck below. The boys waited with paintbrushes and tins of paint in their hands. One of the boys piped up. "Captain Bowman probably wouldn't be pleased if a large blob of paint hits him on his bald patch, and I'd hate to say what would happen if Mr. Harris got hit anywhere." There was a general chuckle at this.

With the ship on a steady course, this was a beautiful place to be. Everywhere the whitecaps glittered in the sun and the waves ran a dark blue-green to the horizon. Gulls hung motionless, almost landing on our shoulders as they stood in the air below the yardarms. The paint was drying rapidly, and very soon the signal was given to haul the sails back aloft. Once they were all properly secured to the yards, we moved to the next mast and repeated the same sequence. I was glad to be wearing Boris's harness, which gave me a feeling of security.

When the job was completed, I was glad to be back on deck looking up at the grey dirty mess now hanging from the yardarms. The brightness of the stripes had been considerably dimmed, certainly enough for the spotter to miss. I could feel the winds picking up from astern and wondered how soon we were in for another blow.

Shipboard activities were intensifying. I saw Bowman and Harris talking to our new helmsman-in-training, Larry. As I joined them, I heard Bowman ask, "How are we faring there, young man?"

"Fine sir. I'm holding the new course true," he replied with obvious pride, "but Mr. Boris is keeping a close watch." I couldn't see Boris anywhere so supposed he'd gone off for lunch, feeling sure that his pupil wouldn't need any real help, especially with the wind blowing steadily.

Bowman eyed the binnacle. "Fine, well done," he said, patting the boy on the back. He peered upward at the sails but the larger mainsail may have blocked his view of the painted-over ones. Bowman had still not forgiven us for having used the striped canvas from the circus, but in the end he'd come to accept it as necessary in order that we'd have enough sails in place to catch as much wind as possible.

"It will still be an embarrassment, anyone looking at those sails," he grumbled.

"Well," Harris said, "they hold wind, don't they?"

"That's right," Edward put in as he disappeared below.

I decided to keep quiet.

Bowman looked up once more with a puzzled air. It was obvious from his manner that Harris had not yet told him what he'd ordered. At first glance, the new paint job hadn't been obvious.

"Would ye look at that!" Bowman exclaimed. "What in blazes has been going on up there?"

"I gave orders to get rid of the colours because of the spotter plane," Harris answered.

Just then Edward put his head back out of the hatchway and barked, "You'd better be after getting down here, there's a weather report to all ships." We all three moved at once to go below.

The BBC didn't broadcast messages to all ships except when there was something serious anywhere in the vicinity of the British Isles. We got to the chart room in time to hear: "*We repeat this warning. To all ships at sea: areas Dover, Channel, Fastnet, Irish Sea, Shetland, Fair Isle, Cromarty, and North Sea. Warning of severe winds blowing from the south-west, west, and north-west amounting to gale force at times in all areas, approaching from the Atlantic. Isolated thunderstorms, squalls, and winds in excess of gale force nine are possible. These conditions are expected to continue for at least forty-eight hours. All ships are advised to take shelter wherever possible. We now return you to...*"

I remember thinking this is the big one where we must keep our wits about us. As for the boys, we needed to emphasise the importance of obeying Harris's and Boris's orders without delay. Having been in more than one gale out of the Atlantic—these sometimes achieve hurricane force—I knew that the helm was going to be our most important weapon against an angry sea. That, balanced against the force of the wind in the sails, was going to call on all of Boris's expertise. I'd always been amazed at the captain's and first mate's ability to read a storm and know when to reef and when to set sails and which to set. Sometimes they weren't quite successful and there would be a tremendous crack as a sail was split, but we usually kept well ahead of the breaking waves at our stern, even when running under nearly bare poles.

Harris said quietly, "One thing you have to say for the BBC, they never sound a bit excited, but everyone knows that when they issue a warning to all ships, that means there's bad weather about to hit. And this time it's for the whole of the British Isles all the way round. Flynn, fetch Boris and Robert. We need to get our duties sorted out." With a grin and a wink, he added, "You'd better let the cook know as well."

Once we were all in the chart room, Harris started detailing duties. This was no easy job because conditions change quickly during storms. We didn't want Bowman overly taxed but there he was, expecting to be assigned some shipboard duties. Harris made him responsible for spotting any potential difficulties we didn't see ourselves and not to be shy about calling them to our attention. Harris also told him to monitor the radio and keep a check on our position. It was nearly midday and Bowman could take a proper dead reckoning then. He was not terribly happy with these lesser duties, but I thought I saw a hint of relief that he hadn't been asked to take a turn at the wheel.

"Well," he harrumphed, "if that's the way ye're going to treat yer captain, I'm off to my cabin to get a bit of rest before the blow starts."

Harris turned to him. "Treat our captain? Uncle Billy, you're the one in charge! You have the most important duty of anyone and that's to make sure everything's done correctly, and if you see otherwise, to order one of us to take care of things. That's what the captain's most important duty is—dare I remind you? I only added monitoring the radio because none of us can it do while attending to duties on deck."

"Aye," Bowman said, "just as long as ye know who's running things. You don't make all the decisions but I suppose there's no harm done with you handing out the assignments, as long as I agree. Well, if you need me sooner, I'll be in my cabin." He made his way off in that by-now habitual slow heavy step, disguised by his upright stance. I wondered if anyone noticed, as I did, the way he was now keeping his left hand in his coat pocket, scarcely using it. Perhaps it was just my imagination but I didn't really think so.

"So that leaves just us four," said Harris. "We're going to be the helmsmen, and the general overall eyes and ears of the ship. We'll not be able to keep a proper lookout, but we need to make sure we aren't going to be pushed by contrary currents too close to the Cherbourg Peninsula. There are some nasty rocks thereabouts and there's no way of telling which way the wind will swing when the storm system starts. Just now the wind is south-easterly, so it looks as though it'll work its way south before westering and we'll have to come over on the other tack at some time. I was thinking of heading round the Peninsula and moving east-sou'east to keep out of sight of that bloody MTB as much as possible. But now, if we have at least forty-eight hours of weather, we must move west as far as we can before he gets here and then try to maintain our longitude as we course north during the storm. I'm sure we're going to have to reef in most of the sails and maybe set the jibs, but we'll see what the weather's really like.

"This is serious now, and we've all got to pull our weight. This is a good ship, but she's been badly neglected and we have to keep her head up at all times. Most importantly, we mustn't strain the masts with too much canvas. Boris, once the boys have finished painting, have them practise on the remaining topgallants and royals for speed of reefing in. Right now let's get a good meal inside us before we're condemned to cold meat and potatoes with warm tea—that's if we're lucky."

Even though it was getting rougher, Katherine had prepared a nice stew and some freshly baked rolls with sausages so we dug in for a quick bite. Bowman returned and sat down with us again. The storm had him pacing like a tiger, a somewhat creaky one, trying to think of everything. He and storms were old acquaintances.

Robert was worried about the boys becoming faint-hearted and hesitant, and not putting their best into combating the on-coming storm. This only seemed to irritate Harris, so I stepped in.

"Never mind about maybes like that, we've much more important things to consider and I don't think that's one of them, so shut up and just leave it," I suggested with some asperity.

"Eh?" Bowman grunted. "Ye're starting to sound like Harris, and that's not flattering."

"I suppose I had a good teacher." I retorted.

Harris made no comment but suggested that we go up and have another look round because no matter how many times we made sure of things, it always seemed there was more that needed doing. We'd finished our meal and now went quickly up to the main deck. Harris was still having premonitions that we'd missed something in our attempts to cover all necessary points before the storm hit.

As we moved out for one more check of the ship, Harris pointed a finger at Boris. "I want to talk to you," he said in his most booming voice.

"Yes, yes," Boris said, "but now I eat."

Boris was stopped by Harris's heavy hand on his shoulder. "I don't think so," he said. "If anything, I'm going to feed you to the bloody bear for his lunch. What do you say to that?"

Boris smiled, "Make him vegetarian?"

"Don't be cheeky! Let's go." And off they went.

I said softly to Robert, "I'm curious about what's going to happen here, so I'm going to take a closer look."

"That's up to you," he said, "but I'm going to do a bit of inspecting of safety lines and secure hatchways, important things like that while you're off being nosey," and he went off forward.

I went aft to number three hatch and got to the 'tween decks in time to see Boris and Harris going down into the main cargo hold carrying a lantern and a bucket. I quickly got myself in a position to observe, because I knew something that Harris didn't know and was about to find out.

As they were descending the companion, Boris started talking in a singsong voice and waving a fish in the air. When Harris got to the bottom, he looked into the greyish dark of the hold where the bear's cage stood, while Boris lit another lantern. There was a low rumbling sound, seeming to come from no particular spot. Boris and Harris made their way quietly forward and then, without saying anything to Boris, Harris grabbed the tarpaulin with one hand and pulled it off the cage. His face grew blank and he looked at Boris.

"There's no bear in this cage."

Boris just stared back at him. "Ah yes, no bear in cage, good."

"So if he's not there…" Harris nearly jumped and spun in the air as Boris pointed off to one side where several bales had been ripped apart. Lying on the straw was the bear, looking much larger than he had when he was loose on deck.

"Bloody hell!" Harris said breathlessly. He took one step backward. "You really did let him out again!"

Boris was very calm. "After him on deck and out of cage, not good to go back in cage, too small. Now cage is broken and no good anyway."

Boris said something in Russian and walked over to the bear carrying the bucket of fish. It seemed that he wasn't really interested in the fish. Instead he raised his nose and smelled the air. Suddenly he rose to his feet and came forward from the straw, giving a low moaning and rumbling sound. Harris stood fast while the bear slowly approached him. As the bear did so, I could see Harris tensing himself. Seeing those long claws, Harris put his hands behind his back just in case the old fellow wanted to shake hands, but he needn't have worried. Once the bear got wind of Harris, his personality altered completely. He lost all sign of wariness and came to a stop with the flat top of his head resting against the big man's leg.

Boris was excited, "Scratch head, scratch ears!"

Harris didn't really need any urging as he reached over and stroked the bear's head. It was obvious that the bear remembered him. Harris looked about the hold and spied a little stool. He drew it up, and sat down. The bear was very docile, and allowed Harris to scratch his ears and his coat. He raised his nose appreciatively, smelling Harris again.

"Why, this bear is quite tame," Harris said.

Boris nodded in agreement. "But not touch feet," he cautioned.

Harris looked closely and saw where the hobbles had rubbed the bear's hide raw around its ankles. "I see," he muttered, his brow furrowing.

Boris reached over and picked up a small tub. "I make this to put on feet."

Harris looked in and smelt it. "Ugh, what on earth is this stuff?" he asked. "Smells absolutely terrible! Was this made to use on the Germans?"

"Oh, very good medicine," Boris replied. "Salve of sorts." In his thick Russian accent, the word salve sounded like something completely foreign to any known language here on earth. "I learned from grandmother in Russia."

"Yes well, has the bear let you put it on him?" Harris asked.

"Well yes," Boris said slowly grinning. "Sometimes lets and sometimes not."

"Oh Lord. Well, I don't—since you've taken on the care and feeding, it'll be your job, along with everything else you have to do, and we damn sure aren't going to put about and take him back again. But right now I have work to do!" Harris exclaimed.

"No, no, now you make friendly with bear," Boris insisted.

"Why's that?" Harris asked impatiently.

"He make good friend with you, same he make good friend with me, and then he knows he welcome. Now I must eat." Before Harris could stop him, Boris was out of the hold and passed me without a word.

I left Harris to his private reunion, a bit embarrassed at having spied. I went back on deck and called down, "Everything all right down there?"

Harris bellowed back from below, "That all depends on what you mean by all right. I'm fine. He's fine, but I can't join you just now."

"Well then, that's fine too. I daresay we'll find trouble enough to stay in until you return," I taunted.

"Always a comfort, Flynn," Harris responded.

And so I left him to get reacquainted and went off to do some inspecting of my own, starting with the galley. Katherine was a little overwhelmed with everyone coming in for food at once. We'd hardly been able to keep to a normal watch rotation and we seniors had been eating at any time we had the chance. I told her the latest with Harris and the bear while I had a mug of tea. I also wanted to emphasise properly the dangers of the coming storm.

"I'm afraid there's a really big blow on its way in from the Atlantic," I said earnestly. "The BBC made an all-ships broadcast, which only happens when the weather is going to be very dirty. I can't guarantee my getting back down here, so when your helpers are called away and you can feel the ship starting to jump a bit, put out the fire and try to save as much hot water as you can. This time it's going to be bad for least two days, so we'll be looking at cold food and cold drink most of the time." I tried not to look gloomy at the prospect.

"I'll see if there's some way we can get warm water," she mused, looking around the galley, "without setting us on fire!"

"Just please be careful first about yourself," I said. "With the ship pitching and rolling worse than you've had it so far, you don't want to be moving about with pots full of hot water. We won't die if we don't have a hot drink. But the other concern," I went on, "is fire. Old salts are always worried about a galley fire. Still, I'm sure you'll manage without any advice from me."

"My, my," Katherine murmured as she leaned against me with her arm about my waist, "I'm sure I'll need your advice most of the time, but when you're not here, I'm certain I can make up my own mind." I put my arms around her and she gave me a playful push as we wrestled briefly, laughing.

Suddenly a voice boomed behind us. "Here now, none of that stuff on my ship, if you don't mind." We turned to find Harris grinning benignly down on us. "Still, it's nice to see young love so happy, but there are times and there are times, and you only have another ten minutes while I eat a bit more." He ladled out a bowl of stew and potatoes. With a cheery, "remember, only ten minutes more, and I'll see you on the poop deck," off he went to the wardroom.

"I've never seen him act so sentimental before," marvelled Katherine. "That bear must have meant quite a lot to himself when he was younger." Then we paid more attention to other matters for our allotted ten minutes.

Harris appeared on the poop later, wiping his mouth with a belch. "Now," he said, "we've got to get from end to end of this ship without interruption, making sure everything is battened down. While you're about it, make sure the emergency steering wheels aft the poop are in order, just in case the cables to the main wheel go."

I'd never looked in the aft poop and was surprised to find an enclosed steering platform with a double wheel like the one forward and an additional place for the binnacle just for emergencies.

Harris and I moved slowly forward, looking for anything that was loose or could come loose. As we went, I became aware of an odd buzzing noise coming from no particular direction. It was like a bee near one's ear.

"Do you hear that?" I asked Harris.

Before he could answer, there came a shout from aloft. "A plane, a plane to port!"

"Damn and blast it!" Harris shouted as we ran for the port rail. Scanning the sky, we finally made out the plane. It was a small single-engine, far to our stern. It was flying on a course diagonally away from us and moving north-east. We watched it for some time in silence as it flew farther away until the sound died off completely. Harris looked after it thoughtfully, "With any luck, he's flying back to base to refuel and didn't see us. Facing this way, he'd be looking into the sun." At this time of year the sun was already quite low in the sky over our starboard bow as we ploughed west.

"He must have been farther east when he came down on his outward leg. We've been lucky!" said Harris.

There were a few boys still standing about when Harris boomed, "All right, back to work. He's on his way home to England to refuel and we won't see him again if we're lucky. Come on, the storm's coming, and he isn't!"

We moved slowly forward until we got to number one hatchway, which was still open. Harris leaned in and called down. "Halloo, brown bear. We're going to have to close you up now, but we'll bring some food down later." As he stood up, he saw me looking on and grimaced. "Yes well, I know he can't understand, but it's just the sound of my voice, to show I know he's being put in the dark." At that, he closed the hatchway down, hammering in the wedges all round.

We seemed fated not to complete an inspection, because the next moment we heard Larry calling from the helm, "Mr. Harris, Mr. Flynn, Edward says we're just getting that submarine again on the radio." I hoped this would give us good news as the storm loomed on the horizon.

Edward was talking when we got to the radio. "Now that's the news we need. Are you sure the MTB's already turned east?"

Johnson's voice crackled from the speaker, "*Roger that. We've got her on radar and she's headed in our direction, over.*"

Edward turned. "Harris has just come in so I'll pass you over to himself," he grunted.

Harris took the handset. "Hello, Captain. It sounds like good news. We were hoping the MTB might get distracted by your plan. What sort of message did you give her, over?"

"I think the fact that he had us on his radar for some time really persuaded him. It takes time to recharge batteries on the surface and thank God we still haven't gotten the effects of a storm that's due, so the sea wasn't choppy. As we got near full charge, I sent the message and within minutes we submerged. I've got some budding actors on board and one of them does a good imitation of an Englishman. The message he read laid it on good and strong for them. It reads: MTB 310, go back to base. Will not obey your orders to give in. Chase us, but you'll never overtake us. We'll never surrender our ship. Whatever you may have been told, you have been pursuing us for no reason. We do not recognise your authority in this matter. None of our crew is here against his will. Break off the pursuit and return to base while you are still able."

Johnson continued, *"I brought the crew into it for a bit of light relief, using the old radio. There's no need to buy trouble, since it's my experience that it usually comes for free! I'll say one thing for sure, there's a captain aboard that MTB who's very upset right about now! The main thing is they have changed course, over."*

Harris was happy. "Now they'll be back in Dover tonight while we tackle the storm just like any other piece of work. If the storm lasts three days, then we'll be out of sight by the time they take a chance coming out again and we hope to be very far away. Thank you very much, and please excuse us as we must carry on working to get everything ship-shape!" We signed off with promises to keep in touch in the future.

Harris said, "We're entirely too lucky, so don't forget to say your prayers. We'll need everything going for us to get through this storm, so let's get to it." And he barged out of the chart room with me close behind.

Outside we could feel the change in the weather. The wind was starting to veer round and gust, lifting the tops of the waves and sending spray over the ship. We were heading into a rack of heavy black clouds, lined with bright yellow sunlight shafting out across the deck. We finally got through the inspection, and I personally checked the safety net under the bowsprit, as we'd be setting the jibs soon. By then Harris had gone up into the rigging and I reluctantly followed, checking every ratline in the shrouds. There was going to be a lot of activity during the next two days.

Once we were back on deck there were the fo'c's'le quarters to check, but I left that for Harris and went below to check the officers' cabins. It was now getting time for our call from Richard, so I got back to the chart room where Bowman and Edward were listening to the latest BBC report. They were now forecasting the storm to be the duration of the next forty-eight hours, possibly longer. No matter how experienced the crew or seaworthy the ship, gale force storms strike fear into the hearts of everyone on board, and Bowman and Edward were no exception. Instead of bickering, after this report they went outside onto the bridge deck, talking quietly and very gravely. Then the radio started its caterwauling and crackling, meaning that someone was calling in on our wavelength and a new voice came over: "*Calling Harris, calling Harris. Are you receiving me, over.*"

I shouted to one of the boys to go find Harris as I picked up the handset. "I'm speaking for Harris. Please identify yourself, over."

"*Is that Flynn? Dick from near Gravesend told me it might be you answering. My name is John Boyd and I'm more than happy to help you in your project. Nil basti carborundum is my motto: never let the bastards wear you down! Anyway, here's Richard with the latest.*"

"Thanks, John," I called. "It's nice to know we've got friends. Hi, Richard, how are things with you this fine day?"

"*Funny you should choose that comment, because the forecast says the opposite, so I expect you to be talking while hanging on to a stanchion or shroud, whatever that may be.*" Richard sounded in good spirits.

"I don't want to break your happy mood," I said, "but the storm is coming, so you'd better batten down all hatches at home and check your house insurance."

"*As bad as that, eh?*" Richard now sounded sombre.

"Yes," I said, "and probably worse. I'm looking out at the ugliest lot of clouds you've ever seen, coming in from the west. The wind is backing and picking up force every minute, but we're ready for it. The boys have become sailors overnight it seems, and are at home on the rigging as they would be riding a bicycle—of course, that would be a bicycle on a tightrope! Two or three of them are thinking of the sea as a career, but I'll wait to see what they say after the storm has blown over."

"*Now that you mention them the public reaction to the story so far is generally the best of luck to you, but there are some doubts about the boys. Some are from genuinely concerned people. Some comments are from those trying to deflect attention from their own shortcomings, like the department that gave O'Connell money all these years without checking on him. At the moment he's been booted out of his comfortable position, and is on suspension pending investigation by the government authorities as well as the police.*"

"But as I say, the public seems to be well on your side so HM's ministers are treading carefully. I've got demands for follow-up stories and more photos. Until someone actually spots you, I can't just jump into a plane and snap some. I also need some biographical material on all of you, since none of you is world famous yet. Central records for the Services are not giving anything away. The police came to the office, but I only said I didn't know where you are and couldn't reveal the sources of my information. Someone may be so unhappy that he'll pull strings to have the police trail me. Nobody followed me today, but I'll keep an eye on my back all the same."

"Well now," I said, "as for biographies, Edward our navigator is here now. While he's telling you his deepest and darkest secrets, I'll round up the others to give their own stories."

"That sounds like a good idea, but before you go," Richard broke in quickly, *"why don't you and I have a little talk about Gretna Green? Even* The Times *has been known to take notice when the story contains a genuine appeal to the interests of its women readers."*

I was a bit taken aback. I didn't like to say anything about Katherine and me without consulting her. I said to him, "I'll have to clear that with the lady first. Why don't you start with Edward? Harris will be here soon. Meanwhile, I'll go and talk with her."

"All right," Richard replied, *"but bring her back with you. I'd like to ask her some questions other women may wonder about, such as can she get a regular bath and has she her own cabin?"*

"Well, you've a point there, but now here's Edward." I handed the handset to Edward to do his blarney and went to tell the others.

When I got to Katherine she wasn't too happy at first at the idea of telling a reporter anything, but I said there was no need to be too detailed. I'd discreetly add that she was a very good cook and that we hoped to find something for a husband and wife team in Scotland.

"You never know," I said to her, "someone might read this and offer us a job. You may even become a celebrity!"

"If we're not all in prison!" she said curtly. I asked her to go up to the chart room and wait for me because I needed to have a word with Boris.

When I found Boris, he was repairing some ratlines in the lower shrouds where they took the most wear. I asked him plainly if he had papers to be living in England. He said he had some before, but they'd expired and then got stolen. "Very bad place I stayed, but no money." I told him about the newspaper reporter wanting to know the crew, but he said better not to include him, in case the police or somebody got curious.

I agreed and started back when I realised that the bear would be my real inspiration.

If the English are stupid about anything, it's about animals: treating them like members of the family, guessing what they're thinking, dressing them up, risking their lives, and sometimes even dying for them. I was sure the bear would cover all our sins. We'd be forgiven even such crimes as stealing the canvas and taking the bear without permission. But first he needed a name, so when people pictured him in their minds, they could make him one of their own. I asked Boris if he knew of any name for the bear, but he said I should ask Harris.

When I got back, Harris was in the chart room waiting to talk to Richard. I told him I'd spoken to Boris and that he didn't care for publicity because of his papers, so no one should mention him for now. I shared my thoughts about the bear and asked if he could remember the bear's name when they were younger. Harris thought it over, muttering to himself, "Brown bear...brown bear," but in the end said that Brown Bear was what everyone always called him.

"I'm going to tell Richard the whole story," I said. "I'm sure he can make use of it and as one brown bear looks much like another, he could use any photo." I grew excited as another idea hit me. "Perhaps we can get some good free publicity for the circus, about how kind they were to the bear, and how they were just looking after it until they were to give it to the retirement home or whoever was asking for it and...and..." I faltered as I thought of the circus in terms of our sails. I'd never really liked the idea of our taking the canvas. This way we might be able to contact the owners before they complained to the police.

Harris declined this with one hard crash of his fist on the table. "You tell nothing of the sort about their giving good treatment to that bear! Those bastards should be in cages themselves with people throwing food in at them! You can tell Richard the story, but if you say one kind word about any of those people, I'll skin you alive and fly your arse from the main-truck!" he thundered. "Do you understand?"

"Of course, it was only an idea. Consider it dropped," I said hastily.

Finally, after we all related our stories, I told Richard about the bear.

He could hardly believe his ears. "*What're you trying to do?*" he shouted with delight, "*get the prize for the most tear-jerking story of the year? I can see it now—big bold headlines reading:* Lovers' Tryst Sealed by Brown Bear *or* Waifs of the Water Need Love and New Homes. *Or, what about* Ship's Mate Meets Childhood Friend? *Oh, I have it!* Bear With a Past, Before the Mast, Mr. Bruin Sails to Gretna Green...*My God, do you know how much this sort of thing sells papers? You'll be in every last one from the* Land's End Gazette *to the* Truro Times, *and all points in between, including the* Dumbarton Dispatch. *As you get closer to port, I can bet you'll have planes flying over for photographs, including one from my people.*

"*Finally,*" he said portentously, "*questions will be asked in the House of Lords, and you'll be the leading item in the six o'clock news everyday. Oh! You're going to come out of this smelling of roses.*" Richard was almost singing at the thought of the scoop this would make.

I left the others in the chart room and went outside where the last of the day was fading, though it wasn't doing so without protest. The sky was almost black and on the horizon lightning was flashing down, with thunder reaching us in a slow grumbling roll with hardly a break between peals. The wind was westering now. Boris and the boys had close-hauled us in while all the radio talk was going on. Soon we'd have to go about on the other tack, trying to make the distance west as best we could against the headwind. The storm was indeed coming.

Chapter 24
A STORM AT SEA

One of the most fearsome forces in nature is the power of the sea and the massive intensity of its violence when aroused. The storm we'd been watching close in from astern was now fully upon us. Just preceding it, and amidst the fury of the first blow, a heavy squall pounded down upon us. Adding to the bedlam of noise, the sails bellied out drum-tight and the sound of the wind through all the rigging became a sharp shrilling amongst the thunderous roar, with the yardarms and masts creaking and protesting against the enormous strain. The wind was coming more from the south and the ship began quickly to gather way, breasting the valleys between the waves, and clipping along through the tops of the raging torrent.

This was the weather the *Bonnie* was designed for. Her sails were there to take advantage of the winds that storms brought and to make journeys quicker. Sailors once preferred that the glass read *storm*—but not in my day. I reflected back on my time in the Royal Navy, when storms were a thing to dread. The ships we sailed were much heavier, but they were no real match for storms, unlike the *Bonnie*. As incredible as it may sound, it is more incredible to have lived this experience.

The waves had grown into mountains, crashing over the bow and washing over the decks. Boris, Robert, and I were leading the two watches, ready for any crisis, and we led the charge from one situation to another. Each one was different, although each had a truly major significance of its own. Harris, being the strongest of us, took up his position at the helm. Steering through a storm was no small task, and we knew that even Harris would need assistance at the double wheel when the going became really difficult. And it didn't take long to reach that point.

Boys were rapidly becoming men in circumstances such as this, scrambling through the rigging and handling the sails exactly as they were trained. Boris was living aloft, yelling orders to some and using his bo'sun's pipe, giving the orders for hauling and bracing the yards. His unique way of getting from mast to mast was surely unparalleled and had certainly never been seen or heard of even by this company of tall ship sailors. He'd rigged several lines in such a way as to allow him to swing from one mast to another without any need of descending to the deck below. We thought this a bit reckless, but his sense of timing and anticipation of movements of the ship were faultless. I doubt to this day if there was ever a soul who could match such a performance. At that moment, I thought he was quite mad.

We'd stopped worrying over the MTB in pursuit. If they were venturing out in this weather, they would have found themselves floating like a cork on a rough millpond while boys tried to hit it with stones.

Above the roar of the wind sounded the shrill whistle of the bo'sun's pipe. Each blast was signalling which sail and what mast. Boris had memorised these commands over the years he'd spent at sea. Still, even though things were running quite smoothly, these were extremely arduous tasks. Time after time, green water swept over the decks taking everyone off his feet. Had it not been for the harnesses Boris rigged up for the boys, some would have been washed overboard so quickly that no one would have noticed. Bowman had taken up position on the deck and Boris referred to him in all matters concerning the sails. It was far too easy for them to blow out if not properly set, and the boys on deck were continually on the go, bracing the yards or hauling on the buntlines.

Each time the call came for all hands aloft, I found my old fear returning with a vengeance. The higher you climb, the more you notice the pitch and roll of the ship. Your focal point must be only that which is in front of you. If you look down or to the side, you tend to freeze and it takes time to regain your equilibrium. I recalled my first conversation with Bowman, when he ranted on about there was nothing romantic about hauling in wet canvas with nothing holding you to the yardarm except the wind at your back. My mind constantly replayed Boris's comments about falling from such a height. The word *splat* was everpresent in my mind. I'm not happy aloft in a storm, but I couldn't let anyone know lest the lads should notice. They were doing a marvellous job weathering this storm and hanging onto the wet cold yardarms safely clipped in Boris's harnesses. When I descended to the deck, a feeling of fatigue overcame my entire body. I looked at my hands. They were raw and blistered, not to mention frozen from the seawater and wind. I could scarcely raise them over my head.

I looked towards the wheel where Harris, now assisted by Larry, was hard at work trying to control the rudder. I thought Larry was a bit lightweight for this kind of sea and started over to relieve him, even though I was exhausted, when another sea came over the side. Once again I lay there soaking wet. I was grateful for the wool I was wearing because it kept me warm, but the wetter I became, the harder it was to move about. The fury of this blow was absolutely unprecedented in my experience.

I'd just got my legs back under me when I heard a call from the rigging, "Help, need help now!" over the sounds of the wind and waves.

The voice was unmistakable. Even over the roar of the storm, I could hear Boris calling for help. I had rarely heard Boris ask for assistance, much less help, so without delay, I immediately started up the shrouds towards the voice in the darkness. The night wind was cruel and the squall was relentless as several of us climbed up against the pitching sea. There was little to see and communication was extremely difficult. I realised he was at the level of the upper topsail yard. By this point I could barely feel my arms—they were reacting in a mechanical fashion. Just then I heard the call again, but I couldn't tell if Boris was on the port or starboard side of the ship. I called out on the darkness, "Where are you?"

"Here!" came the familiar voice from the port side of the yardarm. I carefully set my feet on the footrope under the yard, held fast to the jackstay rail atop, clipped my safety-line to it, and edged my way slowly towards his voice. As I made my way along the yardarm I saw that one of the boys had slipped. His hands were gripping the upper rail, but his feet had come off the footrope. It seemed that only the harness was holding him to the yard along with his frozen grip of terror. Boris was on the other side of him. They must have been trying to furl the topsail when the boy slipped, because now one end of the sail was flailing around in the wind while hanging down from the yard. The real danger would come if a burst of wind blew it over the yard. Getting hit by a ton of wet canvas did not bear thinking of. I thought we should move the boy first, as quickly as possible.

"Are you all right?" I shouted to Boris.

"Yes," he came back, "but boy is not, must move him quick."

"What can I do?" I shouted, my voice nearly drowned out by the shrill winds.

"I will pull harness, you pull boy. Both pull up on yardarm and clip his harness to you," Boris directed.

"All right, tell me when you're ready," I yelled back to him. We both got a good grip and pulled, but couldn't move the boy, and couldn't get him to put his feet back onto the footrope. Boris pulled again. This time I hauled the boy in towards me, until we had him bent over the yardarm enough for me to clip his harness to mine. I double-checked to make sure I was connected to the yardarm, you may be sure!

"Pull boy!" Boris cried. If I thought my arms hurt before, I was wrong. Now the boy's dead weight made them ache so badly I really couldn't control them. I couldn't get the boy to move towards the mast, he was still clinging in terror to the jackstay. There was no time to try persuasion so I simply hit his fingers as hard as I could with my own throbbing hands until he let go. Once he did so, he seemed to come to himself and moved back with me towards the mast.

It was then that a tremendous gust of wind caused the sail to fly footloose up over the yardarm, covering Boris. I tried hard to push against the canvas with my legs but couldn't get enough force into it as I was holding fast onto the young lad. Again the wind hit, lifting the sail like a rag and dropping it to flap wildly under the yard.

Of Boris there was no sign. I couldn't believe my eyes. It was not possible! Even now I find it hard to express my feelings about that moment. It was a combination of shock, horror, and disbelief. Boris was gone!

I continued pulling the boy towards the mast as I called out Boris's name. One of the others, who had heard that first call for help, now reached me. It was Robert.

"Let me give you a hand there," he yelled.

"By God, Robert, the sail blew up over the yardarm and Boris is gone," I shouted in his ear, my throat constricting. Robert looked over at the still-unruly slapping canvas, but before either of us could say another word, a shout came from the darkness on the starboard side.

It was Boris!!

"My God, man, I thought you'd gone for good! What happened?" I shouted against the wind. Boris just shrugged his shoulders.

"This night bad, yes?"

"Yes, it bloody well is," I yelled, trying to make myself heard. "How did you keep from falling?"

At this he just laughed and answered, "Boris not fall, always ready. Get boy down now!"

Robert and I helped the boy down the bucking shrouds, while Boris got the end of the buntline and returned aloft to finish reefing the unruly sail. When we arrived on deck, one of the other boys came over and helped his exhausted friend away.

It was then that it all caught up with me. My arms hung loosely at my sides, my head lolled, as I hung there half-standing and half-suspended from a lifeline. Suddenly I was startled by a shout in my ear.

"You're not getting much done just hanging about there," Harris roared. I looked at him dully.

"I'm bloody well spent," I shouted back, and explained what had just happened.

He didn't seem very impressed. "Oh very well, have a fifteen-minute break, that's all we can afford. All hands are busy at their stations and we need everyone, so be quick about it."

I was no position to argue the point further, so I simply thanked him. As I was making my way below, however, Harris called, "If you can manage any sort of rest or relaxation in fifteen minutes, please let me know how it's done." And he went off along the deck to catch up some pins that were clattering about in the scuppers.

Although my welcome respite truly was necessary, Harris was not very encouraging as to my making much recovery in so short a time, but I was more than willing to try.

I made my way aft and slid back the hatchway to reveal the familiar ladder. Climbing down, I managed to pull it shut. My arms ached and descending the ladder was agony in the tossing ship. At least I was out of the shrieking wind and beyond reach of the continuously breaking waves, but I was hearing the heavy clanging of the freeing ports along the well deck, which made a thunderous clatter.

I made my way to the galley, but didn't find Katherine there. Only a lukewarm urn of tea clamped to a table and some biscuits in a tin were there to greet me. I helped myself to some of each.

I then noticed an unsavoury smell that I knew only too well. Someone here was seasick, maybe more than one. When I reached Katherine's cabin I quite forgot what manners I had learnt and pounded heavily at the door.

"That's Flynn, I suppose. Don't break it in," came her welcome. The door slid open immediately and there she stood in an overcoat and scarf. "Well, is it over yet?" She asked with a laugh.

"Hardly," I groaned. "I came down to see how you're holding up."

She cast an eye over me. "Flynn, you're completely soaked." Well, that was obvious enough.

"Yes, it does tend to happen to people in a storm on a sailing ship." I managed a small laugh for her benefit, but it was quite without mirth. I was absolutely knackered.

"You should get out of those wet togs straightaway," she insisted.

"Oh, it's not worth it. I'm only going up on deck and get soaked again," I sighed. I spotted a most inviting chair hard by the bunk. Perhaps any chair would have looked inviting at that moment, but this chair positively beckoned; I immediately staggered forward and collapsed gratefully into it.

"I hope you don't mind," I said weakly, as Katherine slid the door closed.

"Oh, no, Do make yourself at home," she said. "What's happening on deck now?"

"Everything that possibly can happen, good and bad." I answered, stretching my soggy limbs. "I'm so knocked out now that I just had to have a tiny break." I gave her a short summary of the night, including the retrieval of the boy and Boris's amazing escape. "We're all working as hard as we can, and it's going to take all of us giving everything we have. If the wind veers anymore, we'll need to come about on the other tack and that's a big enough job without a storm. But," I added, "as bad as this storm may seem, the wind has brought us quite a distance from the MTB that was chasing us. She's confined to harbour, as she simply wasn't designed for weather like this. In fact it's just this type of weather we need to help us keep well ahead, and I'm afraid we'll be looking at a few more days of the same."

Katherine looked at me and gave a sigh. "Oh well," she said with a game smile, "I suppose I'll have to stay with it now that I'm here. It's not exactly as if we can get out and walk at this point." Her endurance was remarkable. It gave me the uncomfortable feeling that I was the only one who was making a fuss about my discomfort.

"By the way, how's that bear doing through all this?" she asked.

"He's all right, I suppose. Boris and Harris have been keeping an eye on him, but it's Boris who seems to do all the work." I tried to stretch out my arms, but the effort only gave me pain. "I don't know how he manages it."

Katherine shook her head. "He's an amazing person. I can't believe I once slapped him in the pub," she laughed.

"Just what prompted that?" I asked.

She laughed, "Well, he was remarking about the pies and wondered if we did the baking ourselves. I told him yes, it was all made fresh here and so we used no preservatives. He then made the most outrageous remark about us making good babies together or some such. And that's when I slapped him. It wasn't until much later I learnt that the Russian word *preservative* translates into English as, well, French letters [condoms]." She giggled at the memory.

"I didn't know that," and I managed to laugh. "You never told me."

"Well it was quite embarrassing, you know. I don't think I ever apologised to him," she said.

"He did mention something about a misunderstanding, but he never did say what it was. When he returned to the table, he said, 'She likes me.'"

Katherine's eyes twinkled. "Is that a fact?"

"Oh yes, and Edward, never one to miss a quip, told him that that much was obvious." We both laughed briefly, trying our best to ignore the storm while holding on to the railing in her cabin.

"You know, it's a pity. Boris is soaked up on deck, you're soaked down here, and here I am wrapped up, freezing and getting bounced off the walls."

"That's a bulkhead," I said, pointing to the "wall."

"Whatever you call it," she said, "it's just as hard when you hit it."

It wasn't until my eyes were beginning to roll back in my head that I realized, if I didn't get up soon, I never would. I had visions of an angry Harris coming in search of me. I looked down for my pocket watch, and then remembered I didn't have it.

"How long I been sitting here?" I asked. I told her Harris had given me a fifteen-minute break.

"How benevolent of him," she remarked dryly. "Only fifteen minutes? That's positively inhumane of himself." She asked, "Could you use another hand up there? All I've been doing down here is tending to seasick boys and being thrown about."

"Thanks for the offer," I said, "but you'd be thrown about even more so on deck, and conditions above are quite treacherous. What you could do is try and work out how to boil water without setting us on fire. A hot drink is what we all need. But now I really must get back."

As I was leaving, the ship gave a tremendous roll, first landing Katherine in a heap next to the bulkhead and then flinging me across the passageway as it rolled in the opposite direction.

"Do be careful, Flynn," she cried, giving me a long-armed embrace. "That's all the hug I'm giving while you're soaking wet."

I made my way back to the deck. Stopping at the coal-burning stove I cautiously opened it up and had a look inside. There were still some slight embers burning in it, so I reached into the bin and put two more large chunks of coal inside, briefly enjoying the warmth around my hands.

I climbed the pitching companion, and slid back the hatch over my head to reveal the powerful storm at its best. The cold winds actually did a good part in reviving me.

As quickly as my eyes adjusted to the dark, I noticed that there were now three people at the double wheel keeping the ship steady and on course. Upon seeing me, Harris called for me to go forward and help Boris. I nodded my head to avoid having to yell against the force of the wind. Grabbing hold of one of the safety lines that ran the length of the deck, I began moving forward. To my surprise I met Bowman, who was having difficulty keeping his balance. He had just fallen, so I helped him up, and together we started back aft to the companion. I slid the hatchway open and went down below with him to make sure he was all right. He made no resistance as I helped him to the easy chair in his cabin, and he fell heavily into it. I don't know what he'd been doing on deck in this weather, but he'd obviously done too much.

"I'm all right. The old ticker isn't what it once was, that's all!" He reached into the pocket of his storm coat. Pulling out a flask, he took a sip and passed it to me.

I had a nice long pull of the single malt whisky. "I certainly could have used this an hour ago."

"Take that along wi' ye. Before this night's out ye'll need it."

"What about you?" I asked.

"I'll be just fine. I just need a wee bit of a rest," he said.

"No," I protested, "you keep this with you."

"Nay, nay. There's plenty more of this down here if I should find need." He insisted, pushing the flask back in my direction. "They need ye on deck. Go on then, I'll be fine." He settled himself deeply into the chair and closed his eyes, despite the violent rocking and shaking of the ship. Without further discussion I climbed back up the ladder and secured the hatch.

Back on the storm-tossed deck I again reached for the safety lines and started forward. Halfway along the deck, I met some of the boys and several of us were caught in waves breaking over the ship. For a moment, the group wasn't able to make any headway. I mustered up all the strength I had, "Right now lads, let's go. Move! Move! Let's go!" I shouted.

Slowly but steadily, we reached the seconded set safety lines and carried on. Looking up in the darkness, I watched the sails as the wind filled them, but could not see very much activity on the masts.

Suddenly Boris appeared out of nowhere, as was usually the case.

"Where is Bowman?" he asked.

"I helped him below, he's not feeling well," I told him. He nodded his head and reached into his pocket, producing the bo'sun's pipe. "Okay, Boris knows what to do."

"I have no doubt," I replied. "What do you need?"

"Nothing yet, everything is good. Twenty minutes more and we turn yards—use this," he said, pointing at the giant mechanical winch.

"But we've never used one of these before!" I exclaimed. Boris gave his trademark laugh. "Then we all learn together!"

"You mean you never have either?" I asked, taken aback. "That doesn't exactly inspire confidence!"

But my words were lost in the wind, and Boris was already into his next project. I didn't realise till later that he was trying to be funny as usual. Just another joke at my expense. He knew well that connecting the drive chain from the mast to the pump motor would turn the winch, which I noticed was now secured to the deck properly.

Our preparations had been thorough enough that now the boys were able to get some rest off watch. I checked the forward area and started aft towards the helm. Harris and Robert were struggling with the double wheel trying to use the foot break as the ship was exposed at the top of each mountainous wave. With her rudder half free of the water, it was being pushed by the wind and waves which made controlling the helm even harder.

"Everything okay?" I yelled to Harris.

"Just lovely, can't you tell?" was his retort.

"I just thought you should know I helped Bowman get below. He's not feeling well. Says his ticker is off."

"He has some pills in his cabin. Go below and see that he takes them," said Harris.

"Are you suggesting that I give him an order?" I asked.

"No, but if he gives you any trouble, tell him that I am," he replied.

Before I left, I reached into the pocket of my long coat, and pulled out a flask. "Would you like a drop of this?"

Harris grinned. "Thank you, but I already have one for each pocket."

Why did this news not surprise me? It seemed to me that everyone was well supplied with this lovely amber nectar.

Once again, I threw back the hatchway and pulled it closed against the sea. Down below I saw that Bowman had moved into the galley and now sat by the little stove, which was doing its best to throw out heat from the coal I'd put in before.

"Are you okay?" I asked.

"I thought I told ye ye're needed on deck," he growled, "and don't think I don't know why ye're here. It's that bloody Harris, right? It was he that sent ye down here wasn't it? Those bloody pills!"

"He said if you didn't take them one way that he'd surely give them to you another," I assured him.

"Those're his words, eh?" he muttered. I offered him my hand to help him from his chair, but he refused. Suddenly, the ship rolled and I almost fell against the hot stove.

"Well then, I'll just have to keep my hands for my own personal use," I said, reaching for the stanchion. Bowman managed to rise from the chair and carefully extended one of his hands towards mine. Bracing myself, I helped him along.

We started down the passageway for his cabin, when suddenly the door to the chart room burst open and out flew my wheeled office chair, overturning and dumping its occupant unceremoniously into the passage before us. We recognised the figure sprawled on the deck before us as Edward. He got unsteadily to his feet.

"I haven't seen much of you tonight," I said, trying to hide my amusement.

"I must have fallen asleep in this thing," he muttered.

"Sleep?" Bowman barked. "What the bloody hell are ye doing sleeping, Ned?"

"Because I'm on the next watch, so blow it out your bagpipes!" he replied indignantly.

Bowman grumbled under his breath, then said, "Do ye have any idea where we are?"

Edward took out his pocket watch, "In a storm as I recall, but I'll need nearly three hours before I try to ascertain our position. In fact," he said, picking up the chair, "now that I'm awake, I'm going to have some tea," and he walked unsteadily off to the galley.

Bowman turned and looked at me. "What kind of an idiot goes to sleep in a rolling chair during a storm?" he said, shaking his head in disbelief.

"When you're tired enough, you can sleep anywhere," I responded.

We continued down the passageway until we reached Bowman's cabin. He went into his drawer and found the bottle of pills. Placing two in his hand, Bowman threw them in to his mouth with a sigh. "Sometimes I wonder if they do anything at all. Lying down for a bit usually helps." He crawled into his bunk without any further protest.

I started back down the passage and was greeted by the thunder of many feet coming down the ladder. It was the change of the watch, and everyone was pushing down to the galley for tea and bread. Katherine was there to greet them, pouring tea and trying to get the oven lit for loaves of what would soon be fresh baked bread. This seemed overly ambitious given the way the ship was still rolling in the storm, but she seemed determined to get something started.

I joined the group, who were busily exchanging stories of this night. Picking up a mug and a piece of bread, I mostly listened, for I hadn't the energy to carry on much of a conversation. While I'd been below, the mechanical winch, along with a lot of manpower, was able to turn the gigantic yardarms and sails to meet the wind, which had been veering slowly to west-sou'west. It was well over gale force nine, and we were taking it nearly straight on our port side, with the sails as close-hauled as was possible. If we hadn't already reefed in many of the sails, the strain on the masts would almost certainly have been too much. We were still westering on a long diagonal, thanks to the experience and skill of the crew. Our prayers had been answered in that we were still unharmed and not broached to, with broken masts and fallen yards dragging us down slowly but surely beneath the waves. An awful picture, that!

Even in my woollens I was beginning to feel the cold, so I told Katherine that I'd see what change of clothing I could find in my cabin. Harris sat with his feet propped up, tossing more coal into the stove in an effort to take off his chill.

"Where's that Bowman?" he asked, shivering.

"Resting comfortably in his cabin," I replied. "Who's minding the shop?"

"Robert and two others are on the helm," he responded dully.

I left him to his coal-pitching and made my way down the passage to my quarters. I slid back the door, found my matches, and lit the kerosene lamp. At that moment, I became aware of the disaster that had befallen me.

Water dripped freely from the deck above onto almost everything in the cabin, pouring through gaps in the caulking, as great waves cascaded over the decks. My duffel bag had absorbed much of the falling water. Even though it was a futile gesture, I pulled it to a place where the water wasn't dripping. I then looked at my bunk, which was completely sodden. I slowly lifted my mattress, hoping against hope that it wasn't soaked completely through. My hopes were dashed, as it was totally beyond salvage. There was only one place left, my old sea chest. I'd paid a lot for it when I became an apprentice, as it was guaranteed to keep out water unless completely immersed for some hours. I looked over where it was tied down, and with a last glimmer of hope, slowly opened it. With great relief, I found that the contents were dry, so I flipped through and retrieved a dry change of clothing. At the foot of the bunk were wool blankets that escaped the leakage. I reached for the pillow, but it too was a soaking great mess. The cabin was completely unusable, and hanging things to dry was unthinkable at the moment. Realizing that this wasn't a suitable place to obtain the rest necessary to sustain me, I blew out the lamp and slid open the door. Slowly I backed out, holding clothes and blankets away from my sodden self. As I closed the door, I jumped as a welcome voice piped up from behind me.

"Hullo, sailor, come here often?" Katherine giggled.

"You startled me," I said.

"Flynn, you are a sight. Very fetching!" she laughed, looking me over.

"Thank you very much, but I'm in no mood for flattery at the moment. My quarters are flooded, my mattress is sodden, and prospects for sleep are extremely dismal." I must have looked pathetic, as I tried to keep my aching gear-laden arms clear of all wet surfaces.

"Come over here," she ordered. "I have to get breakfast on." She slid open the door to her cabin. "Go in and get some rest, and have that wet clothing off." As the cabin door was slid shut behind me, I began the task of undressing and hanging my wet things on the hooks on the bulkhead. Throwing my additional blankets onto the bunk, I quickly got beneath the covers. Although the ship was still being tossed about by the storm, I quickly fell unconscious into a blissful sleep. I didn't hear the bo'sun pipe calling all hands when it was time to turn the yardarms.

I awoke when Katherine's soft lips met mine, bringing me back to the reality of the rocking ship. "It's time for you to go on watch. Harris is looking for you," she whispered. I quickly dressed and made my way to the galley.

I found Harris and Ted drinking hot tea with hands that could scarcely hold the mugs.

"Right, Flynn," Harris grunted as he saw me, "duty watches on the wheel are now down to two hours on and four off with two people on the wheel at all times. Your partner is Larry and he's up there just now, with Edward as an emergency stand-in, waiting for you because no one could find you. Everyone's already tired, and the storm isn't yet eight hours old. I have no idea where we'll be at the end of seventy-two hours if this really is a three-day blow. One thing cannot happen, and that's for the ship to broach to. We may have to leave the sails set as they are and sail according to the wind even if that means we move due east, but we must hold her head to the seas at all times." Harris had become very animated while speaking, but I understood what he meant. This project had been built on the idea that we had a crew. Now the crewmen, all young boys, were betraying the neglect of their long years in the orphanage. They had the spirit and the will, but their bodies were simply not as fit as they should be.

I was about to go on duty, when Bowman's cabin door opened and he put his head out. If anything, he looked worse than before his sleep, and I exchanged a concerned glance with Harris. The old captain was clinging hard to the door's frame and blinking in a confused manner. Seeing us, he called, "Here, there was a boy in a white steward's jacket in here just now. He brought me some tea, but now I don't know where he put it. Could ye get me another?"

Harris's breath hissed between his teeth on hearing mention of the boy. He went to Bowman's side and gently pushed him back inside the cabin, talking softly to him. He put his head back round the door and beckoned me, "Get a mug of hot tea quickly and don't talk about what you just saw, all right?"

I got the tea, and then went to take my place at the helm with Larry. As I braced myself against the fury of the storm, I wondered how the builders of this ship, or any sailing ship, expected them to weather storms like this. They had done so many times in the past and would continue to do so, so long as there were any left to sail. As I stood facing forward, holding on to the lifeline with all my might, the scene made a terrifying spectacle. In what little the daylight offered, clouds covered the whole sky, and what could be seen was more in one's imagination rather than what the eyes could actually take in. The wind whipped the wave tops into a white spume of froth, which glowed all round us. One's first indication that a wave was rearing up was when the glow seemed to rise straight up in front of the bow, as the ship plunged down the back face of the wave. When the white would break and fall, it seemed certain that it would engulf the whole ship. But at the last second, the bowsprit would start to rise and most of the wave would crash under the bow, with only a small part actually pouring onto the ship. The waves were higher than the mainmast and as we sank into each trough, the noise of the rigging would change as the wind blew over the top of the masts, only to hit the sails again as the *Bonnie* mounted to the top of the wave. It was this rolling hit of the wind that gave the most life to the ship, shaking her from stem to stern.

As I took one side of the double wheel, with Larry on the other, we became part of this unending fight with the elements. The weather became a living thing, determined to take the wheel and make us founder, using every trick it could devise. It lulled us for a wave or two when the ship held true to course, then suddenly wrenched the head away with a cross wave so that we had to fight to bring it back again, and I wasn't convinced the foot break was doing much to slow the turning of the helm. It was no wonder that Harris now decreed only two hours of this. I didn't know if I could stand even one! But stand them both I did.

I was happy to hand over the helm to Robert and another apprentice. My whole body ached and my hands clenched like claws, cramped with cold and shooting pain as circulation and sensation began to come back.

The wind had settled west-sou'west. To meet our course, we would be using the wheel and not turning the yards to tack with the sails. This gave the two watches more time to recover. I found them in good spirits in the fo'c's'le; some sleeping, others playing cards.

"I just stopped by to see how you are," I shouted, "and listen to any complaints, but not about the weather." This brought a few grins to tired faces. "Does anyone have a white jacket, such as stewards wear?"

They said that none of them had one, but one or two looked at one another questioningly. As I was about to leave I called them over and, as quietly as I could, asked again about the white jacket.

One said with embarrassment, "Captain keeps asking us the same question, Mr. Flynn. He says the boy has been in his cabin, bringing him tea then taking it away before he can drink it. But really, none of us would do such a thing to Captain Bowman."

"Oh well," I said, trying to make light of it. "Perhaps our captain has been taking a bit too much whisky that's stored in his cabin. I must get Mr. Harris to have a word with him." The others lighted up at this explanation. They had obviously been talking among themselves and were worried.

There was one other visit I had to make and I went down the 'tween decks and the companion into the main hold. Boris had the same idea and was now looking at one very seasick bear. He unfolded a paper containing several fish, but Brown Bear was not interested in the slightest. We set to clean up the mess, which was mostly on bedding straw that we replaced with fresh bales. Boris tried to interest the bear in a bucket of fresh water, but this was also greeted with an unenthusiastic response.

Boris said, "He must drink, not drink long time, maybe he die."

"Don't worry," I comforted. "Even if he doesn't eat or drink for the whole seventy-two hours, he's not going to die. You watch, by tomorrow he'll have gotten used to all this shaking and rolling and be just as normal."

Boris accepted this, but I could see he was still worried. As I left, he climbed into his hammock for some well-deserved sleep. When I got back to the passage leading to the galley, I saw Bowman's door open at the other end and went to investigate. Harris and Bowman were in one of their family-like tussles, with Harris calling Bowman Uncle Billy. Although this irritated Bowman, it gave Harris leeway to treat the old man not as a captain but as an irascible but harmless granddad.

Bowman was clearly annoyed. "I'm all right, damn it. My ticker is off, it happens now and then—ye know that!"

"The thing I don't like is when you try to conceal it from people who care about you. You may be the captain of the ship, but you've been my friend the last thirty-some years. I don't have any family left, and you're all that comes close. I resent you shutting me out, so let's not have anymore of it!"

Bowman glared up at Harris, then gave a grudging chuckle. "Well then, thank ye, ye great nursemaid."

"Don't mention it, Uncle Billy. I'm here to give you hell whenever necessary," Harris smiled.

"Always a comfort," Bowman said wryly.

As much as they disagreed and had words, these two would walk across hot coals for each other. This side was seldom shown to other people from the outside. Harris finally walked out, where he found me waiting.

"Harris, have you heard the stories about the white jacketed steward?" I asked.

He looked at me grimly and nodded, "I've heard, but I don't know what it means. Maybe he's getting a bit mental in his old age. He's only seventy and as fit as can be, apart from this heart murmur, as they call it. All we can do is make sure he doesn't do anything like trying to take a turn at the wheel or get into the lower shrouds for a better view. I'll have a word with Edward as well so that they don't have quite such long arguments. I think if they hold them to about ten minutes that should be quite enough!" He smiled wanly and moved off into the chart room to find Edward.

I went to stand next to the helm, where the first light of the approaching dawn revealed what we'd only imagined during the night.

Chapter 25
THE STORM ENDURES

It may have been my fancy, but I felt as though the wind had eased a trifle. Still the prospect was bleak, with great grey walls of water continually in front and behind, as we slid down one side and climbed the other. At the peaks we could see nothing but a whole series of waves, white spume and spray flying in the wind, before diving once more into the next trough. The wind was still in the same quarter, piling the waves across our port beam as we fought our way close-hauled along whatever degrees west of north we could manage. It was just possible that we could break out more sail. That thought was scarcely new before the pipe sounded, bringing the boys pounding onto the deck; some to go aloft and release the gaskets, the rest to downhaul the buntlines as we set more sail. Once again Boris was ahead of me.

The *Bonnie Clyde* took the challenge, and we ploughed more heavily through the peaks as she picked up speed. Driving at fifteen knots in this kind of weather must be one of the greatest sensations there is. I stood and savoured it to the fullest, but not for long. An all-too-well-known voice thundered in my ear, asking whether I was going to stand there all day. Harris pointed out that there were several injuries in need of attention. Indeed, there were the usual casualties of such a night: bruises, scrapes, blisters, one twisted ankle, and a number of seasick cases. This much was to be expected. We could count ourselves fortunate that we'd got off so lightly, as I applied mercurochrome and bandages and plasters, and crepe bandages for the sprains and the twisted ankle. I didn't ask Harris why I was chosen to tend to this, but I'd a basic knowledge of first aid and set up my surgery by the aft hatchway.

Just as I finished my doctoring, I saw Bowman come up on deck to have a look around. He looked frail, but I guessed he was determined to show us that he was still in charge.

"How are you this morning, Captain?" I enquired.

Without answering my question he asked, "Has Edward calculated our course and position?"

"I've been looking at our injured crew, so I'm not certain. I expect he's in the chart room," I responded.

Bowman held onto one of the ropes of the standing rigging with his right hand and carefully looked over each of the sails above us. "Seems they're holding good and true," he observed. "How are the pumps running?" He pulled out a handkerchief and wiped his forehead. His whole face was shining with sweat even though the air was cold, and his hand had a slight tremble.

Turning him round, I made sure his harness was attached to the lifeline and walked him across the bucking deck and through the occasional seas coming over the sides to the hatch so that he could go below to the chart room. Edward was there and I left them together, saying I'd report back once I'd seen the pump situation. I could hear the telltale roar of the generator and looked out to see a steady flow of water being pumped out from below. As I descended, the noise got louder and I found two lads servicing the pumps. They told me the ship hadn't taken on much water from above, but that the pumps had been on since the storm began. This wasn't good news; we preferred to operate the pumps intermittently, in order to save on precious fuel. Given the age of the ship, and her long neglect, we must be taking water into the bilge steadily from loose caulking or old welds.

Before going back up, I had a quick look down into the main hold. I couldn't decide which figure was snoring the loudest, Boris or the bear. Chuckling, I returned to the chart room. Bowman, Harris, and Edward were busy going over a chart as I made my report, including what I thought about the state of our fuel supplies. Harris just smiled in that sweetly ferocious way he had at times and remarked that the hand pump could always be manned by those not occupied with something important! This suggestion gave me pause. I told him that I hoped it wouldn't come to that because that sort of work was unreasonably laborious.

They went back to their discussion, but I pulled Harris back and whispered, "Look at Bowman. Remember what we agreed last night? Let's get these two onto other things before they start their usual disagreements."

"You're right. I didn't think, this damned navigating..." Harris replied. Turning back to the table, he called out, "Right, that's enough discussion. Boris and I will look at our choices. We're heading for Land's End, and we know the course to get there. Now you two gents are off watch, I believe, so get off and have a bit of sleep. You can get some hot tea as you pass the galley, but that's all, and *no arguing*, Edward," Harris caught his eye with a meaningful glance. Talking and chaffing, he got them out of the chart room and headed to the galley.

"Thanks, Flynn," Harris said. "I think I must also be getting old when I can't see that Uncle Billy is overdoing it. I had a word with Edward, but he must keep reminding himself. No small task, that. I also told Katherine to keep the galley fire going and that each lookout boy is to report to her after his turn at the bow. That way, there's always someone on duty ready to dowse any fire that might be thrown out of the stove. All that comes out of suggestions by you," he said musingly. "Are you trying to get my job?" he grinned.

"Not unless it involves a serious pay increase," I sniffed.

Harris said he'd stay in case the radio started up during the next hour or so. I went down to my cabin to try and sort out the mess made by the leaking deck, only to find that my guardian angel was there before me. She'd put up lines across the cabin and hung out my wet clothes. The mattress and bedding had disappeared, and next to the bulkhead there was now a fresh hammock. What a girl, practical *and* beautiful!

A pair of soft hands came over my eyes, and a voice said, "Ugh—you're wet again!" I turned to find her standing off with eyes shining, trying to dab off the damp from her jumper and slacks with the towel she was carrying. Her cheeks were red and her hair was tousled.

"I've just had a wash, and I don't need another," she sniffed. "You just have that jacket off this minute so I can get the thanks I deserve for all the work I've done in here."

I was only too happy to oblige and was rewarded with the pleasure of holding her, if only for a few moments. Of course one of us had to have a hand hanging onto a support at all times. Anyone who has knocked teeth while kissing can testify that it tends to be a passion killer. Finally, we settled for my arms round her and the bunk support, with her half-lying on me.

"I came down to do what you've already done," I said. "I was going to the galley to get a mug of coffee, if you have it."

"Only Nescafe," she said with a grimace.

"That will have to do," I told her.

Nonetheless, I had to get back to the chart room so Harris could get on with the ceaseless inspection of the ship. I knew she understood Harris's anxiety at being responsible for so many crew members in a storm like this. They'd all driven themselves hard for weeks before Robert and I had shown up, making sure the ship was seaworthy, but four men can take care of only so much. According to an earlier conversation in the chart room, everything wasn't as watertight as it should be. Harris's perpetual patrolling was intended to catch trouble before it happened, or failing that, to provide sufficient warning for us all to be rescued or to escape on the life rafts. This was unthinkable, although we had to be prepared in any event. I arrived in the chart room with my mug of coffee in hand.

"Thank you, Flynn, most thoughtful of you," Harris said.

"Oh no, you go get your own," I shot back.

"Okay," he said, "but I was going to embellish that one a bit." He reached into his coat pocket and produced a small flask.

"Well, that would be very nice," I said, setting the mug on the table, at which he obligingly poured a generous amount into it.

Suddenly the radio began its usual rude reception noises, but then stopped. I turned back to find that Harris and my mug had disappeared, except for the sound of laughter floating up through the companion. It had been difficult getting my mug to the chart room without spilling it all. I was contemplating ways of getting even, when Boris came in to ask me for help in moving crates from the hold, but my mood had turned sour. I looked at him and sighed bitterly.

"That damned Harris is always one step ahead of me," I lamented.

Boris scratched his ear and replied, "Then you must walk faster."

Boris was one of the most unflappable people I'd ever met. Maybe it was his being Russian, but he never seemed to be upset by anything. Back at the inn he'd walked through the barroom brawl without touching anyone, and by the same token no one touched him. If there was an emergency, he would take care of the problem and go on with his business as though nothing had taken place. He was as agile as a cat and strong as a bull, with no discernible temper whatsoever. However, there were accounts from Harris about occasions to the contrary when Boris had been provoked beyond reason.

I rose, stretching my stiff muscles, and prepared to assist with Boris's task. We went to the number one hatch and made two trips carrying the crates, heavy ones filled with tinned food, back to the wardroom. As we brought the second load to the open hatch, I refused Boris's offer to help me down the ladder, but did let him carry the crate. There sat Harris with his feet propped up near the coal heater, sound asleep with his index finger affixed to my mug. I walked over and got another mug. As I filled it with coffee, I realized there was one thing yet missing. I glanced over at Harris. His right hand was propped on the table with the mug. The other hung limp at his side, revealing a flask that was clearly visible in the pocket of his slightly open watch coat.

Very carefully I crept up behind him, with full knowledge that discovery might do me serious harm. Using great care with my thumb and two fingers, I slid the flask slowly out of his pocket. Giving it a shake, I was happy to find it half full. I added a liberal dose to my coffee, but thought it best not to try and replace it. I started to put it in my pocket, then realised I still had Bowman's in my possession. Now I had one for each pocket, a comforting thought. I sat for a few moments enjoying long sips of the warm fluid, when I was startled by Boris's sudden re-appearance. Most of his arrivals were sudden and unexpected. Well, he'd come too late to see the crime in commission. I silently congratulated myself on having pulled a fast one without witness and thus far without discovery or repercussions.

Edward descended the ladder, seemingly deep in thought. He looked over and demanded, "What are you doing hanging about down here?"

"I'm enjoying a warm beverage and waiting for our radio contact," I returned coolly. "Besides, I live here, so you needn't get cross with me."

Edward relaxed and coughed his gruff laugh by way of agreement. I pointed over to Harris, his feet up, and sound asleep.

"Now that's a damned strange place to be taking a nap!" Edward burst out at Harris, who stirred and sat upright in his chair.

"Excuse me?" Harris said, snapping awake. "What's that? What do you mean, a strange place? At sea, rest is where you find it. Besides, who appointed you time keeper?" It was clear he wasn't pleased at being awakened, and he might have elaborated on the theme had he not been interrupted by another awakening.

Now it was the radio that awoke, and I could hear a familiar voice. "*Calling Harris, calling Harris.*"

I recognised Martin's voice and quickly keyed the handset. "Hi there, Martin," I called. "Good to hear your voice. How are things with you?"

"*I want to ask you that. Here it's been one hell of a day and night, and today has started the same. The wind is so strong that you can only move outside by holding onto trees, gateposts, and such…and the rain is forever. Despite all this, though, we presently have at the inn a variety of shady Fleet Street characters, and every paper I see has your ship and pictures of whoever was on the tug on the front page. With the exception of* The Times, *of course*," he added in an upper-class voice.

"You watch out," I said, "one day they will, just you wait and see!"

"*Who will what?*" Martin sounded a bit exasperated.

"*The Times* will, they'll have pictures on the front page, even of la-dies," I taunted.

"*Do you want to hear my story, or don't you?*" he asked impatiently.

"Yes sir. Please go on sir. I'm all—"

"*You'll be all dead if you don't shut up,*" we both laughed. "*Still, it was very difficult to get away this morning without one of the reporters spotting me, but I did eventually shake him off. Now where to begin? Oh yes, the favourite photo seems to be the one of Harris laughing, and holding the radio handset in the air. This seems to have caught everyone's attention. The reporters keep on offering me hefty sums of money for the story of the escaping lovebirds or some such, but we never discussed what I should say if asked.*"

"Well, we have promised Richard exclusive rights, but not for money," I admitted. "Why don't you ring up and ask him? We've given Richard all our details now. I should think he used some of it for to-day's AP news service piece. If it's money that's involved, I don't see why you shouldn't say your piece. Of course you might have to answer to Mrs. Beasley, should she find you've been withholding information from her. Do what you think is best."

"*All right then, I will. All the papers have printed something about you. Local news is also interesting. O'Connell has been booted out of his job and residence by the trustees, who decided that they'd better show they won't tolerate this sort of rubbish. But they've not explained how he was able to carry on like this all these years without detection. I'm told that the tax man is already in there looking at the figures, and I'm sure someone has told him about the Bentley. I think a prosecution might be brought soon. Meanwhile, would you believe it? I have to put up with O'Connell here! Mrs. B. has taken him in, at Katherine's old cottage. He's with her most of the time and doing odd jobs for his keep. He really is a nasty piece of work. However, the most worrying thing I have to report,*" he said gravely, "*is the activity of Scotland Yard. There's a team of three coming in from Gravesend each day, and they're asking every-one they can about the crew and the boys.*

"*According to the local policeman, they seem to be trying to work up a case of kidnapping or child abduction. The trouble is, English law can clobber you as well as protect you. If the police wanted to, they could probably make a case for the public prosecutor to issue a summons for kidnap because every one of the boys is under twenty-one and cannot be taken away from their legal guardian. However, my friend assures me that the publicity from this whole incident will give the authorities cause for deliberation before taking any action. By the way, you're going to have to make an honest woman of Katherine as soon as you can.* The Daily Mirror *is insinuating sinful things and I don't know what the Sunday papers will do with that part of the story. Juicy stuff, you know.*"

"Bugger all to them!" I exploded. "Just because Katherine and I are on the same ship—" I paused for a few seconds. I was outraged at the thought of them writing anything to harm Katherine. In the end, I asked him, "Please collect a selection of papers for us, Martin, so we can see how the story was presented when we get to port. There are some things that are going to need explaining, as with the boys, but we're hoping that public opinion will see all charges punished by slaps on the wrist rather than time in prison."

While I'd been talking, the sounds of the ship had been gradually getting noisier. We could hear that the solid thump and swish of water dumping on the fo'c's'le head and well deck were becoming more frequent.

"I don't know if you can hear," I went on, "but the storm is closing down on us again and after a slight lull, is back with a vengeance. The ship is a real marvel and the builder deserves more than praise. Despite all the neglect, the masts and the yards are taking the strain, and the pumps are working to rid us of whatever water that's getting through the hull. The boys have proved themselves men many times over. Apart from a few scrapes and sprains, are all fit, considering the fact that they've been on the edge of malnutrition for so long. That bloody reptile O'Connell really must be made to pay for his neglect."

"*Really?*" Martin was interested. "*Then I'd better say a few words to certain parties to have a good look at the food bills. Even though we all think she's a nag, Mrs. Beasley should also learn about the* other *O'Connell. Oh yes, one more thing. I had a call from a man named Brian yesterday. He says he's a friend of Harris. He'd seen the papers and wanted to send you his best wishes for a successful voyage. He asked if he can help in any way. He says he has a lot of friends in London. That's about all from my end.*"

"And it'll have to be all from my end," I shouted over the wind and crashing seas. "Things are picking up here and I'll be needed to work on deck. Thanks for all your help, Martin. We look forward to your next bulletin." We said goodbye and closed the connection.

Outside, the clouds, which had lightened slightly, were now darker and thicker than ever and seemed to scud over the horizon to envelop us. As they rolled overhead, they brought a squall of hard, driving rain and hail, cloaking the deck with glittering ice that was swept away by the next wave. The watch aloft was battling with flying canvas, with boys getting their feet knocked out from under them. Hanging from the stays, their legs kicked wildly to find the support from the footrope. Harris and Robert were at the wheel, with Larry to help with the brake as the ship slid and fought the waves.

The boys now came stumbling down the ladder, exhausted after having reefed in everything except the mainsail, jibs, foresail, and fore-staysail. Still the ship bounced forward at the peak of each wave.

As the boys crowded down to the galley to get something hot to eat and drink, Boris came hurtling out of number three hatchway and headed for Harris at the wheel. After shouting something, Boris quickly returned. Harris handed over the helm to Larry and went after Boris. I sensed an emergency and ran down through the nearest hatch. The 'tween decks should have been in near darkness, but instead flames lit up the area and smoke was beginning to fill the space. Running forward, I found Boris and Harris attempting to smother the fire, which was burning over and around the generator. It had managed to tear loose from its retaining bolts and was now lying on its side. The petrol from the tank spilt and caught fire from the hot cylinder block, and was now spreading onto the deck.

I ran forward to the number two hatch closest to the galley, which was the nearest place I could think of for buckets. I yelled to Katherine, "Fire! No time to explain." I picked up two buckets, grabbed her helper, and shot back to the number two hatchway. The fire had caught a little on the wood of the bulkhead as well as on the deck. Before I could stop the boy, he had thrown the contents of his bucket on the deck and spread the flames, threatening some of the goods we'd stacked a few days ago. Using buckets of water must be done with care as to not spread the flames by pushing them farther down the deck. Harris and Boris were still wrestling a large tarpaulin to smother the fire. I told the boy to get the watch off duty and form a line from the nearest gunnel, filling the buckets over the side with a rope tied to their handles. The boys proved their mettle again by seeing the problem and reacting without question. Soon the fire was doused with no casualties apart from Harris getting a bucketful over him when he stepped the wrong way after a warning shout.

Once the emergency passed, we all stood and caught our breath. Before the boys disappeared, Boris got them round the generator. With a bit of work, they soon had it standing upright again against the bulkhead in its original position. Harris said a few words of praise for their speed in coming to fight the fire and sent them back to the fo'c's'le to continue their interrupted rest. Boris poured more water over the affected parts to cool them down, especially in the area of the tank. He poured in petrol, pressed the starter, and it caught the first time, running smoothly, so thankfully there was no damage there.

Boris was annoyed. This was the first time I'd ever seen him so, and he surely had ample cause. "I find this cap over there. Means boys not close tank!"

Harris wasn't so sparing of words, "So some lazy good-for-nothing didn't close the tank properly?" He glared at the departing boys. "I'm going to tan the little sod's arse so roundly when I catch him, he won't be able to sit down for a week!" he roared as the boys left by number one hatch. Winking at me he said, "I hope that's enough of a threat not to skimp on their work."

Leaving Boris to affix the generator to the bulkhead, this time using a chain instead of rope that could get hot enough to break again, we made our way back to the wheel, where Robert and Larry appeared to be holding their own.

"Hey, Flynn, it's nearly your watch on the wheel," Robert called out. "She's handling beautifully, but you'd better not relax an inch, for she'll take a mile and it's forever to get the binnacle centred again." Just to emphasise this point, we were staggered by a seventh wave as it flung water down the well deck in a flooding torrent. It beat against the bulkhead below the wheel and threw a sheet of water over us all. Robert forgot to duck his head and had to take a hand from the wheel to wipe his eyes. That was enough. The pressure of his hand had been maintaining the rudder in a certain equilibrium. Taking the pressure away shifted the wheel an inch, just as he'd said, and then suddenly the sea snatched a mile, slewing the head round. If it wasn't for Larry holding on, we would have continued that fatal turn and broached to in the waves.

All helmsmen learn this trick of the sea. When they relax their guard, they're always ready for the counter of full rudder in the opposite direction until the bow picks up, followed by the slow centring. Then they watch the bow and binnacle at the same time until equilibrium is regained. All this takes place in seconds but it's the essence of the helmsman's job, to feel the ship and the sea through the wheel, like a live thing straining at the end of a leash, and to know when to ease off here and when to pull in there. I've usually enjoyed my spells at the wheel of whatever boat, but the sailing ship is the only really live one.

"Give me five minutes," I called back to Robert.

I shouted to Harris, "Come on, I'll buy you a cup of coffee so you don't keep stealing mine."

Leading the way into the chart room, I told him to wait because I wanted to tell him about Martin's call. Katherine was in her element again with the stove burning and making good hot food. I told her quickly what had happened, and then took two mugs of coffee back to Harris.

Having told him what Martin said, I added, "When you think about all we did to make this voyage possible, without people knowing our motives, we must sound like a gang of crooks. Maybe you and Bowman can have a talk before we get Richard's next call, so he can get us the best publicity. We've publicly embarrassed several Whitehall people, and in their rat-pack that means shunting sideways until they retire or resign, so they'll be desperate to get back into their bosses' good graces." I went through the list of our misdeeds, all of which would need to be put in their best light so that public opinion could tread lightly over the obvious criminal acts. "These can easily be considered justified," I concluded.

Harris had been listening in silence, and once I'd finished he took a long swallow of his coffee and said, "Just remind me not to praise you at all in the future. You do rattle on, don't you?" and he grinned briefly before becoming serious.

"Let's not forget that this has been Uncle Billy's outing right from the start. Even though he's tough and cantankerous, when I think how bad public criticism could be—" his face broke a bit, "I'm not going to see him suffer disgrace or obscurity after all he's been through! I want him to have the glory he never got in his working life. Just working one of these ships for thirty years or more should bring a shower of medals."

Harris thought for a moment. "I think you're right about Richard. I'll sit down with Uncle Billy and Edward and get them to agree what to ask of him. Already I can think of using Martin's ex-*Times* man to see about making a connection with one of their leaders. Those articles are usually pretty influential, even getting into *Hansard* when mentioned in MPs' speeches. Then there's Brian. I know he hasn't been in the country long, but he has many friends and family members who got out of Europe in the early thirties. Who knows, he may have a Rothschild or two he can get in to see! Meanwhile, Flynn, get your arse into gear and relieve Robert while I find Boris to come and help you."

I downed the rest of my coffee, adjusted my oilskin, made doubly sure my sou'wester was firmly fixed to my head, and went outside to the helm, where Robert was so glad to see me he disappeared without a word of thanks. Larry was silent and I saw that he was just holding on. He gave a grateful smile when I told him that Boris was on his way.

Suddenly, there was a sound that I hadn't heard before on this ship. It was the clang of a bell, coming from the lookout on the fo'c's'le head. It struck twice, and I remembered my training days, reciting with the mate, almost as huge as Harris but only half as human, standing by me also reciting, "Two bells vessel to port, three bells vessel ahead, one bell vessel to starboard." I was stuck at the wheel, but from my post I watched Harris darting up to the lookout's position, where he pointed off the port bow. I thought I could see the smallest of lights winking just on the horizon. The next instant, Harris was in the shrouds and climbing the ratlines up to the top, trying to get above the continuous spray and loss of visibility as the ship slid into each trough. After some time there, he came back down and checked the binnacle for the light's bearing off our course. Then he went into the chart room, shouting for Edward. I had to hold my curiosity, but I could more or less remember what lay ahead from having studied the charts.

Manning the helm wasn't something I could do when I was an apprentice, but I think it's an exercise that should be allowed all personnel on a ship, providing circumstances allow it. Not only is it good practise for navigation, but especially close to land or heading for a landfall, a good sailor will learn to know what to look for and not be completely surprised when he sees it.

I knew the boys on lookout had been instructed to use the bell for any sightings, including land. I doubted that any ship had been sighted, but instead it could be a fixed light warning of rocks or a shoal. I could see that our course was taking us out of the long indent on the coast of France between Le Havre and Cherbourg Peninsula, to a heading that would bring us near Weymouth. The light we saw must have been at Pointe de Barfleur on the extreme north-east tip of the Peninsula.

After some time, and some argument, which I could overhear through the chart room bulkhead, Harris came storming out with a new course.

"One day—" he shouted, "one day I'm going to roll up all of Edward's charts and bludgeon him to death with them. So bloody much argument about a simple choice! It seems the BBC and all reporting ships agree that this storm is going to carry on at least another twenty-four hours. Before the storm we'd more or less agreed that we should get behind the Peninsula, away from the possible search pattern of the MTB, then swing around Alderney and then head due west, ending up well to the south of the Scilly Isles. I've just been arguing with that stubborn old idiot, Edward, that the storm changed everything and now we should be clawing our way as much due north-west as we can manage, and then come about on the other tack, heading south-west. Once the storm dies we should be in the Channel well to the south of

Plymouth, well placed to take advantage when the wind veers round to the east."

"Harris versus Edward." Quite a picture.

"So who won?" I asked. He didn't reply to this, and merely gave me the course, which I saw would leave us in the best position the next day when the storm died down. As I set the new course, I hoped that we'd not been spotted from land as we very quickly lost sight of the light. The remainder of my watch was a blur of unrelenting effort, as Boris and I fought to hold the course and to maximise the power we could get from the wind. It seemed an eternity until at last my time was up. After handing the helm over to Harris and one of the bigger boys— Tom, I think it was—I staggered back into the chart room and collapsed in the chair in front of the radio.

"Ha ha ha," Edward cackled, "how does it feel to be an old man, just like me?" Now that was a thought. Edward couldn't be much over sixty and with me near thirty, we really were both old men on this ship full of boys nineteen years and younger.

I gave a feeble growl. "That's enough of the old Methuselah. You just get in line for a couple of hours at the wheel in this weather and let's see who's calling who old!" I was too exhausted for further banter, and devoted my remaining mental energy to what Harris had said about our possible position tomorrow afternoon. "Edward, how soon do you think before we reach Dumbarton?"

He thought a moment, then said that if we could get good winds after the storm, and no other delaying factors were involved, it might take us as little as four or five days.

Edward continued, "If we're south of Plymouth by tomorrow and the storm starts to die, then we must keep on southerly to make sure to avoid the hazards off Lizard Point. Rounding Land's End and travelling north through St. George's Channel and the Irish Sea will be very testing. The winds and the current are always contrary. Once swallowed most of the Spanish Armada, they did." He went back to his charts and calculations. He couldn't keep out of the storm, but he'd do all any mariner could to steer our ship out of harm's way.

Boris now came in and, seeing me relaxing, said, "Enough rest. Come, work to do."

"Did I mention that I was completely knackered?" I protested, but I knew there was no arguing with the brute.

I followed him down to the main hold and helped move a number of straw bales for the bear. I'd never spent time around wild animals. I knew a bear only from its reputation, and for me that was near enough.

Boris and I then took on the task of bringing boxes of tinned goods aft to the galley. The boxes were heavy, perhaps because my arms had not yet recovered from their previous tasks. Katherine was busy with the evening meal and had time only for a hasty hello-and-thank you.

Finding that Boris had vanished without telling me whether he wanted me for anything else, I came back up on deck to find young Larry alone at the wheel. As I leaped to put myself next him, I shouted, "What the hell is Harris playing at, leaving you on your own with these seas?" But Larry was quite enjoying himself.

"This is the first time I've had her on my own, Mr. Flynn. It's a lot harder than I expected, but I love it."

"Do you need a relief? It's almost meal time," I asked.

"No sir, actually I'd like a bit more of this," he said. "I don't know when I'll get the chance to go solo again, and I'd be happy to put more time in."

"Okay, but I'm sending your relief in twenty minutes. I can guarantee you'll have other opportunities at the helm." I stood there for a few more minutes, smiling at his enthusiasm. He seemed to know how the ship would react, but it was heavy work. I couldn't understand why Harris had gone off and left him on his own.

As I watched, Harris returned from wherever he'd been and resumed his place by helmsman Larry. My questioning look was obvious, and without waiting, he said shortly, "I'll tell you later." At that I shrugged and turned away.

I was pretty sure I knew where Boris was. Sure enough, I found him tending to the bear. He had got over his seasickness, and with no fish in sight, had to make do with some mess made up by Boris. I helped clean up around the hold—not a pleasant job in a confined space. I found Boris good company because his answers and comments were always so to-the-point. I had a sneaking suspicion that he understood more English than he admitted. I decided to test this, mainly because I wanted to be better friends with him. This was difficult while he hid behind a pretend language barrier.

"Boris, you understand more English than you let on. I think you understand everything I say, but for some reason you pretend not to quite often. Why is that?"

Boris looked at me appraisingly. I suspect that he'd already decided about me some time ago. "Sometimes it is good to have someone explain something when you already understand. Sometimes there are big differences in opinion. I tell you this because I think I can trust you. There are not many people for me to be entirely open."

"But what about Bowman, Harris, and Edward? You've known them for years. Are you trying to tell me you don't trust them knowing how well you can speak and understand English?" I asked.

He smiled. "You see how many fights I never see or get involved in? If Boris doesn't understand, nobody notices the ignorant foreigner. You have seen this?"

"Aren't you the sly old fox," I said, "but is that such a good reason for not understanding?"

He continued to smile placidly. "Understanding English and speaking it are two very different things. But you never heard me say this, yes?"

"Actually it's too windy to hear anything," I said, extending my hand. We shook hands, our understanding quite clear.

"Thank you very good." he said, reverting to his customary primitive speech, and then off he went in his usual abrupt way. For my part I took a lesson from this, always shooting off my mouth when things are just as easily accomplished without yelling. Maybe I should have pretended I understood less sometimes, but I could never work it as well. Oh yes, his secret was very safe with me.

I could sympathize with Boris, for communication was hard when one was even a little foreign. Since my father was American some of the terminology was quite different, and I was forced to endure much teasing from other boys regarding my use of the King's English. It seemed beneath them to even use my name, and they would refer to me only as that south-witted lad. I naturally found this discouraging, and often extremely embarrassing.

I recall a girl I was seeing while attending the university. I met her at my job while working part-time to help pay for my education, and she invited me to her family's house for tea. This was a nice opportunity to chat with her family about all the latest things going on about the campus and the world of politics. "So you met Vera at your job, I understand," her father happened to ask, "and how's the screw?"

I became speechless at this, supposing it to be an enquiry into our non-existent sex life. I was astonished that he could be so casual about his daughter's virtue. My face turned several shades of crimson before my girl whispered that he was simply asking how much money I made at my job. The lads at the university were not as forthcoming with explanations. Their heartless chaff often led to fisticuffs, at which I was soon forced to become very adept, an expert in fact.

The present-day Flynn realised that he'd never got lunch, so I went to see if I could beg anything from Katherine. I found the galley a bit tense, with Katherine looking unsmiling and rather testy herself. Just up the passage Harris, Bowman, and Edward were arguing outside Bowman's door, so I assumed everything was normal. I was about to join them, but Katherine held me back.

"You may be interested in this particular problem," she whispered, pulling me closer. "Let me explain. Somehow I feel partly responsible."

"What exactly is the problem?" I asked.

"Just before dinner I was getting everything ready for the boys, who are always here on the dot, ravenous. Among the things set out was a tray of beer and ale, part of what Martin donated." She looked chagrined, and sighed.

"And the problem?" I prompted.

"Those three," she nodded her head in their direction, "had a fit over young boys drinking."

"Surely, you're not serious?" I cried.

"No, it's absolutely true," she replied, "and now the boys have to wait for their dinner while this matter is being resolved."

It was difficult to believe that I was listening to such rubbish, but I was already working out a solution.

Very soon everyone had come in, crowding into the galley and down the passage, which left very few to run the ship. Bowman, Harris, and Edward had retreated into Bowman's cabin. I'd hoped that Boris and Robert would be on deck steering and keeping a watch on the sails, but I saw Boris among the crew standing there.

A very flushed Bowman came out of his cabin and said, "No one is to come in here until we have this business settled."

Someone had to stop this nonsense, so I spoke up. "Yes, and I intend to settle it for you without any further argument from anyone!" I announced. Bowman stared at me. Harris now emerged from the cabin with that dangerous too sweet expression.

"You're going to do what?" he asked gently.

"Until I'm finished, I'd like you gentlemen not to interrupt," I declared. "Everyone here knows the story of how Bowman went to sea at the age of thirteen, and Harris not much older. In those days, boys became men early. When they went to sea, much was demanded of them and an astonishing bunch they were. They're definitely a vanishing breed of seaman, and we can only hope to learn what they know. I'm sure they've forgotten more than any of us will ever learn. However, they forgot one important thing: how do you measure manhood? Some of the ways you know, such as going aloft in a heavy storm to haul in wet canvas in pouring rain with the ship rocking beneath you, praying you don't get exhausted in the efforts and fall."

I continued, "Each man went through similar trials everyday, and for that they were rewarded, as most seamen of their day, with a measure of grog or a pint of ale. The ale was there because good drinking water was only available on ships at the beginning of a voyage, and only when it rained thereafter, but a drink of plain water didn't seem much reward to men who risked their lives daily.

"Now then, Captain," I asked, "don't you believe these boys have become men since we've been through all of this together?"

Bowman looked around at the company, seeing all eyes upon him. For a moment, he was completely silent. I folded my arms and stood in an attitude of respectful expectation, noticing Edward peering out from the cabin door.

The captain bent a long look upon me, and nodded. "Indeed. I've worked many men, and I suppose I can concede that those who work as crew deserve respect as men." He eyed me quizzically, wondering what was to happen next. Now it was time to play my ace. I reached into my pocket and pulled out the flask I'd acquired from Harris earlier without his knowledge.

"Oh, by the way Harris, you carelessly left this on deck. I believe these are your initials." And with that I threw the flask to him in view of all. At first he looked at it in disbelief and quickly checked the pockets of his watch coat.

Harris held up the flask and shook it, his gaze narrowing at its near-empty state. "You've a strange way of making your point," he muttered in half-amused tones.

I then looked at Boris, who returned my glance blandly. "So Boris, do you think these boys should be treated as men?"

At first he pretended he didn't understand, and I put on my most patient expression, prepared to wait him out.

Boris eyed Harris and Bowman and folded his arms, "Yes, everybody man!" He turned to face Katherine, "Everybody— of course not you," he added in an apologetic manner.

I looked about ready to challenge. "Anyone who's seen these boys in the last few days knows they've become men. Right now they're all men, waiting for their dinners. There's a tray here with various beers and ales from which to choose, but drink wisely." I started to open the bottles, making sure I handed one to Bowman first. Edward now came forward and made sure of a bottle for himself, still looking undecided about the matter.

"Here we are with the ship tossing about like a cork, not knowing when a sail is going to blow out. These boys are hungry for food and drink, and you're going on like three old women at a temperance meeting. Where's your sense of proportion?" I left them to think it over while I went to get my own food and a beer.

Katherine whispered, "That was brilliant—you should have seen the look on their faces!" I smiled and said, "They've been getting at you and making you unhappy with their nonsense, after all."

The boys now tentatively approached the bottles, with many a glance to Bowman and Harris. Larry and Todd each claimed a beer, but didn't try so much as a sip at first. The other boys watched them closely, to be sure of any consequences. I could see the Great Grog Affair would take some time to settle fully.

"Flynn? May I have a word with you?" Harris asked.

"Yes, you may, after I've eaten." I said.

"*Now!*" Harris demanded. He was definitely not in the best of moods. I felt the growing presence of uneasy tension—and it had my name on it.

"How did you come into possession of my flask?" he grated.

"That is your flask, is it not?" I responded, injured virtue writ large upon my face.

Harris looked down, "Yes, of course it is."

"You shouldn't be so careless as to leave it lying about. What would the men think?" I turned away, ignoring his low growl.

With this delicate matter out of the way, I took my seat with the crew in the wardroom. It seems I'd made many friends that evening, for several more lads were very self-consciously enjoying a nice bit of beer or ale. I wondered what Bowman was thinking, as he and Edward sat silently eating their dinner. It's been said that no good deed goes unpunished. I feared that the consequences of my act would be revealed soon enough.

I was getting ready to go on deck when Katherine beckoned me over. "I forgot to tell you, I had one of the crew hang out your mattress for drying, but don't expect to be using it soon. I also took the liberty of hanging up your wet clothing, so I'm afraid you'll find your cabin looking a bit like a tailor's shop."

"That was very thoughtful," I said. "In fact I saw it when I passed earlier, but didn't have time to thank you."

"Just one more thing, I let you have the second part of the afternoon in my room, remember?" she whispered.

"Of course I remember, how could I forget?" I answered.

"Well then, where do you propose to sleep tonight?" she asked. With all of these things going on around me, I forgot about an alternative accommodation completely.

"I couldn't help noticing that hammock, so I can stay out of your way for now," I told her.

"Now you listen here, stop trying to be the chivalrous protector," she scolded. "After all that you and I have been through. Oh, you do sometimes become infuriating!"

"Listen Katherine, I—"

"Enough!" she interrupted. "Quietly, we'll do as we did at the inn. Your trunk and dry clothing were taken into what is now *our* cabin," she smiled.

I reached out and softly embraced her. We'd already made a commitment before leaving the inn together. She didn't force me, but sometimes unless someone shows me the bridge is strong enough, I tend to be reluctant to go across.

Inappropriate modesty perhaps, but I was somewhat shy by nature and certainly was trying my best not to take a good thing for granted. We were now closer than ever before and I didn't want this to change. Again and again, I pondered what we'd do and where we'd go when we reached our destination. All these things Katherine and I would speak of in the next few days. Everything else seemed insignificant by comparison.

Chapter 26
THE WEATHER ABATES

On deck, the constant pounding of the sea and the wind moaning and howling through the rigging made the ship seem like an immense living thing. The bow and bowsprit disappeared every now and again, then came out of the sea with white water cascading over the fo'c's'le head. The triangle of the foremast staysail was taut and sang in a higher pitch as it curved up in front of the foresail. Holding the buntline, one could feel the wind pulling and trembling. With most of the sails filled, the masts creaked and groaned down to their solid footing on the keel as we rode over the top of each wave. Each of us had complete confidence in the *Bonnie*. She could weather anything so long as we did our jobs properly, but the sea was relentless and we couldn't afford to relax our guard even for a second. Tiredness showed in the faces of everyone, as off watch had become just as much a test of endurance as on watch. Sleep was almost impossible, for relaxing meant being flung about in the bunk and even onto the deck.

Bowman had made it his job to get amongst the crew off watch, to encourage the boys and listen to their stories of all that had happened to them on watch. Their spirits rebounded quickly, but their bodies could not, and we were concerned for their general staying power. The earliest estimate for the storm to die down was twenty hours. We were hoping for only one major change of course during that time, depending on the wind bearing.

I was sitting in the chart room after the evening meal, nursing a mug of coffee, idly wondering what the outcome of my pro-drinking cry was going to be, when Bowman and Harris came in.

"Good," Harris said, "just the man we wanted to see." Bowman sat down in the only other chair while Harris used the corner of the chart table.

Bowman cleared his throat and spoke, "I will say that I regret that business about the drinks. Perhaps we did get a wee bit carried away. I suppose it's because we're worried at what's going to happen when we get off the ship, people saying we led those innocent boys into piracy and let them drink as well! Ye were quite right to get it settled quickly. The poor lads needed their dinner. Anyway, let's have nae more about it."

"The next thing on my list is the canvas," said Harris. Here, if the circus owners want to be nasty, we haven't a leg to stand on. We took it without permission, knowing full well that if we'd asked, the answer would have been no. It's called stealing."

"Ah yes," I put in, "but we did have the money to pay for replacement tents, we just couldn't locate a source. Perhaps with the publicity, it's very likely we can, now that factories are changing over to peacetime production again. If we ask Richard to write up how sorry we are for taking the tents, but that after all the circus was closing for the season, that we have the money, and we're now looking for a supplier who can deliver before the season starts again, maybe the owners won't press charges. Also the circus will get quite a lot of free publicity with the papers that use Richard's story."

"It all sounds very reasonable when we sit here analysing it," Bowman mused, "but there are many people involved I canna abide, and the worst are Whitehall twits and lawyers. They'll weasel ye out of yer eye-teeth if they aren't screwed in."

"Well, we can only wait and see," Harris said, "but I'm counting on the publicity, no matter what the lawyers say."

"Next," I pointed out, "is the question of ex-Navy, still-Navy, scrap-Navy stores and…"

Harris waved his hand. "All right, Flynn, less of the funny stuff. What you don't know is that some, but not all, of the new stuff you see stored below is bought and paid for, and I've got the receipts. The only problem is that the receipts are in the name of a non-existent contractor, who was buying stuff for re-fitting an existing ship, which is not, in fact, being refurbished. I thought if I put the *Bonnie Clyde*'s name on paper, some clever little irk up the line would be asking questions."

"So that's the truth of it, is it?" I exclaimed. "That's somewhat of a relief. I'm sorry, but all this time I thought you'd just made everything *walk* out of the yard. My apologies."

Harris gave me a hard look and grinned, "The scrap did walk. All the old items you see, including bits of machinery, most of the ropes, block and tackles, life rafts, pumps, quite a bit of the rigging parts, paint and more that were in the yard, but had been written down to nil long ago and was to be officially disposed of. Scrap merchants refused it because it would cost more to collect it than they would get for selling it, so it just sat there mouldering. I think the worst they can get me for is falsification of documentation, if there is such a crime, but you remember that commander coming around? Some of this is worth quite a bit, but not for the scrap merchants."

At this juncture I added another thought. "What about the bear?"

This did give him pause, and he thought for a moment, then brightened. "Aren't we taking it to its new owner or something?"

"I suppose I'll have to get the real story from Robert," I said. "Richard seems to think the bear story is going to make us out the kindest people since Father Christmas. He's just dying to get some photos. The worry with the bear is telling what we're going to do with it, since we never had any real plan, after all. It's old now and will need special care."

Bowman scratched his beard, remarking, "With all the attention the creature will attract, something should come up. There may be a Scottish Bears Benevolent Society, for aught I know." He rubbed his hands together. "Aye, that seems to take care of everything."

Harris had been pondering over his list for some time, and he now suddenly burst out, "Here you two—wake up! How can you say that takes care of everything when there's a little question of theft still outstanding?" He glared at us but I hadn't much of an idea in my head at this point just which theft he meant. It was late and I was tired and at this point just hoped I could remember how to use a hammock. After giving us a few seconds, he exploded, "What about the bloody ship?"

He did have a point there, but it was one far beyond our legal knowledge to fathom. AP's legal department would probably welcome the problem. There seemed to be two ways we could be attacked, one being that we'd committed an act of piracy. As we hadn't threatened anyone nor used force, I thought piracy was a bit stiff. But it made me think of the tug and I said, "There's another theft we forgot, the handset from the tug's radio. And the fact that by tampering with the compass we led to the tug's having to heave to through a night when it could have well been run down.

"What would be the legal view of stealing something that the owner wanted thrown away?" I told the others what I thought, and we agreed to ask Richard if his legal department would like to have a go at it.

"You know," I added, thinking aloud, "it seems to me that there may be some reluctance to actually bring this pursuit to a conclusion."

"And why do you think that would be?" Bowman asked. I moved a bit closer to them so that no one would overhear our conversation.

"What would you do in their position? No, seriously. If you overtook this vessel and boarded it, what would you possibly accomplish? Let's see, you could arrest everyone. Of course that would be counterproductive because there would be no one to sail or steer the vessel. Also, it would be foolish to try to take this ship under tow because there would be insufficient control without someone at the helm. And one more thing," I said, holding up my index finger, "just where could they possibly tow this vessel when they themselves have absolutely no idea where we're going? Given all that, they'd be forced to tow us back to England, which would be impossible."

"Good points," Bowman agreed, "but those decisions are based largely on logic and I haven't noticed, over many years, their decisions ever have involved much of what's logical!" And he rose, yawning. "That's enough of this business for now, lads."

Bowman was quickly away to his cabin, but Harris and I had a watch together at the wheel before we could think of resting. It seemed as though Richard wasn't likely to be calling this late.

We went outside onto the bridge deck. The sky was so black that the only light came from the binnacle, shining up under the chins of the helmsmen and casting strange shadows across their faces. There was also a small glow on the forepeak that came from the riding lights, but aside from these, we were just another bobbing piece of flotsam in the darkness. Robert and Boris reported for their watch at the wheel and I told them of the conference, but I could see that they both, even the tireless Boris, were feeling the effects of continuously fighting the storm and couldn't muster much interest.

Perhaps I was imagining it, but I thought I could feel a slight lessening in the perpetual violence of the sea, the wind seemed not quite so forceful. If so, it was by only the smallest degree. The ship's bell struck eight, always a welcome sound, as it meant the end of a watch. The old watch crowded down to the galley for a hot drink and the hope of sleep. The new watch groaned at the prospect of four hours of work, all hoping that there'd be no need to set or reef sails, nor to brace the yards. The lookout reported back to the wheel that the navigation lights were burning properly. Harris and I took over for our watch, once again without sleep.

Immediately I got that familiar sensation that I was a part of the ship. Carved in with the wood of the deck, rising and falling with it, the only movable parts were my arms, head, and shoulders. I could feel the sea streaming past the rudder, trying to push it off line. The gusts of wind hitting the topsails tried to make the head fall off ever so slightly, and my automatic turn of the wheel in the opposite direction was intended to counter this.

The night wore on with little or no words spoken between me and Harris, only the occasional debate whether to set more sail or attend to other measures that would let the watches rest as much as possible.

Whatever the state of the storm, we'd have to come about on a new tack soon after first light and we'd need all hands on deck. At last four bells sounded, and we were relieved at the wheel by Edward and Larry.

I quite literally staggered down to the galley for hot tea and was surprised to find Katherine there. She looked tired and sleepy. As we sat leaning on one another she said drowsily, "If only the ship's motion was a regular corkscrew, a person could get used to it and fit one's body to it and get lulled to sleep. But these everlasting odd kicks and sidelong slides, with no rhyme or reason, I really don't…" and her voice trailed off as the effort of thinking was just too much.

After a little longer I carefully disengaged myself. "I'm going to try sleeping in the hammock, Katherine. Tomorrow we'll have to make a big course change, coming on the other tack, so make sure your boy warns you in good time. We're going to need all hands on deck." I kissed her good night, went to my cabin, swung into the hammock, and fell asleep.

What seemed only five minutes was in reality four hours later. I was on my feet at the washbasin in the corner of the cabin, wondering what to do with the toothbrush I was holding in my hand. What can this unfamiliar object be, I remember thinking. The cobwebs gradually cleared from my head, and I went across to the galley.

The *Bonnie* was still rearing and pushing as we set more sail, but the vicious side twists and the sudden slides were absent. Thank goodness the storm was finally easing. Katherine had managed some sleep as well and looked much fresher than the night before.

In answer to my query, she said that Harris hadn't yet been down, so I took two mugs of coffee and made for the bridge deck. He was already there and even thanked me for the coffee. The clouds were breaking now, streaking along as they changed shapes in the early light. To port, the horizon was lined with light as the clouds lifted out of the sea. The wind roared in the rigging but with a lower note, as the sea rose and fell in glistening mountains as far as the eye could see. Boris had been busy during the night, setting more sail so that we continued our north-westerly course at about twelve knots. Taking the helm by myself, I could feel the difference in the ship. It was taking the sea smoothly without all the savage pounding of the past two days. It was still stormy, but the fight had gone out of the weather, and it was now a minor hindrance rather than a hostile force. We were making good time and were steady on course.

"With the storm blowing over like this, it'll take time to die down in the east." I said to Harris. "The MTB might try to get out from Dover this afternoon, and I think he'll travel due west for a while before carrying on the search pattern. He must be a very confused captain, with an unexplained radio message, no sightings reported, and the whole of the Channel to search."

Meanwhile, we were nearly in position to come about on the other tack. The wind was giving no signs of changing, but we had to stay well clear of the coast to avoid a possible sighting. Changing tack on any sailing ship is always fraught with danger. As you set the helm hard over, you're asking the sails to pull the head round. This means being ready with part of the deck crew to brace the yards round using the capstan and the remaining crew to haul down and let out the buntlines on the sails on the yards. Once the helmsman feels the ship responding, he can order the rest of the yards braced and the sails close-hauled. Only then can he relax, while the crew carries on coiling down.

With the wind steady and the sea quieter, the change went more smoothly than we had expected. We were heading sou'sou'west and watching for the wind to back through north as the storm moved over. I just was thinking it was time to be relieved when Edward put his head out the chart room door to shout that Richard was trying to get through.

I shot down to the galley, found Robert and Larry, and chivied them up to the wheel within seconds. Harris and I got ourselves comfortable in front of the radio, together with Bowman. Edward finished greeting Richard and handed the handset to Harris.

"Hello there, Richard," he began, "we missed you yesterday, so I hope all's well with you."

"*Hello, Harris. I'm sorry I didn't get through, but I expect you heard from Martin that the weather hit everything here too. It was difficult to get around, and I needed to see people to check on stories…Anyway, I decided it was better to call this morning with news from my Whitehall friend that the MTB was still confined to harbour in Dover. He said the commander called off his search because of a message that came from you just west of the Straits. How did you manage that? I'm sure you're much further west.*"

"Unfortunately that's a state secret just now and won't be for publication even when I can tell you," Harris replied, laughing. "I'm sorry, but I know the mystery man won't care to let his name be known."

"*You sailors! Sometimes I envy you the assistance you can call on freely given. We landlubbers have a lot to learn from it. The MTB in Dover had strict instructions not to risk his boat, but to get out as soon as he can. According to the latest shipping forecast, I suppose he'll move some time this afternoon.*"

"That's our reckoning too," Harris said, "and it would be nice to know if he carries on with the same search pattern. We also think they'll start using spotter planes again. Just before the storm closed in, the one from near Swindon skimmed near, but didn't see us. Not surprising considering the amount of whitecaps at the time. Has your friend mentioned that they may use another patrol boat based in Plymouth or Cardiff?"

"Not yet," Richard replied, *"but you know better than I that the chances of you being spotted will go up as the storm dies. Forget about spotter planes, it's more apt to be a ferry or freighter that sees you, since they've been told you're suspected of various crimes and they should report your position immediately. On a positive note is the publicity you have so far, including regular mention on the BBC. I'm counting on your seamen's fraternity that not many will report. I'll sound out my friend about MTB stations still operational."*

"Thanks, Richard, you're a great help, and we really do appreciate it. Don't forget, we're ready to answer any and all questions you have. Before that, we have some matters we need to discuss with you. Last night, Captain Bowman, Flynn, and I had a long talk, because we're worried about what will happen when we get to the end of this voyage. Reading plain facts, anyone would think we were just a bunch of crooks, stealing this and that, abducting boys, and maybe a young lady. Why, it's every good citizen's duty to hunt us down."

Richard cut in quickly, *"A lot of that has already been countered by the newspaper reports. Many, many people are on your side."*

"We understand that, thanks to you," Harris continued. "No, our worry is deeper because we know we've bent the noses of some self-important Whitehall officials who are now so personally embarrassed that we think they'll stop at nothing to get us. We need to protect ourselves even further by getting more detail into the papers. What worries us most is the consequences of our taking the boys from the orphanage to be our crew. At the time, it seemed a way of giving them a better life, but having to do it secretly spoilt the effect. We heard from Martin that O'Connell has been exposed for a cheat and embezzler. It's only a matter of time before he's charged. We think if we can get certain information published before then, we'll have a better chance in any court case against us, but we may be completely wrong in our conclusions. Martin has a good friend who used to work at *The Times*, and has contacts in the departments of government subsidies and social welfare. He thinks *The Times* might support an investigation into lax government methods. The story would come out of how O'Connell was appointed guardian in the first place, and how—"

"*No need to go on,*" Richard said in a cheery voice. "*I get what you're driving at. I'll talk to my boss to see if he cares to get involved in what could be a very dirty saga of Whitehall types running for cover and knifing all and sundry as they go. He could finish up with a few enemies that way.* The Times *is seen as an upholder of good government. If he opts for trying to interest* The Times, *I'll phone Martin and have him introduce me to his man. Don't worry, the very worst they can get you for is sailing away without permission, especially after they interview the boys. What else did you discuss?*"

"A small matter of stealing about two thousand pounds worth of canvas," Bowman called out.

Harris interrupted, "You can hear the captain is a bit touchy on the subject, but we wanted to emphasise that we took the tents because we couldn't find any other source of canvas. Just make sure you give our apologies to the owners. But I'm not going to apologise about the bear. I'm quite sure it would have died because of their negligence."

Richard replied, "*I suppose a headline in the paper is better than a small ad. I'll see what I can do. Anything else?*"

"One small thing which we nearly overlooked," Harris laughed. "Only a matter of the ship! If your legal boys like that one, they might look up some points about endangering a ship at sea. I just assumed that the tug captain would have got entry to a harbour anywhere once it got dark instead of heaving to. I suppose he was just too embarrassed, the idiot!"

"*Well, I can be a witness as to that,*" Richard said. "*My advice is not to worry. When you get to Dumbarton, the police are going to have a hard time if they decide to make arrests. I hear the whole town is talking. I've been speaking to the shipbuilders there who say they support you all the way. Hopefully, public opinion will let them speak out in the next day or two, although unfortunately they do depend a lot on government contracts.*"

"It's good to know that people are hearing and supporting us," nodded Harris. "Speaking of shipbuilders, please pass a message to Mr. Reith that we understand and are sorry to have put him into an awkward position. Is there anything you want to know just now?"

"*I want to get started on the legal questions,*" said Richard. "*By the way, how is the storm?*"

"There are signs that it's breaking up," Harris answered. "We've still got strong winds, but the sea has eased a bit. If there isn't anything else, we'd better get ourselves back on deck, and will look forward to your next call."

"*Right,*" Richard said. "*I'll get busy and let you know what I find out. Look after yourselves. Bye for now,*" and he cut the connection.

Bowman said, "He seems hopeful, which I take as a good sign. But see how ye can hurt people and their businesses when ye don't think the whole thing through properly. I wish I'd given Mr. Reith a call." He stood up with some difficulty, struggling against the pitching of the ship, and slowly made his way to his cabin.

Harris and I left, but before we could get the door to the bridge deck open there came a most eerie tortured noise, a crashing sound of splintering wood and twisting metal that finished with a great thud from the fo'c's'le head.

"Hell and damnation, that's a yardarm!" Harris shouted as he hustled through the door with me running right behind him.

The ship had already lost her bounce, and her head was weaving as Larry and Robert fought to hold her steady. Harris raced across the well deck to where a small figure lay crumpled and another sat leaning against number one hatch. Above them a huge shape rose from the fo'c's'le head deck into the air, the other twisted end swaying and banging against the foremast. The lower topsail yardarm had broken in two. One half still held level by the track in the mast and the brace rope from the upper topsail yard, while the other half was held precariously in place by tattered rigging and twisted sail. Confusion was everywhere as boys ran back and forth. Little could be heard above the wind and the flapping of the sails. There was a small centre of order where Boris stood giving out instructions and passing lines to different crew members.

As I got there, everyone seemed to be working to lower a huge piece of sail to the deck. I looked up to see one boy working his way out along the broken yard, releasing the head ropes. Boris pointed towards me, signalling that the dangling part of the yard was to be hauled tight in and lashed to the mast. There are times when no matter what language is spoken, no words are necessary. As I hauled on the line Boris had thrown to me, I saw Harris carefully pick up the fallen boy and head for the chart room, while Larry helped the other one to follow. More boys joined me on the rope Boris had thrown me and, having taken many turns around the broken yard, we eventually felt assured that it wouldn't fall and puncture the deck below.

The torn sail was lowered to the deck and was being replaced with another hoisted up to the empty fore upper topgallant yard. This required a good deal of impromptu rigging in the dark and against the wind with several crew members helping Boris. Remarkably, everyone seemed to know exactly what they were doing and the rest took instruction without question.

At last the gantline was fixed to the centre of the sail, and together with some of the boys, I walked the capstan to raise it to the yardarm, where it was attached to the stayrail while others on deck hauled on the buntlines to prevent it flying out of control. Somehow the emergency had brought out all the strength and knowledge in our bodies and minds just when they were needed, and the new sail was in place and working within an hour of the breaking. Having taken on one problem, Boris was thinking of the next several to follow. Although it never came up on the journey, I was certain he must have been a formidable chess opponent being able to calculate things far in advance.

Looking at the port side of the broken yard, Boris decided that it could stay in place until the storm had gone. Having it securely lashed to the mast ensured that it would hold for the time being.

Finally the bo'sun's pipe signalled everyone to stand down, and I headed for the chart room to see about the casualties. To my relief, both boys were awake and talking with the others who had crowded in. One, however, was still lying on the chart table while Harris and Katherine dealt with the grazes and cuts on his arm and leg. Edward told me that the boy had lain unconscious for about fifteen minutes. With his over-bright eyes and rambling talk, he could still be suffering from a concussion.

At last the bandaging was done and Harris gave the patient two pills labelled For Sleep. Then, despite his protests, Harris picked him up and carried him to the fo'c's'le. Harris sent one of the others to get a couple of extra blankets. He told Larry, "The boy's still in shock and must be kept warm. Stay with him until he falls asleep, and make sure someone wakes him every so often and keeps him covered up."

I then sent everyone off on his duties and went down with Katherine to get coffee for me and Harris, which I carried back to the chart room. He took quite some time to get back, and I was just about to go find him, when he came in and sat down heavily in the other chair. He looked shaken, with a white face and a fine sweat on his forehead. I reached into his coat pocket for his flask and poured a generous tot into his coffee, then handed it to him. He gulped down half in one swallow, and his colour came back to his face and his eyes seemed to focus once more.

"What happened to you?" I asked in concern. "Delayed shock?"

"No," he replied, his face twisted in grief. "It's the shock I got just now. I wondered why Uncle Billy hadn't come out when the yard crashed, so I went to his cabin. As I got there, he was opening the door to his cabin and asked me where the young lad in the white uniform was. You know, the one he says brings him tea?"

"Yes I've heard him say that before, as you know." I said.

"This is the first time he asked me. It was as if I wasn't there, if you know what I mean." Harris darkened, "Then he took my arm and guided me into the cabin. Now, this is the scary part. He took me over to his desk and said, 'Look, there's my tea.' But there was nothing. Oh, Uncle Billy! I don't know what's going on."

After a moment Harris continued quietly, "After that he sat back in his chair, closed his eyes, and went to sleep. We must keep a close watch on him, but without his knowledge. He would never warm to the idea, so try not to notice. Any time he looks frail or tired please speak to me first."

I promised, and reminded Harris that we'd discussed all this before. I was concerned at the thought of Bowman becoming mentally unhinged. This was hard to imagine, since he seemed the toughest person I'd ever met that first day I came aboard ship. We finished our coffee in silence. Harris finally spoke up in his usual booming voice.

"Come on then, let's go see what we're going to do with this broken yardarm."

Outside, the storm was definitely on its way out. The clouds had now broken and blue sky could be seen. The wind had veered to the north, as the waves began a long swelling march to the horizon all round with hardly a whitecap to be seen. Boris had been able to follow the wind by furling the sails on the foremast in order to avoid strain on the broken yardarm still aloft.

"What a mess," Harris groaned in disgust, "what a bloody mess! Both parts are a danger, both on board or overboard, but they must come down somehow. But where the hell am I going to put them?"

Lads were crowding round the foremast where Boris was organising the lowering of the giant half yardarm that had been lashed to the mast. Harris and I went to survey this, both making mental calculations.

"You know," I said, "the whole yard is about sixty feet long, so half will be about thirty." Harris was about to comment but I went on. "This bridge deck must be at least sixty feet long and there's space on each side of the upper part of the deckhouse."

Harris remarked, "How are we to move both parts from the forepeak deck to here? There are winches and hatches all down the well deck, plus getting it over the bulkheads at each end. For that we need Boris—he's the genius with the rigging, pulleys, and braces. This is a stonking great thing and must be handled with the greatest caution."

He was about to go over after him when I said, "Here, let me go while you have a look around here and clear anything moveable out of the way. I'll send up a couple of the boys to help you." I wanted to have a quiet word with Boris out of everyone's hearing so we could talk in proper English, instead of trying to get it all done in his affected broken pidgin.

Taking Boris to one side, I asked him to hold operations for a minute, as Harris and I had a plan. As I presented our idea, his whole concentration went into the problem. He began to prowl up and down the deck, looking up at the yards, touching lines, and going over the capstans and Jarvis winches. When he returned, he said in plain English, "It can be done, but I will have to rig up extra pulleys and lines, and then attach the Jarvis braces, as they can really only take the weight of half the yardarm. It's going to be hard work. Everyone will have to listen carefully and follow my instructions. I will explain so everyone understands. For this I will show people I can understand good English, but knowing and speaking are difficult. I will tell everybody everything so good so nobody will have to pretend to be the interpreter of my bad speaking. Understanding and speaking are not the same," he repeated, to make certain I understood.

"I think it best that you advise Harris of your plans to avoid any confusion that may arise," I responded.

"Now you understand! Is good, yes?" he smiled.

"Yes, is good." I answered.

Boris slapped my knee, "Your English is getting worse!" He laughed at me.

A thought struck me. "Speaking of languages, what does *mudak* mean?" He paused momentarily, looking about as if he wished no one to overhear a top-secret revelation.

"Is like calling someone gigantic arse," he confided, and we both had a good laugh.

Leaving him to get on with setting up, I went back to Harris and found the bridge swept clean of everything not bolted down. I told him what Boris suggested, and he commented, "I've measured the length, and it's just sixty feet inside the rails. The gaps down the sides of the deckhouse are only five feet wide so it's going to be a squeeze. The pieces can't be allowed to swing the least bit. That steel must be well secured." Boris came up just then and Harris repeated what he'd said. Boris waved a hand dismissively.

"No worry, plenty boys hold sides and I can move."

This task seemed impossible, but by using some steel cable, Boris rigged a ropeway from the foremast to the mainmast at the level of the broken yard. Meanwhile a team of boys managed to clear away all the broken lines and stays. They stood waiting while the lashing was untied from the half-yard and attached firmly at its centre by a wire rope from the Jarvis brace. The load was then lifted to the wire ropeway and pulled gently by its rope tether over the top of the deck, until it came to the mainmast. There the second Jarvis winch was attached, and the half-yard was lowered slowly until it could be seized on by boys who started to guide it down one side of the deckhouse. It was hellish heavy. Then another and another, all the time keeping the load level and gently pushing it along at the end of the carrying rope from the Jarvis brace. A cheer went up as the first half gently hit the deck with a clanking of steel.

The second half-yard still in place on the mast was now unshackled. The steel was torn badly as it swung round slowly on the Jarvis brace. The half-yard began its aerial journey to be brought down. Half way, everyone stopped breathing as it billowed up and started to go wonky. Then it evened out and came safely to rest on the other side of the deckhouse. This may have sounded easy, but one slip and the huge weight could have smashed through a few decks and injured many! This could have been a real disaster from which we could not recover.

Harris said to Boris, "you outdid yourself this time, you crazy Russian," and grasped his hand to shake it. Boris quickly snatched it away.

"Not in front of others!" he cried and shook the affected hand vigorously, blowing on it with an expression of terrible suffering on his face. The boys laughed and shook their own hands in imitation, the tension of the last two or three hours exploding out in a maniac few minutes of hysteria.

We were lucky to finish the job before night fell. Everyone trooped off for a well-earned meal and the chance for those off watch to sleep. Harris and I found ourselves at the wheel once more, but he said it seemed unnecessary to have two men on the wheel now.

"You should see your beauty and get your beauty sleep," he said with a leering expression. I was only too happy to get off the deck. I looked up at the sky before I went, seeing the last of the boys flying down the shrouds after they'd finished setting the full display of sails. The wind was now holding steady and we were clipping along due west, bound for Land's End.

Chapter 27
RUNNING HER HOME

It was the end of a long and tiring day as I went below. The smell of warm food from the galley revived me and reminded me that I'd not seen my Katherine for some time. Not only had she prepared dinner, but there was also freshly baked bread. How she was able to manage all this was beyond me. Eating meals proved less difficult, as we could now use both hands at table instead of holding on with one to keep our seats.

I gave her a hug and took my food to the wardroom. There was a small group consisting of Harris, Boris, and Edward. Bowman arrived looking rested, and more like his old self. "Good evening, gentlemen, and I use the term loosely," he said with a grin. "What further troubles are we to review this night?"

Harris and I exchanged relieved glances at his hearty manner.

"The yardarm has been lowered and stowed," said Harris. Bowman told us he had been watching this from the bridge.

"My jaw dropped a few times, but I couldn't find appropriate words," Bowman confided.

"Now there's something ye seldom hear..." Edward's words were cut short by a kick from Harris under the table.

Edward changed the subject, saying the radio started broadcasting a message on many frequencies, telling us to surrender. He thought it came from the MTB. Knowing that we were being warned to put into the nearest port or face further penalties made us feel that we'd really done something wrong.

The others were looking solemn, but not Bowman. "I think we'll have a little game with them later, but let's eat first," he chuckled.

"I agree," Harris boomed. "To hell with the bastards! Dinner's on the table, and we'll wait until we get to Dumbarton before we pay them any mind. We've let this take up too much of our thoughts and nothing can be done about it now!"

We all brightened at his comments. Although the odd law had been broken, none of us cared to pay the penalty. With Harris to lead us into battle, we could put it into our minds that at least we wouldn't have to pay so very much.

Once we'd eaten, Bowman led us to the chart room, where sure enough, the radio was still repeating itself. I pitied the poor operator having to sit there, saying the same things over and over again. Bowman took the handset and, without further ado, started to speak Scots Gaelic. He spoke the ancient words proudly, but at the same time kept grinning to himself. He paused for a moment and the speaker immediately came back with the same language. Bowman jumped as if someone had hit him on the head.

Clicking off the handset, Bowman shouted, "The bloody heathens know the language! Well, I've got two better than that," and he handed the set to Edward. "Ned, read them the weather—in Irish Gaelic."

Edward put on his best BBC voice, which I didn't even know he had, and started to hold forth in the lilting auld tongue of which I understood not a syllable. For aught I knew, he could have been reciting some horribly grisly story. Whatever the text, he was enjoying this immensely and sniggered quietly to himself.

After a bit Bowman said, "Well done Ned, now we'll really confuse them." He then turned to Boris and asked him to tell them whatever he liked—in Russian.

"Speaking language?" he asked with a devilish look in his eye. Warming to his task, he rolled his R's extravagantly and made sweeping gestures to punctuate his oratory. Whatever he was saying, it was certainly expressive, and at the end of it he made a formal bow and added, "Doh svidanya," grinning broadly.

He clicked off and there was silence except for faint yowlings and squawks. Before the same message started over again, a voice yelled, "*Now, Sparks, just what bloody wavelength are you on?*" in a voice to wake the dead. We all had a good laugh as we trooped back to the wardroom.

Bowman asked Boris what he'd said, and he laughed. "Is good borscht recipe. I tell them eat and be happy. Doh svidanya is Russian for goodbye!"

Once the laughter died down, I mentioned something that had been troubling me for a good while.

"We're now somewhere near Lizard Point, well to the south to keep out of the way of that treacherous coastline. As far as we know the MTB will resume its search tomorrow morning, since it's too late now to come and start looking. By tomorrow morning we'll be round Land's End and about four hundred miles away from Dover. Even if the MTB could do it, I don't think his engines would allow it. If they travelled at maximum speed, it would take her a good twelve hours to reach our present position and we'll have been long gone. The real sailors in Whitehall are going to work that out as well, and my guess is they'll have another MTB based at Plymouth, which they'll use instead of the one at Dover. With the storm over, all ships will be on the move, and in fact, they'll have already come out from wherever they sheltered. Once it's dark we could be anyone to a passing ship, except that we need a masthead light as well as port and starboard riding lights going."

Harris swore under his breath and went out shouting, "Boris, Boris," at the top of his voice.

I waited till he came back and then put my idea forward. I opened up a chart and spread it on the table.

"I know we'll be spotted sooner or later, so I'm suggesting we could bring the odds in our favour by not heading due north when we round Land's End." I pointed to the chart. "Instead, let's take a course north-west aiming at the Irish coast somewhere between Cork and Wexford. With luck we should miss any ships on their way due south that will be crossing in a straight line between St. David's Head and Land's End. Ships from Glasgow, Belfast, Dublin, and Liverpool will all be using that route."

Again pointing at the map, I ran my finger up along the Irish coast from Cork to Wicklow and paused there. "If we keep below the horizon of other ships along the coast, I should think we wouldn't be spotted until we get here," and I tapped the map at Wicklow. There was a bit of silence, and then Edward stood and leant over the chart, pulling some crumpled notepapers from his pockets until he found the one he wanted. Taking out his reading glasses, he put them on, looked at his notes, and looked over the chart.

"We've just cleared Lizard Point, the graveyard for many a sailing vessel." Edward said solemnly. He spent a few moments recounting some of the disasters that had happened there. "When we go round Land's End, we'll slowly turn due north up through St. George's Channel, my old sailing grounds of the Irish Sea. I'll grant that the chances of us being spotted are almost a certainty. We'll be passing very close to Land's End Light Station. If we're to be discovered, that'll be the place, even at night and with a masthead light. They'll report a ship that doesn't steer a straight course and someone is going to read that report before morning and guess why the ship didn't steer straight, like a steamer. We were very lucky reaching the end of the Channel. But I say let's head straight north as fast as the *Bonnie* will pull all night. This will be the most crucial part of our journey, and we'll need to sail as close to the wind as possible," he cackled and looked at Harris, who just stared at me.

Again there was a silence until Bowman spoke up, "I suppose I'll be having to make the decision. I like both ideas, but I especially like the idea of getting to the end as quickly as possible." He gave an odd smile and continued, "So I suggest a bit of a compromise." Using a knife, he etched a line from north of the Scilly Isles, to midway between Rosslare and Fishguard, and then up between Dublin and Holyhead. "This way we'll be trying to stay out of sight, but not being too cautious." He gave a laugh. "If we had some train timetables, we could probably stay out of sight of the Fishguard and Holyhead ferries too. I think we'll do this without riding lamps. If we get round unseen, so much the better, but be sure we post lookouts."

"Right," Harris agreed. "You've heard the captain. We should be having a fairly quiet night, so those off watch had better get some sleep while they can. Edward, you'll need to work out the course changes, so make them as quick as you can. Give them to Flynn who's about to take the wheel."

I went up on deck while waiting for Edward's new courses. The clouds were scattered now, and there was a small crescent moon touching their edges with silver. Stars could be seen dimly and the wind was a strong breeze coming easterly. Boris had managed to rig us a masthead light and it was quite bright, though I couldn't imagine where he'd got the material to make a better reflector. Far off the starboard bow I could see a light twinkling low on the horizon. I reckoned this must be the Land's End light.

Edward had come out with his new course calculations and confirmed this. "Indeed it is lad, and you must keep it like that as you steer due west. Only when it's out of sight will you steer north, just as I've written it on the paper," and off he went in his usual shambling walk.

I was glad he was still talking to me, as I'd gone over his head at the impromptu discussion. Still, Bowman had become quite the Solomon in that meeting, because Edward and I accepted the compromise without argument.

I went up to the wheel to relieve Robert. He and I always seemed to be missing each other, but we made a tentative date for early morning fishing for the bear. I told him about the latest developments on the pursuit front. He was about to make a point, when Harris came on deck and I showed him the course corrections.

Robert was anxious to make his point and carried on, "If I were with the Admiralty, I'd be trying to make out how I'd proceed if I did overtake this ship and board her. I could arrest everyone, or I could try to tow her. But for my money, if they finally do catch us up, they'll simply make threatening noises and effectively *escort* us to Dumbarton. But

I'm no thinker, so I'll say good night to you both and go get some shut-eye," and turning around, he went quickly below.

I started to laugh, as Harris rolled his eyes. "Flynn, didn't you and Uncle Billy already have that conversation with me, or do you two have a conspiracy of thoughts?"

"Yes, you know we did," I said, "but Robert wasn't present. This confirms what I was thinking."

Harris was quiet, leaning against the rail behind me. Steering was a joy now. The ship seemed to skip the waves effortlessly. The smack of the bow into the water brought a wave level with the rail to catch the moonlight.

Harris cleared his throat, "I expect you and Robert are right. I care very much about reaching Dumbarton. Bowman sees that as the final worthwhile achievement in his life and has worked for months to achieve this goal. What you're seeing now is the real Bowman. That heart of his is really playing him about, and again just now, he was wandering." Harris's voice was shaking as he went on, "He's been like a father to me ever since I came to sea at the age of fourteen, about thirty years ago, and I don't know what it would be like if he weren't there to fight or cheer at the end of each day. I expect him to snap out of it as he usually does, but it's frightening to have it now going on longer than it ever has. He looked like himself during that chat, and a good compromise was made without fuss."

He was silent and I had nothing to say that could have helped him. After a while he sighed and grumbled. "This won't get the baby bathed," and off below he went.

For the first time I was alone on deck. It was exhilarating to feel the power of the wind and hold the course with the sails set close-hauled, as we headed out towards the Scilly Isles. I felt part of the ship, bending and turning to her every movement.

A voiced whispered softly behind me, "Flynn, you're almost dancing there."

Katherine stepped up to my back and put her arms round my waist. We stood like that for a sweet while, absorbing the peace of the moment and the lack of stress, just thankful to be together. After a little, I explained about the course to follow and showed her the binnacle.

"What a perfect night," she said softly. "This is something for us to remember always. I'm sure we'll never again have the opportunity to sail in a barque and hear the sound of the sea and wind as it is here. In a steamer, all you can hear is the engine and smell that horrible oil."

I pressed her hands against me, trying not to break the spell. "From tomorrow until we dock, life is going to be hectic and I think unpleasant, so we need tonight to prepare ourselves. I keep thinking of our future and wishing I knew how it would be. It would be nice if I could find a job on an inter-island ferry in the north of Scotland, or find a neglected schooner that I could refit as a charter boat for fishing or holidays. We could work together. You could be the cook and I would be captain and crew. When we had no customers, we'd live on the boat."

I was really just weaving dreams, but Katherine came round to face me and spoke up, "Not likely! This voyage has taught me what the sea can be, and I think I'll always be respectful of it, but I'm giving notice to everyone that I'll no longer keep this occupation upon reaching our destination." She then smiled. "The idea of being free to move where and when we like, meeting new people and seeing new places is intriguing, but I'll be more than glad to be on dry land again. Later when we're a bit more settled, I'm sure it'll seem worlds better not to be venturing abroad again." She paused with a little gasp of laughter.

"If I go on like this we'll be old before you know it!" and she threw out her arms. "It feels so good to make plans like this and think of a future that truly is possible. These last seven years have been filled with so much misery and hopelessness that this is like being an eighteen-year-old again." She put her arms around me and kissed me hard enough to make the compass spin. I nearly lost the head and the sails started to flap, but since the dear old *Bonnie Clyde* was also locked into our dream, she came back on course without effort.

"Young lady, you're *dangerous* company," a voice rumbled from behind us as Harris came up from below. "It's about the end of your shift, Flynn, so why don't you go and watch the flowers grow or something *off* the poop deck. I'll see to our course correction. Anyway, you're in no fit state to get it right," and giving me a push, he took over the wheel.

Instead of heading aft, I took Katherine's hand and we went forward. Now the swoop of the bowsprit was slower and more majestic as the bow split the sea, throwing spray no higher than the rail. I showed her how all the sails lined up parallel down the length of the ship and how they bellied out, all set to catch the maximum wind. In the light of the waning moon, they glowed a little, standing solid like tall grey trees. We came down from the forepeak and walked slowly along the well deck. Katherine suddenly looked about in a puzzled fashion, sniffing, and remarked, "That's an odd smell."

I had a premonition of what we'd see next, so I said to her, "Don't be alarmed, he's really very tame." The next moment, a big lumbering shape came waddling round the covered hatch, followed by Boris. After the successive storms and just after our change of course, the bear escaped once more from the hold onto the deck and there'd been no opportunity to take him back down. Since he was so tame, there was no worry, but Harris made a point of having Boris keeping an eye on him. At first Katherine got behind me when the shaggy beast came closer. He stopped as well, and twisted his head from side to side, sniffing loudly.

Boris said, "New smell, must know you," and he spoke in Russian to the bear. While scratching its head and ears, he held out his hand to Katherine and beckoned her to come forward. She was hesitant, but eventually, leaning far forward, she quickly stroked its nose and drew back.

"No good," Boris said, "must give him time."

She went forward again and held out her hand for the bear to sniff, then let him sniff at her feet and at the hem of her dress. All the while he rumbled in his throat, and now he gave a sharp snort and nuzzled up to her. She began to smile, scratching behind his ears, and then held him under his chin to say hello while he peered at her with his short-sighted eyes.

How Boris had got him to walk with him around on deck I didn't know. The bear wouldn't be able to stay in the midst of the rushing boys as they braced yards or hauled down on lines, unless he was on top of the number one hatch cover. It was small but easily climbable and wasn't used for anything besides the cork life rafts.

I said to Boris, "It's seems a pity to leave him below now that you've got him up here. Why not have a word with Harris about keeping him up here?" I explained about the hatch cover. "We've only got a couple more days of sailing, and even if it gets rough, you should be able to make him some sort of safety harness."

Boris looked thoughtful. "I think about it," he said, and prodded at the bear to carry on walking. Although large waves would occasionally break across the deck surface, Brown Bear seemed surprisingly placid as we streamed along, running with all possible sails in place. He never did understand why the water washing over the deck always tasted so bad.

As Boris was passing, I started to tell him about our new course, but he said he was just too tired to be bothered at present and was going off to get some sleep.

"Aren't you interested in our current position?" I asked.

"Why? This will change nothing. Boris will sleep tonight. Wherever we are is where we will be," he said with a yawn. There was certainly no arguing with that logic.

"Well now," Katherine exclaimed, "I can see now why that reporter said we have everything. I sometimes think that all men must be crazy, because they do such crazy things. Here's a problem of getting an old ship from the Thames to the Clyde, and you bring along a huge brown bear for the ride. But men need feeding, and if I don't get some sleep, there won't be any breakfast." We took our last look up at the sky, nearly cloudless and star-filled, before making our way down to our cabin.

Outside her door, I gave a look in both directions before I slid it open and then closed it behind me. There was a small light given off by a trimmed wick turned low. Katherine chuckled in amusement.

"Don't worry. Mrs. Beasley would never look for us here," she said, and we both laughed. "Tired?" she asked.

"Extremely," I replied.

"Well, I don't mean to be pushy, but if you're sleeping here, get undressed and keep me warm," she ordered. I hesitated momentarily, but only momentarily. Then I quickly pulled off my clothes and fled under the covers.

She hastily joined me. "You're freezing!" protested the owner of the warm soft body now shrinking from me.

"I'm sorry, but I haven't been warm all day," I sighed, giving a shiver for emphasis. Katherine chafed my frigid feet with hers impatiently. I wouldn't have blamed her if she shoved me out, but to my surprise she drew near again and kissed my icy lips.

"Cuddle up, I've been looking forward to this all day," she whispered. I needed no further encouragement, and wrapped my arms about her snugly.

"Oh, Flynn, what will we do when we arrive there?" she asked sounding concerned.

"I just want to make you happy," I said, "but I've been worried about making sure everything would work out."

"Aren't we a pair?" she laughed again. "Each of us worrying about the other's feelings while both sharing them. What would you like to do when we arrive?" she asked.

"As long as we're together, it matters little. I'm sure I can get work enough to keep us comfortable, and I've saved most of what I made at the inn. And I never used my ration slips while I was there and have over a month's worth." I said. There was so much I wanted to say, but where to begin? "Katherine?" I whispered.

"Yes?" she said.

"You needn't feel under any pressure this moment," I began, "but I don't want to continue hiding, looking out the door before exiting or wondering what people might be thinking forever." I paused. "Am I making any sense?"

"Of course," she answered. I put my hand on her shoulder and pushed it back so that we were looking at each other.

"At the risk of sounding entirely insecure about this, I've never even been engaged before—but more than anything else in this world, I'd like you to be my wife." There, I've done it! It's now been said and out in the open. We were definitely going in that direction anyway, but I'd never formally proposed. I wanted my intentions to be very clear! My heart was beating uncontrollably and I felt a large lump developing in my throat, about the size of a football. Katherine hugged me tighter. I thought she was beginning to cry. Perhaps my remarks came too early. Her silence was making me nervous.

"Oh, Flynn, I'd like that very much," came her soft reply. "I'd like to be your missus, Flynn."

"You mean yes?" I asked again.

"That's a yes, you dull-witted tarry sailor. Just in case you forgot, my reasons for coming were not just to relocate myself, you know," she said, hugging me closer. Moments passed without either of us saying a word. All communication was with hands and fingertips as I stroked her hair, her dear face, her warm skin.

"You know, your timing is terrible," she laughed.

"And why's that," I asked.

"Because if you think either of us is going to get very much sleep tonight after all this, you're quite daft!" She was half weeping and I could only hold her, realising that a dream long thought about was at last coming to pass, regardless of my bad timing and terrible wording. We lay there in each other's arms for what seemed like an eternity. All else seemed meaningless.

Every couple remembers that magic moment of proposal. What was said, where they were, and sometimes even what they were wearing at the time. Unfortunately, this magic moment was broken by the shrill sound of the bo'sun's pipe calling all hands to stations. The timing couldn't have been more dreadful, as Katherine had said earlier.

I apologised as I made a mad dash about the compartment, gathering my clothing and pulling on my boots. "Someday, I'll make this up to you," I promised.

Without changing her voice she replied, "I intend to see to it!" With one further kiss, I ran to the door and down the passageway and climbed the ladder to the deck.

"What kept you?" Harris asked testily.

"I was being flung about trying to get my britches on," I responded.

"Leave em' somewhere, did ye?" Bowman asked with studied blandness.

"I won't dignify that with a reply," I said coldly, giving Bowman a sour look. "Nice to see you on deck again," I added, to change the subject.

"By the way, the rain and raging seas over the deck completely saturated your room. The waves made it into a virtual shower, or hadn't you noticed?" Harris taunted.

"Actually I did notice," I replied casually.

"Well, if I may enquire, where do you currently reside?" he asked.

"I still have my hammock, and no, you may not enquire," I replied.

"I see. Well, silence speaks volumes, you know. It won't be long till the library is full, eh? And what do you suppose the *men* might think regarding that," teased Harris as though going back to my comments about the lads drinking.

"Well, if anyone is really curious, we happen to be officially engaged," I said, letting a modest note of triumph creep into my voice.

"Well, well, well. I suppose congratulations are in order," Bowman grinned.

Harris raised his eyebrows. "It was only a matter of time," he shrugged and stood smiling.

"Oh, of course. I'd forgotten you know everything, you great wazzock. So why the call for all hands?" I asked, removing my scarf.

"False alarm," Harris said. "Everybody else has been told to stand down."

"But now that you're here," Bowman began, "give me a hand forward. I want another look at the jibs." Harris glanced up at me quickly and motioned for me to stay close to the old man, so the two of us duly made the trip forward to the jibs. After a long study of their setting, Bowman was satisfied that everything was fine, and we walked back to the wheel.

I went below again, but this time I didn't knock on the door or even care if anyone saw. I merely slid back the panel and stepped in. Katherine was just dressing.

"How did it go?" she asked, trying to keep her balance.

"False alarm for once, and I'm very glad there was nothing more to it," I said breathing a sigh of relief. "I say, you're up early."

"Yes, every morning. There's bread to be baked and breakfast to get ready," she pouted wearily.

I gave her a hug. "I told Harris and Bowman about our engagement."

"Did you now? As if they hadn't thought that was liable to happen!"

"Harris asked where my quarters were now, but before he could talk of improprieties, I set him straight."

Katherine rolled her eyes, "I've heard stories about Harris. Himself is hardly one to speak of improprieties! A lady or two in every port I've been told."

"Now that you're off to your duties, I'll get some sleep," I said.

She gave me a sleepy smile and kissed me before slipping off to the galley with a whisper, "Good night, love."

I found myself humming a song and trying to remember the words: Good night sweetheart, see you in the morning. Good night sweetheart, happy days are dawning...till I began forgetting the words and fell asleep.

Chapter 28
SIGHTING THE BONNIE

Early next morning, I awoke to the sound of the bo'sun's pipe and the rush of feet on the deck. The course was set to take us on the long haul up into St. George's Channel. Lying awake in bed, I thought that life seemed fine and uncluttered. All that vanished when I jumped out shivering to face the day.

After the deafening and unceasing noise of the past few days, this was like a Sunday in the suburbs. As if on cue, the ship's bell struck and I looked to see it was 0600. The sun was rising in a clear sky and all seemed bright. I came up on deck to the bite of the easterly wind. If it kept up like this, we'd be home and dry in a day or two, but I felt in my bones that the wind was boxing the compass. The quick change from westerly to easterly meant that the wind and moisture from the Atlantic would start to pile the clouds into a threatening storm. Before that, we were sure to be spotted on this crystal clear day. Sufficient unto the day, I thought, and headed to the galley for hot tea and a morning kiss before presenting myself at the wheel for a stint.

Brown Bear was now settled on top of the main hatchway, sprawled out in the middle of the cork life rafts and enjoying the wind through his thick fur. Rumours were fast circulating that Boris's snoring had finally driven him out. The lads were no longer afraid of him, and he was enjoying life, with scraps from the galley along with the fish. Brown Bear would bury his muzzle between his paws and groan with pleasure whenever someone stopped to scratch him. I even saw Bowman stop to pat him. The old man looked relaxed and walked about normally as he enjoyed the sun.

I relieved Robert at the wheel to his chaffing, "I can't say you got any beauty sleep, Flynn, though you were long enough about it. I suppose I'm going to have to fish by myself if you're taking over here."

I forgot our fishing date, but I was sure that Robert would have plenty of willing help from the boys. Harris came up with his mug of coffee to stand and chat a while. The feeling of calm was everywhere as we continued on our course north. I think we'd all given up worrying about what was to happen when we got to the shipbuilder's yard and disembarked. We'd done something worthwhile and no one had suffered from it, except possibly the two boys who'd come down with the broken yardarm.

I asked Harris how the two injured boys were coming along, and he said, "You know youngsters, in a few hours they can bounce back from something that would kill an elephant. They're all right except for a few cuts and bruises that'll be gone within a day or two."

We were spotted at 0800 by the Fishguard ferry, which set up a series of whoops on her foghorn and changed course to run just aft of us. As she drew closer, we could see an Aldis lamp flashing from the bridge and Harris read out the message: *W-E-L-C-O-M-E B-O-N-N-I-E C-L-Y-D-E and congratulations. Will have to report sighting. My job if I don't. The whole country wants you to win.*

Boris had already brought our lamp the night before, and Harris signalled for quite a while, with a brief reply back from the ferry. By that time she'd come within fifty yards of us and early morning travellers could be seen lined up along the rails. They all seemed to be waving something; a scarf, a hat, a newspaper. I also saw one or two with cameras. We could hear faint cries as their voices were caught by the wind, but could only make out the occasional hurray or well done.

Once they'd passed, I asked Harris what he'd flashed.

He replied, "I told him that after he reported us, to please get a message through immediately to Richard. I gave him the number to call, and he flashed back *done*. As Richard says, the bond of the sea is strong. From his handling of the Aldis lamp, I'd say that captain is ex-Navy."

Edward had been out with the rest of us while the ferry came past, and then disappeared back down to the chart room. He now came back out again with a map in his hand.

"I was after looking at the possibilities of an MTB base and really, you know, the last reasonable one was Plymouth. They were built for only one job and that was to raid the European coast and coastal shipping and get back home as fast as possible. From Plymouth to here is about 250 miles, a six-hour journey for an MTB going flat out. As the engine would probably seize up, and certainly their fuel would be long gone, it's going to be much longer than six hours."

Looking at the map, I calculated that if the MTB travelled in our wake, they would be close to the Scilly Isles before they got a message of the sighting. They made raids on Cherbourg, Le Havre, and Dieppe during the war, but I'll bet they took along spare fuel. I turned to Harris. "Is the range of an MTB, say, about 300 miles at an average fifteen knots?"

"Probably a bit generous, but let's use it as a basis," he suggested.

"All right, assuming that, once they knew our exact whereabouts, the captain would have to decide where to go for fuel without going too far out of the way. Fishguard, itself, is probably a bit too chancy, so it would have to be Milford Haven, say a five-hour journey from their present position. In five hours we'd be farther north by about sixty miles, a two-hour trip for them plus say half an hour for refuelling, another thirty miles for us."

I was laughing at this as I made the calculations, and Harris and Edward were growing a bit annoyed at my merriment.

"What's so bloody funny now, Flynn?" Harris boomed. "I could do with some cheering up."

So I told them my up-to-date version of the race of the tortoise and the hare. "They might catch up with us somewhere opposite Drogheda. If we count 300 miles as their range. Milford Haven to Drogheda is about 130 miles, and it's another 180 miles to Dumbarton. The MTB will have to refuel again at some point before we dock. What's more is," and I couldn't keep the glee from my voice, "by the time they catch up it'll be between four and five this afternoon and not far off dark! You know how much they hate travelling at night!" All of us laughed in delight. We must have looked an odd sight, laughing and holding on to each other and slapping backs, but the arithmetic was so true. The story quickly spread round the ship and everyone enjoyed the joke of it. We were destined to get to Dumbarton, no matter what man or nature could throw at us.

The wind was still brisk but was getting warmer as it veered south, with clouds low on the southern horizon. We were seeing more ships now, mostly freighters, quite a distance off because of our position in mid-Channel. There were occasional flashing messages like *We are with you* or *Scots wha hae*, which brought a cheer from Bowman. It seemed to bear out our own hopes of the public on our side, ready to do battle with bureaucracy.

At one point a two-engine RAF plane flew over. It looked like the wartime observer-cum-light bomber, the Blenheim. I think it was on a training flight, for it did not come closer, but it waggled its wings as it flew on.

About two hours later Edward put his head out the chart room door and called, "Richard's coming through."

This time all the officers crowded in, leaving Larry in charge of the wheel and the deck with dire warnings of what would happen if any one of a number of happenings should occur without his warning us first. He just grinned and turned to Ted, ordering, "Look lively there, I've got the wheel."

Richard was coming through loud and clear. "*Getting spotted eventually had to happen, but it gives me a chance to scoop some good pictures. Give me your current position and heading. I've got a plane warming up in Liverpool, and the pilot is waiting for the position so that he can take off.*"

Edward quickly took the handset and read off the numbers from his chart. We could hear Richard repeating these to someone and then he came back on the air. "*The plane is painted yellow and has a big AP painted in black on the underside of the wings and fuselage. I suppose he'll be overhead in an hour and a half. Right now, have I got news for you! It seems that this story of yours has really woken up something in the soul of the average Briton and quicker than I've ever seen it. People have been writing and calling their MPs by the score, even telephoning them. Questions are tabled for tomorrow and commentators are speculating whose heads will roll. Please be careful when that MTB catches up with you, because his instructions were given to him personally by the head of my friend's department. The orders are only known to the Prime Minister and the First Sea Lord of the Admiralty! Not that I'm suggesting violence but you never can tell when politicians feel their positions threatened. Just be careful! The shipbuilder has decided he can take your side and Mr. Reith sends you his best wishes. He will be there to welcome you when you dock,* or maybe even before *were his exact words.*"

Bowman was smiling from ear to ear, feeling vindicated for his efforts. He called out, "You tell him Scots wha hae from me!"

"*Tell him yourself, you'll see him before I do!*" Richard replied. "*What next? Ah yes. I had a call from a Mr. Barnley. He's the owner of the circus. He said he was angry that he had to read about the tents in the papers. It made him feel such a fool that he hadn't known, especially in front of his wife! However, he said that to others he was able to pretend that he had a contract with you to produce a duplicate of his tents by the time he re-opens next April. He sounds the sort of fellow who will be round with a few* friends *if the* contract *is not fulfilled.*"

Richard continued, "*As regards the ship, my legal boys are divided on that one, because apparently the decisions of judges over the years haven't always agreed, but my people all concur that they think the government would be crazy to bring a prosecution, in the face of public opinion. I think that once you're on shore and we can arrange for interviews and statements in front of newsreel cameras, any undecided public opinion will quickly rally your side.*"

"Bloody hell!" Harris sputtered, seizing the handset. "You mean being on the news in the cinema?"

"*Of course!*" said Richard. "*You're going to be up to your ears in reporters and photographers, so you'd better get used to the idea. Just take the bear angle. I'm getting calls from old ladies who want to give it a good home, from zoos ditto, and the*

RSPCA, who insist that they want to examine the bear to make sure it's healthy. I'm sure you're going to love all this, and let me give you a word of advice. Anyone who comes wanting an exclusive story from any of you, only give it if you want to. Otherwise, ask money for it! Don't worry about me. I've a good contract with AP and they're quite happy with all I've done so far, and for a reporter, there's always the next story. Of course, if anyone wants you to appear in an advertisement, then he'll come to you with a contract but make sure it doesn't bind you to him exclusively for life. As for true love, I'd say you should consider running away right now because they're going to be so nosy and personal that you could easily end up hitting one or two."

We all sat looking at one another in bewilderment, overwhelmed with an idea of what the reality was going to be. All of us pictured a few days of excitement, questioning by the police, then we'd be able to get on with our lives. This was especially true for Katherine and me. We just wanted to arrange jobs, rent a house, and get married, without the whole world looking on.

Richard's voice came on again, "*Hey, are you there? My boss was sympathetic, but he said we simply don't have the influence that* The Times *has. So I got in touch with Martin's friend. He was happy to start digging up the dirt, especially as no one at* The Times *really cares for the new Labour government. That's all from my list. Anything from your side?*"

Bowman took the handset. "Richard, Bowman here. Ye've been active above and beyond the call of duty and ye've certainly set my mind at ease. It'll be a privilege to meet ye. Will ye be there in Dumbarton? We're estimating our time of arrival to be late afternoon tomorrow, provided we can get to Greenock in good time. From there, we're going to need a tug."

"*I'll certainly be there, in fact I've already booked a room because I think there's going to be a shortage,*" Richard replied. "*I'm really looking forward to meeting you, Captain Bowman, and all your crew. I feel I know you all so well that it'll be like a reunion rather than a first meeting. Now I have work to do, and then to wait for the pictures to be wired down from Liverpool once the plane gets back. The photographer says he has the finest telescopic lens available. Don't forget to smile! I'll say goodbye for now and look forward to meeting you tomorrow.*"

We called out our goodbyes and sat there in silence. Bowman was like a new man, his face alight with the satisfaction of a job well done.

Bowman pointed out, "I'll be on an inspection tour within the hour and I'll expect to see every man jack working to clean this ship up. From what I see, she's become a floating pigsty. I want her shipshape and Bristol fashion! Do I make myself clear?"

"Right," I answered.

"See to it then!" We all stood up and saluted as he marched out.

Edward sat down in his chair and said in amazement, "Well, were you seeing that? That was Bowman. He's back! And the rest of you had better mind what you're about. His temper isn't the best, and he can scorch the ears off a man at fifty paces."

And so it was when the AP plane found us. They took pictures of everything, sometimes flying just over the waves, sometimes coming straight at us, and sometimes slowly circling at masthead height, with the photographer standing up in the back seat and leaning out to get a better view.

"Boris, you'd better dig out that paint again but be careful where you put it, we want it dry before we get to Dumbarton," Harris ordered. Soon buckets and a variety of brushes, brooms, and mops were scrubbing away at the dirt and encrusted salt of years.

After the plane had left the work continued, with Bowman making periodic tours round the ship, pointing to this or that dirty brass, frayed rope or missing pins from the pin rails. Occasionally he would bellow for Harris or Boris and everyone pretended not to hear or see as he gave one or another of them a dressing-down for some neglect. Mostly he was there to give advice and encouragement. The boys started to get to know him as Captain, at times a figure to fear but always one to look up to and respect. I kept myself busy below decks helping Katherine with cleaning up the galley. I was rousted out by Harris for shirking and told to go and clean the lighthouses—the brass domes set over the navigation lights on the forepeak. This is a dirty job, and I was happy to answer a summons from Edward, who sent one of the boys to take my place.

"I've been looking at your calculation about the placement of the MTB," he started, "and it checks out. But I was thinking, why does it have to be Drogheda, especially when it'll be only an hour off dark when she catches up? What do you know about horizons?"

My mind went searching back to my apprentice days and our elementary navigation classes and out popped an answer, "An observer with his eye level at five feet above the sea will have an approximate horizon of 2.8 miles, or as near as I can remember. I can't recall anything else, except that the higher you are off the ground, the farther you can see."

Edward eyed me suspiciously, as if I were trying to take the mickey when he was in no mood for teasing. "You young whippersnappers don't know anything. The way you calculate a horizon is to take the height above sea level, get the square root, and multiply it by 1.224 exactly. How's that for memory?" he chortled. "The trouble is I don't know the height, and I need you to find it."

I had a nasty feeling about what he was going to say next.

"Here's a ball of string. Go up and tie one end with a slip knot to the truck at the top of the mainmast and then come back down, unrolling the ball as you come." He held out the ball to me as casually as if I was going for a walk along the deck. I started to protest and suggested one of the boys. "I'm not going begging to that Harris for something I don't even know is going to be workable. No," he said firmly, "you're the volunteer, so up you go."

Volunteer?

The lower shrouds and the ratlines up to the upper topsail yard were easy enough, but then I had to go outward on the futtock shrouds to work my body on to the top, a small platform where the topmast was joined to the mainmast. By that time I was sweating, the drops sliding down my face and back, and my heart was pounding. Next was the long climb vertically up the topmast shrouds, hoping that Boris had replaced all the old ratlines used as steps. I was past most feeling by this time and clung on to the royal mast for a while to get my breath. Then up another, I don't know how many feet, to the royal yard where I just sat, trembling with tension, trying not to notice the swing of the mast across the sky with the pitch forward. This was now exaggerated as the ship drove through the water. I cursed Edward.

I looked up at the last few feet of bare mast. There were no stays or lines to hold. By standing up on the yard and putting my arm up over my head, I could see that I was about a foot short of the truck. I wasn't going to climb unnecessarily, so I bent and tied the string to the top rail on the royal yard. I made my way as quickly as I could back down to the deck, unrolling the string as I went. As I jumped onto the deck, I found I was glad just to be standing there.

Edward had got himself to the foot of the mast and managed to pull the string reasonably tight without slipping the knot. He then tied a knot level to the base, pulled hard, and the string came down. While I'd been up the mast, he marked a line ten yards long on the well deck, and now started to measure the string. Once he'd finished that, he asked me for my estimate of the last few feet of the royal mast and rushed back to the chart room with me following.

He checked off his calculations, "Truck to yard, yard to deck, deck to keel. Right, that comes to 152 feet near as—damn it!" He said pausing.

The square root of this figure took time to calculate, but in the end we agreed the horizon from the truck to be about fifteen miles, using Edward's formula.

Edward said, "Let's get Bowman and Harris, and I'll tell them my idea."

They were waiting next to the wheel and came in as soon as I put my head outside. Edward was a bit agitated and started off by saying that he thought he'd a good idea, only to be interrupted by Bowman and told to "Get on with it, ye daft Irishman!"

Edward scowled at him and continued, "I reckon the longer we're out of sight of that MTB the better, because there's no telling what those Admiralty twits have told them to do." He pulled a chart across the table and pointed to a spot about forty miles due east of Dublin. "This is our approximate position at the moment. We might even see the Liverpool-Dublin ferry. I propose that when we are hull down from it, we start to change course westward, until we're about twenty miles from the imaginary line joining the centres of the gaps between Holyhead and Dun Laoghaire and between Peel on the Isle of Man and the Irish coast." He drew the line on the chart, and then another parallel to it, twenty miles to the west. "It's now about 1200 and we expect that boat to be up with us about 1700. If we start bearing off a little at a time, it'll not be noticed by passing boats. And, when we get far enough away—that's fifteen miles by the calculation of the horizon of the truck on the mainmast of this ship as performed by me and Flynn here—we'll not only be well off the shipping lanes but also out of sight of the MTB. Taking it a further five miles away is to allow for a little bit of contingencies, like the MTB doing some sort of small search pattern based on that imaginary centre line," and he ran his finger along it on the chart.

"If we say that we'll be on this parallel line by about four, then we should have, with any sort of luck, fourteen hours' sailing before first light tomorrow morning when the MTB can easily check which one of the many boats on his radar is really us. That fourteen hours, ending at 0600 tomorrow and counting on a speed of about twelve knots, like she's doing now, will bring us so close to Greenock that you'll be able to water their gardens from full bladders as you wake in the morning!"

In all the time I'd seen Edward and Bowman together, I'd never before known Bowman to be at a loss for words. He started to speak once but it wouldn't come. Finally, he planted himself in front of Edward and said, "Ned, may we never fight again. This time ye have really put us in the shade! Always twittering on about your charts and speed and this and that, enough to drive a body crazy sometimes, but now…" He thumped Edward on the shoulder and grinned at us. "Don't ye agree?" he asked.

I was excited, but thought the whole thing sounded too good to be true. Harris was also enthusiastic, but concerned about the narrows between the two little peninsulas, one west of Stranraer and the other south of Bangor. "It's only about twenty miles wide. The MTB could run back and forth, an hour each way."

"I've thought about that," Edward said. "We'll be going through while she's still deciding which direction to look. If we can keep up our speed, we should be through by midnight at the latest. I'm also proposing for the passage through that we put up extra lookouts and dowse the navigation lights."

"Humph! That's a bit dangerous," Bowman said. "I'll decide about it when we're there." He got up, looking restless. "I'm going for a walk round the deck and enjoy the sun while it's here. Meanwhile, we need a watch to stand on the main royal yard as lookout, round the clock. Make sure he straps himself to the mast, and give him the best binoculars ye have with the hailer tied to him." As Bowman walked away, Harris went to find a suitable boy.

By now more clouds had moved in, as the sun shone through the white cumulous and glittered off the white tops of the waves. The unhurried swells seemed to come from the north as they passed under our keel. Our bow wave was steady as the *Bonnie Clyde* drove along under full sail at twelve knots pushed by a breeze, which grew stronger as it continued backing further south and west, something we'd anticipated as the lower pressure came in from the Atlantic.

A soft step sounded behind, and Katherine was beside me. I told her of the latest developments and how close we were to our journey's end. The time for worrying was over. We stood there, leaning on the rail, living in the moment, and waiting for what tomorrow would bring.

Chapter 29
OVERTAKEN

Our journey along the East Coast of Ireland had been uneventful. The successive lookouts on the royal masthead had seen nothing, and I was thankful when it became too dark for us to be seen and the last of them came down. For the boys, it had been a special part of their adventure and the competition to go up the mast had been pretty fierce. For me, picturing one of them falling had been an anxiety. We were below the horizon of the coastal towns, but a little before dark we could see the Mountains of Mourne off to the north-west and from what I could see they certainly looked as though they did, in the words of the old Irish song, sweep down to the sea.

As night fell, our lookout was cautioned to ring his bell for anything unusual. The wind continued to back and freshen as we made good time hour after hour. For now, Bowman agreed not to use the navigation lights. As we approached the peninsula east of Strangford Lough and started to bear out into the entrance of the North Channel, he ordered them lit, including the one at the foremast head. We were getting into the shipping lanes and crossed the routes of the ferries from Liverpool and the Isle of Man. The lanes were busy with freighters and tankers serving Northern Ireland and Scotland. It would be difficult for the MTB to try to investigate each one. We matched our course with the ships going north. As we got level with Larne, we changed course to nor'nor'east to bring us into the Firth of Clyde.

One of our greatest fears was about to come true.

The accident happened fifteen miles south of Arran and five miles west of the Ailsa Craig. It was six bells on the night watch, a real witching hour, if ever there was one! Those off watch were sleeping soundly, while the deck crew was with Harris, and Larry as lookout. The moon had waxed slightly fuller than the night before, but not enough to give more than a faintly luminous light to the whitecaps.

Whatever it was, we hit it hard enough for the *Bonnie* to shudder all down her length, and the scraping could be heard as we rode over it. Boris, being nearest the bottom of the vessel, was immediately awake. I came out of a dream with a jolt and tipped out to the deck. I could hear Harris's voice and got up to the main deck as fast as I could. Harris and Boris were down in the hold and I followed their voices. In the 'tween decks I could see lanterns round the generator and pumps. When I found Harris and Boris in the bilge, they'd just finished their inspection. They were holding lanterns over the water, trying to assess how fast it was rising. We still had no idea what we'd hit and I'm sure that no one could have seen it in the almost-impenetrable dark of the night.

"We've not been holed, thank God," Harris said. "Maybe the steel plates below the waterline on the starboard bow have sprung and there's a steady inflow. I don't think the pumps can work fast enough to keep up, but we can do one or two things to try to help. Let's get back on deck."

Bowman was already on deck while Harris gave him a full report. As they moved off together, I took the opportunity to go below to reassure Katherine. She'd know something had obviously gone wrong and was already in the galley trying to ascertain what had happened. I told her we'd struck something, but the ship wasn't going to sink, and then got back on deck.

Harris had just issued the order to close-haul the sails to the maximum possible. The wind was strong, coming from sou'sou'west and we'd been sailing all square to catch the maximum power. Now we were close-hauling on the port tack, which was going to slow us and throw us off course towards Ayrshire. We'd have to correct every few miles by letting out our sails again and moving towards Arran. This was an uncomfortable zigzag course, with a great deal of hauling in and letting out of sails. On the starboard tack, with the wind as it was, we were able to lift the starboard bow higher out of the water and so reduce the water intake.

Harris then had a word with me. "Flynn, I'm sending you and several boys down into the hold to trim the ballast. It's a rotten backbreaking job, but if we don't do it, we'll be so far down at the head that we'll scarcely be making headway. It's a serious leak, but so long as we can get to the builder's dry dock by late tomorrow, we'll not have the shame of seeing her sunk somewhere about Greenock, her keel on the bottom and her masts sticking up out of the water."

The ballast was sand covered by huge paving stones, which needed two people to lift, but the worst part of working in the hold was the movement of the ship. Despite lanterns we'd strung up on the overhead beams, it was dark and there was a decidedly unpleasant smell. The enclosed space and the rising and falling of the deck above magnified the rolling and pitching. I was just thankful that we weren't in a storm. I lined up the boys in pairs and we started to move the paving stones from the centre and place them on top of those up against the port bulkhead. As a very rough guide, I made a plumb line from string and a piece of stone so that the boys could see that we were having some effect and that the ship was tilting to port. It was a long slow process and we quickly had to shed our heavy outer clothes as we worked. Bowman came down two or three times and tried to get in amongst us and help, but I told him firmly to go and be captain somewhere else.

After moving enough of the stones, the boys had a great time scooping up the sand with whatever implement they could find and throwing it over the piles of stones and sometimes over each other. Eventually Harris came down to tell us to stop and to check on the way the slabs had been piled.

He sighed. "There's no right way of doing it, except to tie these with wire rope and wedge them in place, but this'll have to do, and we just have to hope that we don't have any weather during the next twenty-four hours." He called out to the boys, "Well done! It's been a great help."

Up on deck, he told me, "We've given her a bit of a skew and with the sails close-hauled, it's reduced the flow by about half. The pumps are nearly keeping up with this. Boris has even managed to get one or two of the old hand pumps mended, but working those was quite a chore. Still, I suppose every little bit helps."

It may have been my imagination but I seemed to feel the drag each time the bow dipped under the water and we were undoubtedly going slower. Edward said that our speed was about nine or ten knots and hoped that it would hold steady now that we had trimmed the ballast.

The wind had strengthened far more, but hadn't yet blown up the surface of the sea into anything more than whitecaps. Our passage through the water wasn't a pounding ride, but rather a slower pitching motion. This brought in long waves moving under us with a consequent longer period on the upward climb helping to keep the damaged bow out of the water. I went up to the bow and found Boris with a group of the boys using a bo'sun's chair to dangle themselves just over the water to inspect the damage.

I crept along the bowsprit and could see the heavy scar across the keel as it fell into the sea and then rose, streaming water. Boris said quietly to me, "Not far to go. We will make it. When we get to where the Firth narrows, the swell will die off." Boris had an instinct for the right word or action at the right time. His usual silence made people forget he was around until there was trouble; then the first thought from everyone was always, "Where's Boris?"

I thanked him for the comfort and went to find Edward. As usual, he was in the chart room, surrounded by charts and calculations. This time he had good cause, for we were coming to the most dangerous part of our journey—not from natural hazards, but from other ships. From Little Cumbrae Island up to Greenock, the average width of the channel was two miles, and even narrower for sea-going steamers with their deeper draughts. Being unladen, our draught could not have been more than fifteen feet, so we could sail outside the buoy-marked channel, keeping a sharp lookout for any unmarked obstacles.

I asked Edward for our current position. He pulled up to the top of the pile what had to be the last chart we needed. A large-scale map of the Firth, from Bute to Dumbarton, that was marked for shallows, buoys, and the main channel. "Here we are," he pointed to the chart, "We are about three miles to the south of Bute and Little Cumbrae. We should be well in sight of both, so let's take this outside and see for ourselves."

We hung the chart over the rail next to the wheel, and there were the two headlands clearly visible almost dead ahead. Edward observed, "You can also see that this is a busy place." It was. Within sight were three ships, one just going through the gap, one heading towards us, and one hull down astern.

"The advantage for us is that we have right of way, seeing that we only have sails and no engine. If a gust should swing us off course, then the other man must do all he can to get out of our way. Apart from that, though," Edward added morosely, "it's still too damned crowded."

It lifted our spirits a bit when we saw a freighter alter its course towards us, winking a message. As she came level, we could see the crew lined up at the rail, waving and shouting. The foghorn boomed from their funnel head, with puffs of steam rising in the air in punctuation.

In the morning we rose before daybreak to perform our various duties. We'd gone through a hard night and there was so much yet to be done. Katherine went to the galley to start the morning meal as I was about to return to the deck above to see what this day would hold for us. We were almost at our destination!

Suddenly I became aware that below decks was almost completely silent, apart from the creaking of the ship and the sound of the waves. No crew chatter, no arguments, no songs, nor any of the accustomed shipboard noise. There didn't seem to be anyone below decks. A strange and uneasy feeling came over me. I bolted towards the ladderway with all haste, reached the deck, and pulled open the hatchway.

There were small groups of lads doing some work, but mostly they were just standing about. It wasn't until I reached the helm that I could see anything definite. There was a lad holding the wheel whose face I remembered, though his name escaped me.

"What's going on?" I asked in surprise. Just then Larry appeared from the other side of the mast.

"Good morning, Mr. Flynn."

I repeated, "What is going on and where is everyone?"

"You mean Mr. Harris and Captain Bowman?" he asked.

"Yes, that for starters." I was getting this near-panicked feeling and there had to be some cause.

"Well, they're forward on the starboard side with Edward, and—" Before Larry could finish, I hastened to that position with an unusual sense of urgency. I was glad to finally see them. Brown Bear, enjoying the breeze blowing through his fur, watched me go by with interest.

"Morning there!" I sang at the group. "I was worried for a moment at not having seen you." Everyone stood looking rather solemn, but acknowledged my presence and waved me over. In the centre stood Boris, who grabbed my arm and pulled me in closer to see what everyone had in view.

There it was, just as Edward had predicted.

Scotland in the distance! Green, lovely, and invigorating was the view. Why everyone stood there so unsmiling was still a mystery to me at that moment. I looked over at Boris. He then pointed out what I hadn't yet seen. On our starboard bow, working into position was a Royal Navy MTB. I had rushed on deck to find the enemy right at our gates!

There sat the long low grey shape of His Majesty's Ship MTB-175. They'd overtaken us at last, after a night of cat-and-mouse chasing and manoeuvring. We were nearly within sight of our new home, and the authorities now stood right before us in the Firth of Clyde, blocking our way.

In our present condition, every minute's delay brought the failure of the whole project closer.

I stood on the deck of the *Bonnie Clyde*, watching the motor torpedo boat with a feeling of helplessness. Surely we were not going to lose everything now. Only fifteen hours ago we had it all before us, and now this. Robert walked up to join the group. Seeing the situation, he put his hand on my shoulder.

"So this is it then, eh?" he said quietly.

Bowman now turned. Seeing the faces round him and those of the lads in the crew, he paused for only a moment before showing why he was captain. "We're not done yet! *Everyone to your posts*! Ned, get on the radio as we discussed, and call up the tugs and our friends. Ask them to bring two pumps and all the petrol they can. Harris, take the wheel. We're coming to difficult waters and we'll be doing a mite of manoeuvring. Boris, get yer boys standing by on the lines and clear the braces. Robert and Flynn, go with Boris. Now let's have at it! This soon brings us through to Greenock, and Dumbarton is just upriver."

The patrol boat was trying to take up a position between the *Bonnie* and the shore to our starboard, possibly to prevent any course change. We still had a good wind and we carried on our way. The relatively calm sea from the night before had given the opportunity for the MTB patrol boat to cover a great distance. She'd missed us in the dark, and had anchored behind the island until she could see us approaching. What she might have forgotten was that a sailing ship can only lose way by furling sails or by a sudden turn of the head into the wind to take the sails all aback. We had no reason to do either. As we reached the main deck, Boris ordered everyone aloft.

"Why are you doing that?" I asked. "We can't outrun them now."

Boris pointed towards the MTB. "You see deck gun?" I nodded. "Everyone up here, they not shoot unarmed boys. Maybe they want shoot masts to stop us. Now cannot. Boris will give them reason why no shooting."

"Sounds a bit over-cautious to me," I said, "but better safe than sorry. You should've been a tactical adviser."

My compliment was largely ignored as he spread crewmen across the yardarms and released all available sail. Robert and I joined the living shield. Edward had run into the chart room, but now put his head back out to give Harris a course change, and we turned to port to steer clear of the MTB. Edward went back in again, presumably to call the friends and the tugs. I was intrigued by who the friends could be.

There were some threatening gestures from the patrol ship, and now their captain appeared, carrying a megaphone. "*This is your only warning. Heave to, or my orders are to board you and take you by force. You must surrender to us, or face worse consequences later.*" Bowman's answer to that was to give him a Churchill V sign, *reversed*. We heard the MTB hailer splutter before he put down the megaphone.

I didn't think they were going to fire on anyone, as there was too much danger of missing and of hitting the land on either side of us. Boris agreed, and we all came back down to the deck. I was supposed to be the official sparks, although Harris was always taking over—maybe Bowman and Edward had forgotten that. No matter now.

Edward was at the radio, talking to several dozen small boats assembling in the basin below Dumbarton. He was explaining the situation and arranging for them to position their crafts across the path of the patrol boat. We'd pass between them, leaving them to fan out in our wake and slow the pursuing vessel. Edward then got in touch with the tug office and arranged for not one, but two tugs, to take us in tow and bring the extra pumps and petrol. Our pumps were getting overwhelmed and our petrol to keep them going was nearly gone.

After finishing with the radio, Edward made some calculations and said, "From here to where we take on the tow at Greenock is about twenty miles. We'll be under tow for about two hours all told, right up to the shipbuilder's yards. I've asked the tugs to radio Mr. Reith that we're going to need dry docking as soon as possible."

Now came the tensest part of the chase. No matter how many times the MTB spoke to us, we ignored her. Just let her try and board! Lying in the scuppers was an assortment of pins and boathooks just in case we were to repel boarders. As time went on, it was obvious their captain had calculated the odds of his crew numbers against ours, and realised we could knock them all back into the sea if they tried to climb aboard. Still her sudden surges across our bow and attempts to throw grappling hooks over the rails kept us busy cutting their lines and casting the grappling hooks back into the sea to sink out of harm. Harris, at the wheel, was calling on all his expertise to ensure that he didn't collide with them nor let them throw us too far off course. The boys were busy adjusting the yards and sails to maintain good speed. This deterred the MTB from contemplating a near ramming. The boat had no weight for such an action.

After an hour and a half of this intimidation, we were about to enter the narrow reach of the Firth at Wemyss Bay. The captain of the MTB decided, literally, to take his last shot at stopping us. He roared into the narrows and then swept round in a tight circle, until he was bows-on to us.

Putting his engine in slow reverse, the captain again picked up his megaphone and came to the bow.

"*My orders are to stop you in any way feasible, even using force. I have a deck gun here—enough to hole you badly at the waterline, so you'll surely sink. I'll give you one more minute to surrender, or I shall fire.*"

We all turned to look at Bowman, who was now standing on the bridge deck with his cap on and his best dress uniform. He was the very picture of a man accustomed to commanding and to being obeyed. I think we could have surrendered right then and there if he'd ordered us to do so. Instead he gave one of his old growls and turned to Harris, saying in a voice loud enough for us to hear, "Harris, d'ye remember when I used to teach ye poker as a youngster, and ye'd go on making remarks about how this hand or that was going to flatten me. What did I use to say to ye?"

"'Put up or shut up,' Uncle Billy," Harris replied, with a bit of a choke in his voice.

"That's right," Bowman roared. "Put up or shut up. He's put up his hand, but it isn't worth the ante. If I were him and had a real hand," he lowered his voice, "I'd be putting it down. I certainly wouldn't be making stupid threats against an unarmed sailing ship, the great numpty. It just shows what twits we have in Whitehall as our masters." There was a cheer as he finished speaking. Now he gave his order.

"Steady as she goes, Mr. Mate. Hold your course."

"Aye, aye, Captain," Harris replied with a smile and held the wheel immobile in a grip of steel.

I suspect the captain of the MTB had no love of the job he'd been given. He must have been thinking of alternatives to the last crazy actions he was ordered to make. He'd been ashore and must have seen newspapers and heard the wireless, enough to know that his bosses at the Admiralty were not popular at all. He must also have realised that actually shooting and, God forbid, hurting anyone would have meant his own court martial, as the high command ran quickly for shelter. Not shooting would mean that he'd have the public with him, and his masters wouldn't be able to punish him without raising even more hands against them.

However he'd worked things out in his own mind, the MTB backed away, then with a sudden roar, shot forward and under our bow, setting us rocking up and down in the wake of her huge bow wave as she roared off, baffled.

Again everyone cheered, forgetting all discipline. Many came up to the bridge to congratulate Bowman, who'd have none of it. "Simple common sense lads, ye've all got it to use," he protested, but was smiling at the praise nevertheless.

We were now well into the river inlet looking up at the 240-foot twin peaks of Dumbarton Rock and the impressive Dumbarton Castle of stone with its many flags flying in the breeze. The River Clyde flowed on one side and the River Leven on the other two. This had been a fortress before the Romans left these shores and had been a military base as recently as the war. The lookout sounded his bell and called the welcome tidings, "Small boats ahead!"

Soon there was a whole flotilla round us. There was a great deal of shouting through the megaphone between the boats and Bowman, Harris, and Edward, as they all greeted one another with long familiar nicknames and broad smiles. One huge figure, even bigger then Harris, in one of the smallest of the boats, spoke for them all when he roared, "Bowman, ye bloody Scotsman! Now ye've really beaten the Sassenachs and they'll never forgive you."

"I dinna care," Bowman roared back. "I'm never going back there anyway."

"Cast down a line," the big man called out. Bowman nodded and I quickly cast one down. He attached a bundle and we hauled it aboard. It was full of newspapers. As we looked at the papers, we saw that these were ones that Richard had saved for us. Banner headlines shouted: GETTING READY FOR THE GREAT DAY, THE BONNIE CLYDE COMES HOME! There was a shot of Harris feeding the bear, headed: BEARING UP. There were also pictures of the ship in full sail, showing her to be a proud vessel and not some old wreck taken by a pack of cranks.

Bowman seemed to be everywhere, encouraging the boys, keeping an eye on the MTB, and talking by megaphone with friends in the boats. He'd dispatched a boy to the royal yard to keep watch for the tugs but it would be another hour before we came in sight of Greenock. It was one of the slowest hours in my life.

The wind stayed in the same quarter so that we didn't have to change the set of the sails.

In the midst of our suspense, Katherine suddenly appeared on deck with two helpers, all carrying trays of coffee and biscuits as if it were a family outing. We laughed and cheered, breaking the tension. Bowman in particular was charmed by her action and invited her to take coffee with him in the wardroom. I was again struck by her ability to read the situation and come up with an idea that helped those involved. When she came out later she gave me an odd look, partly a smile of happiness, partly a little frightened, but I'd little time to think about it at that moment.

At last there came a faint call from the masthead, "Tugs approaching!" Boris pointed out that in order to secure the towlines to the tugboats, we'd have to reef most of the sails. Bowman gave the order to ensure we were nearly at a standstill when the tugs arrived. As we began pulling up sails to the yardarms, I went into the chart room and found Edward bending over the charts, muttering to himself.

The sparks from the MTB was still carrying out his orders and calling on us to surrender. Obviously his captain had forgotten him. To Bowman, who came in just then, these were still fighting words, and growling that he wanted to hear no more of this rubbish, he picked up the handset and snapped, "This is Captain Bowman. Ye willna stop us, nor will ye board my ship. We willna surrender, so cease your endless blathering!" He put the handset down and returned to his cabin.

Chuckling, I went back on deck. Bowman reappeared and was carrying a folded flag under his arm. He took up his position on the bridge deck. Most of the sails had been taken in with exception of the spanker and flying jibs and all hands were on deck. The towering masts were reefed and looked almost as they had been before the voyage began, and we were slowing in the water.

"How much longer until we have the two tugboats alongside?" Bowman asked Harris, who was still at the wheel.

"Not much longer," Harris replied. "Less than twenty minutes."

"All right, let's give them a new thought," Bowman said. Calling Robert, he gave him the flag he was carrying. "Strike the British colours. That they'll take as a sign of surrender. Wait two minutes and then run this up the mast," he ordered. Robert put the flag under his arm, saluted, and went down to the mainmast.

"What have you in mind, and what flag is that?" Harris enquired suspiciously.

"Ye'll soon see. 'Tis not the skull and crossbones," Bowman responded. "Just one of the last cards in the deck to be played out. Now, assemble the crew on deck and get Edward to take the wheel for a spell."

Harris gave the orders, and soon the crew were standing on deck below the bridge deck. Bowman insisted that Katherine come up to stand by me on the bridge.

Once everyone was present, Bowman took Harris by the arm to stand next to him and he motioned to Katherine and me.

"You two stand here," Bowman ordered, and we moved closer together and stood in front of him.

"Well now, we're all gathered here as they say, and everyone knows these two are engaged to be married. I find it unthinkable to release them to be married in front of strangers. For my last act as captain of this ship I have the power to pronounce them man and wife, if they still want one another. What say ye?" and Bowman looked at me expectantly.

I was completely taken by surprise and hesitated, wondering how Katherine would take this—no white dress, flowers, or the whole ceremony. "Well?" He asked louder.

"Yes," I sputtered, looking at Katherine, "I do very much!"

She blinked back at me. "Can he really do this?" she whispered.

"Yes, a ship's captain does have that authority," I confirmed.

She cleared her throat. "Yes, I do very much," she quavered shyly.

"Ye're both sure of that?" Bowman asked sternly.

"Yes!" we chorused, holding tightly onto one another's hands and finding it difficult to breathe.

Bowman looked around, "Normally it's the custom to ask if anyone has an objection to the marriage. Be sure that if anyone speaks now, he'll swim the rest of the way." Everyone laughed. Then, he spoke directly to us and with proper seriousness, "Being a man of extremely few words, most of them irreverent, I'd like to say only that it is now so. That is, I pronounce that ye are now husband and wife."

Cheers and applause went up from every member of the crew. Even Bowman was smiling from ear to ear and applauded with everyone else. "Well?" he asked with raised eyebrows, so I drew Katherine to me and we embraced with a kiss. That drew more cheers and applause from everyone.

Katherine gave Bowman a hug and a kiss on the cheek, which made his face go crimson. "Get on wi' ye now," he rasped, shooing us off the bridge.

As we went down, everyone crowding round to offer congratulations, I held Katherine's hand tighter and she snuggled against my shoulder. I think it was the shortest wedding any of us ever attended, perhaps the shortest on record.

"I'll make sure ye have a licence, because there's a real log on this ship. I've been keeping a record, such as it is. That's one of the pleasures of being in command," Bowman said in a satisfied tone. "But now for something not so pleasant, something we all must understand." He cleared his throat and moved up to the bridge rail.

"Shipmates, I would like ye to know that it's been a privilege and an honour to serve with such brave lads as ye all are, and under such unfavourable circumstances. Every one of ye has brought something to this endeavour, where we've travelled approximately one thousand miles from the Thames to this point. Our average speed has been around twelve knots, although we surely had some quicker times during the storms. We had a great deal of luck getting this far, but none of this could ever have been achieved without the efforts of everyone in this company. I know that I've occasionally been a hard taskmaster, and ye've been more than respectful with me."

Bowman continued, "Your remaining duties now are to assist in securing the towlines to the tugboats arriving to take us upriver. There's nothing the MTB can do now to stop us from reaching our final destination. He'll not use his deck gun. He'll only shoot off his mouth, which he has been. When we're secure and finally tied up at the dock, ye must follow these instructions carefully: I want all ye boys to leave the ship as quickly as possible, taking with ye only what ye can carry. There'll be people waiting for ye, so get into the crowd as quickly as possible. They're good people, so please show them the respect ye've given everyone here."

One boy spoke up. "How will we know them?" he asked.

"They'll know you," Bowman responded. "Harris and I will assume responsibility for anything the English government may dish out but I want ye to understand that ye've done nothing wrong. We invited ye on a holiday and ye accepted, nae more than this. And if you get questioned by these new-fangled National Health people or the police, just tell the truth. Don't make up any stories about anyone.

"We have succeeded! We've come through the English Channel, run the Irish Sea, survived storms and bad situations, and there isn't a man among ye that I would not take pride in serving with again. The point of this voyage is that this ship has reached her destination. People who wish no harm to come to her will be discussing her fate and ye played the largest part in our achieving that. Another major result has been getting a new life for everyone aboard."

At that moment the bear gave a large burp. Boys with tears in their eyes managed a smile. Bowman looked over at the huge beast and said, "Bear with me," which brought outright laughter from everyone.

"My wish is that we all succeed in our lives and with our new friends. We've all become family, and I'd like to ask that ye still help each other and keep in touch with us and each other. Never forget that orphanage! May ye never have to endure that type of treatment from anyone again and try to make sure no one else has to in the future. There's no telling exactly what will happen, but we'll all try to meet up again when the dust has settled. As for the Royal Navy, they sit there defeated. We've outdone them. As for us, this voyage and all that went into it, was done solely by arm, heart, and brain," Bowman finished.

While we were all applauding the speech, few of us without wet cheeks, Boris came and whispered to Bowman, who called to the boys, "Right, the tugs are almost here. Go forward and get the towing hawsers and prepare for the last step of our journey."

For a moment we all stood frozen in silence, tears visible everywhere. Then Larry, as spokesman, stepped forward.

"Captain Bowman, this has been the best home we've known and the closest we've had to family. It's not fair, and I'm speaking for all of us, to leave you to whatever might happen. Well, we just don't want to leave."

Bowman was clearly touched by this gesture and removed his cap to cover his emotion. I noticed his eyes were wet. Pretending to wipe his forehead, he rubbed his eyes and replaced his cap. He said firmly, "Part of my job, or should I say responsibility, was to make sure ye're all here safe and have new homes. I've done my part, so now ye must do the same and make new lives." He turned and called out to Boris, "Take charge!"

All the boys followed Boris forward to prepare the long lengths of hawser needed for the tow.

Edward, Harris, Robert, Katherine, and I stood silent for a few moments before Harris said to Bowman, "Dammit, Uncle Billy, you were nearly eloquent there," and put his great arm around Bowman's shoulder affectionately.

"Ye certainly know how to ruin a moment," Bowman shot back in mock anger, with difficulty shaking off the heavy arm. He glared about him, "Well, what the bloody hell are ye all standing around here for? Get busy! Robert, did ye strike the flag?"

"Yes, sir," Robert answered, showing him the British Ensign we'd flown from the beginning.

"Well, it's been more than two minutes. Run up the new one immediately!"

Bowman went forward to check that the tow was taken up properly, as the two tugs fanned out on each side of the *Bonnie* to reel in the hawsers. Harris and Robert pulled the pumps and petrol aboard tied hastily to a line. One pump had stopped for lack of petrol, and we were now racing time as the other sputtered running low.

Suddenly all hands raised a cheer as the flag of Scotland, the St. Andrew's white cross on a blue field, now unfurled in the breeze as Robert hoisted it up the mast next to the red duster.

"That'll give the English something to think about, don't you agree, Mr. Flynn?" Bowman said with a grin.

"That'll raise some interesting questions, I'll wager," I smiled. With
that he came over and put his hand on my shoulder. "Thank ye, Flynn.
Without you and Robert I don't think we'd be standing here," he said
softly. I put my hand on his shoulder likewise, but I could only choke
out, "Thank you, sir."

Nothing more was said as he went off to oversee another project,
but his eyes exuded gratitude for all we had been through together. At
that moment, besides the respect and admiration I already had for
Captain Bowman, I felt closer to him than ever. It was one of those
moments that would long endure, and on this voyage we had all shared
many such.

As the tugs moved into position, no effort was made by the MTB to
hinder the operation. When we finally felt the heavy hemp hawsers take
up the strain of the tow, everyone seemed to relax a bit, but we were all
still emotionally unsettled till we heard the pumps come alive with a
steady roar. Harris took up the position at the helm to guide the ship
round the right-hand sweep of the Firth at Greenock, leading directly
into the River Clyde. It was hard to take in that Robert and I were
going to split up after seeing more activity than we had known during
our entire service in the Navy.

Our reception at Port Glasgow seemed to have just begun. There
were more small boats waiting for us, led by the Harbour Master's own
launch. I saw one raincoated figure come out of the wheelhouse and
hold a placard over his head. There was an arrow pointing downwards
and the sign read, RICHARD AP. I went rushing down to the port side
of the bridge deck, waving both arms like a mad thing, and then hitting
myself on the chest and shouting, "Flynn!" By this time, the other seniors were all also waving, including the unmistakable figure of Bowman
in his full dress captain's uniform. Richard must have taken the night
train to be here in time to meet us.

As we rounded the bend, all the ships moored up on both sides of
the river began to sound foghorns, whistles, and bells. Stevedores
stopped work and there were some large painted banners hanging from
the sides of the ships: WELCOME TO DUMBARTON, DOWN
WITH THE SASSENACH, CONGRATULATIONS, and WE
LOVE YOU MR BEAR. This last banner looked like one done by
young schoolchildren. All along the bank road by Gourock and Greenock, where there was a space between docks and wharves, there were
groups of people standing, waving small Scottish flags and cheering.

Through binoculars I could see the same thing on the far side of the
river as well. Perhaps we were the only outlaws they'd seen in the his-

tory of their town—or at least the latest. This was much more than I'd expected. That so-called British reserve was a myth—nothing more than a misreading of everyone's wish not to intrude on other people's privacy. Given a real cause or something to capture the imagination, the British could be as sentimental as a Frenchman or as demonstrative as an Italian any day of the week.

Damaged buildings and bombed-out boat docks lay in ruin here just as in London. The Luftwaffe had taken its revenge not only against ships being built here during the war, but also against the Free French Navy Dockyard that the British had provided when France had fallen.

Bowman was now into the spirit of things, waving his hat and ordering signal flags to be hoisted aloft.

After securing the tow, the boys moved off to their quarters to pack. I suggested to Katherine that we should do the same. We went below to combine enough necessary items for the both of us in one small suitcase, though that seemed scarcely possible.

"Now that we're man and wife," I whispered, "this'll have to tide us over until we can return to collect the rest." Once in the cabin, packing was not on our minds and amongst the socks and sweaters we spent a blissful few minutes, kissing and touching. This left us breathless but unable to go further through lack of time. We arranged everything into two trunks, two suitcases, and one over-stuffed duffel. It would mean making several trips, but that seemed no great task after all we'd been through.

I had to dash off because I'd be needed to help with the mooring when we docked. Katherine had a special surprise for everyone and needed to get back to the galley at once. As we left the cabin, Bowman came slowly down the companionway and we again thanked him for our impromptu ceremony.

"It was my pleasure. I haven't done that in many years. I hope it wasn't too embarrassing," he said.

"Not really, just surprising," Katherine answered.

"Too bad, I was hoping for some embarrassment," he said with a smile. "Well then, I shall now retire to my cabin for a brief rest. I'll prepare the marriage certificate and give it to ye later."

Katherine went off to complete preparations for what she called our wedding reception. The ceremony had thrown out her plans, for she'd already drawn the galley fire, and so there was no way to make things hot. Still...off she went to the galley.

I went up on deck to rejoin the rest of the crew, who were just as busy watching as working. The tugs were making good progress, still escorted by the flotilla of small boats. We were being led by the Harbour Master, in front of the tugs, while the rest of the boats formed a skirmish line astern, keeping the MTB at a respectful distance. This would give us time to tie up and disembark without harassment from them if everything went according to plan. But no skirmish line can cover every inch of ground, and the same is even truer of water. Boats are affected by various forces and must keep a reasonable distance apart to avoid collisions.

So now the MTB decided to test the line. The boat suddenly shot off towards the north bank at what must have been its maximum speed, streaking along with the line of boats to his starboard side. After passing the last boat he ordered right full rudder and brought his boat between the line and the *Bonnie Clyde*.

This manoeuvre was successful in getting round the flotilla, but it was a different matter to try playing games with the tugs spread in front of the ship and the Harbour Master leading a civic procession. At this point we'd nothing left to do except stand by, as Harris was now in control of the helm, working with the tugboats to negotiate the narrowing passage of the river.

Up ahead, clouds of grey smoke hung in the sky above the city and the familiar smell of burning coal filled the air, pouring out of blast furnaces, kilns, and chimneys in one of the biggest shipbuilding areas in the world. This smokiness was the first thing to be noticed when returning from a voyage at sea.

Below the haze, the people thronged the banks of the river where they could see, or else came in small boats, or looked out from their houses. The flotilla around us was becoming a huge armada.

Before long the accident waiting to happen, did so. The MTB collided with another boat and a small pier, though little damage was done. It was nothing serious, but it effectively took the enemy out of the picture. The captain had to stay there in order to collect all the information that would be needed by the Official Court of Enquiry. Our company gleefully applauded the mishap as we continued along.

The boys had finished doing their packing and were getting ready to disembark as per Bowman's orders. Their belongings easily fit in small bags and they were now lining up near the starboard rail with them. It's a good thing memories don't take up much space. There were a good many young girls among the people standing to see us pass, no doubt attracted by Richard's newspaper pieces about twenty strapping young men now looking for a new life in Scotland—or whatever he'd written. Their delighted shrieks pierced the other noises around, and I saw several of the boys preening themselves at the thought of a personal welcome from some of them!

At Harris's request I'd been down to the bilge and found the pumps were holding their own now that we were in calmer water. Shifting the ballast had given the *Bonnie* a definite list to port, partly disguised by the way the sails were held, adding to the slant of the deck.

We were still being greeted with foghorns and ship's whistles from passing boats. Along the coastal roads, we could see lorries and cars flashing their lights. It was all very cheering, but for the MTB captain's actions. Having hastily concluded minimal attention to his unfortunate collision, he now settled for following far astern, a brooding presence that might awake at any moment with some new blasted fool idea from his masters, as he must surely be in touch with them over the radio. We cared little for him now!

Suddenly there was a terribly loud jangling noise. When I looked round, I saw it was one of Katherine's helpers banging a big saucepan with an iron spit-rod, getting everyone's attention. He called out that everyone was invited to the wedding reception in the officers' ward-room. Leaving Harris at the helm, the rest of us headed for the wardroom.

What a marvellous spread had been prepared. Pillaging our ample remaining stores, Katherine had sliced up an entire ham and laid out potato salad, smoked chicken, cheese, and tins of fruit. A small side table was covered with bottles of beer and soft drinks. Everyone was in the mood for celebration of our arrival, our wedding, or both. Those still left on deck took part as well, from plates thoughtfully brought to their stations. Katherine had outdone herself with this feast, which she'd prepared without using the stove. I was being congratulated, not only for having married such a beautiful girl, but also for having found such a great cook. She encouraged everyone to collect and take any food left over, for none of us knew when or where we'd have our next meal.

I found Bowman sitting at the end of the table. He looked quiet and thoughtful, and I went and sat next him.

"How are you?" I asked.

"Are you asking for yerself, or is Harris having ye spy on me again?" he said with a smile.

"You just looked deep in thought," I said.

"Aye, wondering what will happen in the next few days and weeks. Actually I hadn't given much thought to anything except arriving here safely—unless it was whether we'd be arriving here at all," Bowman admitted. "How's that old bear doing?"

"So, you've become fond of him, eh?" I said.

He only smiled and told me that he and the bear had a lot in common, although he didn't go into detail about the comparison. "I'm going to take one last stroll about the deck to make sure everything is shipshape, and then I'll take a bit of a rest until we're secured." He rose and climbed up the companionway to the deck above. I was about to follow him when Katherine came over.

"Well, Missus, I wonder where we'll be hanging our hats tonight," I said, giving her a squeeze. She just smiled and began packing a large wicker basket of food to take along with us.

More small boats had emerged from both sides of the river and were all around us waving and cheering. I began to realize we had achieved real celebrity status. In the distance we could hear bells ringing in the churches, but that surely couldn't be for us.

I found myself standing next to Robert. "Did you ever think we'd make it?" he asked.

"Absolutely. Never any doubt," I answered with a grin. "You were aboard to see to it as well," and I let him know the relief I felt with a wink.

Robert was the kind of friend who pops up only intermittently during one's life, and when he does appear, takes up exactly from where he left off. Still, I asked, "How will I find you again once we're in port and everyone splits up?"

"Not to worry," he assured me, "like a bad penny, I'll turn up when you least expect me. Anyway, I'll have more incentive now. You'll have such good food."

I felt sure that the MTB was not going to try anything crazy. I fancied I could read the captain's mind well enough to know that he was just going through the motions. His last manoeuvre swinging round the flotilla was only window dressing for his bosses in Whitehall. He'd been lagging behind, and as more small boats joined in the procession, had been squeezed farther back and was effectively marooned.

The boats spread out, allowing us passage through the crowded waters. As we passed through, the fleet closed in behind us and the MTB took herself out of line and headed for a dock with a large fuel pump. She'd run out of fuel, later than I'd predicted, but out nonetheless!

We could now see the dock ahead, with its arched Victorian wrought iron entrance, spelling out the name of the builder:

ROBERTSON'S. People were everywhere, waving. Boat whistles were going off, and coming from within the boat builder's yard, I could hear the sound of bagpipes. Our reception was becoming quite out-of-this-world! The boys mounted the riggings and were waving in every direction, while we seniors were standing on the bridge deck and joining in. I couldn't see Bowman, but I knew he wouldn't want to miss this. I thought this may have been his finest hour, having defeated all the odds against him to succeed.

Boris had fashioned a collar and lead from rope for Brown Bear and now put it over his head. The bear sensing the excitement became very spry and stood up, much to the delight of the children in the crowd.

Boris now called the boys into position at the forepeak for taking in the hawsers, while those aloft furrowed the remaining sail. Harris turned the ship in towards the yard. First one tug, then the other, slowed and cast off the tow. We'd just enough way for us to slide gently alongside the dock inside the yard. Throwing loops over the bollards, the dockside crew brought the ship to a gentle stop.

The voyage was over.

On the quay I could see a welcoming group that included the Mayor, judging from the heavy gold chain one distinguished-looking gentleman wore round his shoulders. Next to him was a tall grey-haired man in full kilt and velvet jacket, who I assumed must be Mr. Reith, and various other prominent men and their ladies stood by deferentially.

Off a little to one side was a figure in a raincoat and battered trilby, which had in the hatband a piece of white card. Written on it, in letters we could read from the bridge deck were the words PRESS RICHARD AP. I suppose he wasn't quite sure we'd seen him earlier, but he certainly didn't want us to miss him in the crowd of people. I couldn't resist making a funnel with my hands and shouting as loudly as I could: "Hurrah for AP!" at which he flourished his hat and made a low bow. We all laughed and cheered.

More ominously, however, behind the first group was another, consisting mainly of Scottish policemen in their distinctive caps with black and white chequered band, one or two of whom also had one or more silver stars on their shoulders. Included in the group were three men dressed in dark grey suits and carrying neatly furled umbrellas. I also noticed other strapping fellows laden with what looked very like different kinds of weapons, including at least five in traditional tartan kilts with broadswords or claymores on their shoulders among a group standing farther back behind a restraining rope, and there was considerable open ground between the Suits and the Kilts. The tension between the two rival factions was evident, some connected to the British government intent on boarding the ship, the others, who were among our supporters, were doubtless there determined to stop them.

While the gangway was being brought up and fixed in place, I told Robert that he'd better get the boys ready and wait for Harris's signal to move down onto the quay.

I then said to Harris, "If these boys are going to have a chance of getting away, we need a diversion. What about Boris going down first, leading the bear. This would attract the children and their parents. Once he has two or three families over the rope, you, Edward, and Bowman can go down and do an official sort of speech and hand-over. By that time I should be able to get the boys off and into the crowd without too much notice."

"Right," Harris said. "Let me first have a word with Boris. You and Robert stand by to come down with the boys and act as interference if you see anything suspicious."

Boris secured a chain to Brown Bear as a long leash and began to proceed down the gangway. It was funny to watch as the railings bulged out to accommodate the width of this huge animal. Amidst many oohs and aahs from the crowd, Boris and the bear got down to the quay. Brown Bear gazed at the crowd gathered before him, and perhaps his mind must have gone back to happier days of performing and entertaining audiences throughout his life. With a happy groan, he rose onto his hind feet and began slowly to turn as he'd once done for circus crowds when he was a young dancing bear.

Boris laughed, as Brown Bear came down onto all fours, and started down the dock with the bear at his side, waving to the people looking on quizzically, but delighted at the novelty. The police on each side had broken ranks and fled to the end of the dock, remaining there in complete disorganisation and chaos as Russian and bear promenaded past them into the middle of the main yard. As they headed towards the open street, Boris asked for directions to the zoo. With such a very large bear at his side, there weren't many who approached Boris; however, that didn't keep him from being his most jovial as he walked down the middle of the pier waving to the crowd, with all eyes following their passage. I trailed them at a distance to observe developments.

Stopping at a group of onlookers, the bear stood up again and successfully turned round to applause and cheers from many, while others picked up their children and disappeared in terror or perhaps simply disbelief. Boris finally found someone who was pleased to lead them to the zoo. The three of them proceeded down the dock and into the street. Passing one of the local pubs, I could see everyone inside now lining the pavement to watch the spectacle.

One man, completely sotted, blinked at the unlikely sight. "By God, that's the biggest damn dog I've ever seen," he slurred. Another man let the pint glass slip through his fingers and break on the pavement below without changing his fixed expression.

It was an ideal time and Robert started the boys down the gangway, where they quickly entered the crowd. I saw them being approached by nice people, who then led them away. It was a relief to know that they were out of reach of the *law*, at least for now.

What we didn't know until a very few minutes later was that one boy was still on board. This was Larry. He came up from below—white-faced, with tears pouring down his face, and took hold of Harris's arm. My heart sank. Harris motioned me to follow.

We quickly came to the bottom of the companionway and the passage leading to Bowman's cabin, where I became aware of a strange silence. No more crew, no busy discussions, no songs, only an ominous quiet broken by sobs coming from Bowman's cabin. The sounds from outside came through as though from a great distance and the air was still. We stopped at the door of the cabin, which stood open, and slowly entered.

There on his bunk lay Bowman, just as he did when occasionally resting during the day. His arm hung off the side, resting on a chair by the bunk. Harris rushed past everyone inside and went over to attend his long-time friend. When he took Bowman's hand it was plain that our captain was gone. Harris slumped, still holding the gnarled, lifeless hand. He slowly removed his cap and set it down. Silence settled over our company like a chill that had suddenly frozen everyone as still as statues at the realization that Bowman had died. Edward's sobs were the only thing audible in the stillness, while outside, jubilant onlookers cheered the arrival of the ship and the celebration continued.

I opened my mouth to say something, but no words came. I felt as if I should leave these three friends together, but I also felt a deep sense of loss, and a sudden feeling that all our effort had been for nothing crept over me.

I felt a soft hand take mine. It was Katherine, whose tears reflected my own. No one said anything for what seemed like hours, but only minutes had passed before Edward spoke, his voice quiet and shaking.

"You know," Edward said to Harris, "one thing he never told you was that he often repeated the story of you and that chap from the government office in London. You remember the other one you dropped over the side? He thought that the funniest thing he'd ever seen, but he could never tell you that." They were still kneeling by the bunk and Edward continued, "He did really care for you, you know, but you did sometimes try his patience. I suppose I did as well on occasion." Edward was silent for a bit more and then he said quietly, "This time, you know, he did it—as much as I doubted him, he came through again. We all made it here all safely. He said they'd never catch him. He never let me down on a promise," Edward concluded, choking back his tears.

Harris sat down in the chair and gently placed Bowman's hand upon the still breast. He looked slowly about the cabin, when his gaze suddenly fixed on Bowman's desk. He stood up, staring. This made Katherine and me look as well.

We all gasped.

There among the charts and books was a mug of tea with the steam still rising from it.

Harris said slowly, "About fifteen minutes ago, one of the boys said that Bowman had come out of his cabin and asked if he'd seen the boy in the white jacket. The boy told me that Bowman had said, 'He brought me my tea and told me it was nearly time.' The boy said Bowman hadn't seemed alarmed but that he was very quiet."

Harris went over and touched the mug to satisfy his curiosity about it still being hot. For a moment he stood in thought, and then turned to Katherine.

"Who brought Uncle Billy this mug of tea?"

Katherine looked surprised. "I don't know. When we were in the galley everyone knew I didn't light the stove today."

I reached over and touched the small pot-bellied coal stove that was in Bowman's cabin, but it too was cold to the touch. We all looked at one another and at the steaming cup. Some things defy explanation, and from that time, none of us has ever mentioned it again. Perhaps there was something unworldly about this boy in the white jacket, or perhaps Bowman was imagining things as they *were* when he first went to sea. I suppose we'll never know.

A few moments later we heard the sound of several people coming down the companionway. A voice called, "Coming through!" Another voice said, "Stand aside!"

Then another voice in a softened tone asked, "May I come in? My name is Commander Wright, Royal Navy, and I've been sent to speak privately with you."

I went to the door, where I met a man in his mid-forties, in uniform. This was a man with authority and what he said, people listened to, and when he ordered, they obeyed. I could tell when I looked at his service ribbons. I'd met several officers like him during the war. Their ships were happy ships, because the men had absolute faith in the officer's ability to bring them through any action. I asked him to step inside and as he came in he turned to tell his lieutenant to wait outside, then he closed the door after him.

Taking note of the solemn faces Commander Wright said, "I'd like to see your captain." We had all instinctively moved in front of the bunk when we heard a strange voice, but now we stepped aside. The commander immediately removed his cap and fell silent. After a moment of studying each of our faces, he asked if he could pay his respects. Harris agreed, and he stood by the bunk with head bowed for a few minutes. He straightened up and Harris asked him to take the chair in front of the captain's desk. Harris pulled a blanket from the foot of the bunk and covered over Bowman, then drew the curtain that separated the sleeping and washing area from the rest of the cabin.

Harris now came to stand behind the desk and faced the commander. "Harris, First Mate," he identified himself like a prisoner of war might. "I'm in command now, and responsible for anything we may be held accountable for."

The commander had a look of admiration and respect on his face as he looked at Harris.

"I'm extremely sorry for your loss," he said. "I was looking forward to meeting Captain Bowman. I was also looking forward to meeting you, Mr. Harris. Both you and the captain had reputations for independent thought when you were in the Navy during the war, but our paths never crossed. It's a pity because, in my own small way, I'm as unorthodox as both of you, and I suppose we would have made a good team.

"Now, let me tell you the purpose of my visit. I am the personal envoy to the Prime Minister. He is not so stupid as some members of his party, or some civil servants. He has asked me, firstly, to apologise to you for the attitude of the Admiralty when you first suggested saving the *Bonnie Clyde* and for their persistent refusals to listen. The Prime Minister is primarily a statesman, and the uproar you succeeded in raising these past ten days or so isn't something the government would long

N. Jay Young

tolerate. You must know that you've nothing to bargain with," he finished.

Harris, unaccustomed to being defeated, now came to himself. He
went over and opened the porthole through which the sound of cheering and celebration became louder with the sounds of horns and bells
and then closed it. Harris later told us that when Commander Wright
said we had nothing to bargain with, Bowman's words came to him as
they had an hour earlier: Harris, d'ye remember when I used to teach
ye poker as a youngster, and ye'd go on making remarks about how this
hand or that was going to flatten me. What did I use to say to you? Put
up or shut up!

Harris now turned to the commander and said, "Nothing to bargain with? I'll up the pot by a few thousand people, the AP, a few
newspapers, and I call," he answered with a coy look.

Wright smiled back, knowing Harris did indeed have a winning
hand. "If what I've been reading in the papers is any indication, I think
you'd all rather go to jail than admit you were wrong. However, public
opinion would make any politician quake in his shoes. The Prime Minister has suggested that the whole matter be allowed to fade quietly
away, provided you refrain from giving anymore stories to the newspapers. He also asked that you no longer continue in public to
characterise the government as stupid, unfeeling, and not listening to
common sense, and all the other terms the press attribute to you. In
short, the whole episode is to be as if it never happened.

"In return, no criminal charges will be brought against you for taking the ship, taking the condemned stores, taking the handset from the
tug, or taking the boys away from the orphanage. I regret we can do
nothing about the matter regarding the sails, although I've heard tell
that you have a few months in which to replace what you,
ah...borrowed. As for the bear, my orders do not cover wild animals.
So, what do you think of this proposition?"

To say that we were dumbstruck would be an understatement.
Every one of our worries taken care of in one blow, in return for almost
nothing! Now that we'd handed over the ship, there was really no reason for us to be saying anything, except now everyone wanted to hear
about it.

Harris looked at me and said, "That seems to cover all the points
we raised before, Flynn."

I agreed. We could all start with a clean slate and no endless arguments with officials or lawyers.

Harris addressed Commander Wright. "You know you set the captain of the MTB an almost impossible task, especially once the storm had gone. I think he did damn well even to find us."

"I've already noted that young man in my personnel files. He did a rather good job of showing he was following orders in the last few miles. But what do you say to this proposal? Remember that whatever you decide, this conversation never happened and would be officially denied if anyone spoke of it outside of this cabin."

Harris looked at each of us. "Well, I know your answer, Flynn. You'll excuse me for not asking you, Katherine, as you're an innocent bystander in all this. Edward, I hope you can see that this is the best solution."

Edward, though looking pitiably broken and lost at the passing of his old friend, managed to say, "Aye, aye, Harris, whatever you say, so long as you think Billy would have approved. I'm not myself thinking too well just now, but what I do know is we must hold a wake to say a proper goodbye."

Harris then turned to the commander. "Just as you've heard of me, so I've heard of you from men who served under you. I hope that you haven't been changed by over-long contact with Whitehall, but I'll take my chance on what I see now. The answer is yes, Commander Wright. We accept the offer, and may it bind you as it binds us."

Harris stood up with his hand outstretched to shake hands with Wright, who also rose and took it in a firm grip without the painful expression that normally accompanies a Harris handshake.

"You have my word," Wright said. "Excuse me for a moment." He opened the door to call his lieutenant, "Please send this message: Ship found abandoned and empty, and have agreed to relinquish to builder. All other points settled and agreed. After it's been sent, give a copy to this gentleman here," and he indicated Harris. The lieutenant saluted smartly and left.

Commander Wright now relaxed and shook everyone's hand with a reserved smile on his face, and he congratulated us on completing a job he'd have liked to have had a go at himself. He was charming to Katherine, wishing the both of us well and a long life by the sea.

Harris had seen something on the desk while he was sitting there and picked up a paper from the desk. "This must have been one of the last things Uncle Billy did," he said, handing me a piece of paper.

It was our marriage certificate.

Edward now stood up, clearing his throat and wiping his eyes. "We need to get out there and explain matters to all the good people who've

been waiting for us and make the hand-over of the *Bonnie Clyde* official."
He turned to the curtained-off bunk. "I'm glad we did it, but I'm going
to be lonely now." We walked out to the waiting reception. As I closed
the door I looked back at the cup on the desk, no more steam rose from
it.

Katherine and I went ashore to a waving crowd, and tried to participate in some of the festivities going on celebrating the *Bonnie Clyde*'s
arrival. Everyone seemed to know a lot about us because they'd followed the adventure on the radio and in the newspapers.

There were hundreds of questions asked by different people, but
just then I couldn't bring myself to speak. Our emotions were amazingly divided.

Happiness to be married, happiness for our safe arrival, happiness
for not being prosecuted, gratitude for an enthusiastic welcome, sadness
for our journey being over, sadness for losing our captain and friend,
and just plain confusion.

Where do we go from here?

Chapter 30
A SAD FAREWELL

Two days later, several of us were aboard the MTB, heading out towards the open sea. We were guests of the Royal Navy, to bid farewell to an old friend. It was a gracious gesture by the MTB's captain, whom we had after all roundly thwarted, and by Commander Wright, who enthusiastically endorsed it, to offer his vessel to help lay Bowman to rest beneath the waves. The stretcher stood on its trestles aft, covered with the British Ensign and the flag of Scotland, his last colours now struck from the masthead of the *Bonnie Clyde*.

It had been a hectic two days since we arrived. Mr. Reith was visibly taken aback when we told him of Bowman's death. He insisted on attending to the funeral arrangements. "It's the least I can do for my old friend," he said, "and ye have many things to do. He looked so fit when I saw him just three weeks ago," he mourned. Edward told him that the next evening they must hold Bowman's wake, which Edward was going to arrange once he'd contacted some old friends.

Harris explained that Bowman had had a heart problem for some time, but he never cared to discuss it. "I'd take a bet that it was far worse than he ever let on, but he was so determined to save the ship that he overdid it."

We finally met Richard face to face, and he took to us as we to him. Sitting in the hotel lounge, where Mr. Reith had booked us rooms, we told Richard what had happened in Bowman's cabin and the agreement we'd made with the Prime Minister's personal representative, but that it was top secret.

"Don't worry," Richard said, "you've agreed to certain things, but I haven't, nor have any of the other reporters in town. I don't think anyone will continue calling the government rude names, especially after I spread the word round about them going easy on you. No government official has the right to make the press shut up, so we will continue writing. I doubt seriously if the Prime Minister's office would pick a fight with those of us who buy ink by the barrel."

Having had a look at some of the papers Richard brought for us, it was no wonder the crowds were so thick. *The Times* thundered on about the government and the rights of people, while the *Daily Mirror* had Katherine tending the boys like Snow White.

The night before, we went to Bowman's wake. I'd never been to a wake and hadn't known quite what to expect. It was held in the home of a friend, because public health laws in Scotland prohibited the exposure of a corpse in a public place. Despite the stories, it was very respectful. The door was left open so that Bowman, lying on the bed, could be said to be "taking part" in the drinking that was going on in the next room, up the stairs, in the kitchen, indeed anywhere there was space. Bowman's friends and shipmates seemed to be legion, and none of them came without bringing "a little something" to help the wake along. Early on, there were some fine tributes made and we learnt a lot of Bowman's career and his character, but what came over most was the affection these people all felt for him, which they now needed to celebrate.

Katherine and I, having our own private celebrating to do, left early to the sound of various lewd remarks. Harris, Robert, Boris, and Edward stayed till the last man left the house.

Now, as we continued out to sea, they were all feeling and showing the effects of the affair.

This was the first time Robert had met Commander Wright, who now tried to find out something of our involvement. "Two former Royal Navy officers, eh? Just how did you get mixed up with all this, if you don't mind my enquiring?" Robert and I looked at each other for a moment.

"I'm afraid that needs a great deal of explanation," I answered. "It seemed the thing to do at the time. Besides, we succeeded in saving a grand old ship, a group of unfortunate lads, and went on an adventure few would have thought possible these days."

"And the large bear?" Wright smiled.

"Well, everyone needs a pet," Robert replied with a laugh.

"What about this Russian?" Wright asked.

"His name is Boris and he's one of the finest riggers and seamen I've ever known," I told him. I looked aft where the stretcher rested and saw Boris sitting next to it with one hand holding the rail. He sat very still looking aft at the white wake churned up by the machinery below, which gave off a steady roar.

Harris and Edward were seemingly arguing over something so I went over to see what the problem was. The pair of them couldn't agree that the stretcher should be covered with both the flags: England, under which Bowman had served most of his time at sea, and the flag of Scotland, his heritage.

I whispered savagely, "Stop your drunken bickering and show some respect!" They both blinked at this, stopped, and then looked sheepish.

I walked forward with Katherine, the wind blowing her chestnut hair about as she tried to tie it back. We spoke with several of the crew members as we stood beside the forward deck gun that just days earlier had been pointing at us, demanding our surrender. It was covered over now and from behind was looking far less ominous. Eventually the roar of the engines softened as the boat slowed in the water.

Mr. Reith found us a fine piper from one of the Scottish regiments home after the long war. I suggested that he play a set of good Highland marching tunes, because I was sure Bowman wouldn't want dirges as we journeyed out. The lilting wail of the pipes seemed like elemental voices borne on the wind, sea-spirits chorusing a welcome to a son of the sea coming among them.

The bagpipes now fell silent with a last moan, as the bo'sun's pipe rang its whistle. Everyone snapped to an unrehearsed salute as two crew members moved to lift one end of the flag-draped stretcher to send Captain Bowman to his eternal resting place in the deep silence below. When the stretcher was lowered, only the flags remained, and they were folded quickly with skilled hands and presented to Harris, who made no attempt to hide the tears that ran down his face.

I asked for a lament and Commander Wright read a short prayer.

Harris had made one request; that nothing be read from the Bible. "It's fairly well documented that the Bible was written by people who thought the world was flat," he told the commander. "Captain Bowman always thought that it was a ridiculous contradiction for a sailor to believe all that's written there."

"That's odd," Wright said, "I never thought of it that way before."

We returned to the builders' quay where the *Bonnie Clyde* stood in the dry dock and thanked our hosts for their generosity.

Commander Wright turned to Harris, "I assume that I'll never know exactly what was taken from the scrap yard. I mean taken and paid for," he added quickly.

"I don't suppose you brought a list along with you," Harris grinned.

"Unfortunately not. And there's one thing more I'd really like to know. Just how did you make radar contacts come and go, and have radio transmissions coming from different sources?"

Harris gave an engaging smile. "There are some answers, I'm afraid, that Captain Bowman has taken with him, and that's one."

Wright looked closely at Harris. "You're sure that you've no idea how these things were done?"

"Oh yes, quite sure," Harris assured him. "Uncle Billy had many secrets that now will forever be his. Even as his first mate, I was only let in on so much."

"You must have known about the other ships," the commander persisted.

Harris looked innocently surprised. "What ships would those be?"

"The other sailing ships. The—oh, never mind!" Commander Wright sighed, throwing up his hands in resignation. "I wish I'd known him. There were some tactics I'd love to have known about. Positively brilliant." He looked keenly at Harris, who refused to be drawn out. He was surely aware that Harris would never tell even if he knew, but he had to try, after all.

After we disembarked and the MTB had sped out of sight, we stood at the dock and paused for a few moments, looking at the river. I asked Harris why he hadn't given the commander the answers to his questions.

Harris only laughed. "Sometimes it's nice to have a legend live on despite our knowing how it started in the first place. We still must protect those who helped us. As Richard said during the wake, 'When the legend becomes too factual, print the legend.'"

Harris reached into his coat pocket and produced a flask. "Here's to Uncle Billy," he said, taking a drink before passing it to me. I also toasted dear old Bowman. Boris, Edward, and Robert each did the same. Just as Harris was about to place the flask in his pocket, Katherine spoke up.

"Ah, aren't you forgetting someone?"

"Excuse me," Harris said graciously and passed her the flask. After all, she'd been as much a part of this as everyone else. Bowman would have been insulted had she not been allowed to participate. He'd really become extremely fond of her during the voyage.

Suddenly a thought struck me. I reached into my jacket pocket, and feeling the silver flask, pulled it out of my inner pocket. It was Bowman's flask that he'd loaned me during the worst of the storm, and I completely forgot about it till now.

"Harris, I believe Bowman would have wanted you to have this," I said unsteadily, holding out the flask.

He gazed at it for a long while, and seemed once more at a loss for words. Then he shook his great head. "No, Flynn," he murmured, "you hold on to it, will you?" He raised his own flask once more in a last toast. "To the memory of Captain Bowman—a fine sailor, a good man, and one of nature's gentlemen."

"Hear, hear," we all agreed, and took another wee drop in his honour.

Chapter 31
TWO YEARS LATER

Spring had again returned to the serene view overlooking the river, as I walked along the stone path leading down to the harbour. The streams that flowed into it were swollen from winter weather, seemingly too big for their bridges, and the afternoon sun warmed my face on the first day free of winter. There was a sky full of brightly coloured kites, held up by the winds blowing from the river, anchored to the earth by small children. The grass along the hillside glittered bright green from the shower that just passed. The snowdrops and crocuses were everywhere.

Katherine and I had managed to find a small cottage on the outskirts of town, and by now were accepted as part of this community, where we'd made some firm friends. I'd given up the idea of the sea and established a small gardening business and nursery. I had local customers, including two of the big estates in the area around Loch Lomond between Dumbartonshire and Stirlingshire. It was always a challenge to negotiate prices with people who thought of landscaping as merely playing with dirt. After trying it themselves, they eventually came around.

We very often have the whole crew over for tea. We're always delighted with their company, and the camaraderie is something we all cherish. Every anniversary of our arrival in Dumbarton, we take a small boat to the mouth of the river and throw a wreath of flowers into the sea, to remember Bowman and his part in our lives. Harris hands everyone a dram of whisky for a toast and then throws one over the side for his long-time friend. When we get back, it's time to celebrate our wedding anniversary as well. There will be other anniversaries to celebrate in the future as the "boys" marry. Just recently, we went to Larry's wedding. He married a wonderful girl he'd met when we first arrived. He now works as an assistant river pilot, carrying on his maritime training. He's become well respected by the other river pilots for having held the wheel of such a ship as the *Bonnie* through her voyage here.

The boys found good homes with the people who first took them in, with some of the younger ones being legally adopted. As a result of all the publicity, one or two were reunited with family, but they would return each year for the anniversary of our arrival.

At times I go to see Edward on his favourite bench in a park overlooking the river. It's a lovely park, with spectacular views over Port Glasgow and the Firth of Clyde. He often sits for hours reflecting on years past, and we talk about our voyage, still laughing about all the things that happened since the first day we met aboard the *Bonnie Clyde*. His eyes are often sad as he talks about old friends who are no longer of this earth. This makes him feel more alone, because there are few people left who can share the memories of his life since he was a young man. Being so close, he often makes the trip to his old haunts in Ireland. Given that, he makes a trip to visit old friends in Clochan Leigh, also known as Donegal.

Edward teaches navigation at the local college and treats people to the hundreds of stories that have made his life one they can only envy. One of the things that annoys him most is using a cane to get about. This seldom slows him down in the occasional confrontation with some argumentative soul, who will quickly find that Edward is quite adept at using it as a club, or hooking a leaned-back chair off its pins by the leg. He was never one to withdraw from a good argument!

Harris and Boris have a small boat repair business on the waterfront and are often consulted about ship restoration. They also teach technical skills to some of the small boat captains, always an appreciative lot, as well as at the local technical college. I'd often thought of the storm that seemingly ripped Boris off the yardarm that stormy night. How he managed to escape was to remain a mystery, for he would never elaborate on it. I've often thought of that one terrible moment. Without Boris the voyage could have never succeeded. And having developed a friendship with him, I don't know how I would have taken it if he'd been injured or lost, but I'm sure I'd never have properly gotten over it. Still, through the years that followed he would only say that he saw it coming and was thus able to escape unharmed. He would never elaborate on the details, like a magician who never discloses his professional secrets.

Every now and then, we meet for an evening's serious drinking at the Elephant and Castle Pub in Dumbarton. On one occasion, we had a surprise reunion.

We were sitting in our usual corner, when an American tourist and his wife came to sit at the next table. He looked over at us, and then looked again, as if he couldn't believe his eyes. He came straight over and as he stood by us, I looked at him properly for the first time, and then we all recognised him. It was our submarine skipper, Captain Johnson! He told us he was pursuing his hobby of finding tall ships to photograph and maybe sail aboard. He'd just arrived to see the ship down by the river. As he was speaking, he realised that we weren't there by accident, and that the ship must be the same one he'd been on two years earlier. We had a grand time telling him what had happened on the rest of the voyage. That turned out to be a truly memorable evening!

The people in the town never forgot our adventure in bringing the old ship back and often ask about different stories they'd heard. Sometimes I find it remarkable just how much the stories can change when I hear them repeated by other people. Still, it's good for many a pint in the local when we're asked to recount our adventures "in the interests of accuracy." No one ever grows tired of a good story.

Martin corresponds with us every so often and tells us the latest from the Beasley Inn and news from around the village. Once in a while we get together with a ham radio operator here and have a lively chat with him. Ever since the orphanage closed down, the building continued to fall to ruins, until a decision was made to dismantle what was once a grand old building and various contractors carried off the materials to other jobs. As for O'Connell, he'd been dealt with severely and was rarely seen in the company of Mrs. B. The inn went on as usual, but we seldom discussed what happened there. Occasionally Martin can't resist treating us to an amusing story from his many years serving under the Beastly One. Eventually, the old sunken coal ship had been cleared away, and there was talk about preserving the area as a bird sanctuary.

Harris still keeps in touch with Brian and his family, along with Richard and the many mates who helped us on our journey, and those who supplied us with provisions and information prior to and during it. I never knew so many people were involved or how much planning had gone into it until it was over. I now understand why Bowman, Harris, and Edward didn't give over much information.

Earlier that day I went with Harris and Boris to the local zoo. The regular staff knew them well, and had been there when Boris came marching through the main gates with a large brown bear two years earlier. We went over to a concrete wall where we could see into the bears' enclosure: a grassy mound with trees, rocks, and water running by the perimeter.

We stood quietly and watched a female play with her two cubs in the morning sunlight. After a while, Harris opened his coat and took out a large package of sausages. After unwrapping them, he threw several to the bears, who immediately gobbled them up. Two young keepers, who didn't know us, were working nearby and saw this happening.

"Ye there," one of them shouted, "can ye no read the sign, mon? It says dinna feed the animals!"

Harris was bent over looking at the bears and began to straighten, but Boris grabbed his scarf and pulled him back down.

"Let me say something," he told Harris. Boris then stood up and called out, in impeccable English, "Yes, I can read, but my friend here doesn't speak much English. I speak Russian so I'll tell him what you said." Boris then addressed Harris earnestly in Russian, as if translating. "There you are, now he knows," Boris called again.

The young zookeeper waved in appreciation and walked over to us. "Lovely creatures, eh? 'Tis a shame we lost the auld one. Ye should hae seen them together. They were a happy lot, and the cubs are a proper nice addition. Tell yer friend there to enjoy himself," he told Boris, "but dinna feed the animals."

Harris had been looking in astonishment at Boris. As the zookeeper walked away, he said, "I'm going to kill you! Since when has your English become so good?"

"Only when I try very hard without thinking," Boris replied through his greying moustache.

"Tell your friend, indeed!" and Harris seized Boris in a make-believe headlock, as I laughed like a fool.

"Not so loud, you're supposed to be stupid," Boris laughed. Harris watched as the zookeeper walked off, then threw the remaining sausages to the bears.

"I really do miss that old boy," Harris sighed, "but I'm glad his last years were happy here."

"Look!" cried Boris with sudden excitement, seizing us by the arms and pointing towards one of the young cubs. It was standing upright on its hind legs and was turning just as its father had been trained to do, smelling the air and making a tiny roar.

"You know," Harris said, "despite all the things that were reported missing after our sailing, Brown Bear was not among them. They never missed him, because they never really cared."

"You did," said Boris. "If not for your reaction, I wouldn't have known."

"It was you who managed to get that organized and get him on board without anyone noticing. I would never have thought that possible," Harris snorted. "You little weasel!"

I left them and got a ride from a friend to the river. Walking down to the harbour, I sat down on the spring grass next to Katherine. We looked down at the old ship, now shining with a new coat of paint. The standing rigging had been overhauled, and the sails had been removed from the yardarms and long since discarded. The broken yard had been repaired and hoisted back up the mast. Katharine had managed to charm much of the cookware from the ship's galley, that would after all never serve as one again, and each of us had a keepsake from the *Bonnie Clyde* in our homes.

She sat in the sunshine gleaming, and on her bow was inscribed *Bonnie Clyde* in gold, with Dumbarton added on the stern. She was now on permanent display for everyone to share in the history of shipbuilding in the region, the grand story of the age of sail.

Katherine said the ship had never looked so good. "Almost makes me want to do it all over again," she smiled.

"Really?" I asked, in mock surprise.

She wrinkled her nose at me. "I said almost."

After a while, a group of boys were introduced to us by friends who were returning from a tour of the ship. We lolled, reclining on the grass in the lovely afternoon sun, as I told them how the ship came to be here, as I'd been asked to do by their parents. It was a very abbreviated version of the long story I'd told so very many times before.

They sat there listening, mesmerised by the story of the run through the Channel under sail, being chased by the Royal Navy, the circus tent sails, our mates, the brown bear, and our own part in the saga. Later, as we were preparing to leave, one of the young boys came over to me.

"Mr. Flynn, is that really how the ship came to be here?" he asked. I stood up with Katherine, and brushed the grass from my trousers. I looked down at the boy and smiled, then reached over to take Katherine by the hand.

"Could be," I answered. "But then again, it might be just another ship's tale."

Acknowledgments

I would like to thank the following for their assistance and inspiration.

Admiral Willamette Flamillie Jr.: Clearly showed that an officer doesn't necessarily a gentleman make.

Chief Warrant bo'sun William F. Flamillie: Spent time showing me the ropes and masterful seamanship. He was the most resourceful of scavengers in obtaining useful items that appeared almost magically.

Chief Warrant bo'sun Robert O'Conner: A truly remarkable seaman who had served in the Spanish-American War, World War I, and taught seamanship during World War II. He could rig just about anything, and was a valuable teacher and revered master of his trade.

Beth Mueller: Was my voice when I could not speak.

Ann Callicrate: My most avid supporter, without whom this book might never have been published.

Gayle and Dick Newman: Supported this effort.

Dr. Viktor Buzin: Helped me install and learn the voice recognition program used to write this book. He also advised me on Russian vocabulary.

Nancy McAllister: My publisher, shepherded this project into print.

William Waller: My British research adviser, who grew up near this area during the World War II.

Annie Lore: Helped keep my British intact and added some ideas and suggestions.

Valerie, Al, Stan, and Garnet Rogers: Whose music, long chats, and quotations were always inspiring.

Alan Arkin: Told me this was a good story and to "at least write it down."

Martin Harris: Research advisor.

The ships and crews of many vessels, whose names are too numerous to list, but whose memories will long endure.

I regard *Seafaring Under Sail* by Basil Greenhill & Denis Stonham of the National Maritime Museum, Greenwich, the most comprehensive reference written on the subject.

Most of the characters in this story are based on people I met around different waterfronts. I consider myself lucky to learn about ships and the sea from those individuals with actual nautical experience. They gave me first-hand knowledge of a variety of shipboard situations. Some served during actual wartime and throughout the area I describe here.

Although the age of sail has passed, the charm and glory of those days have not. Many ships of this era are being restored and reconstructed by dedicated people, many of them volunteers, who give of themselves so that this   in history will endure for generations to come.

These ships do not number many, and keeping them afloat and intact is an extremely expensive endeavour.

Quite a few countries now use them as training ships and ambassadors of good will. I volunteered many hours, helping to restore and maintain ships that were on display for the public and are now used as museums and tourist attractions. It was a deeply gratifying experience.

During that time, I enjoyed the company of people and animals similar to or exactly like the characters I have woven into *A Ship's Tale*.